Economic Regionalization in the Asia-Pacific

Challenges to Economic Cooperation

M. Dutta
Professor of Economics, Rutgers University, USA

Edward Elgar
Cheltenham, UK • Northampton, MA, USA

Published by
Edward Elgar Publishing Limited
Glensanda House
Montpellier Parade
Cheltenham
Glos GL50 1UA
UK

Edward Elgar Publishing, Inc.
6 Market Street
Northampton
Massachusetts 01060
USA

A catalogue record for this book
is available from the British Library

Library of Congress Cataloguing in Publication Data

Dutta, Manoranjan.
Economic regionalization in the Asia-Pacific: challenges to economic cooperation / Manoranjan Dutta.
Includes bibliographical references.
1. Asia—Economic integration. 2. Pacific Area—Economic integration. 3. Asian cooperation. 4. Pacific Area cooperation. 5. Regionalism—Asia. 6. Regionalism—Pacific Area. 7. Asia—Economic policy. 8. Pacific Area—Economic policy. I. Title.
HC412.D88 1998
337.1'5—dc21 98–9827
CIP

ISBN 1 85898 825 X

Printed and bound in Great Britain by Biddles Ltd, Guildford and King's Lynn

To the loving memory of my sister,

BASU DUTTA

who was too young to leave us on April 11, 1996.

Contents

Figures

Tables

Abbreviations and Acronyms

ABAC	APEC Business Advisory Council
ADB	Asia Development Bank
AFTA	ASEAN Free Trade Area
ANZ-CER	Australia-New Zealand Closer Economic Relations
ANZCERTA	Australia-New Zealand Closer Economic Relations Trade Area
APEC	Asia-Pacific Economic Cooperation
ARF	ASEAN Regional Forum
ASEAN	Association of Southeast Asian Nations
BAC	Budget and Administration Committee
CAB	current accounts balance
CPI	consumer price index
CTI	Committee on Trade and Investment
DFI	direct foreign investment
DMC	developing member-country
EAEC	East Asian Economic Caucus
EC	European Community
Ecu	European Currency Unit
EEC	European Economic Community
EFTA	European Free Trade Area
EMI	European Monetary Institute
EMS	European Monetary System
EMU	European Monetary Union
EPG	Eminent Persons' Group
ESCAP	Economic and Social Council of Asia and the Pacific
ESCB	European System of Central Banks
EU	European Union
Euro	Common Currency of the EU
FTA	free trade area
FTAA	Free Trade Area of the Americas
GATS	General Agreement on Trade in Services
GATT	General Agreement on Tariffs and Trade
GDP	gross domestic product
HRD	human resource development
IMF	International Monetary Fund
IOG	Indian Ocean Group
LAFTA	Latin America Free Trade Area

MFN	most-favored nation
MOFERT	Ministry of Foreign Economic Relations and Trade (China)
NAFTA	North American Free Trade Area
NATO	North Atlantic Treaty Organization
NIE	newly industrialized/industrializing economy
OECD	Organization for Economic Cooperation and Development
OPTAD	Organization for Pacific Trade and Development - or - Organization for Pacific Trade, Aid and Development
PAFTA	Pacific Free Trade Area
PBEC	Pacific Basin Economic Council
PBF	Pacific Business Forum
PECC	Pacific Economic Cooperation Council (formerly Conference)
PFP	Partners for Progress
PLG-SME	Policy Level Group on Small and Medium Enterprises
PRC	People's Republic of China
ROW	rest of the world
SAARC	South Asian Association for Regional Cooperation
SME	small and medium enterprise
SOM	Senior Officials' Meeting
SPF	South Pacific Forum
WB	The World Bank
WTO	World Trade Organization

Preface

The textbook paradigm of a perfectly competitive market of n sovereign nations engaged in international economic relations by way of exchange of m final products, given the comparative taste patterns and production maps of member-economies, continues to elude us. I argue that economic regionalization becomes an option, of course, with a firm commitment to globalism. Regionalism and globalism have become ways to maximize the welfare of all microeconomic units - households and business corporations - in all economies of the world.

The pre-World War II model of economic regionalization brought distant economies under an umbrella wherein the home governments of respective regions provided the stability of the macroeconomic core with monetary and fiscal policy formulation and effective coordination. The satellite economies soon rebelled against the authoritarian home governments. The post-World War II model of economic regionalization grouped the sovereign national economies into two major groups - the North and the South, with the United States dollar, given its fixed gold value, being the anchor of the free world's macroeconomic stability. The rich nations in the North and the poor nations in the South often became hostile bargainers and ended up by establishing a duopoly-duopsony market pattern, contributing to the failure of welfare maximization of the world economies. Neither of the two above models survived. On August 15, 1971, the U.S. dollar ceased to be the anchor of the global macroeconomic stability. Needless to add that the hostilities of the Cold War caused much havoc to the post-World War II global economic relationships.

In Part I, Chapter 1, I review the newly emerging concept of the supra-national, regional macroeconomic core, wherein sovereign nation-state based economies elect to join a regional compact, toward mapping a common economic space onto a common geographic space, well defined by a map-of-the-world view of the region. Chapter 2 presents a historical profile of economic regionalization which belonged to the imperial model. Chapter 3 outlines the progressive emergence of an economic community in the Asia-Pacific. The recent experiment in economic regionalization in Western Europe is examined in Chapter 4. In Chapters 5, 6 and 7, I evaluate (i) Pareto optimality condition in the context of economic regionalization, (ii) Asia-Pacific economic regimes, and (iii) geo-economics and regionalization.

Beginning with the 1960s, a novel experiment in Western Europe gave birth to a unique model of economic regionalization, now known as the European Union (EU). The EU model is based on a three-tier economic plan.

1. *A map-of-the-world* view of the region defines the core. Both the earlier models failed to have their identification with a map-of-the-world view of a region. Membership of the regional group has expanded over time with its commitment to a map-of-the-world view region remaining firm.
2. Intra-regional free flow of trade in final products - goods and services, and of factors of production - physical as well as human integrates the market mechanism. Free trade and investment flows provide the foundation of intraregional free market contributing to the maximization of economic welfare for all microeconomic actors in all member-economies in the Union.
3. A shared commitment to a macroeconomic agenda of monetary and fiscal policy guidelines was viewed as a necessary condition for the maximization of economic objectives of microeconomic actors - households and business firms - in each sovereign member-economy of the Union.

Economic Regionalization in the Asia-Pacific historically followed the experiments in Western Europe with a finite time lag, finding its eventual institutionalization in the Asia-Pacific Economic Cooperation (APEC) in 1989. Over the past decade, APEC has been in the process of evolution. It is "a moving target" and much remains to unfold. Let it be noted with emphasis that APEC is not a replica of the EU, but it does essentially provide a paradigm of economic regionalization in the Asia-Pacific. It is too early for APEC (1989-1997) to present a comprehensive blueprint. APEC begins as a regional institution for trade and investment liberalization. Its emerging agenda remains to evolve.

The terms "free trade area" and "free trade in the area" appear in APEC literature. Extension of free trade facilities, with or without reciprocity, to non-APEC economies continues to be a point of discussion. How will the intra-APEC subregional groupings affect the functioning of APEC? Does the American hemispheric economic regionalization further promote APEC's trade liberalization agenda? The extension of APEC membership, which was frozen in 1994 for three years, will become yet another point of debate at the end of 1997. Will APEC work to develop an intra-regional macroeconomic agenda of shared commitment to monetary and fiscal discipline? With progression of industrialization and consequent graduation of APEC member-economies from labor-surplus to labor-shortage status, will there be a discussion of the thorny issue of intra-APEC mobility of labor and/or illegal migrant labor? Formalization and standardization of goods and services in intra-APEC trade remains an issue of concern. Will APEC be WTO-consistent, as is the EU?

To find answers to all such questions I was happy to be able to arrange personal conversations with members of Eminent Persons' Group of APEC in several member-countries, and with a select group of scholars and public officials. Indeed, APEC's institutional agenda has been the end product of the hard work of a group of eminent persons, one from each APEC member-economy, designated by respective governments. The EPG was judged to have done its work and the group became defunct at the Osaka Summit in 1996.

In Part II, Chapters 8 through 21, I am pleased to be able to share with my readers my conversations with eminent persons of Korea, the United States, Indonesia, the People's Republic of China, Singapore, Australia, Thailand and Malaysia, and with four Professors of Economics in Canberra and Kuala Lumpur and the President of the Asian Development Bank.

The "Lake Pacific" defines the map-of-the-world view of this enormously vast region. APEC is struggling to define its shared macroeconomic agenda. The APEC intraregional free market with free trade and investment flows is targeted to be achieved by a relatively distant time horizon, 2010 for industrially advanced member-economies and 2020 for others.

In Part III, I present an outline of APEC organization in Chapter 22, and follow it up in Chapter 23, by a discussion of APEC vision: action agenda and action plan. In Chapter 24, I review how trade for 1970-1989 propelled the founding of APEC. Specific challenges to APEC are summarized in Chapter 25.

The robustness of the map-of-the-world view of the APEC region, based on the Lake Pacific, very much appears to be an open issue. In Part IV, I discuss intra-APEC geo-economics in Chapter 26. The issue of subregion-specific economic regionalization within the APEC region of the Lake Pacific merits an evaluation. In Chapters 27 through 31, presentations on the ASEAN in Southeast Asia, the ANZ-CER in South Pacific, the NAFTA in North America, the SAARC in South Asia, and the Golden Triangle of China: Mainland Taipei and Hong Kong follow. A search for a more immediate map-of-the-world view of a specific region warrants additional investigation.

M. Dutta
January 7, 1998

Acknowledgments

First, my very special thanks are due to EPG members - Professor Jang Hee Yoo (Korea), Dr. C. Fred Bergsten (U.S.), Professor Suhadi Mangkusuwondo (Indonesia), Mr. Zhao Gong-Da (People's Republic of China), Professor Lee Tsao Yuan (Singapore), The Hon. Neville Wran (Australia), Dr. Narongchai Akrasanee (Thailand) and Dr. Dato Noordin Sopiee (Malaysia) who generously shared their thoughts on APEC with me at personal conferences. My conversations with Heinz W. Arndt, Peter Drysdale and Ross Garnaut - all of the Australian National University, and Mohamed Ariff of the University of Malaya, and with Mr. Mitsuo Sato, President, Asian Development Bank, Manila, greatly aided my understanding of the APEC movement. I thank these distinguished scholars.

Research of this monograph has been facilitated by my participation and presentations over the years at seminars and conferences at many institutions in most APEC member-countries and beyond. I wish to express my sincere appreciation to my fellow economists at all these institutions: Rutgers - the State University of New Jersey at New Brunswick, Columbia University in the City of New York, Brandeis University at Waltham, Federal Reserve Bank of San Francisco, Federal Reserve Bank of Atlanta and Federal Reserve Bank of New York in the United States; Hosei University, Tokai University and Chuo University in Japan; Korea Institute for International Economic Policy, Korea Development Institute, Korea Energy Economics Institute, Korea Rural Economics Institute, Seoul National University, Korea University, Hanyang University, Konkuk University at Chenju City campus and Chung Ang University in Korea; Huazhong University of Science and Technology in Wuhan, Shanghai Academy of Social Sciences in Shanghai, Chinese Academy of Social Sciences in Beijing, People's University in Beijing and The North China University of Technology in The People's Republic of China; The Chinese University of Hong Kong in Hong Kong; The National Taiwan University and the Chung-Hwa Institution for Economic Research in Taipei; Asian Development Bank in Manila and the University of the Philippines at Quezon City in The Philippines; University of Indonesia in Jakarta, Gadjah Mada University in Yogyakarta and Udayan University at Bali in Indonesia. The University of Malaya in Kuala Lumpur, Malaysia; Chulalongkorn University in Bangkok, Thailand; Singapore National University in Singapore; The Australian National University in Canberra, University of New South Wales in Sydney, Australia; the Vietnam Chamber of Commerce and Industries in Hanoi, Vietnam; Jawaharlal Nehru

University and the Indian Center for Research in International Economics in New Delhi, India; the SAARC Secretariat in Kathmandu, Nepal; the APEC Secretariat in Singapore.

I owe personal thanks to Professor Lawrence R. Klein who taught me economics and econometrics. My personal thanks are also due to my fellow economists - Robert J. Alexander, Kiyoshi Kojima, Hugh T. Patrick, Dwight H. Perkins, Hyung Yoon Byun, Lawrence B. Krause, Yoko Sazanami, Arnold C. Harberger, John M. Letiche, Robert E. Baldwin, Gregory C. Chow, T.N. Srinivasan, Peter J. Lloyd, Chang Peikang, Zhang Zhongli, Liu Guoguang, Huang Fan-Zhang, Masumi Kishi, Duk Choong Kim, Dong-se Cha, Yoshihiko Hirata, Tzong-shian Yu, Chyau Tuan, Chung H. Lee, Thienchay Kiranandana, Ashok Guha, James C. Riedel, Romeo M. Bautista, Detlef Lorenz, Marzuki Usman, Anwar Nasution, Kazuo Sato, Robert H. Aten, Richard Hooley, Richard F. Kosobud, George Rosen, H. Peter Gray, Gary Clyde Hufbauer, Gary H. Jefferson, Ching-ing Hou, Joel Popkin, Frank S.T. Hsiao, Mei-chu Hsiao, Anthony M. Tang, Kanta Marwah, Linda F.Y. Ng, Edita Tan, Mahani Zainal Abidin, Edna E. Ehrlich, Rosemary Scanlon, Swadesh Ranjan Datta-Gupta, Toshiaki Hasegawa, David Jay Green, James T.H. Tsao, Chia Siow Yue, Arsenio M. Balisacan, Amit Shovon Ray, V.V. Bhanoji Rao, Saleem M. Khan, Suthiphand Chirathivat, Steven L. Husted, Christina Y. Liu, Yang-Taek Lim, Widjanarko, Michael Plummer, J.C. Liu, Kiseok Lee, Daniel T. Tantum, Amiya Sharma and Edwin Milan.

My wife, Kanak, gave much of her love and time to help me in this project. She accompanied me in my several field trips to Japan, Korea, China, Taiwan, Hong Kong, India, the Philippines, Indonesia, Singapore, Malaysia, Thailand, Vietnam and Australia, and but for her help I could not have accomplished what I set out to do. The Kauls of Manhattan - Usha and Ashok, Kavery and Bhupender - have always been there to give me their love and support. They alone could and did help me overcome the challenges which came to overwhelm me as I worked on this book over the past three years.

My good friends in the Rutgers University Economics Faculty Office - Laura Ford, Dorothy Rinaldi, Kathy McGuire, Michelle Villalva, Marie Felber and Janet Goodstein lent me their ungrudging help at successive stages of my working on this book and have earned my sincerest thanks. Marie Felber gave me very special help to revise my manuscript.

Michelle Villalva extended her generous and helpful cooperation to complete the final phase of preparing the manuscript, and she has earned my very special thanks.

May I take this opportunity to thank Jane Croft, Editor, Julie Leppard,

Managing Editor, and Christine Boniface, Desk Editor, of Edward Elgar Publishing Ltd., for successfully piloting the production of the book.

Finally, I must thank Richard Rose and Debajyoti Chakrabarty for adding all their efforts to this end-product.

I serve as President and Chief Executive Officer of the American Committee on Asian Economic Studies (ACAES), an inter-university, not-for-profit, educational program for studies in Asian economics. The views expressed here are, of course, exclusively mine, and I remain responsible for any and all errors.

M. Dutta
January 7, 1998

PART I

Economic Regionalization - A Perspective

1 Toward a Supranational Regional Macroeconomic Core

People only accept change when they are faced with necessity, and only recognize necessity when a crisis is upon them. (Monnet 1978, p. 109.)

THE PERSPECTIVE

In the 1990s and beyond, the search for an optimum framework for studies in international economics is very much in order. The dynamics of two sets of economic events - one in Europe, especially in Western Europe, the emergence of a single economic region, the European Union (EU); and the other in Asia, especially East Asia, Japan's economic achievement plus the industrialization and economic growth of a select group of Asia-Pacific economies - suggests that a new multipolar world economy has emerged. In the post-Cold War global order, the EU is a unique paradigm of economic regionalization, providing a macroeconomic core for microeconomic optimization - consumer satisfaction for households and profit for business corporations in all member-economies and it very much warrants our attention. The progression of the European Economic Community (EEC) to the European Community (EC), and then to the EU in 1992 is a notable event in the emerging new international order.

The historic liquidation of hostilities between the East and the West presents yet another challenge. The Cold War that plagued the world ever since World War II concluded has now come to an end. In the process, the two international arrangements that dominated the political and economic dialogues over the past several decades have come to outlive their usefulness.

The two superpowers had their respective allies and nuclear arsenals in the two political clubs - the East and the West. At the summit meeting of the North Atlantic Treaty Organization (NATO) in London, June 1990, we happily witnessed the celebration of its total reordering. A new view of Europe from "the Atlantic to the Urals" is increasingly becoming the focus.

The post-World War II bipolar *economic* grouping of the nations of the world into two blocs - the North and the South: rich nations in the North and poor ones in the South - can hardly be useful in the post-Cold War decades. Historically, it did serve its purpose but it can no longer be an optimum framework for studies in international economics in the 1990s and beyond.

If in 1958 the Treaty of Rome (signed in 1957) was seen as a feeble expression of Jean Monnet's (Monnet, 1978) intellectual one-Europe concept, the EC got a new momentum by the signing of the Single European Act in 1985, and in the 1990s, following the signing of the Treaty of Maastricht 1992 (signed in 1991), the EU is approaching a new realism by the end of the century.

The other overriding economic fact is the industrialization of selected countries in Asia, often referred to as "new Japans". Japan has for some years been an economic superpower and earned its membership of the northern bloc. The fact, however, is that Japan is in Asia. Add to this the fast-growing economies of the "new Japans" in East Asia - Korea, Taiwan, Hong Kong and Singapore. As a result, a new Asian economic awareness has become a reality.

The prospect for rapid industrialization in the rest of Asia - ASEAN economies, China, India and other South Asian countries in the SAARC - has been the subject of research by many. Asian industrialization, and structural changes in Asian economies have recently been the subject of much discussion (Dutta, 1985, 1987a and 1987b, 1988; Dutta and Tantum, 1988; Bradford and Branson, 1987; Ito and Krueger, 1997). Australia and New Zealand have now taken their firm places in the Asia-Pacific economic community.

Thus, the dynamics of the two sets of events, one in Western Europe and another in Asia-Pacific, in the context of liquidation of hostile political confrontation between the East and the West, warrants a search for a new international economic order. A new multipolar regional arrangement of world economies may now replace the North-South bipolar arrangement (Dutta, 1987a and 1987b, 1990).

Linder (1986) writes of the emergence of the Pacific century and presents an Asia-Pacific economic profile comprising the western states of Canada and the United States, Japan, Asia's newly industrialized economies (NIEs), plus ASEAN, Papua New Guinea, Australia and New Zealand. He, however, elects to limit his treatise on the Pacific economies to East Asia and excludes China "because of the different economic system obtaining there".

Given the historical progression of the Industrial Revolution and the economic potential of the mega-technologies of our time, the exclusivity of nation-state-based economies merits reexamination. Students of economics have studied how production frontiers of various economies have moved out to the newer spaces. It has indeed been a continuous process, albeit uneven at times. Scholars tell us that the world is at the threshold of the Fifth Industrial Revolution which will bring us to the fuller manifestation of robotics, bio-tech and superconductivity. The production maps of world economies will then be substantively altered. Indeed, the historical process has been in progress.

Dominant economic factors defining the new international economic order warrant attention. First, the scale of production has grown larger and larger, and it will grow even larger as the full potentials of new mega-technologies progressively broaden production frontiers of competing economies. Second, the world financial market has been electronically integrated in an unprecedented way. Third, given the proliferation of fast-developing super-speed communication modes, or call it "information super-highway", flows of capital - human and physical - have become truly global, contributing to the emergence of a new paradigm of industrialization, based on the concept of "adaptive innovation" (Dutta and Tantum, 1988; Dutta 1992a, 1992b, 1992c, and 1992d). Fourth, with an increasing awareness of the new economic parameters of environment, such as acid rain and global warming, the isolated nation-state-based economy, even if it is as large as China or India (population), Canada or Soviet Union (land mass), United States, Japan or Germany (gross domestic product), is fast becoming anachronistic.

As and when the one-currency-based EU inaugurates itself by the turn of the century, the new order of regionalization will certainly replace the present *ad hoc* arrangement of the G-7, the Group of Seven industrialized nations. The four European members - Germany, France, Italy and England - will have become constituent members of the EU, with its respective currencies defined in terms of the European common currency, call it by any name, Ecu or Euro. The United States and Canada, the two members of the G-7 from North American regional space, will have their interrelated currency as their two dollars continue to relate to each other via a free float in the market. The seventh member of the G-7, Japan, as the principal actor in the Asia-Pacific economic region, will progressively have its yen as a core currency for the region. The case can be made that the G-7 may evolve into the G-3 (Dobson, 1990; Dutta, 1990). Or, the U.S. dollar and the Japanese yen may jointly anchor the monetary system for APEC. The core issue is coordination of intraregional macroeconomic policies by a supranational, multilateral arrangement, *not one common regional currency*.

Former UK Prime Minister Margaret Thatcher at the G-7 Economic Summit statement in Houston (July 1990), straightforwardly referred to the three regional economic power centers based on the Deutschmark (DM), the U.S. dollar (US$) and the Japanese Yen (¥), respectively. Of course, the pronouncement might have been made too early, but it did make an articulate reference to the emerging new order of tomorrow. Kojima (1990b, pp. 19-34) makes an imaginative proposal that these three currencies plus gold be made the basis of a new international monetary system.

Ideally, uniting "sovereign" nation-state-based macroeconomies in a regional economic union with one "common" currency for the region may constitute the core of the new international economic order. This is not to suggest that the process will be easy and smooth. The challenge will be to institute the new order of a supranational macroeconomic core where sovereign member-states will elect to commit to a shared agenda of monetary and fiscal discipline, not necessarily a common currency, without compromising the sovereign authority of each individual nation-state (Dutta, 1995a and 1995b).

A strong currency member-economy in a region will have to be able to make sure that it wins and continues to enjoy the basic confidence of the member-economies of the regional compact. They must also be ever ready to accept the role of preeminence of other member currencies of the region, as and when their comparative economic productivity will have warranted it. At the same time each member-economy must fulfil its responsibility to keep its vigil in an institutional form over the intraregional monetary and fiscal management of its region. The issue is one of rational and *multilateral* management of the region's economy and its monetary-fiscal system by a well-structured regional institutionalization.

Member sovereign states in a regional union will be free to engage in a two-track competition - intraregion and interregion. The choice of remaining "delinked" is hardly a choice for an individual nation-state-based economy and an act of "delinking" by itself does not ensure sound economic management and growth.

The twenty-fifth anniversary symposium of the Organization for Economic Cooperation and Development (OECD) Center in Paris in 1988 provided a forum for the debate on "One World or Several?". Noting that the new era will be one of "a growing impotence of purely national decision-making", Louis Emmerij (1989b, p. 25) spoke for "increasing economic globalization combined with growing multipolarity". Okita (1989, p. 41) at the same forum emphasized, "Globalism and regionalism are the two main currents in the world today".

During the Cold War decades, we witnessed several regional groupings, mostly on defense and security considerations, which will remain beyond the scope of our study. Some of them have now outlived their usefulness and have become non-functional, while some others have been reorganized with an intraregional economic agenda. One can indeed define the regional grouping of economies of the world in the earlier period as "strategic", not economic.

The compactness of an economic space in terms of geographic contiguity has been the prime focus of economists studying the location theory. Rational economic regionalization will have to be defined by a common economic space mapped on a common geographic space.

Naturally, it should be a simple exercise to look at the map of the world, and define the core of economic regionalization in terms of the common continental economic space of (i) Europe, "from the Atlantic to the Urals", (ii) Asia inclusive of China, India and South Asia, the Pacific Islands, Australia and New Zealand, and the Southeast Asian countries, for political reasons hitherto excluded from Asia-Pacific economic cooperation framework, and (iii) Africa from its northern rim to the southern cape, and (iv) the Americas - North and South. Specific regional affiliation of independent states of the former Soviet Union and East European countries, and of the countries in the Middle East remain to emerge.

It is instructive to note that the emerging core of the economic region in Europe centers in Western Europe while that of Asia centers in the Pacific Basin. A specific regional core in a common economic space, in Europe or in Asia, can and will progress to broaden its space and scope to embrace the geographically contiguous sovereign economies in its common fold.

This continent-based regionalization may be constrained by subregional conflicts and/or other considerations. But the invitation to accept the continental regionalization should be general and should remain "open" for those countries which for one or another reason may fail to join a given regional market at its inception. Progressive regionalization in Europe in the EU is certainly one model. The principle of *inclusion*, not exclusion, will be the key to the success of the new order of regionalization. Each region should be a compact, defined as *naturally* as possible. China with its "different economic system" can and must coexist in the *Asian Economic Community.* Simultaneous admission of both China and Taiwan to the Pacific Economic Cooperation Conference (PECC) membership is a point to take note of in support of "international economic pluralism" (Drysdale, 1988).

Similarly, for India and other South Asian countries, their belonging to Asia is a fact. With its rich endowments of human capital and their science and technology base, Walt Rostow (1985, p. 286) identifies India as a country ready "to bring about the partnership of scientists, engineers and entrepreneurs, the absorption of the Fourth Industrial Revolution requires".

One can be hopeful that, following the meltdown of the superpower Cold War, before long one should be able to reidentify North Korea, Mongolia, Vietnam, Cambodia, Laos and Myanmar on the map of Asia. Indeed, for these economies, geographically belonging to Asia's economic map remains to be appreciated. It is instructive to note that in July 1995, Vietnam became a member of the subregional compact, ASEAN and foreseeably, membership of ASEAN will pave the way for Vietnam to become a member of APEC.

The lesson from Western Europe points to the bold fact that at successive stages, Portugal, Spain, Italy and Greece, once considered weaker sisters of Southern Europe, became full and effective members of the EU. In 1995 the 12-member EU was joined by three other sovereign economies in Europe - Austria, Finland and Sweden.

Lessons of economic groupings of rich and poor economies of the world in the two rival institutions, the North and the South, have been learned. One wonders if such a bipolar economic grouping of the national economies of the world prompted regimentation of the haves and the have-nots, and contributed to a duopoly-duopsony bargaining framework in a confrontational imperfect market order of the world economy, failing to satisfy the optimality condition.

AN AMERICAN HEMISPHERIC ECONOMIC REGIONALIZATION

For the Americas, the free trade pact between Canada and the United States may have initiated a historic process. On June 27, 1990, President George Bush spoke for a free trade zone for the Americas, the North and the South. In December 1994 came the initiative for the American hemispheric free trade area at a conference of all the states in the North and South Americas, except Cuba, hosted by President Bill Clinton. The debate on the free trade area of the United States, Canada and Mexico was concluded in 1993, and the North American Free Trade Area (NAFTA) was established on January 1, 1994.

A one-currency-based economic community of the Americas will be a natural corollary of the one-currency-based EU. Indeed, the U.S. dollar, which has a free float with the Canadian dollar, has historically been the principal international currency for the Americas. Following the EU model where the Ecu, now Euro, is the creative term for its common core currency centered on the German mark, the U.S. dollar may become the core of the monetary system of the Americas. Will there soon be a well-structured Asian money (AM)? The G-3 will then have its natural birth, with explicit commitment to accommodate the leadership role of other regional member currencies, as and when economic developments will so warrant.

THE ISSUES

A return to the idealized paradigm of international trade wherein *n* sovereign nations engage in trade in *m* final goods and services with their respective sovereign currencies irreversibly linked to a 100 per cent pure gold standard and settle their respective national accounts with the rest of the world in terms of gold is hardly an option. "Other things" have *not* remained "equal", and there are too many "other" economic and extraeconomic variables to be taken into consideration.

International trade and investment flows involving microeconomic actors - household consuming units as well as investing business organizations - in *n* national economies are affected by macroeconomic policies of the respective nations. Indeed, in our free-enterprise capitalist market economies in historically defined sovereign nation-states, monetary and fiscal measures of macroeconomic management are generally crucial for coordinating microeconomic activities. In the absence of a common, effective macroeconomic core of *n* nations engaged in international exchanges, the management has been *ad hoc* and the world has witnessed so many binational/multinational negotiations at several familiar forums such as the General Agreement on Tarrifs and Trade/World Trade Organization (GATT/WTO), the International Monetary Fund (IMF), G-7 and free trade areas (FTAs).

Stability of economic structures at a given time provided the rationale of our education in international trade and investment by our great teachers. The Theory of Comparative Advantage taught us how trade in wine and clothes across the borders of sovereign nation-states would optimize gains for both England and Portugal. At successive stages of progress of economics science, the Heckscher-Ohlin Theory of Factor Endowment, the Kravis Proposition of Factor Availability, and the Ruttan Product Cycle Theorem became integral parts of teaching in international economics.

The sovereign nation-states remained the micro units. The monetary-fiscal policies adopted by each sovereign state became the macroeconomic core for microeconomic optimization of economic welfare, however defined, of microeconomic units - households and business corporations and private firms - belonging to each sovereign nation-state-based economic unit engaged in international economic transactions. Income and price elasticities of traded goods were extensively, often laboriously, estimated and each micro nation-state was ideally free to do its share of competitive buyer-seller meet in the free and competitive world market.

The idealized textbook paradigm often met with real-world challenges and there was the often quoted saying that foreign trade of any sovereign nation-state, as pursued by its government, became the "hand-maiden" of the individual nation's foreign policy. Off-the-market negotiations and security and strategic considerations often were allowed to overwhelm the market.

In the real world, international economics, as and when it was limited to trade in final products - goods and services - was relatively simple. Soon, free flow of capital - financial as well as physical - became a part of the tradables. In the recent decades, free-flow of human capital has become routine in international economics. Perhaps it began with the importation of "cheap" or low-wage "indentured" or "slave" labor. It was then followed by liberalization of immigration laws as demand for skilled and professional manpower became a point of consideration in a given national economy. The phenomena of international refugee crisis on successive occasions added to the momentum of mass migration of human capital.

Another facet of human capital flow across the borders of sovereign nation-state-based economies warrants further attention (Dutta, 1990; Dutta and Tantum, 1988). International transmissions of research results and frontier knowledge in science and technology have become a part of academic freedom. Transnational movement of knowledge is fast, often instantaneous by global computer linkages. Availability of scientists and engineers are no longer limited to specific economies.

Transmitted scientific/technological findings which are essentially in the public domain, can be tested, replicated, refined and further developed with comparative ease. They can then be put into the production process. This is no "copying" in its orthodox sense, and no establishment of industrial intelligence protection agency, however sophisticated, will be able to challenge the process. Indeed, free flow of human capital, disembodied as it is, now works without physical migration of human bodies. This international free flow of disembodied human capital provides the core base for the new paradigm of adaptive innovation.

The world market has progressed to a level of unification wherein the concept of stability of traditional sovereign nation-state-based economic units seems to have become outdated. A move toward one integrated world market is still a long way off. Much remains to be built upon the limited regional achievements in this regard. Historically drawn borders of the sovereign nation-states on the map of the world continue to change. Strange is the course of history! A new regional macroeconomic core in a common economic space with natural geographical contiguity seems to be in order.

It is difficult to accept the changes and no one has said it better than Monnet (1978, p. 109), as we have quoted him at the beginning of this chapter.

2 Historical Profiles of Economic Regionalization

Economic regionalization has a history of its own. Pre-World War II economic regionalization was rooted into specific currency regimes, established under various imperial orders. Historical events dictated economic ties of most Asia-Pacific economies to one or another currency regime: the British pound sterling, the French franc, the Dutch guilder, the U.S. dollar and the Japanese yen - each played the role of an anchor currency in its respective regional sphere of dominance.

It was the colonial mold of economic regionalization, wherein monetary-fiscal policies, designed by home governments of the respective currency regimes, provided a macroeconomic core for microeconomic agents in the respective "satellite" economies. Its agenda was not to establish a supranational macroeconomic core for a specific economic region in a geographically common economic space. Rather, a *supernational* and *superpower* hegemony of monetary and fiscal discipline became manifest.

Thus, the concept of economic regionalization, as known earlier in its pre-World War II manifestation, centered on currency regions, authoritatively established in a given sphere/space of political domination. Indeed, this historically explained a strong economic tie-up, contributing to the growth of intraregional trade and investment flows among distant lands in a given currency region in a superpower regime. This mode of intraregional economic bonds united the Netherlands and Indonesia, the United Kingdom and a host of economies in Southeast and South Asia, plus Australia and New Zealand, France and Indochina, Japan and several East Asian economies, the United States and the Philippines. A gravity model for this regime would have to be sought in imperial political ties, not in physical distances - air mile, water mile, land mile, tunnel mile - between the home market of a specific currency regime and its remote satellite economies.

The system liquidated itself under its own burden as it failed to define the optimum specification of the welfare function of all microunits in the remote satellite economies in a given currency sphere. Its tilt in favor of the home economies became all too obvious. Much has been written on the rise and fall of the old-fashioned imperial economic regionalization.

THE POST-WORLD WAR II ERA

In the post-World War II era came a new order of economic globalism, as opposed to specific superpower-centered imperial regionalization, and its macroeconomic core was based on the U.S. dollar, for US$ 35 an ounce of pure gold. The progress to a unipolar one-world macroeconomic core was soon challenged by the hostilities of the Cold War.

Kindleberger (1986) has forcefully argued that the delivery of the international public goods in the form of free-world monetary-fiscal stability eventually became too costly for the United States. The cost of providing the military security component of it in the context of the Cold War increasingly proved too much to be borne by the United States, he added.

The U.S. dollar-based international monetary system was officially signed off on August 15, 1971. There was a delinking of the U.S. dollar from its fixed gold value and a free float of the world's currencies became the order. Some economists hailed it as the dawn of a new era for a possible return to 100 per cent pure gold standard. The market paradigm, however, proved short-lived. In September 1985, the free float of currencies was summarily replaced by a managed exchange rate regime, first by the G-5 regime (Group of Five), then by the G-7 (Group of Seven). We have noted earlier that some economists have argued that the G-7 system has in effect reduced itself to a G-3 or a G-2 regime.

The experience from August 1971 through September 1985 has been instructive. The monetary-fiscal policies of the major trading countries failed to be coordinated in the free market. The resulting chaos in the absence of an institutional mechanism was responsible for the outcome. The point was straightforwardly made that in the absence of a macroeconomic core, closely and *intelligently* coordinating monetary-fiscal policies of the major trading/investing economies, the system could not optimize economic gains (welfare) for micro units - households and business firms - belonging to all trading sovereign nation-state-based economies. Blame for the failure to adopt generally cohesive and coordinated monetary-fiscal policies can, of course, be widely shared.

The basic argument we make is that pure market forces, *à la* idealized perfect competition, have been found to provide an ineffective and unrealistic paradigm. International efforts to make it work by politically powerful collaboration were institutionalized by the setting up of the General Agreement on Tarriffs and Trade (GATT) in 1948. Its original membership of 23 nations grew to 103 in 1991, and approached 150 in 1992. For GATT, an international economic grouping of some 150-plus members, multilateral trade liberalization has proven to be too burdensome a task. The six-year long negotiations of the Uruguay Round point to this. Finally, the GATT Agreement, signed in 1994, has witnessed the institution of the World Trade Organization (WTO) in 1995.

ALTERNATIVE PARADIGMS OF ECONOMIC REGIONALIZATION: CUSTOMS UNION / FREE TRADE AREA / TRADE PREFERENCE ASSOCIATION / COMMON MARKET

As global coordination of economic relations, especially in terms of trade liberalization, continued to prove a difficult task, efforts to resolve conflicts by way of bypassing the macroeconomic core issues resulted in various *ad hoc* arrangements.

Jacob Viner's treatise on customs union is a reference point (Viner, 1950). The debate has been joined if a customs union's contribution is to trade creation or trade diversion (Park and Yoo, 1989). In the 1960s, several customs unions were formed especially in Africa and Central and Latin America (see Table 2.1). Tables 2.2 and 2.3 present a comprehensive listing of special trade regimes.

The fact remains that the Vinerian customs unions presented a framework of economic regionalization; a recognition of the fact that nation-state-based economies increasingly proved to be inadequate macroeconomic units for trade liberalization, and as such, for maximizing the global economic welfare.

Indeed, Viner's thesis on customs union has recently found its articulate expression in the FTAs (Schott, 1989a). Recently, the United States has signed two FTA treaties, one with Canada (1989) and another with Israel (1985).

Formation of a customs union involved a two-step process:

1. one hundred per cent elimination of trade barriers ensuring a free flow of merchandise imports from one another among member-countries in a union,
2. a common trade barrier, especially a common tariff schedule against imports from all non-members.

A customs union, however, differs from a free trade area (FTA) and also from a common market. Various customs unions adopted their own schedule for their specific agenda. Their accomplishments, which have been varied, are not reviewed here (see Table 2.1).

The "fast" track initialization of the North American free trade area of Canada-U.S.-Mexico in October 1992 and its adoption in 1993, effective January 1, 1994, add another chapter.

Indeed, many Latin American sovereign states, no longer concerned about high-handed economic domination by the United States, appear to welcome a hemispheric trade area, Free Trade Area of the Americas (FTAA). In 1994, the Miami Initiative, led by the United States, brought together all sovereign nation-state-based economies in the North and South Americas, except Cuba, at a hemispheric conference and explored the agenda for FTAA. In 1996, the second hemispheric meeting of the trade ministers of the Americas added further momentum to the FTAA movement.

An instructive argument in support of NAFTA must be noted. It has been argued that member sovereign nation-states in NAFTA will augment their economic welfare (gains) by eliminating all trade barriers among themselves in 15 years without creating new trade barriers against their trading partners in the rest of the world. The economic gains of FTA members will result from no loss to economies outside. The Pareto-optimality condition has thus been addressed. Economists accept the second best, as the idealized *best* continues to elude them.

In addition, a case for NAFTA, or for that matter for an FTA, has been made that as member-economies augment their economic gains by intra-area free trade, their trade with others outside the area will grow and add to the economic gains for households and business firms in all economies outside the area.

FTAs are a lesser form of multinational arrangement for economic cooperation. Members in an FTA, as in a customs union, fully eliminate trade barriers among all member-countries in an area, as per a mutually agreed upon timetable. However, unlike in a customs union, each FTA member is free to maintain its own individual trade barriers against all non-members (see Table 2.2, Panel A).

A trade preference association is a limited version of an FTA; they take many different forms, all involving preferred trade terms for member-countries *vis-à-vis* non-members. It does not necessarily ensure total elimination of trade barriers. Imports of merchandise from a member-country receive preferred tariff terms (see Table 2.2, Panel B).

A common market sets its agenda to ensure full and free flow of both final output, goods and services, as well as of factor inputs, labor and capital, among its members. Ideally, a common market ensures removal of any and all barriers guaranteeing a free flow of all forms of economic transactions among the member-economies (see Table 2.3).

A customs union with its total elimination of trade barriers among member-countries and a common trade barrier against non-members can eventually progress into a common market.

To the extent that sovereign nation-state-based member-economies in an FTA or in a customs union fail to straightforwardly address a common monetary-fiscal economic policy agenda, they remain less than a supranational economic regionalization. The critique of the NAFTA Treaty seems to address issues which may very well transform NAFTA into an economic community of the Americas.

A common market, as was the EC, following the Single European Act of 1985 and the Maastricht Treaty of 1992, became the EU providing for a common monetary-fiscal policy agenda, a supranational macroeconomic core.

ECONOMIC REGIONALIZATION: STRATEGIC OR DEEP

Economic regionalization in the form of a customs union/free trade area/trade preference area or a common market (until the EC adopted its comprehensive charter in the 1980s and 1990s) presents one core lesson. In general, they are by and large instances of strategic regionalization, not a "deep" integration with a common monetary and fiscal policy agenda. Of course, optimization of economic gains, and/or minimization of economic losses, for the intraregional member-states, have been the immediate motivating argument for a given regional group. Individual sovereign nation-states experienced specific limitations for their respective economic gains and opted to become members of a regional compact.

The sovereign nation-states, as on the map of the world, are at best "accidents of history" and their places on the map of the world are subject to sanctions of history. Recent disintegration of the former Soviet Union and several East European nation-states, such as Czechoslovakia and Yugoslavia, must be viewed as "accidents" of history. History is replete with such happenings (Dutta, 1995b).

Often a shared history of hostility involving wars and mass destruction may prompt an effort for regionalization. Economic regional arrangements in specific cases may have been attributable to defense and security considerations of the Cold War decades. Others may have come into existence because their regional economies are naturally too integrated and their continued failure to join a regional compact may deny all member-economies in the region a share in the economic prosperity of the continental region.

Economic rationale of the nation-state-based macro units belonging to a specific geographic region joining a compact is the key issue. The member-states of a compact belong to a region, a common economic space, as is identified in a given case. Indeed, the location theory remains a key issue (Lorenz, 1993). The unit transportation cost of a given economic transaction is less and a gain in terms of comparative advantage follows. The case of deep integration warrants further analyses.

Table 2.1 Customs union: year formed; member-countries

Year	Member countries
1959	Communauté Economique de l'Afrique de l'Quest (CEAO) -West African Economic Community: Benin, Burkina Faso, Cóte d'Ivoire, Mali, Mauritania, Niger, Senegal
1960	Central American Common Market (CACM) -Costa Rica, El Salvador, Guatemala, Honduras, Nicaragua
1964	Union Douaniére et Economique de l'Afrique Centrale (UDEAC) -Economic and Customs Union of Central Africa Cameroon, Central African Republic, Chad, Congo, Equatorial Guinea, Gabon
1969	Southern African Customs Union (SACU) -Bophuthatswana, Botswana, Ciskei, Lesotho, Namibia, South Africa, Swaziland, Transkei, Venda
1973	Mano River Union (MRU) -Guinea, Liberia, Sierra Leone
1981	Organization of Eastern Caribbean States (OECS) -Antigua and Barbuda, Dominica, Grenada, Montserrat, St. Kitts-Nevis, St. Lucia

Sources: Fieleke (1992), Dutta (1992a and 1992b)

Table 2.2 Free trade area: year formed; member-countries

Panel A

1960	European Free Trade Area (EFTA) - Austria, Finland, Iceland, Liechtenstein, Norway, Sweden, Switzerland (Pacts with Czechoslovakia, Poland, Hungary, Turkey, Israel in 1991 and 1992)
1967	Association of Southeast Asian Nations (ASEAN) - Indonesia, Malaysia, the Philippines, Singapore, Thailand; Brunei Darussalam in 1985; Vietnam in 1995
1974	Finland and Eastern Europe (various agreements from 1974 to present) - Finland, Hungary, Czechoslovakia
1983	Australia-New Zealand Closer Economic Relations Trade Agreement (ANZCERTA) - Australia, New Zealand
1985	Israel-United States Free Trade Area: Israel, United States
1989	Canada-United States Free Trade Area: Canada, United States
1991	European Economic Area: Free Trade between EC and EFTA
1991	Andean Pact - Colombia, Ecuador, Bolivia, Peru, Venezuela
1991	MERCOSUR -Argentina, Brazil, Paraguay, Uruguay
1992	Association of Southeast Asian Free Trade Area - Brunei, Indonesia, Malaysia, the Philippines, Singapore, Thailand (Laos and Vietnam have expressed interest in joining the group)
1992	Sweden and the Baltics - Sweden, Estonia, Latvia, Lithuania
1994	North American Free Trade Area (NAFTA) - Canada, Mexico, the United States

Panel B

1972	Industrial Free Trade Area: Member-countries of EC and EFTA
1976	Trade Preference Association: Bangkok Agreement - Bangladesh, India, Laos, South Korea, Sri Lanka

1980	Trade Preference Association: Latin American Integration Association (LAIA) - Argentina, Bolivia, Brazil, Chile, Colombia, Ecuador, Mexico, Paraguay, Peru, Uruguay, Venezuela
1981	Trade Preference Association: Preferential Trade Area for Eastern and Southern African States (PTA) - Burundi, Comoros, Djibouti, Ethiopia, Kenya, Lesotho, Malawi, Mauritius, Mozambique, Rwanda, Somalia, Swaziland, Tanzania, Uganda, Zambia, Zimbabwe
1985	South Asian Association for Regional Cooperation (SAARC) - Bangladesh, Bhutan, India, Maldives, Nepal, Pakistan, Sri Lanka
1994*	The Hemispheric Conference of the Americas: Free Trade Area of the Americas (FTAA) 34 members: Antigua and Barbuda, Argentina, Bahamas, Barbados, Belize, Bolivia, Brazil, Canada, Chile, Colombia, Costa Rica, Dominica, Dominican Republic, Ecuador, El Salvador, Grenada, Guatemala, Guyana, Haiti, Honduras, Jamaica, Mexico, Nicaragua, Panama, Paraguay, Peru, St. Vincent and the Grenadines, St. Lucia, St. Kitts and Nevis, Suriname, Trinidad and Tobago, Uruguay, the United States of America, and Venezuela (excluding CUBA)
1995**	Indian Ocean Group - 47 littoral and landlocked sovereign nation-state-based economies; Australia, Southeast Asia: Brunei, Indonesia, Malaysia, Mayanmar, the Philippines, Singapore, Thailand; SAARC: Bangladesh, Bhutan (included with India), India, Maldives (not separately reported), Nepal, Pakistan, Sri Lanka; West Asia: Afghanistan, Bahrain, Egypt, Iran, Iraq, Kuwait, Oman, Qatar, Saudi Arabia, U.A.E., Yemen (unified); North and East Africa: Burundi, Djibouti, Ethiopia, Kenya, Madagascar, Malawi, Mozambique, Rwanda, Somalia, Sudan, Tanzania, Uganda, Zambia, Zimbabwe; South African Customs Union: Botswana (in SACU), Lesotho, South Africa, Swaziland; Indian Ocean Islands: Comoros, Mauritius, Seychelles

Sources: Fieleke (1992), Dutta (1992a, 1992b, and 1992c), Bradsher (1992), Summit of the Americas, Denver, Colorado, June 30,1995.
Kalirajan and Shand (1996).

Notes: Panel A includes formally designated FTAs; Panel B includes associated groupings.

* The Free Trade Area of the Americas (FTAA) is at its preparatory stage.

** The Indian Ocean Group (IOG) is at its exploratory stage.

Table 2.3 Common market: year formed; member-countries

1957	European Community (EC) - Belgium, Denmark, France, Germany, Greece, Ireland, Italy, Luxembourg, Netherlands, Portugal, Spain, United Kingdom (present membership - original membership six countries and six others joined later: initially a free trade area); now European Union (EU) as of 1992
1964	Middle East and Africa: Arab Common Market (ACM) - Egypt, Iraq, Jordan, Lebanon, Libya, Mauritania, Syria
1969	Andean Common Market (ANCOM) - Bolivia, Colombia, Ecuador, Peru, Venezuela
1973	Caribbean Common Market (CARICOM) - Antigua and Barbuda, Bahamas, Barbados, Belize, Dominica, Grenada, Guyana, Jamaica, Montserrat, St. Kitts-Nevis, St. Lucia, St. Vincent and the Grenadines, Trinidad and Tobago
1975	Economic Community of West African States (ECOWAS) - Benin, Burkina Faso, Cape Verde, Côte d'Ivoire, The Gambia, Ghana, Guinea, Guinea-Bissau, Liberia, Mali, Mauritania, Niger, Nigeria, Senegal, Sierra Leone, Togo
1981	Communauté Economique des Etats de l'Afrique Centrale (CEEAC) - Economic Community of Central African States: Burundi, Cameroon, Central African Republic, Chad, Congo, Equatorial Guinea, Gabon, Rwanda, Sao Tome and Principe, Zaire
1981	Gulf Cooperation Council (GCC) - Bahrain, Kuwait, Oman, Qatar, Saudi Arabia, United Arab Emirates
1989	Arab Maghreb Union (AMU) - Algeria, Libya, Mauritania, Morocco, Tunisia
1991	Southern Cone Common Market (MERCOSUL/MERCOSUR) - Argentina, Brazil, Paraguay, Uruguay

Source: Fieleke (1992).
Note: EC was instituted January 1, 1958, following the Treaty of Rome, signed in 1957 (this text).

3 An Economic Community in the Asia-Pacific Region

The concept of an economic community in the Asia-Pacific Region is not new and it has progressed in two historical phases (Drysdale, 1988, pp. 209-22, especially footnotes 42 and 45, pp. 224-5). The concept of an Asia-Pacific economic community seems to have its root in a proposal for a counterregional economic grouping to the European economic community as it began to unfold after the signing of the Treaty of Rome in 1957. It must be noted that economic rationale of the discussion continued to remain limited in this U.S.-Pacific response to face the emerging challenge of a "fortress Europe".

For an overview of the growth of the process of Asia-Pacific economic cooperation, a tabular presentation of the historical institutional profile follows (Table 3.1). Let us review the movement for economic cooperation in the Asia-Pacific region, exclusive of South Asia, in *two* successive phases.

PHASE I: OPTAD

The first two plans, using the acronym OPTAD, came from Kojima and Drysdale (Kojima, 1968). Kojima used the term for the Organization for Pacific Trade and Development (OPTAD) while Drysdale referred to the Organization for Pacific Trade, Aid and Development. The concept of a Pacific Free Trade Area (PAFTA) was introduced by Kojima as early as 1964, and in the following year a proposal was developed, a response, as it were, to the formation of the European common market in 1958 following the signing of the Treaty of Rome in 1957.

A series of annual conferences on Pacific trade and development, beginning with the first one in Tokyo in January 1968, became its regular agenda. The 19th conference was held in May 1991 in Beijing with "Economic Reform and Internationalization: China and the Pacific Rim" as its theme. In September 1992, the 20th conference in Washington, DC discussed "Pacific Dynamism". In July 1978, Drysdale and Patrick coauthored a position paper for the U.S. Congress (Drysdale and Patrick, 1979) discussing the economic argument for regional economic cooperation.

PHASE II: PECC/APEC

A new Asia-Pacific regional expression, the Pacific Economic Cooperation Council, formerly the Pacific Economic Cooperation Conference (PECC), was an output of the Canberra seminar on the Pacific community in September 1980. In 1992, PECC membership consisted of Australia, Brunei Darussalam, Canada, Chile, China, Hong Kong, Indonesia, Japan, Korea, Malaysia, Mexico, New Zealand, Peru, the Philippines, Russia, Singapore, Taiwan (China), Thailand, the United States and the Pacific Island Nations. In addition, OPTAD and PBEC became its institutional members.

Both China and Taiwan were admitted to full participation at the fifth session of PECC in Vancouver in 1986 and became a new reality in the 1980s of an organized expression of Asia-Pacific economic regionalism. PECC continues to be a non-governmental forum. It remains to be noted that this Asia-Pacific initiative followed the European Community's adoption of the Single European Act in 1985.

In November 1989, at a special ministerial conference held in Canberra, the Asia-Pacific Economic Cooperation (APEC) became the elevated institutional expression of the process. Until 1993, APEC functioned as an intergovernmental agency with full official standing at the "ministerial level", at the level of foreign ministers (not heads of governments as is the case in the G-7).

The second APEC ministerial meeting, held in July 1990 in Singapore, set up seven working groups to study specific areas of regional economic cooperation: (i) investment and technology transfer, (ii) human resource development, (iii) marine resource conservation, (iv) energy cooperation, (v) trade and investment data, (vi) telecommunications and (vii) trade promotion.

Following the successful Korean initiative to include China, Taiwan and Hong Kong in its membership at its third meeting in November 1991 in Seoul, the APEC membership included 16 economies: Australia, Brunei Darussalam, Canada, China, Hong Kong, Indonesia, Japan, Korea, Malaysia, New Zealand, Pacific Islands, the Philippines, Singapore, Taiwan (China), Thailand and the United States. (In addition, PECC, ASEAN and SPF participate as institutional observers.)

In 1993, the APEC membership rose to 17 with the admission of Mexico to the group. It must be noted that the APEC Summit at Seattle in 1993 for the first time in the history of the organization witnessed participation by Heads of most member-states - indeed, a historic symbolic step to underscore the economic significance of Asia, "an economic era of Asian primacy". It is evident that APEC and its agenda remain in a process of evolution. In 1994, at the APEC Summit in Bogor, Indonesia, Chile became its eighteenth member.

The APEC calendar of activities, including its fourth ministerial meeting in Thailand in September 1992, fifth in Seattle, United States in 1993, sixth in Indonesia in 1994, most certainly point to the growing emphasis on the institutionalization of Asia-Pacific economic cooperation. Indeed, an APEC headquarters in Singapore has been in function.

At its ministerial meeting November 12-14, 1991 in Seoul, representatives of the APEC members signed a policy declaration which reinforced its twofold commitments: (i) Asia-Pacific regional economic cooperation and (ii) global economic partnership. The case for a "fortress" regional economic grouping is, of course, rejected. The Seoul Declaration proposes a marriage between "regionalism" and "globalism" and very rightly so. Naturally, a successful conclusion of the Uruguay Round (of GATT negotiations) is proclaimed by APEC ministers as "the most critical issue facing the international community" (PECC 1992, p. 119).

The Seoul Declaration clearly states APEC objectives:

(i) to sustain the growth and development of the region for the common good of its peoples and, in this way, to contribute to the growth and development of the world economy;
(ii) to enhance the positive gains, both for the region and the world economy, resulting from increasing economic interdependence, including by encouraging the flow of goods, services, capital and technology;
(iii) to develop and strengthen the open multilateral trading system in the interest of Asia-Pacific and all other economies;
(iv) to reduce barriers to trade in goods and services and investment among participants in a manner consistent with GATT principles, where applicable, and without detriment to other economies. (PECC 1992, p. 115)

Economic regionalization in the Asia-Pacific, or for that matter in Europe, or in any other continent, must be an "open" - not a "fortress" - regional bloc. It follows that regionalization of sovereign nation-state-based macroeconomic units results in the optimization of economic gains for the micro units - households and business firms - belonging to all intraregional member-economies. In other words, left to an individual sovereign national economic unit, in a regional non-cooperative game, optimization of economic gains of its micro units would not have been achieved. It further follows that the process must extend to global economic cooperation among all regional groupings. We have argued at the outset (see Chapter 1) that each individual sovereign nation-state-based economy will now engage in a two-track free competitive economic game: (i) intraregional and (ii) interregional.

We have also argued that the geographical borders of an economic region cannot be predefined. The experience of the EC in Western Europe points to a progressive broadening of the limits of its geographic space. APEC can and will draw upon the Western European experience. Historically, we argue that the phased development of the framework of economic cooperation in the Asia-Pacific region has been a progressive response to the European experience.

We have noted above that the initial move for Asia-Pacific economic regionalization came in 1968, a decade after the Treaty of Rome was signed in 1957. As the EC moved ahead with its agenda of regionalization, the Single European Act of 1985 and then the Maastricht Treaty of 1992, the Asia-Pacific region made its response by progressively moving from its early informal arrangements of OPTAD (1968) and PBEC (1967) to PECC (1980) and then to APEC (1989).

Membership in regional cooperation has increased from the five industrialized nations in OPTAD (1968) to 18 in APEC (1994). The same has been the experience in Europe. The EC's original membership of six progressed to the 12-member EC and now to the 15-member EU in 1995, with several other European nations being candidates for membership; still others in Eastern Europe and the former Soviet Union are eager for associate membership. Whether EU membership will encompass all sovereign nation-state based macroeconomic units of Europe "from the Atlantic to the Urals" remains an open question.

We have argued that continent-based economic regionalization is a proposition based on geographical contiguity, and as such, economics of location theory. The 1991 Seoul statement of APEC ministers is specific on the subject. "Participation in APEC will be *open* (italics ours), in principle, to those economies in the Asia-Pacific region which (a) have strong economic linkages in the Asia-Pacific region; and (b) accept the objectives and principles of APEC" (see Declaration above), subject, of course, to "a consensus of all existing participants" (PECC, 1992, p. 117).

Two other Asia-Pacific economic regionalization schemes have been referred to: (i) an *ad hoc* regional framework with the Pacific economy consisting of western states of the United States and of Canada on this shore of the Pacific and Japan and Pacific Basin economies on the other (Linder, 1986); and (ii) another option is to relate economic regionalization to sovereign nation-state- based macroeconomic units in geographically defined continents on the map of the world (Dutta, 1992a). Four alternative economic regionalization schemes: (i) OPTAD, (ii) APEC, (iii) the Linder, and (iv) the Continental, are presented here (Figures 3.1- 3.4).

The question is whether APEC as a common economic region should become a compact of deep integration, relative to its common regional economic structure, rather than a pact based on a consideration for "strategic optimization", allowing strategic rather than economic factors to be prime motivating factors for the formation of an economic region. With its stated goal to develop a common monetary and fiscal agenda in the 1990s, the EU is now engaged in an experiment of deep economic integration. Should APEC follow the same track? For the present, it has been very well stated that APEC is neither EC nor NAFTA. We argue that the location theory by itself may not explain the new paradigm of economic regionalization. Belonging to the same region meets the necessary condition for a map-of-the-world view of a geo-economic region. A supranational macroeconomic monetary-fiscal policy coordination by the sovereign member-states of the regional group will satisfy the necessary and sufficient condition. A common geographic space only then will have become a common economic space.

JAPAN AND THE U.S. IN THE ASIA-PACIFIC REGION

Both Japan and the United States are members of APEC. Japan's leading role in the Asian continent and in the emerging economic regionalization in the Asia-Pacific has to be noted.

Saburo Okita (1989, pp. 45-6) presents an outline of Japan's multistage initiative in this regard. Around 1965, Japan introduced its third stage. "Economic cooperation agreements were concluded with Taiwan and the Republic of Korea . . . . taking an active part in the establishment of the Asian Development Bank . . . . The emphasis was clearly on development assistance for East and Southeast Asia". Okita adds, "Most of Japan's assistance has gone to the Asian countries especially the ASEAN. Approximately 70% of Japan's total disbursements went to Asia, including China and India, while Africa, Latin America and the Middle East received roughly 10% of the total each".

Okita (1989, pp. 46-7) continues, "Considering Japan's close relations with the other Asian countries and Japan's responsibility to contribute to the economic stability of this region with its huge population and immense development needs, Asia will continue to receive the lion's share of Japanese Official Development Assistance [ODA]".

However, he reminds his readers that as an economic superpower, Japan

Table 3.1 APEC: historical institutional profile

1947	Economic and Social Commission for Asia and the Pacific (ESCAP): an Agency of the United Nations all UN member countries of Asia (plus associate members from other continents).
1967	Pacific Basin Economic Council (PBEC): a non-official forum for business executives from countries involved.
1967	Association of Southeast Asian Nations (ASEAN): an inter - governmental organization - Indonesia, Malaysia, the Philippines, Singapore, Thailand; Brunei Darussalam in 1985; Vietnam 1995.
1968	Organization for Pacific Trade and Development Conference (OPTAD): an academic forum - Australia, Canada, Japan, New Zealand, the United States.
1971	South Pacific Forum (SPF): an inter-governmental organization - Australia, Cook Island, Federated States of Micronesia, Fiji, Kiribati, Marshall Islands, New Zealand, Niue, Papua New Guinea, Solomon Islands, Tonga, Tuvalu, Vanuata, Western Samoa.
1980	Pacific Economic Cooperation Council (PECC), formerly, Pacific Economic Cooperation Conference: a non-official forum - Australia, Brunei Darussalam, Canada, Chile, China, Hong Kong, Indonesia, Japan, Korea, Malaysia, Mexico, New Zealand, Peru, the Philippines, Russia, Singapore, Taiwan (China), Thailand, the United States and the Pacific Island Nations.
1985	South Asian Association for Regional Cooperation (SAARC): an inter-governmental forum - Bangladesh, Bhutan, India, Maldives, Nepal, Pakistan, Sri Lanka.
1989	Asia-Pacific Economic Cooperation (APEC): an official inter-governmental forum - Australia, Brunei Darussalam, Canada, China, Hong Kong, Indonesia, Japan, Korea, Malaysia, New Zealand, Pacific Islands, the Philippines, Singapore, Thailand and the United States; Hong Kong, Taipei and Mainland China in 1992; Mexico in 1993, and Chile in 1994.
1995	Indian Ocean Trading Group 47 littoral and landlocked sovereign nation-state based economies (see Table 2.2, Panel B).

Sources: PECC (1992), Dutta (1992a & 1992b), Arndt (1993), Kalirajan and Shand (1996).

Figure 3.1 OPTAD

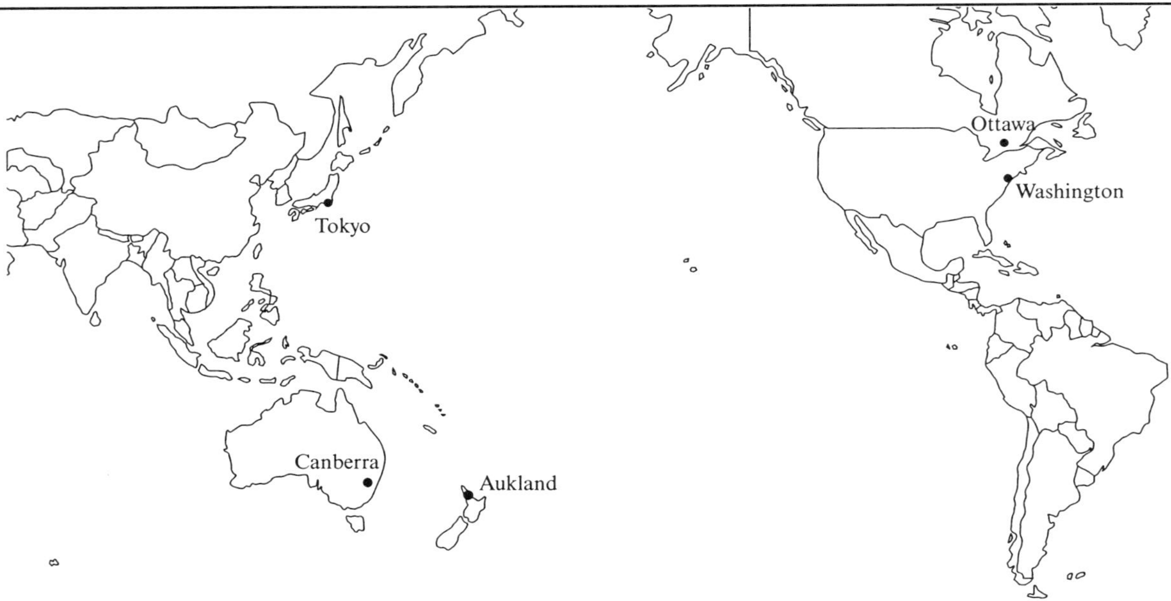

Note: see Chapter 1

Figure 3.2 APEC

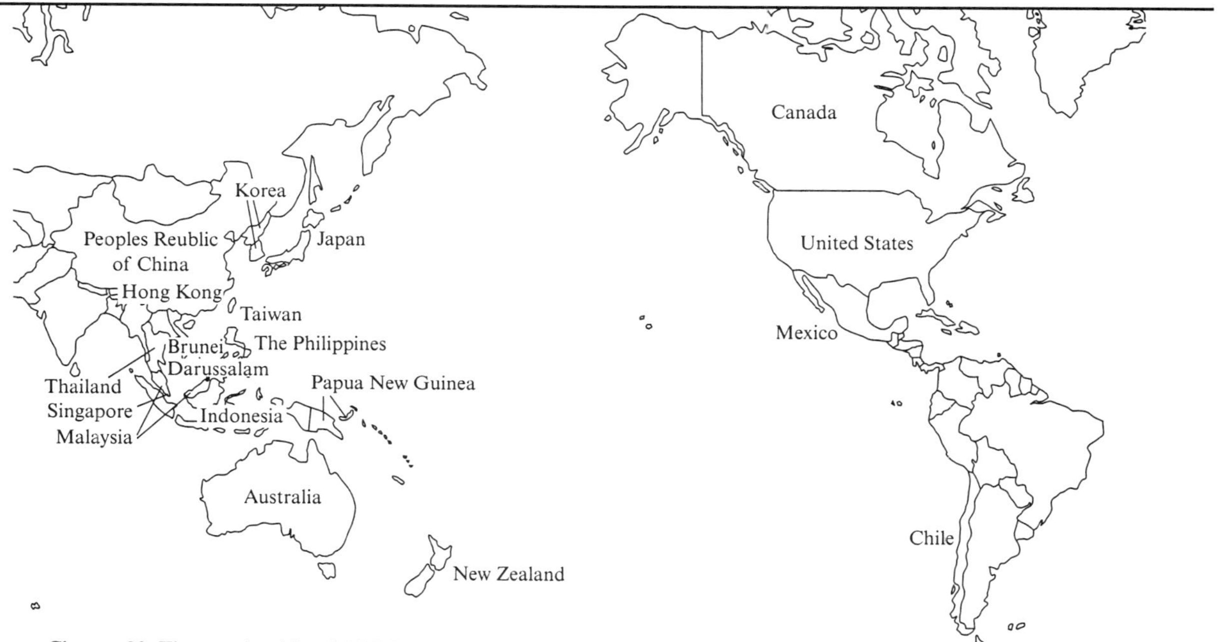

Note: see Chapter 22. The membership of APEC was frozen at the Bogor summit in 1994 for a 3-year period. In the Vancouver summit in November 1997 three new members have been admitted, not included in the sketch.

Figure 3.3 Linder scheme: Asia-Pacific region

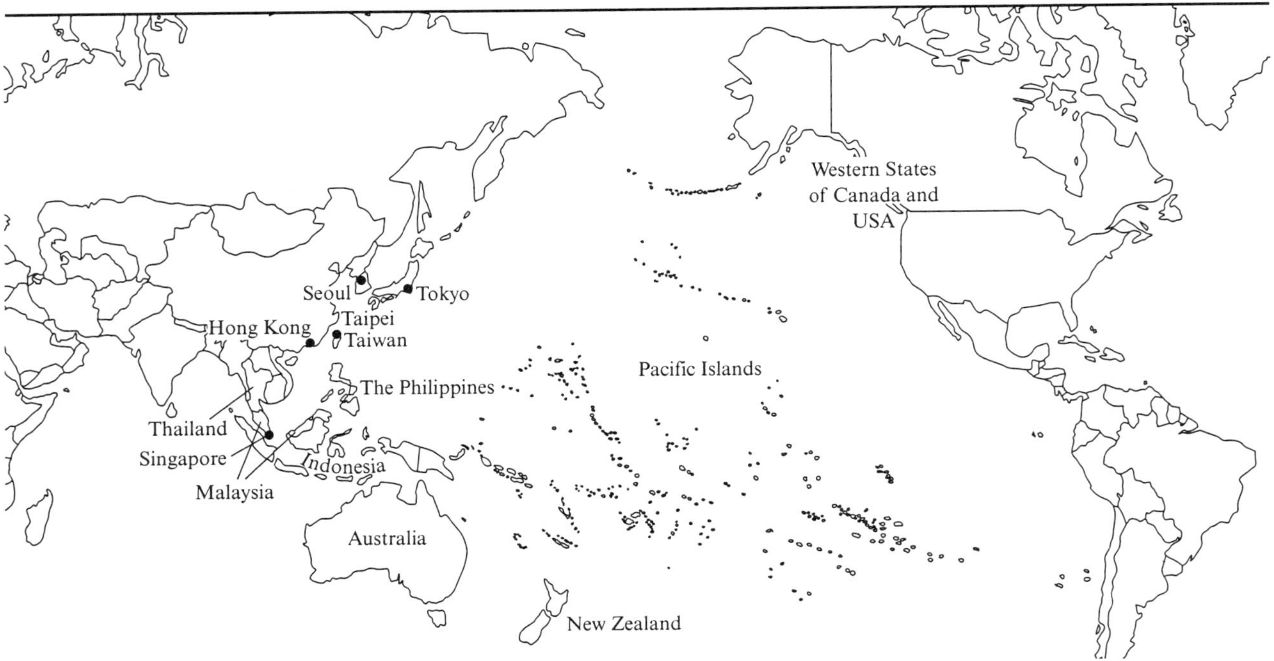

Note: see Chapter 1, p. 4; see also Linder (1996)

Figure 3.4 Continental

Note: see Chapter 1, p.7, also Dutta (1990 and 1992d)

will assume its share of responsibility in terms of economic assistance to the economies in other continents. His focus is to outline the Japanese official approach to the Asian economic community. Recent studies (Drysdale, 1988, pp. 191-2), indicate that Japan has emerged as the dominant source of foreign capital in East Asia and the Pacific.

Around 43 per cent of all Japan's capital exports to developing countries went to East Asia at the beginning of the 1980s. For the United States the figure was just over 12 per cent. The concentration of Japanese direct foreign investment within East Asia is exceptionally marked: East Asia ranks with North America as an outlet for Japanese direct foreign investment, each accounting for just under 28 per cent of all Japan's direct foreign investment.

Japan's development assistance and direct foreign investment (DFI) have progressively extended to India and South Asian countries.

The U.S. role in the Pacific economies came to a new focus as it crossed "a milestone" in 1981, when the U.S. for the first time in its history, did more trade on the trans-Pacific routes than on the trans-Atlantic ones (Dutta, 1987a and 1987b, pp. 93-100). In 1981, U.S. trade with Europe was $115.1 billion as against its trade with Asia-Pacific totalling $131.4 billion. In 1980 the Asia-Pacific total came to $117.4 billion compared with the European total of $119.0 billion. The gap in favor of the Asia-Pacific trade continues to widen.

The United States is a Pacific economy and its interaction with the Asia-Pacific market continues to grow (Dutta, 1990). Given its share of economic interaction across both the oceans - the Atlantic and the Pacific - the United States is indeed at once an Atlantic and a Pacific economy. Its continental economy is robust and it is a market of great magnitude by any statistical measure for both European and Asian economies.

Lorenz (1991 and 1993) notes the U.S.A. appears to be pursuing a strategy facing in both directions at once, Canada/Mexico plus East Asia/Pacific. Some European economists may indeed wonder if the U.S.A. will join a U.S.-Pacific bloc, *vis-à-vis* the EU, effectively in a bipolar economic order, or a vertical hemispheric economic regionalization of the Americas (FTAA), in a multipolar world economy.

From an Asia-Pacific perspective, Park and Yoo (1989, p. 86) state with emphasis that it is simply unrealistic to expect Japan to grow into an export market for other Pacific Asian economies large enough to supplant the U.S. market in the near future, no matter what it does to transform its economic policies and lifestyle. In 1987, they add, the total volume of Pacific Basin exports to the U.S. was larger than the total value of the intraregional trade in

Pacific Asia. Japan purchased less than 10 per cent of the total manufactured exports of the East Asian NIEs, ASEAN and China, while the United States absorbed more than 30 per cent. U.S. imports from all of East Asian NIEs, ASEAN and China in 1987 . . . [were] six times as large as the Japanese imports from these countries.

Based on an extensive empirical study comparing Japan's exports of machinery and capital goods to a set of its neighboring economies and its imports of manufactured goods from them, Shinohara (1987, pp. 23-8) concludes that Japan has acted as "a growth pole" from the supply side, not from the demand side. Balassa (1987, pp. 49-68) reports a parallel finding to point to Japan's limited imports of manufactures from developing countries.

The role of the United States in absorbing exports from the Asia-Pacific economies, especially the NIEs and Japan, is the principal thesis. Gray (1989) examines the role of the U.S. as a "locomotive" economy. Klein (1990) reviews the Asia-Pacific perspective and examines whether export-led growth can continue *indefinitely*.

Certainly, any form of American hemispheric economic regionalization cannot be viewed as a plan for "fortress Americas", resulting in the closing of the U.S market to the East Asian NIEs or to any other economies/regions in a new international economic order, firmly committed to the principle of "regionalism and globalism". The U.S. is an *open* economy, and the scale of its economy, especially the consumer market with its $7 trillion plus gross domestic product (GDP), has been an attractive market for all economies in all continents. Similarly, to study the United States as a Pacific economy is in no way to suggest that the Pacific economies in APEC will become an economic fortress closed to other continent-based regional blocs.

In the Asia-Pacific region, Japan, South Korea and Taiwan have earned trade surpluses and have been exporting capital. Japan has greatly expanded its FDI (see Kojima, 1978, 1990a). For the United States, its unipolar supremacy in the post-World War II global economic system has long ceased to exist.

4 Economic Regionalization in Western Europe: Search for a New Paradigm

BEYOND A CUSTOMS UNION/A FREE TRADE AREA

Jacob Viner's pioneering work, *The Customs Union Issue* (1950) remains the classic treatise on economic regionalization. Removal of trade barriers, Viner argued, would add to the flow of trade among trading countries. In addition, free flow of trade would contribute to competitive price rationalization in all trading economies, much to the gain of consumers in all countries.

No economic principle ever works without qualification. The question has been raised whether Viner failed to adjust his simple model of customs union for "trade diversion" (Schott 1989a, pp. 1-50), and/or for "trade repression" *à la* Stolper-Samuelson Condition (Park and Yoo, 1989, pp. 143-4).

Notwithstanding the fact that a customs union and a free trade area are not identical expressions of multinational regional grouping, Viner's thesis on customs union has been the core economic rationale for FTAs, and its critiques question whether they are basically superior to GATT (Wonnacott and Lutz 1989) and WTO as of 1995, except for the fact that the pace of negotiation in an FTA may be relatively fast, as it generally involves "like-minded" peoples/countries (Canada-U.S. FTA, U.S.-Israel FTA).

A bilateral FTA, irrespective of the fact of "like-mindedness" of the two parties to the agreement, is certainly not comparable to GATT negotiations where negotiations among its 150-plus sovereign member-states have been known to be painfully slow. Illuminating discourses on bilateral FTAs, U.S.-Japan (Makoto Kuroda), U.S.-Korea (Park and Yoo), U.S.-Taiwan (Tsiang), U.S.-ASEAN (Ariff), U.S.-Mexico (Trigueros), U.S.-Australia (Snape), a Pacific FTA (Drysdale and Garnaut), point to the limited, if not dubious, merit of FTAs (all in Schott, 1989a).

Bilateral FTAs can work only in very exceptional situations. Others have made a strong case for GATT and trade negotiations under GATT, should it ever be able to conclude its successive negotiating rounds (Krause, 1987).

Currently, the United States is signatory to two bilateral FTAs and a brief comment on each of them is in order. First, the U.S.-Israel FTA (Rosen, in

Schott, 1989a), signed in April 1985, "within the context of historically strong political, military, and economic ties between the United States and Israel", was implemented on September 1, 1985. It calls for removal of all tariffs and most other forms of trade barriers between the two trading partners in ten years. Rosen gives "high marks" to the performance to date of the U.S.-Israel FTA, 'a product of the special relationship' between the two countries.

Second, the U.S.-Canada FTA (Lipsey and Smith in Schott, 1989a), effective early 1989, also calls for 'a complete removal' of all tariffs and most non-tariff trade barriers between Canada and the United States in a ten-year period. Lipsey and Smith note this special case, when GATT negotiations continued to be held up.

As noted earlier, in 1992, the U.S.-Canada FTA has been extended to include Mexico, following the fast track initialization of NAFTA. Indeed, NAFTA with its supplementary agreements covering provisions for comparability of labor market and environmental protection arrangements among the three signatory countries to the agreement, has resulted in the institutionalization of the North American Free Trade Area in 1994.

The agreement seems to have the potential to progress into a common market of North America, setting the pace for an American hemispheric free trade area (FTAA).

LESSONS FROM THE PARADIGM OF EUROPEAN REGIONALIZATION:

Economic regionalization in Western Europe cannot be studied within the Vinerian customs union paradigm. The EC, which originated as a free trade area, progressed far beyond a customs union, or a free trade area (European Commission 1989a, 1989b, 1990). Extraeconomic issues, sociopolitical parameters inclusive of war and peace, noted to be important, will, however, remain beyond the scope of the present study.

The EU indeed presents a paradigm of its own. Jean Monnet (1978) said it best: "*We are not forming coalitions between States, but union among people*". As of 1992, the EC became the EU, with a supranational macroeconomic core. Obviously, Monnet foresaw much of what was to come.

In March 1971, following the Werner Report in 1970, the EC member-states expressed "their political will to establish an economic and monetary union". In 1979 the process of monetary integration was renewed with the creation of the European Monetary System (EMS) and the European Currency Unit (Ecu). The goal is the creation of a *zone of increasing monetary stability with provisions for multilateral surveillance* within the EU. It is a "mini-lateral", intraregional, supranational monetary system with the Deutschmark as the anchor currency for participants' monetary and intervention policies. It goes far beyond the concept of a region-based International Monetary Fund (IMF). At the center of the EMS is the Ecu, *a reserve asset and a means of settlement for EMS central banks* (European Commission, 1989a and 1989b, 1990).

The EMS, however, continues to function with its limitations, at least for three reasons, the Commission's *Report* (1990) adds:

1. First, several member-countries have not yet joined, or have been forced to withdraw from, the exchange rate mechanism and/or a specific member country enjoys the privilege of wider fluctuation margins.
2. Second, absence of a higher order of convergence of fiscal policies remains a challenge for the monetary policy towards effective exchange rate stabilization.
3. Transition of the EMS to the European Monetary Union (EMU), the goal set in 1978, remains to be completed. (See also Lamfalussy, 1989; Ungerer, et al., 1986; Allen, 1990)

Adoption of the Single European Act of 1985 marked the first major revision of the Treaty of Rome (1957), introducing four important changes:

1. First, it greatly simplified the requirements of harmonizing national laws by limiting harmonization to the essential standards and by systematic adoption of mutual recognition of national norms and regulations.
2. Second, it established a faster and more efficient decision-making process by extending the scope of qualified majority voting.
3. Third, it gave the European Parliament a greater role in the legislative process.
4. Fourth, it reaffirmed the need to strengthen the sovereign member-states' economic and social cohesion.

Over the last three years, the *Report* (1989) continued, considerable progress has been made insofar as implementation of the internal market program is concerned. As many as eight of the twelve member countries *fully liberalized capital movements by July 1, 1990*. The remaining four members will join the process after a specified transition period.

As of 1994, the EU has made substantive progress as its basic membership became enlarged from 12 to 15 member-nations with Sweden, Finland and Austria joining the Union. Should Norway, Liechtenstein, Switzerland and

Iceland soon become members of the Union, a common economic region of Europe with 380 million people will extend from the Arctic to the Mediterranean. However, the EU is yet to achieve its final stage of deep integration with one common currency and one regional central bank. Acutely aware of its difficulties, the EU continues to press its agenda toward progressive deepening of the process of integration of the member-economies.

However, the single most important step in this regard came in 1993, when 12 member-states of the EU resolved to set up the European Monetary Institute (EMI) in Frankfurt, Germany. The EMI became operational on January 1, 1994 and it is expected to evolve into the European Central Bank by the end of the century.

The *three* necessary conditions for the *EU's monetary union* are stated to be:

1. the assurance of total and irreversible convertibility of currencies;
2. the complete liberalization of capital transactions and full integration of banking and other financial markets; and
3. the elimination of margins of fluctuation and the irrevocable locking of exchange rate parities.

The need for a new monetary institution, a *European System of Central Banks* (ESCB), to coordinate the activities of the central banks of the sovereign member-countries, is very much recognized.

The *four basic elements of the economic union* are stated to be:

- the single market within which persons, goods, services and capital can move freely;
- competition policy and other measures aimed at strengthening market mechanisms;
- common policies aimed at structural change and regional development; and
- macroeconomic policy coordination, including binding rules for budgetary policies.

In the budgetary field, three binding rules to be observed are: *first*, imposition of effective upper limits on budget deficits of individual member-countries in the Community; *second*, exclusion of access to direct central bank credit and other forms of monetary financing, while permitting open market operations in government securities; and *third*, limiting recourse to external borrowing in non-Community countries.

It is difficult to evaluate the ultimate success of European economic regionalization (Hufbauer, 1990). However, those of us who subscribe to a positive view of the EU paradigm remain optimistic. Commenting on the growing generalized trend towards regional union, Lorenz (1989) argues that if regionalism is understood not as a defensive or aggressive bloc building as in the thirties, but as a regional grouping that is open towards the world economy, it appears to have something to offer as an alternative to the old international economic order.

Achievements as of this date encourage many to believe that economic regionalization in Europe is deep enough and thus goes far beyond Viner's customs union or its subsequent manifestations as FTAs or any other alternative forms of regional preference, based essentially on the concept of strategic optimization.

A European Union of 15 sovereign member-states in Western Europe offers a unique paradigm of economic regionalization, notwithstanding the happenings in 1992-93. EU is a progressive movement toward institutionalization of a supranational macroeconomic core for the optimization of economic gains (welfare) of microeconomic units - households as well as business corporations - belonging to all its sovereign nation-state-based member-economies (Dutta, 1992b).

The Treaty of Rome was signed in 1957, and in 1958 the grouping of five Western European economies became functional. Soon seven other Western European economies joined the Community membership. The Single European Act of 1985 and the Maastricht Treaty of 1992 are the next two important dates in the progressive manifestation of the paradigm of Western European regionalization.

Since its founding in 1958, the economic regionalization in Western Europe has experienced an uneven course of progress. However, its commitment to a supranational intraregional macroeconomic core has prevailed. It continues progressively to address its stated goal: creation of a zone of monetary-fiscal stability with provisions for surveillance of the sovereign member-nations.

Thus, the three important dates for the EC are: first, 1958 when the Treaty of Rome, as signed in 1957, became operational. Second, 1985 when the Single European Act was adopted. Third, 1992 when the Maastricht Treaty, signed in 1991 by 12 sovereign member-nations, became effective. Under the terms of the Treaty, it can be enforced only after the approval by sovereign authorities of *all* 12 member-nations who were signatories to it in 1991. To date, all 12 members have approved the Maastricht Treaty. Denmark voted down a referendum on the Treaty in 1992 only to substantively reverse the decision by a second referendum in 1993. The parliament of the United Kingdom finally voted for the Treaty in 1993, surviving a subsequent court challenge by opponents. The German parliamentary approval of the Treaty also survived a court challenge.

Two points merit attention. First, definitive judicial verdicts at the highest level of legal authorities both in the United Kingdom and in Germany firmly rejected challenges that membership of the EU would compromise the sovereign authority of a member-nation. Second, Denmark, a member-country which has achieved as high as a 90 per cent score on its overall performance on intraregional integration of laws (see Table 4.1) voted to reject the membership of the Union in its first referendum, quickly reversing itself in the following year.

On the road to a single market, each member government must enact about 170 legislative measures that bring individual national laws into accord with other members' laws and European Community policies. A progress report as of mid-August, 1992 has been published. Of course, these are crude indices, but they do shed some light on the situation.

Table 4.1 On the road to a single market: percentage of measures enacted

Belgium	64.3	Spain	67.3
Luxembourg	69.9	Italy	70.6
Ireland	72.5	Britain	73.1
Netherlands	75.0	Greece	75.3
Portugal	78.4	Germany	78.6
France	83.4	Denmark	89.8

Source: European Commission (*New York Times*, November 16, 1992).

THE PERIODS OF CRISIS

In 1992, there had been much news about the vulnerability of the EMS, which was set up in 1979. The Ecu has since then been in acceptance as the unit of accounting, although *not* as the medium of exchange.

Hesse (1993) points out that in the first eight years of the EMS, only 12 realignments were necessary, while between January 1987 and September 1992, over a period of about six years, no major EMS realignment took place.

The EMS has been sufficiently robust to arrange accommodations for the exchange rate crisis for specific member currencies.

The development of a regional institutional mechanism to forge a common monetary and fiscal policy agenda among its sovereign members is a crucial step to the success of the process. To this end, Hesse emphasizes, the Treaty of Maastricht explicitly states four major guidelines (Hesse, 1993). They are:

1. coordination of the average inflation rate by relating increases in consumer price indices (CPI) in member-economies to an average of the best performance by any three members;
2. coordination of current national budget deficit and national debt as percentages of gross national product (GDP), i.e. current deficit/GDP and national debt/GDP ratios, by a regionally accepted code of fiscal discipline;
3. control of unilateral changes in values of currencies of respective nation-states and the management of exchange rates of all member-economies in terms of a historical bench mark; and
4. limiting fluctuations of national interest rates on long-term bonds within the band set by an average of any three member-states with the best inflation performance.

The EU leadership is very much aware of the practical constraints and have set fairly elaborate escape clauses to enable each individual member - each a sovereign nation-state - to mend its "home" macroeconomic system, as may be necessary.

Commenting on the reports of relatively less than enthusiastic public attitudes in Denmark, France and England, and the difficulties of establishing one European Central Bank, as envisaged in the EU agenda and also in the Maastricht Treaty, one U.S. central banker has observed that the debate over the process of establishment of the U.S. Federal Reserve System bringing together its 12 regional federal reserve banks was no less difficult. Drawing upon the historical experience of the United States, Forrestal forthrightly reminds students of the EC's monetary union and its related difficult experiences that although, " [the U.S.] had achieved a single currency shortly after the Civil War in the mid-1800s, we did not have full monetary union until the establishment of a central bank, the Federal Reserve System, in 1913". He adds: "Even after the Fed was founded with its twelve Reserve Banks, the U.S. did not have a common discount rate for some time" (Forrestal, 1993, pp. 132-3).

The *four* elements of the EU's macroeconomic core, as noted earlier, are:

(i) the single market with free mobility of goods, services, capital and labor; (ii) free and perfectly competitive market economy; (iii) common intraregional policies aimed at structural and regional development; and (iv) coordination of intraregional monetary-fiscal policies.

The emphasis on *intraregional structural development*, the third of the four elements above, is very much in order. Indeed, it makes the EU's paradigm of economic regionalization different from other recent economic groupings of nations, placing the rich nations in one group and the poor ones in another.

The EU paradigm seeks to define itself in term of a contiguous *continental* geographic space relating itself to a common economic space.

Of the 15 sovereign member-economies of the EU, four - Spain, Portugal, Greece and Ireland - are relatively weak, and appropriate provisions will enable them to draw upon the intraregional structural development fund set up with contributions made by more affluent member-economies.

The process of intraregional integration toward its targeted goal of a deep economic union is in progress. Its agenda for the institutionalization of a supranational regional macroeconomic core, straightforwardly defined, remains to be achieved; however, the process is in place and the system has immense flexibility and the ultimate success may very much be conditioned by its in-built principles of accommodation. Provision for the safety net is essential for the success of any system of economic union. It must be noted that the EU has refused to be limited to the traditional teaching of location theory. Belonging to a common geographic space in Western Europe proved to be too inadequate. Hence, the EU agenda is *to map a common economic space on to the geographic space in the map-of-the-world view of the continent of Europe.* The search is for a new paradigm of economic regionalization.

5 Pareto Optimality Condition and Economic Regionalization

Regionalism without globalism, often referred to as "fortress regionalism" is an antithesis for maximizing the global output and therefore for global economic welfare. Thus, regionalization is no substitute for interregional cooperation. Given the actual state of international economic relationships, not observed to be governed by perfectly free and competitive market rules, *à la* Adam Smith's "invisible hands", they are indeed complementary.

Each economic region must be fully and wholly open to interregional global economic relations. The intraregional free flow of outputs and inputs can and must operate to maximize global economic gains. If a given region can add to its economic gains without diminishing such gains for any other region, the second best condition for Pareto optimality will have been achieved.

There exists no "true" measure of a Pareto-optimality condition in terms of economic welfare. Indeed, based on the trade-flow data, the EU has made economic gains for its members by way of augmenting the intraregional trade. At the same time its share of trade with other regions - North America, the Asia-Pacific region, Africa and elsewhere - has continued to increase. The interregional trade flow is a contribution to globalism and adds to global economic welfare. Intracommunity gains have not limited the EU's intercommunity economic activities. Of course, economic welfare is hardly a concept for unique measurement by trade flows.

The debate on "trade creation" *vis-à-vis* "trade diversion" remains to be resolved. The Vinerian paradigm argued for trade creation by way of economic regionalization as the total regional output increased with each member-economy of the regional compact producing, and then freely trading in, goods and services as per its comparative advantages. Critics have pressed the trade diversion thesis as output and/or trade share of a non-member-economy, earlier engaged in "free" trade with some or all members of the regional group, might decline, for their failing to compete against trade barriers. Preferential or free trade arrangements among the regional member-economies would place the non-member-economies at a comparative disadvantage. Of course, the case will be true in the context of the idealized global market wherein, given taste and technology, perfectly free and competitive market rules prevail for all member-economies.

The fact that the sovereign nation-state-based macroeconomies of today are simply "accidents" of history remains to be further examined. No wonder that the GATT negotiations have been so baffling and painfully slow. Thus, factors such as "like-mindedness", and proximity/familiarity/transportation cost advantage of a common economic space bordered by a common geography, have been noted to play dominant economic roles in economic regionalization. Studies in "gravity models" to explain the emerging economic phenomenon are familiar (Frankel and Kahler, 1994).

The EU is the most systematized expression of post-World War II economic regionalization paradigm and there exists *prima facie* evidence of both: (i) that the EU has not closed its market to U.S. exports, much to the relief of many who feared a regime of fortress Europe, and (ii) that the increase in intra-EU trade over time has not caused a corresponding decrease in the EU's trade with the rest of the world.

American exports to the EU have more than doubled between 1992 and 1986 when imports from the EU rose only 27.3 per cent. In 1985, the U.S. had a deficit of \$18.65 billion in its current account with the EU, while in 1991, it earned a net surplus of \$16.73 billion.

EU INTRA- AND INTERREGIONAL TRADE

The phenomenon of EU intraregional trade growth is to be noted. Provision for a common macroeconomic core should explain much of it. Fieleke (1992) presents annual data on total trade (exports + imports) volume in 1980 prices and on trade shares for 1960-89.

Disaggregation of total trade volume by regions - U.S., Canada, Japan, ANZ and the OPTAD total, ASEAN-6, NIE-3, China, Pac.Isl. and non-OPTAD total, APEC (OPTAD + non-OPTAD), SAARC-6, EU (then EC), LAFTA (Latin America and Free Trade Area) and ROW (rest of the world) - points to the fact that the EU trade, both intraregional and interregional has grown. There has been a shift from OPTAD to the non-OPTAD subgroup within APEC (see Table 5.1). Trade shares point out that in 1960 the APEC share of total EU trade was 19.8 per cent, while in 1991 the share was 16.8 per cent. The EU intraregional share in 1960 was 39.8 per cent and the figure rose to 63.9 per cent in 1991.

Further disaggregation of total EU trade by export and import shares, intraregional *vis-à-vis* interregional APEC shares, presents the following results: for the EU's total export trade, the intraregional shares are 41.2 per cent and 66.1 per cent in 1960 and 1991, respectively. Corresponding figures for interregional APEC shares are 17.1 per cent and 14.3 per cent. For the EU's total import trade, the intraregional shares are 38.5 per cent and 61.8 per cent in 1960 and 1991, respectively. The corresponding figures for interregional APEC shares are 22.3 per cent and 19.2 per cent, respectively.

It is instructive to review the Figures 5.1a-d. Figure 5.1a presents trade shares of APEC and EC (now EU). Further disaggregation of interregional (APEC and the EU) trade shares follow: the United States and Japan (Figure 5.1b); Taiwan and Korea (Figure 5.1c), and ASEAN-6, China and ANZ (Figure 5.1d).

The intraregional EU trade by total trade, and also by exports and imports, has grown. The EU's interregional APEC trade shares, total trade, exports and imports have marginally declined. The EU's intraregional performance can be explained by economies of a common economic space. The overall interregional performance can be viewed as comparable to the world trade growth and its share distributions.

One can then argue that if with the relative stability of an intraregional macroeconomic core, EU intraregional trade, both by volume and share, has risen, as is evident, then a Pareto-optimality condition is approached, in the general sense that the EU region has made economic gains (welfare) for itself, that is, for its sovereign member-states, as measured by the trade index, without making any other sovereign-state-based national economy *poorer* (Dutta, 1992a).

Tables 5.2 and 5.3 present the decennial growth rates of intraregional and interregional trade of selected regions of the EU and APEC and major trading countries such as the U.S. and Japan for the 1960s, 1970s and 1980s. Evidently, a pattern for an interregional trade profile is emerging, except for Japan. There is no substantive evidence that a specific region is increasing its intraregional trade share, at the expense of its interregional trade shares. Both intra- and interregional trade flows generally follow the decennial economic growth patterns of trading partner countries in respective regions.

It is important to appreciate that the concept of fortress Europe does not belong to the EU economic regionalization paradigm. The EU is in the process of approaching a supranational macroeconomic core for the region's sovereign nation-state-based 12, now 15, member-economies resulting in the gains of microeconomic units - households and business organizations - of all member-countries. The EU market is open to the rest of the world, and the world market is open to the EU, as it must be in a free global market, albeit with its limitations, subject to GATT negotiations.

A further review of a set of findings, based on EU trade flows of 1948-90, both intra- and interregional, reported by Fieleke, lends support to the argument presented above. Fieleke argues that the year 1948, the base year for the comparative study, is "neutral" and follows market rules. The neutrality argument, the author rightly adds, is indeed not so crucial as the objective is to examine the *change* over time beginning with 1948. The neutral trade share so estimated is equivalent to the actual share, the author reports.

For following years, the trade reported as neutral is that which would have taken place among EC members if the share of intra-EC trade in EC total trade had risen (or fallen) by the same percentage as the EC share of world trade (Fieleke 1992, p. 11).The evidence presented, however, must be considered in the context of the argument of Pareto optimality as discussed above. The observed growth in intraregional trade share over time is attributable to comparative advantage due to (i) gains in transportation cost for trading in a common economic space, *à la* location theory (Lorenz, 1993) and (ii) economies of scale of trading in a common economic space of a shared monetary-fiscal agenda. We argue that intraregional monetary-fiscal policy coordination played a significant role. In its absence, extraeconomic factors - political, social, religious - historically overwhelmed the transportation cost advantage of location theory.

It is important to note that the shares of both intra-EU trade and EU-world trade follow a comparable growth path.

More importantly, the fundamental question for us to address is whether there is a case for Pareto optimality. The evidence in each case is that growth in the intraregional trade has *not* been achieved by a corresponding decrease in the specific region's trade share with the rest of the world. We compare the interregional-trade share *vis-à-vis* the intraregional trade share. There is an absence of significant support for the trade diversion hypothesis.

In the absence of any evidence to the contrary, the growth of intraregional trade, as is observed, can be attributed to the trade creation hypothesis. In addition, the trade profile, albeit a limited measurable index, *prima facie* satisfies the Pareto-optimality condition of second best.

A simple schematic presentation follows (Figure 5.2). Intraregional trade and economic gains of A have grown more concurrently with its growing shares of interregional trade and economic gains with regions B, C and D. Each of these regions has added to their respective shares of trade and economic gains with region B, albeit region B's intraregional gains are relatively more pronounced.

Table 5.1 Share distribution of total EU trade

YEAR	US	CAN	JAPAN	ANZ	OPTAD	ASEAN6	NIE3	CHINA	PAC	NOPT	APEC	EC	SAA /LAF	ROW
60	10.6	2.8	0.8	3.4	17.6	1.0	0.5	0.6	0.1	2.2	19.8	39.8	7.2	33.2
61	10.0	2.6	0.9	2.8	16.3	1.1	0.4	0.3	0.1	2.0	18.3	42.2	6.9	32.6
62	10.1	2.3	0.9	2.8	16.1	0.9	0.5	0.3	0.1	1.7	17.9	44.3	6.6	31.3
63	9.9	2.1	0.9	2.7	15.6	0.8	0.5	0.3	0.1	1.7	17.4	45.9	5.9	30.8
64	9.9	2.2	1.0	2.7	15.8	0.7	0.5	0.3	0.1	1.6	17.4	46.9	5.5	30.2
65	10.0	2.2	0.9	2.5	15.6	0.7	0.6	0.4	0.1	1.8	17.4	47.6	5.2	29.8
66	10.2	2.1	1.0	2.2	15.5	1.2	0.6	0.5	0.1	2.4	17.9	48.0	5.0	29.1
67	10.1	2.0	1.1	1.9	15.2	1.1	0.6	0.5	0.1	2.3	17.5	48.3	4.9	29.3
68	10.6	1.9	1.1	1.8	15.5	1.0	0.6	0.4	0.1	2.2	17.7	49.2	4.4	28.7
69	9.7	1.8	1.2	1.7	14.4	1.0	0.7	0.4	0.1	2.1	16.6	51.2	4.2	28.0
70	9.6	1.9	1.5	1.6	14.5	1.0	0.7	0.3	0.1	2.1	16.7	51.9	3.9	27.5
71	9.1	1.8	1.5	1.5	13.8	0.9	0.7	0.3	0.1	2.1	15.8	53.0	3.7	27.4
72	8.5	1.6	1.6	1.3	13.0	0.8	0.7	0.3	0.1	2.0	15.0	54.7	3.5	26.9
73	8.2	1.4	1.7	1.2	12.5	1.0	0.8	0.3	0.1	2.2	14.7	54.8	3.4	27.2
74	7.8	1.4	1.5	1.2	11.8	1.0	0.8	0.3	0.1	2.2	14.0	51.4	3.3	31.2
75	7.2	1.2	1.5	1.0	11.0	1.0	0.8	0.4	0.1	2.2	13.3	51.4	3.3	32.1
76	7.1	1.2	1.7	1.0	10.9	1.1	0.9	0.3	0.1	2.4	13.4	52.5	3.0	31.1
77	6.9	1.1	1.8	0.9	10.7	1.1	1.0	0.2	0.1	2.4	13.2	52.5	3.3	31.1
78	7.1	1.0	1.8	0.9	10.9	1.1	1.1	0.3	0.1	2.7	13.5	53.8	3.1	29.6
79	7.0	1.0	1.8	0.8	10.6	1.1	1.1	0.4	0.1	2.8	13.4	54.6	3.2	28.8
80	7.2	1.0	1.8	0.7	10.6	1.2	1.1	0.4	0.1	2.7	13.4	52.4	3.2	31.0
81	7.8	1.0	2.0	0.7	11.5	1.2	1.2	0.4	0.1	2.9	14.4	50.5	3.5	31.6
82	7.8	0.9	2.0	0.8	11.6	1.3	1.2	0.4	0.1	2.9	14.4	51.9	3.3	30.3
83	8.0	0.9	2.2	0.8	11.8	1.3	1.2	0.4	0.1	3.0	14.8	52.9	3.1	29.1
84	8.8	1.0	2.3	0.8	12.9	1.3	1.3	0.4	0.1	3.1	16.0	52.5	3.2	28.2
85	9.0	1.0	2.3	0.9	13.3	1.2	1.3	0.6	0.1	3.2	16.5	53.5	3.1	26.9
86	8.3	1.0	2.9	0.8	12.9	1.1	1.6	0.7	0.1	3.4	16.4	56.8	2.7	24.1
87	7.8	1.0	3.0	0.8	12.6	1.2	1.9	0.6	0.1	3.8	16.3	58.2	2.6	22.9
88	7.6	1.0	3.3	0.8	12.7	1.3	2.1	0.7	0.1	4.1	16.8	58.6	2.5	22.1
89	7.7	1.0	3.3	0.8	12.7	1.4	2.0	0.7	0.1	4.2	16.9	58.4	2.5	22.2
90	7.9	0.9	3.5	0.7	13.1	1.7	2.0	0.7	0.1	4.5	17.6	64.7	2.6	15.0
91	7.5	0.9	3.5	0.6	12.6	1.8	1.5	0.9	0.1	4.2	16.8	63.9	2.6	16.7

Source: Fieleke , 1992; see also Appendix Chapter 6

Figure 5.1 (A) Interregional trade (with APEC): EC (EU)

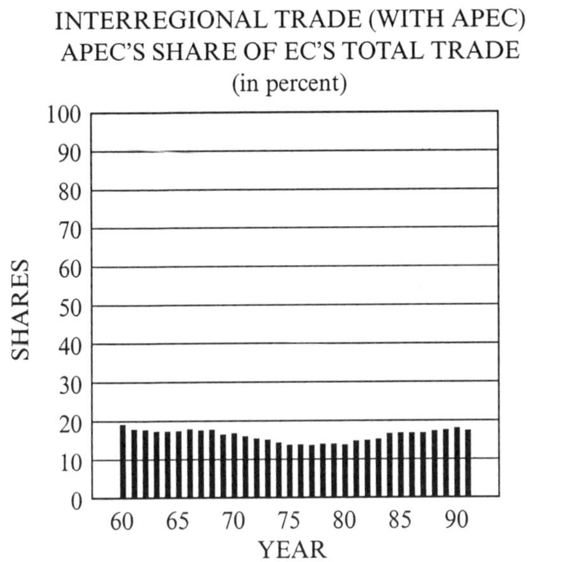

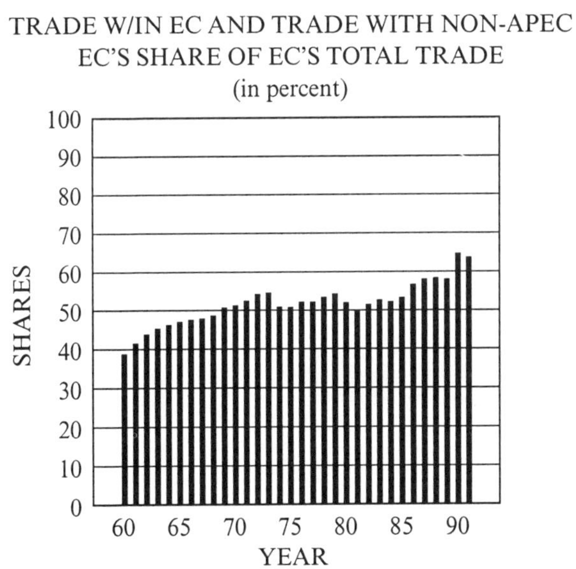

Figure 5.1 (B) Interregional trade (with APEC): USA, Japan

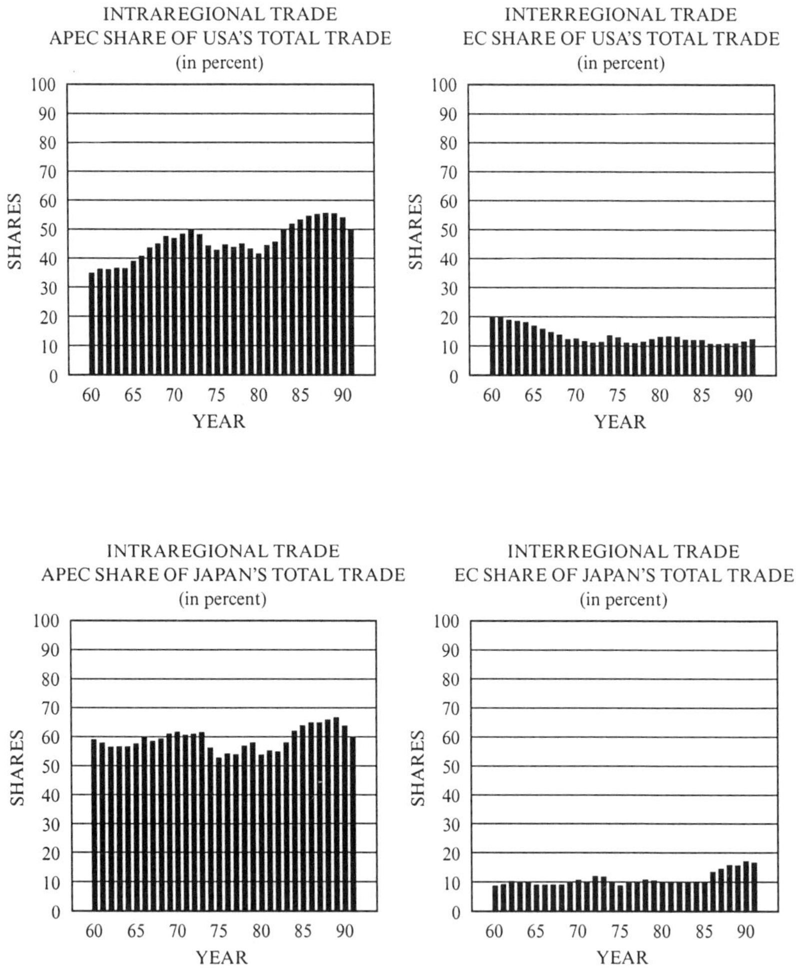

Figure 5.1 (C) Interregional trade (with APEC): Taiwan, Korea

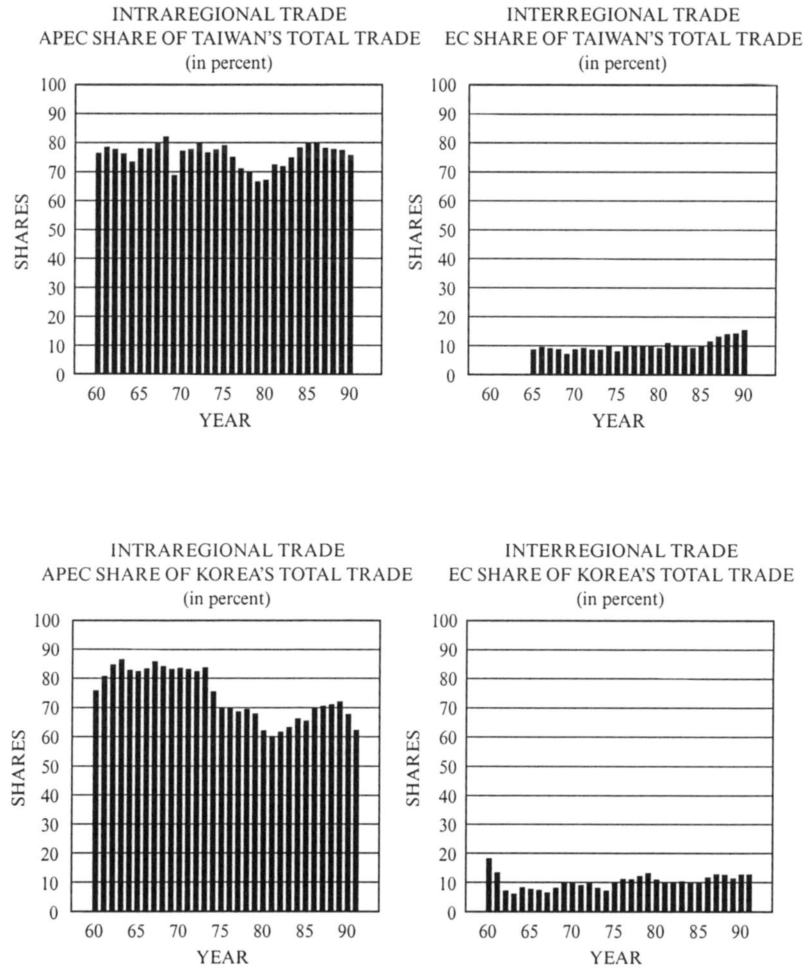

Figure 5.1 (D) Interregional trade (with APEC): ASEAN-6, China, ANZ

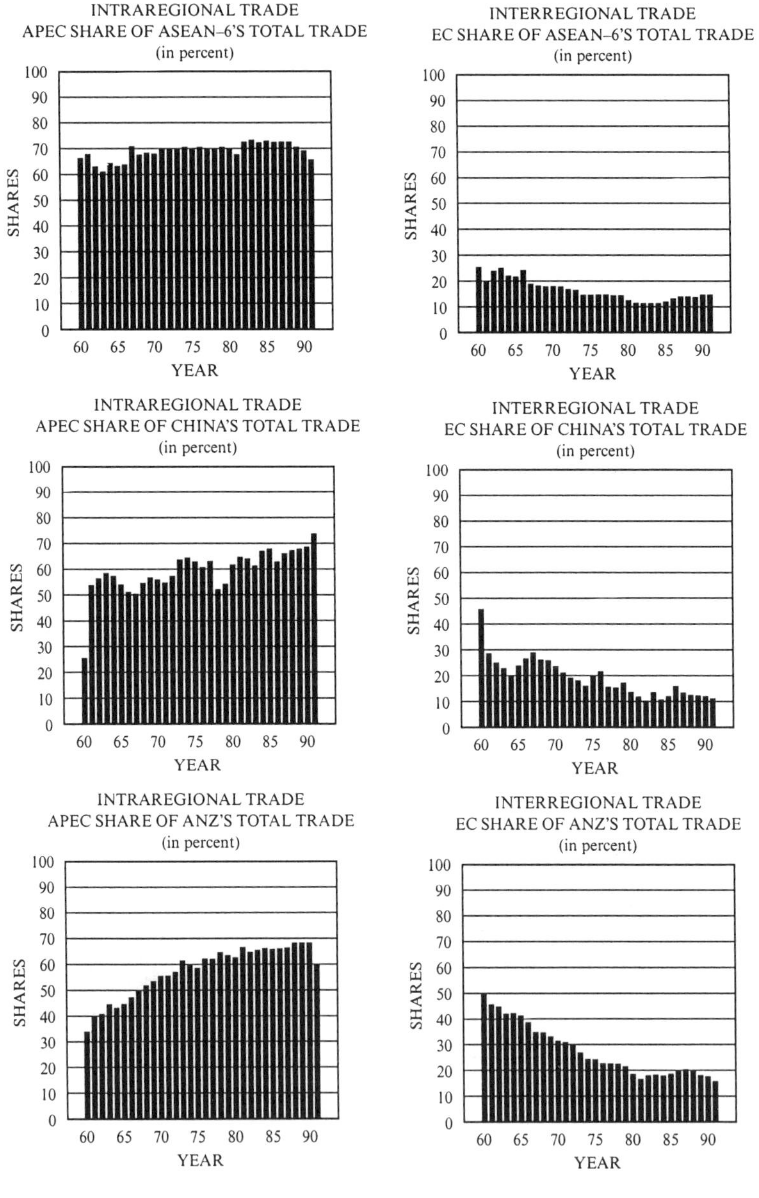

Table 5.2 Annual growth rates: APEC and EU

REGION	SUBJECT	PERIOD	TOTAL	EU	APEC
APEC	EXPORTS	1960-69	8.7	5.2	11.9
APEC	EXPORTS	1970-79	7.0	5.3	6.8
APEC	EXPORTS	1980-90	5.3	5.5	7.3
APEC	IMPORTS	1960-69	10.5	9.4	12.7
APEC	IMPORTS	1970-79	5.5	0.9	4.6
APEC	IMPORTS	1980-90	6.7	9.7	8.3
APEC	TRADE	1960-69	9.9	7.6	12.5
APEC	TRADE	1970-79	6.2	3.0	5.6
APEC	TRADE	1980-90	5.8	7.3	7.6
EU	EXPORTS	1960-69	7.7	9.9	7.9
EU	EXPORTS	1970-79	5.5	5.6	2.0
EU	EXPORTS	1980-90	1.6	2.5	6.5
EU	IMPORTS	1960-69	8.6	11.0	6.5
EU	IMPORTS	1970-79	4.0	4.0	2.5
EU	IMPORTS	1980-90	1.6	3.4	3.7
EU	TRADE	1960-69	8.2	10.5	7.1
EU	TRADE	1970-79	4.7	4.8	2.3
EU	TRADE	1980-90	1.7	3.0	4.9

Source: See Appendix Chapter 6
Note: regression estimates of log of real values with time

Table 5.3 Annual growth rates: NONOPTAD, OPTAD, U.S. and Japan

REGION	SUBJECT	PERIOD	TOTAL	EU	APEC
NONOPTAD	EXPORTS	1960-69	12.9	9.9	14.0
NONOPTAD	EXPORTS	1970-79	9.0	8.0	9.0
NONOPTAD	EXPORTS	1980-90	7.9	9.0	8.9
NONOPTAD	IMPORTS	1960-69	16.1	15.3	16.3
NONOPTAD	IMPORTS	1970-79	8.0	5.0	7.4
NONOPTAD	IMPORTS	1980-90	7.7	9.8	8.7
NONOPTAD	TRADE	1960-69	15.6	14.2	16.0
NONOPTAD	TRADE	1970-79	8.5	6.5	8.3
NONOPTAD	TRADE	1980-90	6.9	8.3	7.9
OPTAD	EXPORTS	1960-69	7.8	4.5	11.2
OPTAD	EXPORTS	1970-79	6.4	4.7	5.9
OPTAD	EXPORTS	1980-90	4.2	4.4	6.5
OPTAD	IMPORTS	1960-69	9.6	8.6	12.0
OPTAD	IMPORTS	1970-79	5.0	0.1	3.9
OPTAD	IMPORTS	1980-90	6.4	9.7	8.2
OPTAD	TRADE	1960-69	8.9	6.7	11.7
OPTAD	TRADE	1970-79	5.6	2.3	4.7
OPTAD	TRADE	1980-90	5.4	7.0	7.4
USA	EXPORTS	1960-69	5.4	4.6	8.1
USA	EXPORTS	1970-79	6.5	5.1	5.9
USA	EXPORTS	1980-90	3.8	3.3	6.6
USA	IMPORTS	1960-69	9.3	10.4	13.2
USA	IMPORTS	1970-79	5.3	-0.0	3.2
USA	IMPORTS	1980-90	6.7	8.3	9.4
USA	TRADE	1960-69	7.6	7.6	11.2
USA	TRADE	1970-79	5.7	2.4	4.2
USA	TRADE	1980-90	5.5	5.8	8.3
JAPAN	EXPORTS	1960-69	17.2	17.5	19.1
JAPAN	EXPORTS	1970-79	8.9	9.8	7.6
JAPAN	EXPORTS	1980-90	3.9	7.7	6.0
JAPAN	IMPORTS	1960-69	12.6	11.9	11.7
JAPAN	IMPORTS	1970-79	4.9	2.2	3.8
JAPAN	IMPORTS	1980-90	6.3	16.7	8.3
JAPAN	TRADE	1960-69	14.1	14.1	14.2
JAPAN	TRADE	1970-79	6.6	6.3	5.4
JAPAN	TRADE	1980-90	5.1	11.3	7.1

Source: see Appendix Chapter 6
Note: regression estimates of log of real values with time

Figure 5.2 Pareto optimality and economic regionalization

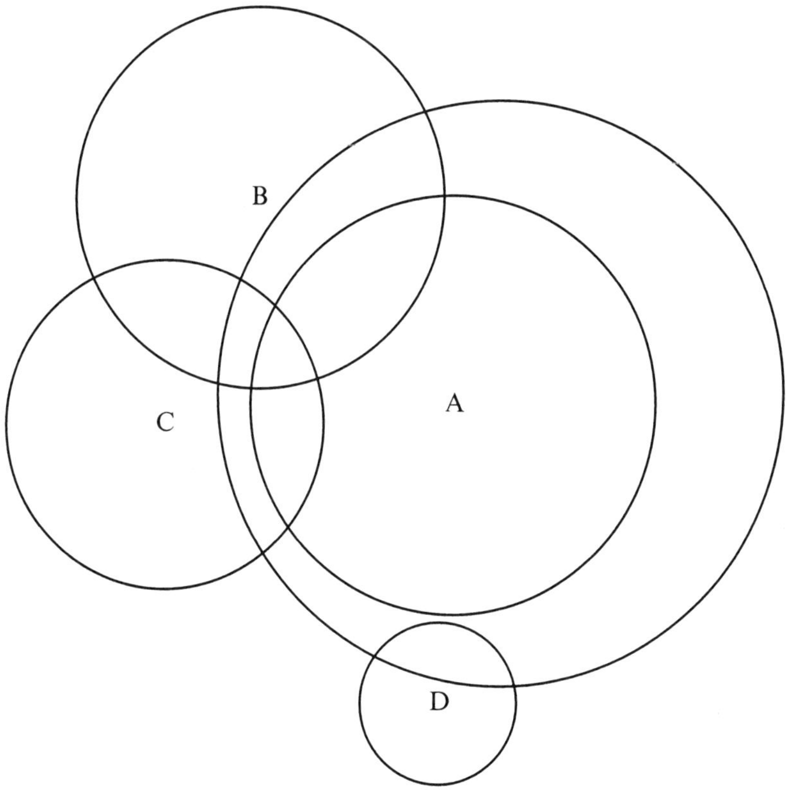

6 Asia-Pacific Economic Regimes

Historical events, as we have reviewed earlier, once dictated economic ties of many Asia-Pacific economies: Korea and Taiwan to Japan, the Philippines to the United States, Indonesia to the Netherlands, Vietnam (Cambodia and Laos) to France, Singapore, Malaysia, Burma, Australia-New Zealand, and India and South Asia to the British Raj. World War II signalled the liquidation of the old imperial model of economic regionalization, anchored to a paradigm of colonial economic regimes.

The post-World War II new economic era that followed was centered on the U.S. dollar, and then the demand pull of the post-World War II U.S. economy sustained the new economic regime of export-led growth that progressed during the 1960s through 1980s. Stability of this economic regime was made possible because the United States provided what Kindleberger (1986) calls "international public goods" in the form of monetary stability and international liquidity (in addition to a defense and security umbrella, of course).

On August 15, 1971, the freely flexible exchange rate, defined by the fixed gold value of the U.S. dollar, ceased to be in operation. Automaticity of the operation of the international free market failed to correct the imbalances that continued to plague the stability of the global economic order. In September, 1985 an *ad hoc* international regime of currency management by the G-5, then the G-7, was put in place.

A new international economic order appears to be emerging and is likely to be in place in the 1990s and beyond. The new order is not anchored to one single currency as was the post-World War II regime to the U.S. dollar. On the other hand in the absence of the idealized competitive world economy, the new order can hardly work with a free float of all currencies of nation-state-based member-economies, each too proud to compromise its sovereign authority to issue and manage its own currency. It follows that the international currency management led by selected strong currency regimes will be the core of the new international economic order.

We now return to the Asia-Pacific economic regimes. Indeed, there is strong evidence for an emerging regionalization of the Asia-Pacific economies. Linder (1986) argued how the Asia-Pacific economies' shares in world output, world trade - both exports and imports, U.S.-Asia trade - both exports and imports grew in the 1960s and 1970s. The trend of growth continued through the 1980s.

Drysdale (1988, pp. 63-4) lists three factors: (i) Japan's industrial might, (ii) the economic development of Asian NIEs and ASEAN and (iii) the relative economic decline of the role of Western Europe, inviting global focus on Asia-Pacific economies and its regional economic cooperation.

The first two factors are universally acknowledged, while the third we must reread in its positive context. Indeed, we argue that economic regionalization in Western Europe presents a learning model for Asia-Pacific regional economic cooperation.

Drysdale studies intraregional Asia-Pacific trade by its disaggregation into two basic components, complementary and biased. Trade complementarity within the Pacific region, based on the theory of comparative advantage "revealed" or otherwise, is shown to be " twice as large as might be expected from regional trade complementarities and world trade share" (p. 102). Regional trade "bias", that is, " bias towards trade among the countries within the region" (p. 103) is noted (pp. 85-107, especially Tables 4.2 and 4.8). Drysdale's finding compares to that of Fieleke (1992).

In the earlier econometric studies of international trade, distance or a proxy variable thereof was often used in specifying trade equations. "Familiarity with trading environments" or "like-mindedness" (Schott, 1989a) has been noted to be important. The "gravity models" (Frankel and Kahler, 1993) further investigate the issues.

We began with a brief reference to history showing how the imperial economic regionalization models defined the intraregional trade routes of most Asian economies.

Much has been said about the basic homogeneity of member-nations of the EU. Heterogeneity among member-economies in the Asia-Pacific region is said to be too pronounced. History has witnessed how homogeneity in Europe was put to the test through the two world wars in the first half of the twentieth century. There is certainly much to be said about the shared experiences of the horrors of death and the economic devastation of those fateful wars. If there is now an effort to identify the basic unity of the structure of Europe's continental economy, it must be welcome.

A unique structure of a continental economy is as real for Asia as it is for Europe and any other continent. Historic progression of the Industrial Revolution, we argue, has made sovereign nation-states with independent national currencies suboptimal economic units for the new international economic order. Regionalization in a map-of-the-world continental framework may be the key to the economic order of the day. One global economic unit with one currency may still remain the order of tomorrow. But simple location theory failed to define one common *economic* space in Western Europe. Distance between the Hague and Jakarta, London and Sydney, Paris and Hanoi became "closer", and transportation-cost considerations remained ignored. The imperial order of monetary-fiscal policy management united these remote economies. Intraregional trade within Western Europe remained limited by the fact that its common *geographic* space failed to be specified as a common *economic* space. The EU regime presents a correction, and the core of this new *gravity model* must be sought in intraregional monetary-fiscal policy coordination.

In what follows, we present the pattern of trade flows of Asian NIEs and ASEAN in terms of regional distributions. The terminal dates for our presentation are 1970 and 1989. By 1970, the selected Asian economies (excepting the Philippines) adopted an open economic policy, replacing their erstwhile import-substituion regimes. And, in 1989 came the institutionalization of Asia-Pacific economic cooperation in the form of APEC.

Our analysis of trade data for 1970-89 (Dutta, 1992a, 1992b, 1992c, 1992d) of three Asian NIEs - South Korea, Taiwan and Hong Kong - and five of the six ASEAN countries - Singapore, Thailand, the Philippines, Indonesia, and Malaysia - shows that only one-fifth to one-third of trade of these eight countries takes place with countries outside the APEC region and that their major trade is within the region inclusive of the U.S. and Canada. The shares of their intraregional trade, export as well as import, have remained high, approximately 70 per cent. As an individual economy grew over time its share of intraregional trade concurrently expanded.

Trade shares of the selected countries with the U.S. can be compared with the shares of Japan, ANZ, and Asia-4. The total U.S.-Pacific trade shares constitute a significant subtotal of their respective shares of total world trade (Tables 6.1 and 6.2). The three major trade regions would appear visibly dominant if the EC trade data were disaggregated from the ROW subtotal.

Further disaggregation of trade data (1970-1989) by destination of trade shows that for each of the eight above countries, the intra-APEC trade share, exclusive of the U.S. and Canada, has remained generally stable, ranging from a third to two-thirds of their respective total trade, exports plus imports. With the exception of the Philippines, this subset of APEC countries has increased its intra-APEC (exclusive of the U.S.-Canada) trade share in 1989, compared with its respective shares in 1970 (see Tables 6.3A-H).

Second, their respective trade shares with non-APEC economies in the region, India and the South Asian countries, have also been increasing.

Third, our analysis disaggregating trade shares of the above APEC countries with the United States shows that compared to 1970, in 1989 their respective shares of trade, imports plus exports, have marginally declined or remained at the same level. Exceptions are for exports of Thailand and for both exports and imports of Singapore and Malaysia. If their respective trade shares with Canada are added to the U.S. totals, the profile of economic interdependence between the two subsets of APEC economies on the two shores of the Pacific may be better appreciated.

In general, one-fifth to one-third of the trade of these countries has been with the rest of the world (ROW). Their major trade is within the Asia-Pacific region inclusive of the U.S. and Japan. As an individual economy experienced growth over time, its share of intraregional trade concurrently expanded. The share of trade of Asia's newly industrialized and industrializing economies, export plus import, within countries bordering on the Pacific is presented in Table 6.1. Table 6.2 shows the intraregional trade share vis-à-vis the share with the U.S.

Data on intraregional trade shares of selected Asia-Pacific economies over the 1970-89 period, in general, present a stable pattern. For Korea and Taiwan, intraregional export trade shares remain stable while shares of import trade have declined. The two countries' trade shares with the U.S. of both exports and imports have declined. Hong Kong's shares in intraregional trade of both export and imports have greatly increased, while its trade shares with the U.S. have declined.

Table 6.1 Trade flows of Asia-Pacific economies' export and import trade share distributions

	U.S.	Japan	Asia-4	ROW
Korea				
Exports				
1970	47.1	28.2	4.4	20.3
1989	33.6	21.6	10.9	33.8
Imports				
1970	29.4	41.0	9.3	20.3
1989	25.7	28.6	11.2	34.5
Taiwan				
Exports				
1970	38.1	14.6	11.5	34.5
1989	38.7	13.5	13.5	31.3
Imports				
1970	23.9	42.8	6.9	23.2
1989	21.5	29.1	9.4	37.2
Hong Kong				
Exports				
1970	35.8	7.1	13.0	40.6
1989	25.3	6.2	40.3	26.2
Imports				
1970	13.2	23.8	30.2	30.1
1989	8.2	16.6	57.9	16.2
Singapore				
Exports				
1970	11.1	7.6	29.5	48.0
1989	23.3	8.6	31.9	32.9
Imports				
1970	10.8	19.4	29.8	34.9
1989	17.1	21.4	28.0	31.6

	U.S.	Japan	Asia-4	ROW
Thailand				
Exports				
1970	14.9	26.6	24.2	33.6
1989	21.2	16.5	20.8	39.3
Imports				
1970	11.6	34.6	8.4	42.6
1989	11.1	30.7	24.6	31.3
The Philippines				
Exports				
1970	41.6	40.1	6.5	11.3
1989	37.8	20.4	13.4	26.6
Imports				
1970	29.4	30.6	9.3	25.3
1989	19.1	19.5	24.4	32.6
Indonesia				
Exports				
1970	13.0	40.8	23.7	19.0
1989	15.8	42.2	20.9	19.1
Imports				
1970	17.8	29.4	15.7	34.3
1989	13.5	23.3	24.2	32.8
Malaysia				
Exports				
1970	13.0	18.3	30.0	36.0
1989	18.7	16.0	38.6	24.2
Imports				
1970	8.6	17.5	28.3	39.0
1989	23.0	32.9	43.5	22.8

Source: Export and import trade share distributions (Directory of Trade Statistics, International Monetary Fund, Machine Readable Dataset Tape). *Asian Development Bank Outlook* - Asian Development Bank, Manila. *Economic and Social Survey of Asia and the Pacific*, United Nations, New York (various issues). For Taiwan, *Taiwan Statistical Yearbook,* 1989.

Note: Asia-4 = ASEAN + SAARC + China + NIEs (excludes Japan, ANZ). Figures for Asia-4, Korea and Taiwan do not include China.

Table 6.2 Trade shares in the Asia-Pacific region: Asia-4 + ANZ + Japan

		1970	1989
Korea	Exports	32.8 (47.1)	34.4 (33.6)
	Imports	51.1 (29.4)	44.0 (25.7)
Taiwan	Exports	27.5 (38.1)	30.0 (38.7)
	Imports	52.8 (23.9)	41.3 (21.5)
Hong Kong	Exports	23.6 (35.8)	48.5 (25.3)
	Imports	56.6 (13.2)	75.7 (8.2)
Singapore	Exports	40.9 (11.1)	43.8 (23.3)
	Imports	54.3 (10.8)	51.3 (17.1)
Thailand	Exports	51.5 (14.9)	39.4 (21.2)
	Imports	45.9 (11.6)	57.6 (11.1)
Philippines	Exports	47.1 (41.6)	35.6 (37.8)
	Imports	45.2 (29.4)	48.3 (19.1)
Indonesia	Exports	68.0 (13.0)	65.1 (15.8)
	Imports	47.9 (17.8)	53.8 (13.5)
Malaysia	Exports	51.0 (13.0)	57.1 (18.7)
	Imports	52.4 (8.6)	82.6 (23.0)

Source: see Table 6.1
Note: Figures in parentheses are shares of trade with the United States.

For the Southeast Asian economies, intraregional trade shares have generally grown or have remained relatively stable, exceptions are the export trade shares of Thailand and the Philippines. Other than the Philippines, which was exposed to a set of adverse extra-economic events, ASEAN economies have generally gained on their respective trade shares with the U.S.

Table 6.3 (A) Korea: exports and imports (per cent)

YR	WORLD	USA	JAPAN	ANZ	ASIA-4	CHINA	NIEs-3	ASEAN-5	SAARC-4	ROW
70	100.0	47.1	28.2	0.2	4.4		2.0	2.4	0.0	20.3
71	100.0	49.6	24.5	0.5	4.4		1.7	2.5	0.2	21.5
72	100.0	46.7	25.1	0.6	5.3		2.1	2.6	0.6	22.9
73	100.0	31.7	38.5	1.0	5.2		2.3	2.9	0.1	24.6
74	100.0	33.5	30.9	1.7	6.1		2.7	3.3	0.1	29.5
75	100.0	30.2	25.4	1.6	5.2		2.2	3.0	0.1	39.1
76	100.0	32.4	23.3	1.4	4.9		1.8	2.6	0.6	39.4
77	100.0	31.1	21.4	1.3	5.6		1.7	3.0	0.9	41.9
78	100.0	32.4	20.9	1.3	7.3		2.0	3.7	1.7	39.5
79	100.0	29.2	22.3	1.2	8.7		2.5	4.6	1.5	39.9
80	100.0	26.5	17.4	1.5	11.8		3.3	6.5	2.0	44.2
81	100.0	26.7	16.5	1.5	10.5		3.2	5.1	2.2	46.3
82	100.0	28.8	15.6	1.7	11.7		2.8	6.1	2.8	43.9
83	100.0	33.8	13.8	1.5	10.7		1.7	5.8	3.3	41.7
84	100.0	36.0	15.8	1.5	10.9		1.7	4.8	4.4	37.4
85	100.0	35.6	15.0	1.3	8.8		1.3	5.0	2.6	40.5
86	100.0	39.7	15.5	1.7	ERR		1.4	3.7	2.4	37.2
87	100.0	38.4	17.6	1.6	ERR		1.6	4.1	1.8	36.5
88	100.0	35.4	19.8	1.7	8.8		2.1	5.0	1.6	36.1
89	100.0	33.6	21.6	1.9	10.9		3.1	6.2	1.6	33.8

Table 6.3 (A) (continued)

YR	WORLD	USA	JAPAN	AUSNZ	ASIA4	CHINA	NIEs-3	ASEAN-5	SAARC-4	ROW
70	100.0	29.4	41.0	0.8	9.3		2.4	6.6	0.3	20.3
71	100.0	28.3	40.1	1.7	10.4		3.2	6.8	0.4	21.1
72	100.0	25.7	40.9	2.1	10.6		4.2	6.3	0.2	22.8
73	100.0	28.3	40.7	2.5	13.3		4.9	8.2	0.3	17.7
74	100.0	24.8	38.2	2.1	11.1		4.7	6.0	0.3	25.9
75	100.0	25.9	33.4	3.0	9.0		3.7	4.9	0.5	31.7
76	100.0	22.6	35.6	2.7	9.9		3.6	5.9	0.4	31.9
77	100.0	22.6	36.3	3.0	10.6		4.1	6.2	0.2	30.5
78	100.0	20.3	39.9	3.6	9.2		3.7	5.3	0.3	30.5
79	100.0	22.8	33.0	3.4	10.8		3.8	6.5	0.5	33.4
80	100.0	22.2	26.5	3.4	10.4		3.4	6.7	0.3	40.9
81	100.0	23.1	24.4	3.8	9.1		2.5	6.2	0.4	43.4
82	100.0	24.6	21.9	4.2	11.5		3.6	7.2	0.7	42.1
83	100.0	24.0	23.8	4.1	10.7		2.3	7.0	1.3	41.6
84	100.0	22.5	24.9	4.0	11.7		2.9	7.5	1.4	40.9
85	100.0	21.1	24.3	4.0	11.9		3.0	8.0	1.0	42.6
86	100.0	20.4	33.9	3.7	9.2		2.4	6.1	0.8	36.4
87	100.0	21.0	32.7	3.4	10.6		3.5	6.4	0.8	35.7
88	100.0	24.5	30.6	3.9	10.4		3.5	6.2	0.6	34.5
89	100.0	25.7	28.6	4.2	11.2		4.0	6.4	0.7	34.5

Source: see Appendix

Table 6.3 (B) Taiwan: exports and imports (per cent)

YR	WORLD	USA	JAPAN	ANZ	ASIA-4	CHINA	NIEs-3	ASEAN-5	SAARC-4	ROW
70	100.0	38.1	14.6	1.4	11.5	0.0	4.1	7.4	0.0	34.5
71	100.0	41.7	11.9	1.7	10.8	0.0	3.9	6.9	0.0	33.9
72	100.0	41.9	12.6	1.7	11.2	0.0	4.0	7.2	0.0	32.6
73	100.0	37.4	18.4	2.4	11.4	0.0	3.8	7.6	0.0	30.4
74	100.0	36.1	15.0	3.4	11.8	0.0	5.1	6.7	0.0	33.7
75	100.0	34.3	13.1	2.4	14.4	0.0	5.6	8.8	0.0	35.8
76	100.0	37.2	13.4	2.7	10.8	0.0	3.6	7.2	0.0	35.8
77	100.0	38.8	12.0	2.6	10.6	0.0	3.5	7.1	0.0	36.0
78	100.0	39.5	12.4	2.6	10.9	0.0	3.5	7.3	0.0	34.6
79	100.0	35.1	14.0	2.6	11.0	0.0	3.5	7.5	0.0	37.3
80	100.0	34.1	11.0	2.7	10.8	0.0	3.8	7.0	0.0	41.4
81	100.0	36.1	10.9	3.0	9.7	0.0	3.1	6.6	0.0	40.4
82	100.0	39.4	10.7	3.2	11.4	0.0	2.8	7.9	0.7	35.3
83	100.0	45.1	9.9	2.8	11.0	0.0	2.6	8.0	0.4	31.3
84	100.0	48.8	10.5	3.0	8.9	0.0	1.9	6.7	0.4	28.8
85	100.0	48.1	11.3	2.7	8.6	0.0	1.7	6.4	0.4	29.3
86	100.0	47.7	11.4	2.5	8.0	0.0	1.9	5.7	0.4	30.3
87	100.0	44.1	13.0	2.4	8.3	0.0	2.0	5.9	0.3	32.2
88	100.0	38.7	14.5	2.6	10.2	0.0	2.6	7.3	0.3	34.0
89	100.0	38.7	13.5	3.0	13.5	0.0	3.6	9.6	0.3	31.3

Table 6.3 (B) (continued)

YR	WORLD	USA	JAPAN	ANZ	ASIA-4	CHINA	NIEs-3	ASEAN-5	SAARC-4	ROW
70	100.0	23.9	42.8	3.1	6.9	0.0	1.8	5.2	0.0	23.2
71	100.0	22.1	44.9	3.3	6.4	0.0	1.7	4.7	0.0	23.3
72	100.0	21.6	41.6	3.0	8.0	0.0	2.3	5.7	0.0	25.7
73	100.0	25.1	37.6	2.7	10.1	0.0	3.8	6.3	0.0	24.5
74	100.0	24.1	31.8	2.4	10.1	0.0	3.6	6.6	0.0	31.6
75	100.0	27.8	30.4	2.7	9.0	0.0	3.8	5.2	0.0	30.1
76	100.0	23.7	32.3	2.4	8.6	0.0	3.8	4.8	0.0	33.1
77	100.0	23.1	31.1	2.5	11.2	0.0	4.9	6.3	0.0	32.1
78	100.0	21.5	33.4	2.9	8.9	0.0	4.2	4.7	0.0	33.3
79	100.0	22.9	30.9	3.1	9.2	0.0	4.3	4.9	0.0	34.0
80	100.0	23.7	27.1	2.6	8.7	0.0	3.8	4.9	0.0	37.9
81	100.0	22.5	28.0	2.8	7.9	0.0	3.6	4.3	0.0	38.9
82	100.0	24.2	25.3	3.4	5.7	0.0	2.6	3.1	0.0	41.4
83	100.0	22.9	27.5	3.8	7.7	0.0	2.5	5.1	0.2	38.0
84	100.0	23.0	29.3	4.0	9.3	0.0	3.0	6.1	0.2	34.4
85	100.0	23.6	27.6	4.4	9.6	0.0	3.0	6.4	0.2	34.9
86	100.0	22.4	34.2	4.0	8.6	0.0	2.8	5.6	0.1	30.9
87	100.0	21.8	33.9	3.2	9.0	0.0	3.1	5.7	0.1	32.1
88	100.0	26.2	29.9	3.0	8.3	0.0	3.0	5.2	0.1	32.7
89	100.0	21.5	29.1	2.8	9.4	0.0	3.5	5.7	0.1	37.2

Source: see Appendix

Table 6.3 (C) Hong Kong: exports and imports (per cent)

YR	WORLD	USA	JAPAN	ANZ	ASIA-4	CHINA	NIEs3	ASEAN-5	SAARC-4	ROW
70	100.0	35.8	7.1	3.5	13.0	0.4	3.6	8.8	0.2	40.6
71	100.0	35.2	6.6	3.6	14.2	0.4	4.3	9.2	0.3	40.5
72	100.0	33.5	6.8	3.4	14.5	0.5	4.8	8.9	0.3	41.8
73	100.0	28.1	9.6	4.3	18.1	1.0	6.2	10.5	0.3	39.9
74	100.0	26.5	6.9	6.0	18.7	1.0	6.0	11.2	0.6	41.9
75	100.0	26.4	6.4	4.7	17.1	0.5	4.8	11.3	0.4	45.4
76	100.0	29.1	7.0	4.5	15.0	0.4	4.4	9.8	0.4	44.4
77	100.0	32.2	6.1	3.8	17.9	0.5	6.1	10.8	0.5	40.0
78	100.0	30.4	7.7	3.7	18.4	0.5	5.6	11.4	0.9	39.9
79	100.0	27.3	6.8	3.2	19.3	2.5	5.2	10.7	0.9	43.4
80	100.0	26.2	4.6	2.7	23.8	6.3	5.5	11.1	0.8	42.7
81	100.0	27.8	4.7	3.1	27.8	9.0	6.6	11.4	0.8	36.7
82	100.0	28.9	4.5	3.2	29.0	9.3	6.9	12.0	0.8	34.4
83	100.0	32.2	4.4	2.7	28.8	11.4	5.8	10.7	0.9	31.9
84	100.0	33.2	4.4	2.7	31.7	17.8	4.9	8.1	1.0	28.0
85	100.0	30.8	4.2	2.3	37.4	26.0	4.0	6.4	1.0	25.3
86	100.0	31.4	4.7	2.1	33.4	21.3	4.5	6.5	1.1	28.4
87	100.0	27.9	5.1	2.0	35.6	23.3	5.0	6.2	1.1	29.4
88	100.0	24.8	5.8	2.0	40.4	27.0	6.4	6.1	0.9	27.0
89	100.0	25.3	6.2	2.0	40.3	25.7	7.1	6.6	0.9	26.2

Table 6.3 (C) (continued)

YR	WORLD	USA	JAPAN	ANZ	ASIA-4	CHINA	NIEs-3	ASEAN-5	SAARC-4	ROW
70	100.0	13.2	23.8	2.6	30.2	16.1	6.4	5.7	1.9	30.1
71	100.0	12.5	24.4	3.2	32.0	16.5	6.8	6.2	2.5	27.9
72	100.0	11.9	23.2	2.9	35.9	17.7	8.5	6.8	3.0	26.1
73	100.0	12.8	20.2	2.9	37.3	19.5	7.9	6.9	3.0	26.9
74	100.0	13.5	20.9	2.6	37.8	17.6	8.2	9.9	2.1	25.2
75	100.0	11.8	20.9	2.6	41.2	20.3	8.7	9.6	2.6	23.5
76	100.0	12.3	21.6	2.6	41.3	17.9	11.1	9.7	2.5	22.3
77	100.0	12.5	23.7	2.4	37.8	16.6	10.0	9.7	1.5	23.6
78	100.0	11.9	22.9	2.4	37.0	16.7	9.6	8.8	1.9	25.8
79	100.0	12.1	22.5	2.3	39.0	17.6	10.1	9.6	1.6	24.2
80	100.0	11.8	23.0	1.9	42.6	19.6	11.0	10.4	1.6	20.7
81	100.0	10.4	23.2	1.8	45.5	21.3	12.1	11.1	1.0	19.0
82	100.0	10.8	22.1	2.0	44.9	23.0	10.3	10.5	1.2	20.2
83	100.0	11.0	23.0	1.9	45.1	24.4	10.3	9.3	1.2	19.1
84	100.0	10.9	23.6	1.8	45.4	25.0	11.1	8.5	0.8	18.3
85	100.0	9.5	23.1	1.8	46.7	25.5	12.6	7.6	0.9	19.0
86	100.0	8.4	20.4	1.7	50.3	29.6	12.8	6.9	1.1	19.1
87	100.0	8.5	19.0	1.5	52.8	31.1	13.7	7.1	1.0	18.1
88	100.0	8.3	18.6	1.3	54.5	31.2	14.8	7.4	1.2	17.2
89	100.0	8.2	16.6	1.2	57.9	34.9	14.3	7.4	1.2	16.2

Source: see Appendix

Table 6.3 (D) Singapore: exports and imports (per cent)

YR	WORLD	USA	JAPAN	ANZ	ASIA-4	CHINA	NIEs3	ASEAN-5	SAARC-4	ROW
70	100.0	11.1	7.6	3.8	29.5	1.5	1.1	25.4	1.5	48.0
71	100.0	11.8	7.1	5.2	29.9	0.9	1.3	26.6	1.2	46.0
72	100.0	15.4	6.4	5.5	29.0	0.9	1.6	24.9	1.5	43.7
73	100.0	17.0	8.0	4.5	26.1	1.4	1.6	21.2	1.8	44.4
74	100.0	14.9	11.4	6.1	24.3	0.9	1.9	19.8	1.6	43.4
75	100.0	13.9	8.7	6.7	26.3	0.8	1.5	21.8	2.2	44.5
76	100.0	14.6	10.2	6.1	23.1	0.6	1.7	19.0	1.8	45.9
77	100.0	15.5	9.5	5.9	25.0	0.7	2.7	18.6	3.0	44.1
78	100.0	16.0	9.7	4.9	27.6	0.6	2.6	19.3	5.0	41.8
79	100.0	13.8	9.6	5.0	28.6	1.2	2.5	20.3	4.7	43.0
80	100.0	12.5	8.1	5.8	30.5	1.6	2.6	20.8	5.5	43.1
81	100.0	13.2	10.1	5.3	29.7	0.9	2.3	21.1	5.4	41.6
82	100.0	12.6	10.9	5.5	31.8	1.2	2.3	23.0	5.3	39.3
83	100.0	18.1	9.2	3.9	32.3	1.0	2.9	23.9	4.6	36.5
84	100.0	20.0	9.4	4.2	31.1	1.0	2.7	21.9	5.5	35.3
85	100.0	21.2	9.4	4.4	29.9	1.5	2.4	20.6	5.4	35.1
86	100.0	23.4	8.6	3.8	29.4	2.5	3.0	19.5	4.4	34.9
87	100.0	24.4	9.0	3.1	29.7	2.6	3.5	19.9	3.8	33.8
88	100.0	23.8	8.6	3.1	30.8	3.0	3.8	20.3	3.6	33.7
89	100.0	23.3	8.6	3.3	31.9	2.7	4.9	20.6	3.7	32.9

Table 6.3 (D) (continued)

YR	WORLD	USA	JAPAN	ANZ	ASIA-4	CHINA	NIES-3	ASEAN-5	SAARC-4	ROW
70	100.0	10.8	19.4	5.1	29.8	5.1	2.0	21.0	1.7	34.9
71	100.0	12.7	19.7	4.7	27.6	4.7	2.0	19.2	1.6	35.3
72	100.0	14.0	19.7	4.6	27.0	4.2	2.5	19.0	1.4	34.7
73	100.0	15.1	18.3	3.9	28.6	4.6	3.2	19.1	1.8	34.0
74	100.0	14.0	18.0	3.2	22.8	3.2	2.3	16.0	1.3	42.1
75	100.0	15.7	16.9	3.8	21.1	3.5	2.5	14.0	1.1	42.4
76	100.0	13.2	16.0	3.0	24.4	2.9	3.3	17.0	1.2	43.3
77	100.0	12.6	17.5	2.9	23.4	2.6	3.2	16.5	1.1	43.5
78	100.0	12.7	19.2	2.4	23.1	2.6	3.4	16.1	1.0	42.6
79	100.0	14.3	17.0	2.6	23.9	2.3	3.5	17.3	0.8	42.1
80	100.0	14.1	18.0	2.6	23.0	2.6	3.4	16.1	0.8	42.3
81	100.0	12.6	18.8	2.5	21.4	2.8	3.3	14.5	0.8	44.7
82	100.0	12.9	17.9	2.7	23.3	3.1	3.2	15.6	1.3	43.2
83	100.0	15.1	18.0	2.2	25.5	2.9	4.0	16.8	1.7	39.2
84	100.0	14.6	18.4	2.8	27.9	4.7	4.3	17.9	1.0	36.3
85	100.0	15.2	17.1	3.1	31.9	8.6	5.0	17.1	1.2	32.7
86	100.0	15.0	19.9	2.1	29.4	5.6	6.0	16.9	0.9	33.6
87	100.0	13.9	22.5	2.1	29.3	5.2	6.5	16.6	1.0	32.2
88	100.0	15.6	22.0	2.3	29.4	3.9	6.7	18.0	0.9	30.7
89	100.0	17.1	21.4	1.9	28.0	3.4	7.5	16.2	0.9	31.6

Source: see Appendix

Table 6.3 (E) Thailand: exports and imports (per cent)

YR	WORLD	USA	JAPAN	ANZ	ASIA-4	CHINA	NIEs-3	ASEAN-5	SAARC-4	ROW
70	100.0	14.9	26.6	0.7	24.2	0.0	7.5	15.5	1.3	33.6
71	100.0	13.2	24.8	1.1	22.1	0.0	4.8	15.2	2.1	38.9
72	100.0	12.6	20.7	1.0	31.0	0.0	7.5	19.4	4.0	34.7
73	100.0	10.1	26.1	0.9	30.1	0.0	9.3	19.8	1.1	32.8
74	100.0	7.9	25.8	0.9	31.0	0.0	12.2	17.9	0.9	34.3
75	100.0	11.1	27.6	1.0	28.8	0.9	6.7	17.2	4.1	31.5
76	100.0	10.0	25.8	1.1	30.0	2.1	9.3	17.1	1.5	33.1
77	100.0	9.7	19.7	1.0	32.6	2.9	9.6	18.0	2.1	36.9
78	100.0	11.0	20.3	0.9	22.4	1.9	4.1	15.4	1.1	45.3
79	100.0	11.2	21.2	1.1	25.7	1.5	5.9	16.7	1.6	40.8
80	100.0	12.7	15.1	1.1	24.9	1.9	5.8	16.2	1.0	46.2
81	100.0	12.9	14.2	1.2	24.4	2.6	5.7	14.6	1.4	47.3
82	100.0	12.7	13.7	1.3	26.6	4.4	5.4	15.5	1.3	45.7
83	100.0	15.0	15.1	1.7	23.8	1.7	4.5	15.6	2.1	44.5
84	100.0	17.2	13.0	1.8	24.2	2.5	4.2	14.1	3.5	43.8
85	100.0	19.7	13.4	1.9	25.2	3.8	4.5	14.3	2.6	39.9
86	100.0	18.1	14.2	2.0	24.9	3.1	5.2	14.2	2.4	40.8
87	100.0	18.8	14.7	2.1	22.4	3.4	3.6	13.5	1.9	42.0
88	100.0	20.1	15.9	2.0	21.1	3.0	4.3	11.5	2.3	40.8
89	100.0	21.2	16.5	2.1	20.8	2.9	4.0	11.3	2.6	39.3

Table 6.3 (E) (continued)

YR	WORLD	USA	JAPAN	ANZ	ASIA-4	CHINA	NIEs-3	ASEAN-5	SAARC-4	RO W
70	100.0	11.6	34.6	2.9	8.4	0.0	2.8	5.0	0.6	42.6
71	100.0	14.2	37.7	3.8	7.5	0.0	3.4	3.3	0.8	36.8
72	100.0	15.7	36.9	3.9	8.1	0.0	3.7	3.4	0.9	35.5
73	100.0	13.3	36.0	4.0	7.8	0.0	4.5	2.7	0.7	38.8
74	100.0	13.5	31.4	3.4	5.8	0.1	2.9	2.1	0.7	45.9
75	100.0	14.8	32.4	2.7	6.7	0.5	2.9	2.7	0.6	43.3
76	100.0	13.5	32.5	2.5	9.9	2.0	3.1	3.4	1.5	41.6
77	100.0	12.4	32.4	2.4	10.1	1.5	3.4	4.3	1.0	42.7
78	100.0	13.7	30.7	2.6	13.4	1.6	5.1	5.9	0.7	39.6
79	100.0	15.7	25.7	2.6	16.5	3.4	5.0	7.5	0.6	39.4
80	100.0	14.5	21.2	2.3	19.5	4.5	4.5	9.6	0.8	42.6
81	100.0	13.0	24.2	2.5	17.7	3.2	3.6	10.1	0.7	42.6
82	100.0	13.4	23.5	2.4	20.1	2.7	4.6	12.0	0.7	40.7
83	100.0	12.6	27.4	2.2	20.8	2.6	5.3	12.0	0.9	37.0
84	100.0	13.5	26.9	2.4	23.2	3.1	5.9	13.7	0.6	33.9
85	100.0	11.4	26.5	2.0	23.1	2.4	5.2	14.6	0.8	37.1
86	100.0	14.3	26.4	2.1	22.3	2.9	6.1	12.2	1.1	34.9
87	100.0	12.5	26.0	2.1	25.6	3.9	6.5	13.7	1.4	33.9
88	100.0	13.7	27.3	2.0	23.7	3.4	7.4	11.4	1.5	33.4
89	100.0	11.1	30.7	2.3	24.6	3.1	8.8	10.9	1.8	31.3

Source: see Appendix

Table 6.3 (F) Philippines: exports and imports (per cent)

YEAR	WORLD	USA	JAPAN	ANZ	ASIA-4	CHINA	NIEs-3	ASEAN-5	SAARC-4	ROW
70	100.0	41.6	40.1	0.5	6.5	0.0	5.2	1.2	0.1	11.3
71	100.0	40.4	34.9	0.5	7.7	0.0	5.6	2.0	0.1	16.5
72	100.0	40.6	33.5	0.7	7.1	0.3	5.2	1.4	0.2	18.1
73	100.0	36.4	43.4	1.0	7.7	0.3	5.1	2.1	0.1	11.5
74	100.0	42.4	34.9	1.2	4.8	0.5	2.8	1.3	0.2	16.7
75	100.0	29.2	37.8	1.5	7.2	1.0	3.0	2.7	0.5	24.4
76	100.0	36.0	24.3	2.0	7.8	1.5	2.7	3.1	0.4	30.0
77	100.0	35.3	23.2	2.0	9.9	2.9	2.7	4.0	0.3	29.6
78	100.0	33.8	24.2	2.3	13.7	1.4	6.1	6.1	0.2	26.0
79	100.0	30.2	26.4	2.1	11.0	1.1	5.7	4.1	0.2	30.3
80	100.0	27.5	26.6	1.8	15.3	0.8	7.4	6.5	0.6	28.8
81	100.0	31.0	21.9	2.2	17.9	1.4	8.3	7.2	1.1	27.0
82	100.0	31.6	22.9	1.9	15.4	2.1	5.5	7.1	0.7	28.2
83	100.0	36.3	19.9	1.7	13.6	0.5	5.5	7.1	0.5	28.5
84	100.0	38.0	19.4	1.8	15.9	1.1	4.5	9.7	0.6	24.9
85	100.0	35.9	19.0	2.1	18.0	1.8	4.3	11.4	0.6	25.0
86	100.0	35.6	17.7	1.6	15.6	2.1	6.1	7.2	0.2	29.5
87	100.0	36.2	17.2	1.7	16.8	1.5	6.3	8.9	0.2	28.0
88	100.0	35.7	20.1	1.7	15.0	0.9	6.1	6.9	1.1	27.4
89	100.0	37.8	20.4	1.8	13.4	0.6	5.4	6.8	0.6	26.6

Table 6.3 (F) (continued)

YR	WORLD	USA	JAPAN	ANZ	ASIA-4	CHINA	NIEs-3	ASEAN-5	SAARC-4	ROW
70	100.0	29.4	30.6	5.3	9.3	0.0	3.9	5.2	0.3	25.3
71	100.0	24.9	29.3	4.9	11.6	0.0	5.4	6.1	0.1	29.3
72	100.0	25.8	31.1	6.4	6.9	0.1	2.4	4.1	0.2	29.8
73	100.0	28.3	34.7	5.8	5.8	1.4	2.0	2.1	0.3	25.4
74	100.0	24.1	26.8	6.0	5.1	0.8	1.7	2.3	0.3	38.0
75	100.0	22.1	27.2	4.9	11.0	1.4	4.3	4.8	0.5	34.9
76	100.0	22.2	27.1	4.5	14.0	1.4	5.4	6.5	0.7	32.2
77	100.0	20.5	25.2	5.7	15.9	1.9	6.9	6.4	0.6	32.7
78	100.0	21.1	27.5	4.7	15.4	2.3	7.2	5.6	0.3	31.3
79	100.0	22.9	22.8	4.5	15.3	1.9	7.4	5.7	0.2	34.6
80	100.0	23.5	19.9	4.0	15.5	2.7	6.4	6.1	0.4	37.2
81	100.0	22.8	19.0	3.8	16.7	2.5	7.4	6.6	0.2	37.8
82	100.0	22.5	20.1	4.1	16.0	2.7	6.6	6.5	0.1	37.3
83	100.0	23.3	17.1	3.4	17.8	1.0	7.4	8.6	0.8	38.4
84	100.0	27.4	13.6	3.0	24.1	3.6	8.7	11.6	0.2	32.0
85	100.0	25.1	14.0	3.9	32.0	5.4	12.0	14.2	0.3	25.0
86	100.0	24.8	17.0	3.9	24.8	2.3	12.2	9.8	0.6	29.5
87	100.0	22.2	16.6	4.0	23.0	3.1	10.8	8.8	0.3	34.3
88	100.0	21.0	17.4	4.3	26.1	3.1	12.8	9.4	0.7	31.2
89	100.0	19.1	19.5	4.4	24.4	2.2	12.1	9.6	0.5	32.6

Source: see Appendix

Table 6.3 (G) Indonesia: exports and imports (per cent)

YR	WORLD	USA	JAPAN	ANZ	ASIA-4	CHINA	NIEs-3	ASEAN-5	SAARC-4	ROW
70	100.0	13.0	40.8	3.5	23.7	0.0	2.8	20.9	0.0	19.0
71	100.0	15.6	44.6	1.9	22.5	0.0	4.9	17.6	0.0	15.3
72	100.0	14.9	50.7	2.3	15.8	0.0	6.2	9.6	0.0	16.3
73	100.0	14.5	53.2	1.7	16.7	0.0	4.8	11.7	0.2	14.0
74	100.0	21.3	53.5	0.3	12.9	0.0	3.7	8.7	0.5	12.0
75	100.0	26.3	44.1	0.3	14.8	0.0	3.8	10.3	0.7	14.6
76	100.0	28.7	41.7	0.4	13.4	0.0	4.1	8.8	0.4	15.8
77	100.0	27.8	40.2	0.6	16.5	0.0	5.2	10.6	0.8	14.9
78	100.0	25.4	39.2	1.0	18.1	0.0	4.9	12.7	0.5	16.3
79	100.0	20.3	46.1	1.5	20.0	0.0	5.4	14.2	0.4	12.0
80	100.0	19.6	49.3	2.0	16.8	0.0	3.8	12.6	0.4	12.3
81	100.0	18.3	47.9	2.8	15.5	0.0	3.2	11.9	0.3	15.5
82	100.0	15.9	50.1	4.1	19.8	0.1	3.9	15.7	0.2	10.0
83	100.0	20.2	45.8	2.0	19.9	0.1	3.2	16.4	0.2	12.1
84	100.0	20.6	47.3	2.3	16.5	0.0	4.6	11.4	0.4	13.4
85	100.0	21.7	46.2	1.2	17.5	0.5	5.8	10.7	0.7	13.3
86	100.0	21.6	41.3	1.7	20.4	1.0	8.4	10.3	0.7	15.1
87	100.0	19.5	43.1	2.0	19.9	2.0	7.2	9.9	0.8	15.5
88	100.0	16.2	41.7	1.7	21.7	2.5	7.5	10.7	0.9	18.7
89	100.0	15.8	42.2	2.0	20.9	2.4	6.7	10.9	0.8	19.1

Table 6.3 (G) (continued)

YR	WORLD	USA	JAPAN	ANZ	ASIA-4	CHINA	NIEs-3	ASEAN-5	SAARC-4	ROW
70	100.0	17.8	29.4	2.8	15.7	3.2	3.3	7.4	1.9	34.3
71	100.0	15.8	33.5	3.1	15.8	2.5	4.0	7.7	1.6	31.8
72	100.0	15.5	34.0	3.6	18.4	2.5	5.0	9.2	1.7	28.5
73	100.0	18.8	29.3	3.5	18.1	1.8	4.3	8.6	3.3	30.4
74	100.0	15.9	29.4	3.7	18.9	2.9	4.8	9.3	1.9	32.1
75	100.0	14.0	31.0	3.6	18.6	4.3	4.5	8.7	1.1	32.8
76	100.0	17.4	26.2	3.7	23.6	2.3	4.7	14.0	2.6	29.2
77	100.0	12.5	27.1	3.4	23.0	2.5	4.7	14.3	1.6	34.0
78	100.0	12.5	30.1	3.8	19.7	1.8	6.0	9.6	2.3	33.9
79	100.0	14.6	29.1	3.7	22.5	1.8	7.1	11.6	2.0	30.2
80	100.0	13.0	31.5	4.2	21.4	1.8	6.6	12.4	0.5	30.0
81	100.0	13.5	30.1	3.5	22.4	1.9	6.9	12.8	0.8	30.5
82	100.0	14.3	25.4	2.7	26.7	1.4	4.3	19.6	1.5	30.9
83	100.0	15.5	23.2	2.9	30.8	1.2	5.0	23.9	0.6	27.6
84	100.0	18.4	23.8	3.2	20.2	1.6	4.0	14.0	0.6	34.3
85	100.0	16.7	25.7	5.2	16.9	2.4	4.7	9.4	0.4	35.4
86	100.0	13.8	29.2	4.5	19.2	3.1	5.1	10.4	0.5	33.3
87	100.0	11.0	28.0	4.2	22.3	3.2	5.5	13.0	0.5	34.5
88	100.0	12.9	25.4	5.0	21.6	3.0	7.9	9.8	0.8	35.1
89	100.0	13.5	23.3	6.3	24.2	3.3	9.8	10.2	0.9	32.8

Source: see Appendix

Table 6.3 (H) Malaysia: exports and imports (per cent)

YR	WORLD	USA	JAPAN	ANZ	ASIA-4	CHINA	NIEs-3	ASEAN-5	SAARC-4	ROW
70	100.0	13.0	18.3	2.7	30.0	1.3	3.2	24.8	0.7	36.0
71	100.0	12.7	18.2	2.3	31.8	1.1	3.2	26.7	0.8	35.0
72	100.0	13.8	17.2	2.3	31.6	1.6	2.4	26.4	1.2	35.2
73	100.0	10.6	17.7	2.4	31.0	2.7	2.7	24.4	1.2	38.3
74	100.0	19.5	23.1	3.3	32.5	0.0	4.1	26.8	1.6	21.7
75	100.0	21.3	18.2	2.6	32.8	0.0	3.8	26.8	2.1	25.2
76	100.0	15.6	21.1	2.6	25.7	0.8	2.2	21.5	1.1	34.9
77	100.0	18.2	20.5	2.1	26.2	2.0	2.0	18.9	3.3	33.0
78	100.0	18.6	21.7	2.4	24.6	1.5	0.3	18.6	4.3	32.7
79	100.0	17.3	23.4	2.4	26.7	1.6	2.1	20.0	2.9	30.3
80	100.0	16.3	22.8	1.8	29.6	1.7	2.3	22.4	3.3	29.3
81	100.0	13.1	21.1	2.0	35.6	0.8	4.1	26.5	4.2	28.2
82	100.0	11.6	20.3	2.2	38.6	0.9	4.0	30.0	3.7	27.3
83	100.0	13.2	19.7	1.6	41.0	1.1	7.6	28.2	4.1	24.6
84	100.0	13.5	22.8	1.7	40.1	1.0	7.9	26.0	5.2	22.0
85	100.0	12.8	24.6	1.9	39.3	1.0	8.6	25.6	4.0	21.5
86	100.0	16.4	23.3	2.2	35.2	1.2	8.0	21.7	4.4	22.9
87	100.0	16.6	19.5	2.4	38.5	1.6	8.9	23.7	4.3	23.0
88	100.0	17.4	17.0	2.6	39.4	2.0	9.1	24.1	4.2	23.7
89	100.0	18.7	16.0	2.5	38.6	1.9	8.9	25.2	2.6	24.2

Table 6.3 (H) (continued)

YR	WORLD	USA	JAPAN	ANZ	ASIA-4	CHINA	NIEs-3	ASEAN-5	SAARC-4	ROW
70	100.0	8.6	17.5	6.6	28.3	5.3	5.1	16.0	1.8	39.0
71	100.0	6.7	19.6	6.9	24.5	4.6	3.6	14.3	2.0	42.3
72	100.0	9.0	20.7	8.9	25.5	4.3	3.6	15.9	1.7	36.0
73	100.0	8.2	21.6	8.1	25.0	5.9	2.7	14.5	1.9	37.1
74	100.0	9.1	17.0	6.6	31.4	0.0	2.2	28.0	1.2	35.9
75	100.0	11.1	16.0	7.6	34.3	0.0	2.2	31.1	1.1	30.9
76	100.0	12.7	21.2	8.0	21.3	3.5	1.8	14.3	1.7	36.7
77	100.0	12.3	23.4	7.0	20.8	3.1	1.8	14.6	1.4	36.4
78	100.0	13.9	23.1	7.5	20.9	3.7	1.6	14.3	1.3	34.5
79	100.0	15.0	22.4	6.9	20.9	2.8	2.3	14.5	1.2	34.9
80	100.0	15.1	22.8	6.5	22.5	2.3	2.6	16.4	1.1	33.1
81	100.0	14.6	24.4	6.4	23.3	2.4	2.0	17.9	1.0	31.2
82	100.0	17.6	25.0	5.4	28.2	2.2	5.2	19.9	0.8	23.9
83	100.0	16.1	25.4	4.9	27.1	2.0	5.2	18.9	1.0	26.6
84	100.0	16.3	26.3	4.8	28.1	2.0	5.6	19.5	1.0	24.6
85	100.0	15.3	23.0	4.8	31.4	2.0	6.0	22.4	1.0	25.4
86	100.0	18.8	20.5	5.0	31.9	2.6	6.8	21.5	1.0	23.8
87	100.0	18.7	21.7	4.9	32.5	2.9	7.8	20.8	0.9	22.3
88	100.0	23.0	30.0	6.5	41.1	3.8	11.6	24.5	1.2	22.6
89	100.0	23.0	32.9	6.2	43.5	3.7	12.3	25.7	1.8	22.8

Source: see Appendix

APPENDIX

Terminology

NIE 3	- (South) Korea, Taiwan, and Hong Kong
ASEAN 5	- Singapore, Thailand, Malaysia, the Philippines, Indonesia
SAARC 4	- India, Pakistan, Bangladesh, Sri Lanka
ANZ	- Australia and New Zealand
ROW	- (Rest of the world) trade with countries other than U.S., Japan, ANZ, and ASIA4

Notes on data

Data for all countries other than Taiwan from 1970 to 1987 are taken from the International Monetary Fund (IMF)_*Directory of Trade Statistics* (DOTS) machine-readable dataset tape, 1988 edition. This tape does not include data from Taiwan.

Data for 1988 and 1989 are taken from the DOTS Annual, 1990 edition. This annual figures contains exports and imports data from 1983 to 1989. Though Taiwan is not included in the IMF member-countries, data for trade going to and from Taiwan for the years mentioned as reported by the member countries are published in this annual.

Direction of trade statistics for Taiwan from 1970 to 1988 are taken from the *Taiwan Statistical Data Book*, 1989 edition. The1989 figures are taken from its partner countries' statistics from the 1990 DOTS Annual. The figures for Taiwan shown under Korea, Hong Kong, Thailand, the Philippines, Singapore and Indonesia are the same as the figures shown in the Taiwan series.

When the source country's data are not available, the partner country's reported figures are used and is footnoted below. Except in these circumstances, all exports figures are in their FOB values while imports are in their CIF values.

Individual country notes

Korea: Trade with China is not available for the period covered.

Taiwan: Trade with China is not available

Thailand: 1970 data for all countries are partner country figures.

Philippines: Exports and imports to and from Japan in 1973 is partner country figure.

Indonesia: Exports to Korea data for 1970, 1971,1972, and 1973 and imports from New Zealand for 1970 and 1971 are partner country figures.

Malaysia: All exports and imports data for 1974 and 1975 are partner country figures.

Data for New Zealand, Sri Lanka and India are partner country figures.

7 Economic Regionalization and Geo-economics

GEO-ECONOMICS - A CHALLENGING CONCEPT

Geo-economics, we argue, is the core concept that provides the foundation of an economic regionalization model in the post-Cold War era. Let us recall that geo-politics was at the core of the Cold War regime of strategic regionalization. Indeed, it was so, even for the imperial model of economic regionalization.

Geo-politics anchored itself to a superpower hegemony which assumed the responsibility of providing free "international public goods", a defense and security umbrella as well as monetary and fiscal stability. The nation-state-based economies of the world, excepting only a few in the Non-aligned Bloc, elected to join one or another of the two superpower regimes and drew upon their supplies of "international public goods". The cost of providing the two-fold public goods - political and economic services - eventually proved to be too real. The end result was the liquidiation of the geo-politics-based Cold War regimes. It can be argued that in the pre-World War II imperial economic regionalization models, the superpower hegemony worked, very much with its authoritarian imperial enforcement. The monetary-fiscal stability in the respective regimes, anchored to related imperial currencies - the French franc, the British pound sterling, the Dutch guilder, the Japanese yen or the U.S. dollar - was enforced and secured by the political might of the ruling powers in historical circumstances.

Geo-economics must be appreciated as the post-Cold War revolutionary concept. It rejects the superpower hegemony, and its focus is on *supranational, multilateral, coordination of monetary-fiscal policies* for the sovereign member-economies in a regional compact. The meltdown of the Cold War has earned the sovereign nation-state-based economies a degree of freedom. The cry is for economic stability by way of intraregional economic cooperation. If global cooperation is yet to be effectively operational, the next best choice is the regional economic cooperation. Geo-economics *maps a common economic space on to a common geographic space*, replacing geo-politics. Indeed, geo-economics is a robust concept.

In what follows we present its core characteristics. First, it must be appreciated that the core of this concept is the acceptance of *a map-of-the world view of a region.* Western Europe is the map for the EU. For APEC, the Lake Pacific is the common geographic space. Asia-Pacific economic cooperation is anchored to the Pacific region. The borders of the region must remain open. The principle of *inclusion* has been the guideline for both the Western European and the Asia-Pacific economic regionalization. A natural belonging to a map-of-the-world region initiates the process of bringing together the sovereign nation-state-based economies in a regional group.

Second, the focus will have to be on a well-specified economic agenda, ensuring optimization of economic gains for all micro actors, households and corporations, in each member-economy belonging to the regional group. The pull-and-push factors of the competitive market must be allowed to play their effective role. The agenda must include provisions for the intraregional free flow of both inputs of production, labor and capital, and the final output in goods and services. An agenda for free trade in goods and services, and for free flow of capital input via investment engages much attention. Free flow of labor input, however, brings to the fore issues relative to labor laws and illegal immigration, warranting intraregional coordination of policies of much complexity. In addition, coordinated, multilateral, intraregional policies for education, health and environmental parameters affecting human capital development will be very much in order.

Geo-economic grouping can optimize global economic gains only by a firm commitment not to raise any barriers to non-member-economies. In this regard, a regional economic group must work consistently with the specific instructions adopted by the WTO.

Third, importance of extra economic factors, such as, race, religion, language, life style and political system may not be allowed to overwhelm the process of economic regionalization. Considerations for economic gains may become a cementing bond.

Fourth, an effort to play the superpower game by a member-economy of a regional group will compromise its common geo-economic agenda, and will eventually be counterproductive. Let the competitive market forces in its own course relate to the magnitude of the GDP of a member-economy, such as the U.S. or Japan, and the high growth rates of the GDP in Asia's newly industrialized and industrializing economies.

Fifth and finally, a geo-economic, intraregional grouping can hardly remain tactical and/or strategic. Efforts to limit it to a traditional free trade area or a Vinerian customs union will be unsuccessful. Dynamics of events will result in its evolution into an economic union with intraregional macroeconomic policy coordination, with or without a common currency. Thus, acceptance of geo-economic regional economic grouping will essentially involve a commitment to some variation of deep integration.

In 1957, the Treaty of Rome hardly anticipated the eventful changes in the economic map of Western Europe. Historic progression of economic regionalization in Western union has now become institutionalized in the EU which presents the best scenario of the geo-economic regionalization.

The EU does seek to offer a supranational macroeconomic core to support economic regionalization in Western Europe. Extraeconomic issues apart, economic regionalization in the EU presents a paradigm of its own, providing intraregional public good, especially in the form of monetary and fiscal stability, for optimization of gains for microeconomic actors - households and firms - belonging to all its sovereign member-economies, concurrently ensuring a degree of economic pluralism for its member-economies (European Commission 1989a and 1989b, 1990).

By addressing the need for providing a common *supranational* macroeconomic core in terms of monetary and fiscal stability and the need for structural integration of member-economies within the regional Union, the EU is indeed a paradigm of what Richard Cooper (1974) called "deep" integration. At the same time it combines with a unique blend of economic pluralism for member-nations. It thus significantly differs from Viner's customs unions, or FTAs, or any other bloc formation, basically based on the concept of "strategic" optimization.

In December 1994, the leaders of sovereign nation-state-based economies in the North and South Americas, excepting Cuba, met at a hemispheric summit in Miami with the United States as the host. The Miami Initiative, as I have referred to it, projected the vision for a free trade area from "Alaska to Argentina", a Free Trade Area of the Americas (FTAA).

The trade ministers of the 34 member-countries - Antigua and Barbuda, Argentina, Bahamas, Barbados, Belize, Bolivia, Brazil, Canada, Chile, Colombia, Costa Rica, Dominica, Dominican Republic, Ecuador, El Salvador, Grenada, Guatemala, Guyana, Haiti, Honduras, Jamaica, Mexico, Nicaragua, Panama, Paraguay, Peru, St. Vincent and the Grenadines, St. Lucia, St. Kitts and Nevis, Suriname, Trinidad and Tobago, Uruguay, the United States of America and Venezuela - met in Denver, Colorado, on June 30, 1995, and in Cartagena, Colombia, on March 21, 1996. The immediate program was "to prepare for the initiation of negotiations of the Free Trade Area of the Americas (FTAA) in which barriers to trade and investment will be progressively eliminated", no later than 2005. The FTAA will be fully WTO-consistent, as per Article XXIV of GATT 1994 and its Uruguay Round Understanding, and Article V of the GATS (General Agreement on Trade in Services). Commitment "to facilitate integration of the smaller economies and increase their level of development" has been "reiterated". This facilitated the concurrent operation of MERCOSUR, the trading bloc and customs union of Brazil, Argentina, Paraguay, Uruguay and Chile joining it in 1996. Be it noted that the Group's commitment to "transparency in the FTAA process" has been reaffirmed.

The working groups in areas of Government Procurement, Intellectual Property Rights, Trade in Services and Competition Policy have been appointed with instructions to work on specific details. The conferees agreed to include environmental and labor standards in the trade negotiations.

In 1995 came the proposal for the Indian Ocean Group (IOG) consisting of 47 littoral and land-locked sovereign nation-state-based economies in the Indian Ocean region. The IOG is in its exploratory stage, but merits attention. Seven APEC member-economies (Australia, Brunei, Indonesia, Malaysia, the Philippines, Singapore and Thailand), along with 40 others (eight from South Asia, 11 from West Asia, 14 from North and East Africa, four from the South African Customs Union, and three from the Indian Ocean Islands), belong to this common geographic space. Will it map to a common economic space?

APEC is still in a fluid stage. APEC is neither EU nor NAFTA. One must not hasten to compare the European experience with the one in North America: NAFTA, with Canada, the United States and Mexico and its 380 million people, became effective as of January 1, 1994. But NAFTA with its present statutory structure is most certainly distinguishable from the EU.

What is APEC? Some have called it a paradigm of "open regionalism" (Ariff, 1994; Garnaut, 1994) - a forum for friendly communication on economic issues of mutual concern. The APEC charter has no agenda for constituting a supranational macroeconomic core by way of intraregional coordination of monetary-fiscal policies or by a specific agenda for intraregional structural economic development. There is no suggestion that the Asia-Pacific region can and/or should replicate the EU experiments. Indeed, there is a general consensus to the contrary. If APEC is not EU, it is not NAFTA either, albeit the APEC Summit in Bogor 1994 adopted a free trade agenda of the member-economies by 2010/2020.

Can APEC-centered "open regionalism" survive? Or, is it only an oxymoron? This issue will have to be faced as the EU emerges in its full bloom with or without one currency managed by one European Central Bank by the end of the century, and as the American hemispheric free trade area assumes its fuller manifestation. Any speculation of the future of APEC at this stage will indeed be unwarranted. We outline a schematic model explaining the fast-growing phenomenon of economic regionalization in its many and varied institutional forms.

A CONCEPTUAL/THEORETICAL MODEL

Historically, the free market economic system has progressed to its present successful standing by an interaction of *deepening and widening,* a twofold interactive process.

The historic progression of the Industrial Revolution is a part of the global economic history. Indeed, economic development by successive stages of industrialization presents the process of deepening of the system.

In the context of existing macroeconomies, the process of deepening of the economic systems has been rooted into a free market economy with its framework well defined and determined by a macro core in the context of a sovereign nation-state. The provision of necessary "public goods" by the macroeconomic core has been a necessary condition for the success of the deepening processes in various industrialized market economies.

There have been those who would have preferred a total absence of a macroeconomic core with or without an automated moneysupply institution. The consensus has been to balance optimization of gains (welfare) for microeconomic units - households and business firms - within a macro core by a policy of prudent coordination of momentary-fiscal policies.

An industrialized mature economy progressively deepens, if and only if it has been provided with necessary public goods, rich in economic as well as extraeconomic contents. Literature in search of a micro foundation of macroeconomics is extensive.

There is more to it than simple aggregation. The individuals belonging to the group constitute the group action agents - the macroeconomic structure. It is more than the provision of law and order, national security and defense, as the bill of duties for the institution of government. To paraphrase Kindleberger (1986), the provision of monetary and fiscal stability is an essential component of the macroeconomic core.

The deepening of a market economy cannot be achieved without institutionalized manifestation of the group entity. Adam Smith, the Guru of our free market economy, rightly reminded his students that what would be good for the East India Company might not necessarily be good for the people of England.

THE MARKET "WIDENING" AND ECONOMIC REGIONALIZATION

The other facet of the growth of the capitalist market economic system has been sustained by the process of widening of the market. The immediate issue for us is to examine how the process of economic regionalization relates to the facet of widening of the free enterprise market system. We have referred to its many and diverse manifestations at successive stages of history, especially in the context of Asian economies.

1. The earliest phase was the imperial mode of economic regionalization and it collapsed since what it offered was *a supernational/superpower* macroeconomic core, *NOT a supranational* core. It did not offer a cooperative, intraregional, multilateral coordination of monetary-fiscal policies. Its power base had its root in the home economy where unidimensional policies were formulated. Sooner or later the satellite economies came to delink their linkages with their respective home economies and currencies.
2. The Cold War period witnessed many variations of "strategic" regionalization with basic focus on security parameters, given the confrontation between communist command economies and capitalist free market economies. With the liquidation of the Cold War, they have all come to outlive their usefulness. Indeed, they are widely perceived as greatly cost-ineffective. It became obvious that the U.S. alone could not pay for the provision of "international public good" to all economies belonging to its many and varied friendly political alliances.
3. As we have discussed earlier, the idealized one-world paradigm anchored to the U.S. dollar at a fixed gold value could not continue to be operational. Indeed, on August 15, 1971 we signed off to delink the U.S. dollar from its gold redemption obligation.

APEC AN EXPERIMENT IN SUPRANATIONAL MARKET WIDENING

The post-Cold War paradigm of widening of the free market economic system thus must be based on a new and innovative model. The Western European model became one option, if not the only option. The FTAs do not meet the agenda of providing public goods to the intra-FTA member-economies. Should NAFTA adopt an effective enlarged agenda by including intraregional North American common and cooperative, multilateral control measures for human capital (labor) environment, an extra mile will have been traveled. Even so, the need for an intraregionally coordinated monetary-fiscal policy would be left open.

We have noted that there is a growing and organized effort to bring all economies in the American hemisphere - North and South - into a free trade area, transforming NAFTA into a new entity, the FTAA. Will FTAA remain limited in providing free "public goods" with a combined package of security and defense and monetary and fiscal stability to all its sovereign nation-state-based member-economies?

APEC is an ideal forum for communication with a limited agenda, if not too limited for effective market widening. Within APEC there are three subregional FTAs. One FTA is NAFTA in North America, and it has a full legally binding agenda. The second FTA is in Southeast Asia, the ASEAN Free Trade Area (AFTA). The six sovereign nation-state-based economies - Brunei Darussalam, Indonesia, Thailand, Malaysia, Singapore and the Philippines - of some 350 million people, constitute ASEAN. As of July 1995, Vietnam with its 70 million people joined ASEAN. The third FTA is ANZ-CER, in the South Pacific (see Part IV).

Note that the ASEAN-FTA (AFTA) is different as it is in no way formally/legally institutionalized as is NAFTA. However, it does maintain an intraregional economic structure by agreements among member governments with its headquarters in Singapore (see Part IV).

The prospectus of economic data at the present time based on the rates of growth of real GDP, savings/GDP, and investment/GDP ratios, however, point to the call for progressive widening of the market system in the Asia-Pacific region.

We shall argue that two sets of factors brought APEC to its present status. One was the pull factor and another a push factor.

First, the pull factor - the fast industrialization and the relatively high growth rates of real GDPs of most of these economies present them as an attractive, profitable market. The pull factors of Asia's new capitalism are rooted in the profitability of these economies and have been responsible for competitive attention for both trade and investment flows. The world's savings-surplus richer economies in Asia, North America, Europe and Oceana are engaged in a robust competition for their respective shares of the Asian market.

The Asian economies followed a paradigm of economic growth, which we describe as an *Adaptive Innovation Paradigm* (Dutta and Tantum 1988). For convenience, let us characterize the basic innovations which at successive stages of the progression of the Industrial Revolution contributed to the process of deepening of the market economy as Schumpeterian innovations.

Asia's new capitalism has successfully experimented with a new paradigm of industrialization. Successful as it is, it has been the result of a process of adaptation of innovations, as existed elsewhere. Importation of the alien technology and know-how became the key. To pay for these imports, foreign exchanges were to be earned by exporting finished products.

The inflow of foreign capital was serviced and then paid off as has been the illustrious case of Taiwan, and also of South Korea. The same mode of operation has been noted in other Asian NIEs - Singapore and Hong Kong. The parallel mode of operation is progressively in evidence in most Southeast Asian economies, notably in Malaysia, Thailand and Indonesia. Recently, China and India have made significant strides.

One notes that increasingly in the Asian economies - ASEAN, China, India and South Asia - much more reliance has been placed on Direct Foreign Investment (DFI) which helped their sharing of risks, as they planned for accelerated economic development by way of industrialization *à la* importation of technology from abroad. Repatriation of profits, at least a reasonable part thereof, to the home stockholders of foreign investors became possible through emphasis on export earnings. Indeed, the DFI brought with it not only technology and management, but also *access to the world market.* Thus, the term export-led growth continues to prevail in the literature. The process involving import of capital goods to be paid for by export of products is truly *a paradigm of import-export-led growth, an open economic policy of industrialization by way of internationalization.*

Their exports could not have been sold in the world market if the products they manufactured with the help of imported technology failed to be competitive both in terms of unit-cost/price and its quality parameters. The process of adaptive innovation paradigm began by their skillful adaptation of the imported technology to their respective indigenous economic structures, given its comparative advantage which rested, at least to begin with, more on relative cheap labor and low wage cost per unit of output. A key element in the success of the adaptive innovation paradigm in Asian economies has been the availability not only of cheap labor, but also of cheap, *skilled, engineering* labor.

The successful Asian economies rejected the much criticized "turn-key" model and adapted the imported technology to their comparative advantage to become cost and quality competitive, and thus gain access to the world market and capture an increasing share of it. The process was more than a simple act of copying.

The new paradigm worked only when the necessary macroeconomic core brought into operation coordinated monetary-fiscal policies. Management of money supply and inflationary threats, budgetary imbalances and current account balances (CAB) were seen as necessary components of the macro core of Asias successful NIEs.

Second, the push factor came from the Western European economic regionalization beginning in the 1960s. The Western European effort to integrate their sovereign nation-state-based economies into a paradigm of economic regionalization following the Treaty of Rome, January 1, 1958, as we have noted earlier, moved the five richer APEC economies - the United States, Canada, Japan, Australia and New Zealand - who conceived the non-official economic forum, later known as OPTAD, as early as the late 1960s.

With the progressive manifestation of regionalization in Western Europe through its successive stages - European Economic Community , European Community, and now European Union - a growing push, a friendly challenge to the rest of the world to make a response became manifest. Is APEC a response?

APEC is an evolving, yet-to-be structured forum for economic regionalization in the Asia-Pacific. A structure needs to be set up. The structure must be *a supranational* arrangement for intraregional economic cooperation by way of intraregional monetary-fiscal policy coordination, thus ensuring the delivery of *intraregional public goods.*

A return to the classical model of supernational economic hegemony by the superpowers is indeed a non-option. The economic map of the world has changed and the change is irreversible.

In the context of a sovereign nation-state, we have argued that a macroeconomic core exists and provides public goods consisting of parameters, both political - security and defense, and economic - monetary-fiscal stability. The EU progressively seeks to deliver such a package of public goods to its sovereign member-economies. Can APEC be expected to offer a comparable model?

Asia-Pacific economic cooperation in the context of Asia's new capitalism presents a historic intersection of the twin processes of *deepening and widening* of the free enterprise market economic system. Industrialized rich, savings-surplus economies in the North Bloc, inclusive of Japan, in their search for a post-Cold War paradigm of widening their respective shares of the global markets enthusiastically noted the pull factors of Asia-Pacific economies. Under the set of historical circumstances, economies of these rich nations already became deepened with capital-intensive production maps.

The economies in the Asia-Pacific, hitherto traditional, began by initiating the process of deepening their respective home economies. Their agenda for accelerated industrialization and economic development extended an invitation to the international economies who sought widening across the Pacific. Rational choices of the market forces were allowed to work and the intersection of the twin processes yielded positive results. NIEs deepened, and in turn, joined the process of further widening to neighboring economies in Southeast Asia, China, and to India and South Asia. The "Flying Geese" model became the reference point.

A part of the success of the Asia-Pacific experiment must be attributed to strategic regionalization which brought several of the East Asian economies to an alliance with the United States and its allies in North America, Oceana and Western Europe. The market access was mutually shared at an accelerated pace. The intraregional trading economies in the Asia-Pacific thus became exposed to a unique experience of economic regionalization. The movement continues to build upon its own momentum.

THE GRAVITY MODEL

Many researchers have recently reported their findings on the gravity models of many variations. Hans Linnemann (1966) discussed whether the distance factor could be a possible explanatory variable in his econometric studies of international trade flows. This author made unsuccessful efforts to quantify the distance factor in his studies on foreign trade in the early 1960s.

Under specific historical circumstances, the distance between Sidney and London was found to be the shortest, as was the distance between Jakarta and The Hague. For several decades since 1948, China did not exist to the rest of the world. Since the 1970s, China is one of the fastest-growing and most lucrative markets and a share thereof has become the coveted target of most nations.

Some researchers have explained economic union of a free trade area between the two far-distant economies of the United States and Israel in 1985 by a social-anthropological factor, "like-mindedness" (in Schott, 1989). On the other hand, the fact of like-mindedness failed to retain the historically integrated economic link between Australia-New Zealand and the United Kingdom, when the latter opted to join the EU. Economic history is replete with many such not-so-common phenomena.

Recently, distance factors, based on land and water, have been subjects of intensive scrutiny in the context of gravity models in support of economic regionalization (Frankel and Kahler, 1993). The opening of the Euro-tunnel in 1994 will foreseeably be a subject of further extension of the gravity model. Then, as now, economists will continue to make efforts to quantify the distance factor by land or water or tunnel or air.

Man's ever-increasing knowledge in conquering physical distances among trading nations remains to be fully integrated into the gravity models. One wonders if the fast growing information super-highway will further revolutionize parameters of gravity models.

We shall seek an economic core to specify a gravity model which can explain rational market behavior of sovereign nation-state-based economies in their intraregional economic relationships. We argue strongly that the gravity model in economics must be anchored to an *intraregional supranational macroeconomic core* with an intraregional agenda and a commitment to make intraregional public goods available to all regional member-economies. A shared agenda for providing such public goods to member-countries is being sought in different international economic forums with varying degrees of success. The essence of economic regionalization is to present a gravity model which fits the bill.

THE EXCHANGE RATE: THE HOME PRICE/THE WORLD PRICE

Dornbusch (1990a and 1990b, 1987, 1980) has extensively and forcefully argued the role of exchange rate parameters in explaining economic relationships among sovereign macroeconomies. The World Bank has recently computed the GDPs of its member-nations both in home prices and world prices. The Bank presents interesting evidence showing China and India as the third and sixth largest economies of the world when GDP is measured in their respective home prices.

The literature on exchange rate is required reading in international economics. The term "currency war" has been noted. Only recently in the 1980s, the world's seven richer nations at their various G-7 summits debated how monetary-fiscal policies pursued by one of them could be counterproductive for the group. The overvaluation of the U.S. dollar *vis-à-vis* the Japanese yen, or the under-valuation of the dollar *vis-à-vis* the yen, the two currencies that dominate much of the world trade, continue to be a crucial factor in the U.S.-Japan trade negotiations. Efforts to correct this exchange rate imbalance by U.S.-Japan binational negotiations have failed to produce the optimum result. Nor have the G-7 summits yielded better results.

The situation merits additional attention as the role of the IMF to manage the exchange rate globally has become increasingly limited. The G-7 nations have taken their debates and discourses effectively out of the IMF. In addition, the member-nations of Europe in the EU have elected to manage their intra-Union exchange rates and related issues independently.

Should there be an institutionalization of intra-APEC exchange rate management for its member-economies to *multilaterally* manage their exchange rates? Or, should there be a total restoration of the IMF regime by inviting the G-7 and the EU economies to its original format? The situation is more complex when one notes the fact that four of the EU-economies - the United Kingdom, Germany, France and Italy - concurrently are members of the G-7 and articulate their policies through its summits.

Kojima (1990b) argues for a gold-plus multiple key currency model for exchange rate management. Following the Ecu anchored to the German mark, may one argue for an Asian money anchored to the Japanese yen?

An option is to have the APEC exchange rate *concurrently* anchored to the U.S. dollar and the Japanese yen with open provision for other APEC currencies - the Australian dollar, the Korean won, the New Taiwan dollar, the Singapore dollar, the Hong Kong dollar - to attain the anchor currency status, as the economic rationale warrants.

It is to be noted that the convertibility of the Chinese yuan by the year 2000 is under discussion and the Indian rupee has recently been made convertible (excluding capital accounts).

The core argument for APEC is to face squarely the issue of intraregional monetary-fiscal policy coordination and work toward developing an intra-APEC exchange rate management mechanism. To shelve the issue by limiting the debate to binational negotiations, as is the case between the United States and Japan, is at best a suboptimal choice. Experience shows that the success of such a binational approach has been constrained by the relative ability of the two economies to absorb exchange rate "shocks" as agreed upon.

Others continue to argue that the free market will *in the long* run ensure the equilibrium in the world exchange rate market. We have earlier noted the painful and unsuccessful experiment between 1971 and 1985, and we returned to the managed exchange rate regime.

We conclude that in the absence of a multilaterally coordinated monetary-fiscal policy regime, exchange rate management can hardly be left to the market, and that in the absence of an effective global coordination of such macroeconomic policies, an intraregional approach is an option.

THE ROLE OF GOVERNMENT

By providing public goods as commonly defined in a given sovereign nation- state-based macroeconomy, the government plays an economic role. This has been a fact more pronounced in Western Europe and in Japan. The role of government in providing public goods remains to be recognized in all cases, including the United States. Existence of an economic agenda and a national economic policy - monetary and fiscal policies - targeting its fulfillment has been universal. Relative ineffectiveness of such an agenda in the United States in recent decades has been cited to be one of the six arguments of the U.S. for its loss in global competitiveness (MIT Commission 1989).

In the case of Asian industrialization *à la* the paradigm of adaptive innovation, the role of governments in these economics has been well known (Wade, 1990). They came in the form of successive five-year economic plans as in Korea or in some variations of formal economic planning as in Taiwan and Singapore. Malaysia, Thailand and Indonesia have followed a parallel course.

China, of course, has a far more comprehensive economic planning, given its form of *socialist market economy.* India adopted "a mixed economic policy" in its successive five-year plans since the 1950s. In 1978, China adopted its open economic policy and marketization of its economy. In 1991, India's new economic policy, substituting its erstwhile import substitution plan by an export-led growth program, has become a new focus for Asia's new capitalism.

In each newly industrialized/industrializing economy in Asia, monetary and fiscal policies were carefully and closely targeted. Was it indeed a happy marriage between capitalism and socialism? We argue that it was a careful recognition of society's role to institute a macroeconomic core ensuring the supply of public goods with effective provision for its core economic parameters. They would not be able to import alien technology and know-how and pay for these precious imports by their export earnings in hard currencies without gaining access to the world market for merchandising their exportables. To that end, each of these economies needed to orchestrate its respective monetary-fiscal policies.

The binational approach to correct imbalances in the economic relationship of the individual Asia-Pacific economy with the United States will be of limited result. The United States is an economic superpower. However, the ability of a superpower, as the United States is, to enforce a supernational economic regime in a superpower-dominated economic hegemony is not expected to be successful and can hardly be the optimum U.S. agenda.

The threats of Super-301 against friendly economic allies may be counterproductive (Lipsey, 1992). Economic/commercial diplomacy has recently been much in vogue and is being aggressively followed by most advanced industrialized economies. Their respective national security administrations are called upon to guard their industrial/economic copyrights/secrets carefully. Economic communications to be punctuated by considerations for human rights, prison labor and non-proliferation of nuclear arsenals can at best yield suboptimal results. An effective option in the absence of a one-world government is a supranational regional approach at an intraregional forum. Can APEC be the forum for such debates?

PART II

Asia-Pacific Economic Cooperation (APEC) - "A Moving Target"

8 APEC is a "Moving Target"

Asia-Pacific Economic Cooperation (APEC) is no longer "talk only". It is an institutionalized forum of 18 sovereign nation-states: the United States, Canada, Mexico and Chile on the American shore of the Pacific, Japan, South Korea, the People's Republic of China, Taiwan, Hong Kong, the Philippines, Brunei Darussalam, Indonesia, Singapore, Malaysia and Thailand, on the Asian shore, and Australia, New Zealand and the Pacific Islands in the South Pacific. The principal item of its agenda is to liberalize intraregional trade and investment flows with a target for free trade by 2010/2015/2020.

The many and varied issues before APEC include harmonization of tariff rules, standardization of products in trade, formulation of an investment code, human resource development, environmental parameters, energy resource exploration, employment and growth and coordination of monetary-fiscal policies toward facilitation of its agenda.

Annual APEC Summits with the participation of the heads of the member-states since 1993 have become an event of global economic significance. Each member-state has designated an eminent person, and the eminent persons' group (EPG) works to prepare blueprints for the summit meetings. At the Osaka Leaders' Summit, the designation of EPA was discontinued. However, parallel functionaries will certainly be in order. Each APEC member-country may designate an Advisor Plenipotentiary. Regular meetings of APEC finance ministers review monetary-fiscal issues. The senior officials at the national capitals of APEC member-states have their assignments and the Senior Officials' Meetings (SOM) have become a regular feature. Then, there is the APEC Secretariat in Singapore.

APEC is neither an FTA, as is NAFTA, nor is APEC an integrated, intraregional economic union, as is the EU. What is it? It has been rightly suggested that APEC is indeed "a moving target" which very much defies a textbook definition.

Soon after the Treaty of Rome became operational on January 1, 1958, giving birth to what is now the EU, concerned economists in the Asia-Pacific region articulated the concept of OPTAD. The movement continued to gain momentum, as it were, in tandem with the progress of economic regionalization in Western Europe. Shortly after the Single European act was adopted in 1985, APEC became formally institutionalized in 1989. In 1992, the Maastricht Treaty became yet another turning point for the EU, and in 1993, APEC attained its heightened visibility by convening an annual summit with the participation of the heads of APEC member-states, for the first time in its short history. The APEC Summit in Bogor, Indonesia in 1994 was a great success. In 1995 the next summit was held in Osaka, Japan. "As more summits are held, APEC's vision becomes clearer every year", asserts Jang-Hee Yoo. Annual summits have also been scheduled for 1996, 1997, 1998 and 1999 in the Philippines, Canada, Malaysia and New Zealand, respectively. "It is too early to say how APEC will really evolve", says Fred Bergsten, adding that for the present, "APEC is a regional institution for trade and investment liberalization". The EPGs of Indonesia, China, Singapore, Australia, and Thailand further confirm: "APEC is a consultative forum for trade liberalization", "a consultative forum for its member-countries", "a political commitment to the whole area of trade liberalization", "economic regionalization based upon the concept of voluntary association with its focus upon free trade in the region", and "a trade forum, trade and investment forum". The EPG of Malaysia adds, "We must make sure that APEC succeeds in creating this Pacific community and this effective economic entity". The APEC initiative continues to unfold.

APEC is a historic movement and its emerging agenda will have to be studied with care. We have argued that the core of post-Cold War economic regionalization centers on a common economic space being mapped on to a map-of-the-world view of a common geographic space. The Lake Pacific is the common geographic space for APEC. The intra-APEC subregional grouping in North America, Southeast Asia and South Pacific is an issue. In addition, one must study the two other initatives for economic grouping, (i) the American hemispheric free trade area and (ii) the Indian Ocean grouping, each one of which has been joined by several APEC members.

To find an answer to what APEC is, in what follows I present my recorded conversations in June 1995, and during August to December 1994 with EPG members from South Korea, the United States, Indonesia, the People's Republic of China, Singapore, Australia, Thailand and Malaysia; the president of the Asian Development Bank, and four concerned scholars in APEC studies at the Australian National University, Canberra, and the University of Malaya, Kuala Lumpur.

How will APEC, which is different from the EU, be consistent with the WTO? How does one distinguish between the two expressions, "a free trade area" and "free trade in the area"? How do the 18 sovereign member-states of APEC, at varying levels of industrialization and economic development, plan for harmonization of tariff, standardization of tradables, formalization of an investment code, and coordination of employment, environment and energy goals? How can an intraregional free trade program be operational without a necessary, if not sufficient, level of coordinated macroeconomic agenda?

How will the Americanization of the American hemisphere, encompassing all sovereign states in North and South America, fit into the broader APEC agenda? Will a competing agenda for Asianization of Asia become a challenge? Will the Lake Pacific framework for APEC be robust enough for a progressive expansion of its membership to economies in the Asia-Pacific region?

One can argue that APEC is an Asia-Pacific response to the movement for economic regionalization in Western Europe, and it will develop its agenda with no attempt to replicate the EU.

9 A Conversation with JANG-HEE YOO

Q. *Let us begin with the question many of us seem to be concerned about. APEC, Bogor in 1994 became a high point since its founding in 1989, while APEC Osaka 1996, people perceived, became a low point. How will you explain this situation to your readers?*

A. An important point that people often miss is that APEC is still in the process of growing and developing. So far we have had three leaders' meetings, or "summits" as they are referred to in the media. The first summit was held in Seattle in 1993, the second in Bogor 1994, and the third in Osaka in 1995. As more summits are held APEC's vision becomes clearer every year and APEC's programs become more concrete. In the Bogor Declaration of 1994, all of the member-economies decided to complete APEC's trade liberalization program by the year 2020 for developing economies and by the year 2010 for the developed economies. Even though the year 2020 may be a long way off, this is a major step towards economic integration in the APEC region that should not be underestimated. What is so significant about the Bogor Declaration is that all 18 member-economies were able to come together and decide to accept this concept of APEC, despite the fact that each economy varies a great deal in terms of economic development status, relative size of economies, and economic systems. This is definitely one of the most remarkable developments in the APEC movement.

Last year in Osaka the leaders decided to have each country submit the plan of action for trade liberalization before the summit meeting in 1996, which is this year. Writing these action plans for trade liberalization and trade facilitation, I think you would agree, is not an easy task. It is an extremely complicated, cumbersome, and in some cases, an extremely painstaking task, especially for some of the economies whose trade systems are not already as liberalized as some of the other economies. Even so, all leaders decided to submit their respective action plans before the summit meeting in Manila in 1996. I think this was a remarkable, and courageous decision, aptly illustrating the progress of the APEC movement. I strongly believe that APEC will be growing even further. I am optimistic that APEC will be able to form a very unique kind of cooperative economic integration in the future.

Q. *I share your optimism, but we must first be able to answer questions as they come up. In terms of trade liberalization, I would like to ask a two-part question as a follow up: first, there were 2010, 2015, 2020, three dates for the three groups of APEC members, based on economic development. What was the argument for having only two groups?*

Second, liberalization of trade, it seems, has been limited to tradable goods. Services, we have not discussed, or even intra-APEC free flows of investment remain to be discussed.

A. You are correct. When the EPG report came up in 1993, our recommendation was first to divide the 18 APEC member-economies into three groups: (i) less-developed economies, (ii) mid-developing ones, and (iii) developed advanced economies. At the Bogor leaders' meeting the leaders decided on a two-group system instead of a three-group system. Presenting two groups of 2010 and 2020, rather than three groups of 2010, 2015 and 2020, simplified the scheme. As we dichotomize the system this way this fact has become even clearer. Canada, the United States, Japan, New Zealand and Australia are advanced developed economies, and for the time being everybody else will belong to the group of 2020.

Furthermore, I think some of the faster-growing economies like Singapore, Hong Kong, Taiwan and Korea will not have to wait until the year 2020 to complete their liberalization.The bottom-line date is essentially 2020. All the APEC member-economies must become liberalized by 2020. If one member-economy becomes much more advanced and developed than the others, it can voluntarily join the group of 2010 at its own discretion.

Indeed, that is one of the unique features of APEC. All other regional economic integrations have drawn a strict line at a specific date, and all member-countries must conform to this target date. APEC is more flexible. There are some items that we see in the declaration that allow each member-country to make its own decisions on a voluntary basis. If a member so elects, it can liberalize its trade much earlier than the year 2020. I believe that Korea is going to be one of these examples.

The second part of the question is about trade in services and investment flows. Indeed, the Bogor Declaration of 1994 and the Osaka Statement of 1995 stated that all goods and services are to be included in the liberalization programs. While GATT's rule indicated substantially all goods and services, APEC's rule eliminated the term "substantially" as adopted by the ministerial meetings in 1994. APEC's movement for liberalization is going to apply to all goods and services.

Q. *How about the investment flows? To my best understanding there is no specific directive regarding intra-APEC free flow of the investment. In addition, one must take note of the fact that the intra-APEC labor movement is increasingly becoming a crucial issue. How is APEC going to confront the mobility of labor within the APEC countries?*

A. First of all, investment is going to be made free across the borders, which is the concept adopted by the APEC Committee on Trade and Investment [CTI]. They are presently working on the APEC principles of investment liberalization. I believe that the CTI will be ready to present them in the near future.

As I understand it, the CTI begins with the position that the investment liberalization goal adopted by the leaders' meeting in 1994 was "non-binding" insofar as its enforcement is concerned. Investment principles will become binding if a member-economy decides to adopt the non-binding principles and go along with the principles of investment liberalization. An individual member-country is free to make its own judgment to postpone adoption of the principles until later, or to go ahead and give effect to the principles immediately. Once a member-economy elects to adopt the investment liberalization principles, it must make a declaration by itself and must become bound by the principles. That's what the CTI is working on at the moment, as I understand it. Once again, this voluntary basis differentiates APEC from other regional economic integrations.

The issue of labor mobility is somehow connected to this concept. As investment becomes more and more liberalized in general, economies that have adopted these liberalized investment principles earlier must and should be able to hire the foreign workers. Nevertheless, for member-economies that did not adopt the investment liberalization principles early, labor mobility is going to be somewhat limited. It all depends upon how soon the investment liberalization principles are adopted by an APEC member-economy. There are some differences of opinion in terms of the timetable, that is, how fast the principles of investment liberalization could be feasibly adopted. It is also important to emphasize that member-economies will have different needs in terms of adjustment.

Q. *As you know, some economists studying intra-APEC mobility of labor have established dates when several APEC members migrated from labor-surplus to labor-shortage economies, meaning the aggregate demand for labor becoming greater than the aggregate supply of labor. Several economies on this shore of the Pacific, perhaps Korea included, have passed that cut-off point in time. What would you like to see the arrangement to be for intra-APEC labor mobility, which could effectively face the fast-growing challenge of illegal immigrant workers?*

A. Well, as the intra-APEC investment flows become increasingly freer, the industry relocations will follow. Chances are that labor-intensive industries will be moving towards the labor-surplus economies and vice versa. A capital-intensive industry will be moving towards those countries whose capital supply is relatively better and more abundant. Through the process of relocation of industries, part of the labor problems will have been addressed too. Secondly, labor itself could be mobile, moving across the borders. For example, in Korea, to meet the growing demand for industry, quite a few unskilled workers from China/Philippines/Indonesia are offered employment. Accordingly, Korea's immigration law had to be changed. Thus, our labor market, particularly the unskilled labor market, has been generally stabilized. Recently the rate of growth in wages and salaries for unskilled workers has also been relatively stable compared to the period when foreign workers were prohibited from coming in.

It follows that all newly industrialized/industrializing APEC member-economies should adjust their legal systems or immigration systems to match their respective economic needs. Whether or not this is possible for the member-economies depends upon what APEC, as a system, can offer to each member-economy. If APEC is institutionalized enough so that it can develop its own policies or guidelines that each member-country must observe and abide by, intra-APEC adjustment processes will be accelerated. If APEC as a system cannot accomplish this, the adjustment process would be delayed accordingly.

Q. *That's very important. Your comments on this important issue are indeed very welcome. If I had read it right, between Bogor and Osaka a great deal of emphasis has been placed on issues of formalization/standardization of tradable goods and custom rules, important as they are for liberalization of intra-APEC trade. From your vantage point, would you care to comment on the importance of these steps?*

A. I think it is very important, and not only important for facilitating trade in the APEC region, but also for contributing to globalization of world trade. It seems to be one of the front runners of APEC's unique projects. We may say that the Committee on Standard and Conformance, one of the working groups of APEC, seems to be most active at the moment. As I understand it, they have even proposed some rules of standardization, conformance, and safety and so on at the Senior Officials' Meeting recently. The focus of the proposal seems that the new rules should center on regulated products. That is, the most serious barriers to trade are government regulations which mandate how a product meets government standards. This should be changed. The private sector should take the initiative to form a new standard/conformance rule.

Q. *In 1994, I had occasions to have conversations on APEC with members of the Eminent Persons' Group in Australia, China, the Philippines, Indonesia, Singapore, Malaysia, Thailand and the United States. If I have understood them correctly, trade liberalization efforts by way of normalization/*

standardization of traded products may have more adverse impact on the less developing APEC member economies - China, Indonesia, the Philippines - and thus may load the dice against them. They cannot compete and then their trade may be hurt. Have you noticed this, or whether or not the EPG group has addressed the related issues that divide the advanced industrial members against the less-advanced / less-industrially-developed members?

A. Well, surprisingly, these less-developed economies [LDEs] would like to see the standardization even more anxiously than the developed economies. This is because the LDEs are having a tough time producing quality tradable goods by uniform standardized measures. They feel this standardization and conformance movement of APEC will be a building bloc and an operational mechanism they could utilize to homogenize the production standard in their respective economies. The developing economies will then have the legitimacy to say that all APEC member-economies should use the uniform standardization, measurement, and the safety standard. At that point, all the domestic industries would have to go by this rule. The government of an individual member-economy alone would not be able to exercise this new standardization. Together with APEC's rules and recommendations, they will be able to enforce conformance rules and achieve product standardization.

Secondly, as they adjust to new standardization and conformance, they will be able to more comfortably produce their own products and facilitate the export of those traded goods to advanced countries. This will automatically mean that export of the member-economies will be able to find more opportunities and larger markets.

Q. *I'm glad to know that standardization and conformance act as a positive force. One other question that strikes me is that, in the fairly lengthy EPG recommendations there is one paragraph, less than 100 words, on intra-APEC monetary policy coordination. Some of your fellow EPGs argue that it is too early to talk of such macroeconomic issues. Others argue that such issues do not truly belong to the APEC agenda. You have served as Korea's EPG from the inception of APEC, could you elaborate on this topic? We all know that APEC finance ministers/central bankers hold annual meetings, of course, at a cost to the taxpayers in all member-countries.*

A. Indeed, EPG members didn't talk much about macroeconomic policies and financial policies. There has not been a proposal for intra-APEC standardization of these policies. They have been rather left to individual member-countries. EPG discussion was more or less concentrated on the international financial market order, particularly the order for exchange rate determinations. Recently, we have seen the Mexican peso crisis. No international institution was able to deal with this peso crisis directly. Nor was any single individual government able to deal with this crisis effectively. One reason was that the international monetary organizations like the International Monetary Fund didn't have too much of a stabilization fund. With a larger fund, the IMF could have quickly purchased pesos on the international financial market so that the sudden drop of its values could be prevented.

Mexico is an APEC member-economy. APEC/EPG members had dealt with this issue quite intensively and proposed that the IMF's stabilization fund must be increased. If something unusual happens in the international financial market, the IMF could then quickly get involved and use the funds to minimize the unexpected fluctuations of the currency values. It is to be noted that a good number of APEC member-economies maintain a very high level of foreign exchange reserves, and, therefore, there could be a way for APEC members to raise the extra money to increase the IMF's stabilization fund.

Q. *I would like to press that question a little bit if you will permit me. Suppose APEC leaves intra-APEC exchange rate stabilization to the IMF or the World Bank. That will enable the 18 APEC members passing on their intraregional responsibility to 150 other member-nations of the IMF, who are not within the APEC regional grouping. If APEC developed a set of guidelines to limit unilateral currency devaluation, increase of money supply, raising of public borrowing, APEC would be better prepared to attack any such problem: today the Mexican peso, tomorrow the Chinese yuan, after tomorrow the Indonesian rupiah, the Thai bhat or the Malaysian ringet, or another member currency. Taiwan, an APEC member, with its huge foreign exchange surplus, would be able to help correct intra-APEC exchange rate stabilization. Would you care to comment?*

A. You are right that the IMF is working for the whole world, not just for the 18 APEC members. At one point of time we even contemplated forming a mini-IMF that would just serve APEC countries alone, leaving the other members of the IMF aside.

Nevertheless, given the fact that a major part of global financial transactions, and a major part of the world trade are taking place in the APEC's region, the probability of having another financial crisis or payment crisis within the APEC region seems to be higher. The IMF may not be able to avoid getting involved.

Secondly, APEC's most important objective is to work for the multilateral economic order globally, not just regionally. APEC'S effort is to supplement/complement the World Trade Organization's multilateral efforts to strengthen the unity of a world economic order. In terms of exchange rate stabilization, if APEC contributes to the IMF's stabilization fund, APEC will have done its share for the global stabilization of exchange rates/financial markets. The recommendation was to strengthen the IMF's stabilizing function for the benefit not only of APEC, but of the world.

Q. *You will forgive me for pressing this question further. We have seen it done before when the G-5, later the G-7, was formed. The most industrialized and richest economies of the world essentially took the job of exchange rate stabilization away from the IMF. Did the rest of the APEC members do their share in correcting the problem for a fellow APEC member directly? Was it viewed more as a problem of the American administration? Would you prefer specific APEC intraregional effort in regard to intraregional exchange rate stabilization?*

A. This leadership of the G-7, earlier the G-5, is certainly subject to much debate. Some have argued that the United Nations as a world body is not going to function as well as it did in the past, because these selected rich, industrialized nations are doing their things outside this world forum. Some also argue that the IMF is no longer functioning as effectually as it had in the past, because the G-7 financial ministers choose to address their issues within their exclusive forum. Some are concerned that the WTO system, even though it was launched after a painstaking seven years of negotiation, will not work as effectively as expected, because the G-7 will do most of what they would prefer to do in the same forum.

That was the way that this world's politics and economics were run in the decades past. Now there is an even stronger development taking place in the world that is more convincing and effective than the G-5/G-7 - that is, multilateralism. Presently, all the countries of the world, big or small, developed or developing, in the West or in the East, are participating in the decision-making process for liberalization of international trade and global monetary-fiscal stability. Let me further add that the G-5/G-7 are important because the world decision making does need some kind of leadership. But that doesn't mean these five or seven countries need to dominate all major economic decisions.

Look at the disputes settlement mechanisms that the WTO has set up. Each country on the disputes settlement panel has one vote. It doesn't matter if it's the U.S. or Monaco, each has just one vote. Thus the majority will rule the process.

In the long run, I am convinced that this principle of multilateralism/ globalization will be working for the betterment of the new world order. Exactly what the new world order formed in the twenty-first century will look like is anybody's guess. As far as I'm concerned, the new world order will accept multi-lateralism as its core principle. All countries big/small, east/west, will participate in the decision-making process and the opinion of the majority will rule so that universal values of the human society could be upheld. No member-country will have any special privilges.

Q. *Let me move on to a separate question that is now being debated. Some have very adamantly challenged the proposition that the European Union, now with 15 member-nations in Western Europe, is consistent with the WTO charter. The principle of GATT-consistent economic regionalization and the concept of "open regionalization" are oxymorons. How would you join this debate?*

A. I believe that APEC's agenda of open regionalism is valid and that APEC can find its own place even within the WTO system. This is true according to the GATT Article 24, which stipulates that regionalization is absolutely legal if this specific regional grouping does not erect any further trade barriers against other non-member economies of the regional group.

I'm quite optimistic on the issue. If a country of one regional group extends its liberalization program(s) to non-member economies that have not adopted parallel trade liberalization program(s), then it will be a case of an open regionalism. The real question is whether a member-economy within a regional group, say APEC, would offer the liberalization program, as effective within the group, to a non-member-economy, conditionally or unconditionally. Personally, in the context of APEC, I am definitely in favor of open regionalism, the choice of conditionality/unconditionality being left to the individual country's decision. The rule of an individual member's freedom of choice has been the norm for APEC and it should continue to be so.

In Korea's case within the APEC system, let us assume that it is the year 2020 and we have established a free trade region. Korea, China, the U.S., Japan and every other APEC member are enjoying the free trade system. No tariffs or non-tariff barriers exist. What will Korea do for Nigeria or any other non-APEC country? Korea could offer the same kind of liberalization program with zero tariff and no non-tariff barriers. That will be APEC's picture in the year 2020.

In my view, Korea would go ahead and provide the same zero tariff and zero non-tariff free trade arrangement to a country like Nigeria. Whether Nigeria reciprocates it or not, Korea would not change its trade arrangement. That is what we call unconditional provisional most favored nation [MFN] principle. Chances are, sooner or later, Nigeria will be affected by Korea, and it would appreciate Korea's effort and offer to reciprocate by cutting down tariff and non-tariff barriers, or at least gradually lower them in each successive year. Nevertheless, Nigeria's appreciation of Korea's policy of open regionalism will foreseeably be manifest in various ways.

Even if Korea's story may be so, on the other hand, other APEC members' position may be different. Suppose a country would like to provide a fully liberalized trading scheme to Nigeria, if and only if Nigeria does the same. This will be an example of conditional open regionalism. That country would like to go conditionally, and Korea would like to go unconditionally, and that should be the choice of each country. That is open regionalism based upon individual choice.

Q. *How about the multinational Korean corporation, based in Taiwan, or Taiwan's incorporated in Seoul? Should each follow the rules of their respective home country? Or, follow the rules of the country of their incorporation?*

A. In the APEC non-binding investment principles, we call for transparency, national treatment and non-discrimination principles. According to these APEC nonbinding investment principles, member-economies should extend to investors from any economy equal treatment in relation to the establishment, expansion, and operation of their investments.

Q. *Returning to the case of Nigeria, how do you expect a Korean corporation incorporated in Taipei, and a Taiwanese corporation incorporated in Seoul, to behave regarding the conditional/unconditional deal with Nigeria?*

A. If a Taiwanese company is in Korea, that should be treated as a company of Korea by the year 2020. This sort of national treatment is one of the objectives of APEC to be accomplished by the year 2020. Even though the name carried is Taiwanese, it is treated as a Korean company based upon the national treatment principle; thus, it must abide by Korea's unconditional MFN regime, and vice versa. A Korean company incorporated in Taiwan must act like a Taiwanese company. Even though the company's nationality is Korean, the company must abide by Taiwan's conditional open regionalism if Taiwan's trade policy is elected as such.

Q. *Let us move on to the American Hemispheric Conference of all sovereign countries of North and South America, excepting Cuba, hosted by the United States in 1994. The potential of these American hemispheric initiatives is a hemispheric expansion of the North American Free Trade Area into the Free Trade Area of the Americas. How does Korea view this "free trade area" of the Americas?*

A. Should APEC succeed in applying open regionalism, some cases conditionally, others unconditionally - I don't think it makes any difference. Assume FTAA has been formed and Argentina, not an APEC member, is a member of FTAA. Let us say by the year 2020, Korea has provided an unconditional MFN to Argentina. The effect is transparent to other members of APEC and FTAA. One way to view this is to assume that all countries, APEC members and FTAA members, are members of a larger free trade regime. Both Korea and Argentina act as if they both are members of a free trade area regardless of their existing regional membership.

Q. *How do you respond to the concern, shared by some of your fellow EPGs, about a potential hostile response from the United States to the proposal of an East Asian economic community, excluding all the APEC members of the Americas?*

A. To make such an exclusive grouping, the East Asian Economic Caucus [EAEC], one needs specific economic rational in its support. APEC has its Asia-Pacific regional identity. The Pacific Ocean is there and so are Asian countries, the U.S., Canada and others. Now the question is where you have to draw the dividing line in the Ocean and why does one need to form the EAEC.

Secondly, economic merits for forming that kind of regional arrangement are missing. APEC does have substantive economic rationale because the intra-APEC trading is more than 50 per cent of the total world trade. The EAEC does not generate this level of trade. The fact of the matter is that the intra-regional EAEC trade is not so substantial. With the exclusion of the United States, Canada and Australia, the intraregional trade volume would become much smaller. The intraregional EAEC trading among Japan, Korea, China, Taiwan and the Southeast Asian countries alone is simply not comparatively significant enough to warrant formation of another East Asian regional integration.

It must be noted that in the absence of a strong economic argument, the only identity EAEC can possibly have would be rather racial, that of East Asian people. Any such non-economic regional agreement will not help our commitment to multilateralism under the WTO or the GATT. Our goal must be to make the whole world a single integrated market. Thus, EAEC could be a source of much misunderstanding or misconception unless it delivers an economic identity and agenda. It would be extremely counterproductive to promote a race-based regional grouping.

At the same time, APEC's development is rapidly progressing. All prospective members of EAEC are APEC members, and turning our back on APEC is not a feasible option. Further, discussions at the Asian-European Meeting, held in Bangkok in March 1996, indicate that we would rather optimize mutual economic gains by trying to strengthen linkages between Asian and European countries. As we observe the new developments toward intercontinental economic integration, we are pretty much convinced that the whole world is becoming one barrier-free market for multilateral economic cooperation. We know that APEC is here and APEC can be an institution to help all its members move to this global agenda.

Q. *I must ask you one more question. Are you fully convinced that the*

European Union is not a fortress Europe?

A. The EU is considered by many economists to be a fortress in Europe and I do have the same concern that the EU could become a very exclusive club for its member-countries. But I think, at the moment, the EU is based on a regional identity and no major changes in the characteristics of the EU in terms of a fortress image can be observed. I also believe that in the future, whether they like it or not, they will subscribe to the concept of open regionalism. They cannot allow them to become isolated from the rest of the world. The open regionalism concept has not been officially adopted by the EU. Many economists from the EU who visited the Korean Institute of the International Economic Policy [KIEP] and gave guest lectures indicated that sooner or later the concept will prevail even in the EU. The economic integration of the whole world should inevitably be their goal.

Concerning the MFN principles adopted by most countries, the EU members happen to be the only ones in an economic regional grouping who do not subscribe to the spirit, which will prove detrimental to their own economic development. As they realize such disadvantage sooner or later, they will come to subscribe to this open regionalism, that is to say, that EU members will also provide zero tariff and zero non-tariff liberal trade facilities to non-member-countries.

Q. *May I press the question further? The EU has progressed into one economic unit, with a much higher order of regional integration. Even if they have yet to establish one currency, they already have one accounting unit of currency, the Ecu. Following the Maastricht Treaty in 1992, the EU members have voted for an agenda for the intra-EU free flow of trade and investment and labor. The EU is a case of what some have called deep integration; some others may call it the United States of Europe. The EU has accepted the GATT Agreement and the 15-member EU is one member of the WTO, subscribing fully and wholly to its goal for liberalization of the global trade. What is wrong with the arrangement for GATT-consistent economic regionalization in Western Europe?*

A. There is nothing wrong with that. The real trouble is that the United Europe or EU, as one integrated economic unit, does not offer zero tariff and zero non-tariff trading facilities to non-member countries, while all the others, especially APEC member-economies, propose to do so with its agenda for complete trade liberalization.

Q. *If and when 18 APEC member-economies achieve their trade liberalization goals in 2020, hopefully with free flow of capital and labor, it will certainly be a different world.*

A. Right, free flow of capital is possible and is very much desired. Free flow of labor must be discussed in a separate context. Labor is not just services embodied in the human agents. Whether the labor should be freely moving around all over the world market also depends on an individual human agent's decision as well. Services of labor can hardly be treated as a commodity in international trade. Pending in-depth research and detailed discussion of the many and varied aspects of the human factor mobility, the discussion of free flow of labor across national borders should be shelved.

We have no knowledge whether the British people would like to work in Korea, or whether American labor would like to work in Nigeria. Even if labor could move freely around the world, it does not necessarily mean that all the people would opt for it. It is unlikely that a large number of workers could elect to move with their respective jobs around all the countries in the world.

Q. *I would like to go back to the EU, which has been referred to as a case of "deep integration". Would you care to comment on both the words, "deep" and "integration" in the context of APEC?*

A. When Professor Richard Cooper used those terms, he had in mind, I think, the emerging scenario of a European entity with economic integration, reinforced by a process of political as well as social and other types of integration. The EU has achieved economic integration based on its agenda. Political, social and monetary integration may follow in the future. The APEC agenda is quite different from that of the EU, and it is limited to free trade and investment.

Trade and investment are economic activities that belong to enterprises in the private sector. We in APEC believe that the private sector will increasingly lead the market economy, nationally, regionally and globally, as we go into the twenty-first century. APEC development is pretty much a market-driven phenomenon. As the governments of the APEC member-countries set up the environment, the economic decisions are going to be made by the private sector enterprises. The free market system will find its own order.

The European integration is different. It's not market driven, it is government driven. The EU is even talking about political integration, a process that will involve many delicate hurdles and difficult struggles. I am afraid that the process will exact a great deal from the EU member-countries.

On the contrary, in the APEC system, we don't talk about political, monetary, social and cultural integration. I think that the APEC agenda limits itself to facilitating the working of the free market economy in the region. We in APEC believe that this process will eventually help build the global free market economy.

Q. *How about making a few comments on what I refer to as "geo-economic" regional groupings within APEC, Closer Economic Relations of Australia and*

New Zealand, Association of Southeast Asian Nations , Northeast Asian group, North American Free Trade Area of Canada, the U.S. and Mexico? Then, there is one more, not at all formal but still very real regional grouping: the Golden Triangle of China consisting of Taiwan, Hong Kong and Mainland China.

A. Let's see. We are talking about small regional trade arrangements within APEC. In Northeast Asia, we don't have any special institutionalized organization. However, in APEC, discussions of such small regional trade arrangements have been limited. Linkages among the small regional arrangements would not be contrary to APEC's agenda. The EPG members have concluded an idea that the annual APEC Leaders' Summits will be able to iron out any and all differences among smaller regional trade arrangements. Indeed, the differences have not been that large, and foreseeably, they will continue to function as small-scale regional arrangements.

Q. *May I point out that Professor Peter Lloyd of Australia writing on ANZ-CER states: "it [ANZ-CER] should be completely like EU". In the context of the noneconomic as well as economic contents, ANZ-CER should be a better approximation to the EU.*

A. I don't know. I do not see how Australia and New Zealand can become one political entity.

Q. *Apart from political union, Australia and New Zealand have achieved a higher, if not deeper, order of monetary policy coordination.*

A. Economists like Peter Drysdale and others don't see it that way. The ANZ exchange rate system is fine. The monetary coordination is very productive. Why then do they have to use just one currency?

Q. *Would you then say there is a case for APEC intraregional exchange rate coordination?*

A. KIEP is working on it. The Institute for International Economics in Washington, DC, is working on it as well. In fact, the two Institutes are working together to find some mechanism that could be used to stabilize the intra-APEC exchange rate system. Let me add that we are running into some difficulties as to how best to define the equilibrium exchange rate. Also, we do have a question whether there is an optimal methodology to sustain the equilibrium exchange rate. Thus, defining the equilibrium exchange rate and maintaining its stability within the 18-member APEC system remain subjects for ongoing research. We are studying these issues of definition and of stability. I think that our progress is still in its very early stage.

Q. *Leaving aside monetary policy coordination, there are models for intraregional exchange rate management. One option would be to accept whatever the exchange rates are on a specified date, with provisions for unilateral changes strictly limited to a plus/minus range, as may be agreed upon. An additional provision for deviations by an individual member with prior APEC approval may add to the flexibility of the overall system. Appointment of an APEC Standing Committee to periodically review the progress would be quite appropriate.*

The other model is to make the exchange rate totally free, which is not practical. However, I have argued that any effort to stabilize the intra-APEC exchange rate in the absence of intra-APEC monetary-fiscal policy coordination must remain wide open.

A. I don't have much to add to that. I know that the issue of the intra-APEC exchange rate stabilization is currently under study by a team of economists in the two Institutes, the one in Seoul and the other in Washington, DC, as I stated earlier.

Q. *I am pleased to note that an aspect of the larger issue of intra-APEC monetary-fiscal policy coordination has been engaging the attention of APEC experts. One final question. Will Korea vote for the admission of Vietnam to APEC?*

A. Well, the moratorium until 1996 will apply to the new membership issue. Next year, however, Vietnam's membership may come up. The Southeast Asian members of APEC will foreseeably have a great deal to say on the subject. Korea will wait for their recommendation. Korea has no strong position one way or another. Korea will have no objection to Vietnam's joining APEC, if so recommended.

Member, Eminent Persons' Group. This conversation was taped on May 27, 1996 in Seoul, Korea.

10 A Conversation with C. FRED BERGSTEN

Q. *You have said that APEC is neither European Union, nor NAFTA. We know what it is not. How would you give a positive definition of APEC?*
A. It is too early to say how APEC will really evolve. However, based on the blue print or the vision of the Eminent Persons' Group , I say that APEC is a regional institution for trade and investment liberalization; as it will be reducing variance within the region, APEC will concurrently be promoting reductions of barriers outside the region.

The concept of open regionalism is to be appreciated. In the EPG Report, a very specific four-part definition of it has been outlined. It is a concept that we think has never really been operationalized or defined carefully before. The strategy would be to ensure that APEC, far from causing new problems for the world system, will be a building block for further liberalization for the global system. To our knowledge, no previous regional arrangement has ever done that. We would see APEC, for example, offering to extend its own liberalization benefits to any outside countries who agree to liberalize with APEC on a reciprocal basis. The European Union certainly never did that. NAFTA has certainly never done that. It has never been done before.

There are specific cases where the EU did an arrangement for a free trade area with the ASEAN Free Trade Area [AFTA]. NAFTA may take on specific members, but there has never been a case where a regional grouping adopted a general principle to generalize its benefits to outsiders on any basis, reciprocal or non-reciprocal, or any other way. APEC will do just that.

APEC will simultaneously develop a meaningful, substantive regional institution to help expand the environment of trade and investment, economic exchanges in general in the Asia-Pacific, and at the same time to become a leader for promoting global trade liberalization. In 1993, the APEC Summit in Seattle did play an important role in bringing about the Uruguay Round to a successful conclusion in December, 1993.
Q. *Taking a historical overview of economic regionalization in Western Europe since the Treaty of Rome in 1957 and then the emergence of the European Union, do you think that developments in Western Europe have acted as a push factor for Asia-Pacific Economic Cooperation?*
A. I think there has been more general, positive interaction between a whole set of regional arrangements around the world and the global system. To illustrate, when the European Community was initially formed the U.S. supported that, but immediately wanted to reduce the discriminatory effect

toward itself and other parts of the world. The United States, therefore, proposed the Kennedy Round of global trade negotiations. So, in the very first instance the new European Common Market promoted global liberalization through the Kennedy Round. The same thing happened again in the 1970s when the European Common Market expanded to take in Britain and a couple of other nations as its members. It meant more and more discrimination against the outsiders when the U.S. took to the Tokyo Round of trade negotiations to reduce the common external tariff, and thus reduce adverse effects on the world system. Then, in the 1980s when the U.S. tried to get another global round, the Europeans resisted. The U.S. then took some regional initiatives, free-trade agreements [FTAs] with Israel, and then with Canada. The Europeans noted that the U.S. had an alternative course of action and then decided to return to the global trade negotiations, the Uruguay Round.

In the late 1980s, when the Uruguay Round looked like it was faltering, many countries began to look for alternative approaches; that was one of the reasons for creating NAFTA. Both the perceived possible failure with the Uruguay Round and the creation of NAFTA led the Asians to get worried. Among other things, came the Mahatir proposal for forming the East Asia Economic group, which in turn, caused alarm in the U.S. Quite rightly, the notion of an Asia-only group was not acceptable. The U.S. then worked with the initiative that became APEC. Then finally, the creation of both NAFTA and APEC raised the specter that the U.S. might go regional, which induced the Europeans to come back to a final deal that sealed up the Uruguay Round in Geneva. The chief German negotiator for the Uruguay Round noted that the most decisive element in bringing the Uruguay Round to a successful conclusion was the APEC Summit in Seattle, November 1993. He told us that the U.S. had an alternative and that the Europeans did not.

Thus, I think that the bottom line has been a positive ratcheting up of trade liberalization in regional and global levels. Concerns continue to be expressed that regional trade arrangements could undermine the global system. What has happened in fact is a positive interaction. Certainly, right from the start, all the planning for APEC would try to make sure of that.

Q. *If Western Europe has been a push factor, economic miracles in Japan and new Japans have been a pull factor for APEC, as some of us see it. Would you briefly comment on that?*

A. I think there are several pull factors for APEC, one is, of course, the economic dynamism of the entire region. A second factor is the heavy and growing inter-dependence of economic relations across the Pacific. Trade within the Asia-Pacific region is even greater than trade within the Western European regional market. From the standpoint of the Asian countries, most of them still depend on the U.S. for between one-quarter and one-third of their exports. It will be an economic disaster for them to be in any way divorced from the U.S. market and discriminated against. That is one reason they have disliked NAFTA and would prefer to see an Asia-Pacific arrangement that would bring an end to any other regional agreement in which the U.S. is participating.

A third factor relates to the security of the Asia-Pacific region. The Asians desperately want the U.S. to remain engaged in Asia for security reasons, more so when the Soviet Union no longer means a counterweight to China. Uncertainty about China's defense strategy is widely shared. In addition, some uncertainty about the future of Japan's military power persists. There is a very strong desire on the part of all the Asian nations, ranging from Japan to Southeast Asia, for the U.S. to remain involved. There is a fear that if the U.S. economic participation in the region were to wane, the U.S. might scale down or might even withdraw its presence in security terms.

There is a whole web of pull factors cutting across economic and security issues, running both westward and eastward across the Pacific, and really giving a very high level of intra-regional interdependence, as has been laid out in some detail in the first EPG Report in 1993.

The mix has changed over time, and as we report in our second EPG report in 1994, the successful conclusion of the Uruguay Round of global trade negotiations had a lot to do with it. Some doubt that the Uruguay Round will succeed lingers. Countries throughout the region were worried about a substantial erosion of the global trading system, as they feared the risk of inward-looking regionalism most significantly embodied by the European Community.

Prior to the end of 1993, I'd say that the push factor was considerably more important than it is now, now that the Uruguay Round has succeeded, generating more confidence in the global system. There is a sense that not all problems have been solved, but the global system is alive and well. It also provides a safer global context in which to pursue regional arrangements without such a fear that they will be viewed as undermining the global system. So at this point in time on a scale of one to ten, I'd say the pull factors are probably eight, and the push factors are one or two.

Q. *It has been suggested by some [Yoichi Funabishi, Foreign Affairs, Winter 1991-1992] that the North American Free Trade Area [NAFTA] is a step toward Americanizaton of America with its implicit call for the North American co-prosperity sphere. Your comments please.*

A. NAFTA is really a small fry in terms of world trading arrangements. The free trade arrangement of Canada and Mexico with the United States does not significantly alter the picture, as it exists in reality. They add at most 10 per cent to 15 per cent of the American economy. One could view NAFTA as a simple ratification of the enormous trade dependence of both Canada and Mexico on the United States. For a long time, with three-fourths of their trade with the U.S., the three economies of North America have been closely related. The situation is very different from that in Western Europe where four or five economies of roughly the same size function with no single dominant power even after the German unification. The U.S. economy *vis-à-vis* the economies of Canada and Mexico within NAFTA present a far different scenario. The U.S. alone accounts for 85 per cent to 90 per cent of the total North American economic activity. The underlying economic structures of the two regional groupings in Western Europe and in North America are very different. The integration processes in the two regions have also been different. Western Europe has already gone from a customs union to a single market, and on to an active discussion of a common currency. Nothing like that is envisaged in NAFTA.

The one thing to say about NAFTA is that it breaks a new ground in terms of creating a free-trade area between highly industrial and still quite underdeveloped economies in a given region. The ratio between the per capita income of the U.S. and Canada on one hand and Mexico on the other is much greater than the per capita income between Northern and Southern Europe. NAFTA is a pioneer in this respect and that I think is important for APEC because APEC, of course, is trying to forge economic cooperation and free trade arrangements among countries with even greater disparities in per capita income levels and economic development than NAFTA. Thus, a truly positive economic rationale for NAFTA must be noted.

There is a possibility of some trade diversion due to NAFTA, as is the case for any free trade area [FTA] arrangement. So, there are countries in Asia unhappy about it. Some of them want to be a part of NAFTA. Others want to create some superstructure like APEC that would subsume NAFTA and generalize any preference treatment.

I don't think there is much concern that it will develop into a co-prosperity sphere, anything like the historical analogy that gave rise to that phrase, either in terms of its military implications or in terms of the sweeping nature of the economic integration involved. Those analogies are pretty easy to refute with very little educational effort.

Q. *Two successive U.S. Secretaries of State stated that NAFTA and APEC will be complementary. You have also stated the same. Do you see any problem?*

A. I think it is very important for NAFTA and APEC to be complementary. It's basically up to the U.S. to assure that, because it is the biggest single economy in both APEC and NAFTA. I don't suggest there will be no problems; there will be some technical problems, at a minimum, if NAFTA is extended into the Western Hemisphere more broadly, and comes to include some countries that are not in APEC. For example, if APEC really limits its membership to countries on the Pacific, excludes Brazil, Venezuela, a few countries that over time could accede to NAFTA, as NAFTA becomes a Western Hemispheric free trade agreement, then there could be at a minimum some problems, with rules of origin, trade shipment, and the like.

But I think there is a broader policy question. If the U.S. and its partners in both directions really pursue these two regional groupings, then there is a very strong logic over time in merging the two. In the APEC context, we in the EPG meetings have talked about the need to incorporate the subregional groupings - NAFTA, the ASEAN Free Trade Agreement, and the Australian/New Zealand CER - in APEC. All of those subregional preferential arrangements should over time be rolled into one broader free trade arrangement of APEC.

Now, a Western Hemisphere (North and South Americas) agreement could be a little more complicated. It might include countries outside the two regional groupings. The U.S. already has a free trade agreement with Israel, and technically the problem already exists. But there the volume of trade is very small, but very important pragmatically. Already, Mexico, which is a member of APEC, has its own free trade agreements with Colombia and Venezuela, countries that are outside APEC. So, some problem could come up in modest circumstances. One way to answer any such problem will simply be to broaden the regional arrangement.

The real long-term answer, and this is what we would like to see APEC promote, is the elimination of trade barriers on a global basis.

Q. *Indeed, this is the argument of some of our fellow economists who argue that all this regionalization should be scrapped and that the way to go is the global free trade regime.*

A. I think the ideal outcome is free trade, and most economists and trade officials should support that. In practice, of course, it is not so easy. European countries historically agreed to free trade through reciprocal negotiations. Many countries, particularly smaller countries, developing countries, countries with high protection, have done some unilateral liberalizing. But when it comes to the big countries and the really tough trade barriers, the only way you can get it done through your domestic politics is reciprocal liberalization. Some of that happens globally, some regionally.

The most promising route now to globalization is to approach the issue first through the regional efforts, particularly through APEC, and then be willing to generalize regional success to the global level. In my opening remarks I did refer to this positive interaction for the last 30 years between the regional and global efforts. The U.S. must keep a global focus and continue to make use of the regional efforts as building blocks for the global trade liberalization. I think that positive interaction will continue, and in fact, will be the most expeditious and rapid way to achieve globalization. It is correct to say that we should all keep our eyes on the ultimate goal of maximum global liberalization for both economic and political reasons. It will eliminate or minimize trade diversion and avoid the risk of intragroup conflicts. Everything APEC does will, I believe, move in both those directions.

Q. *You seem to suggest that regionalization is a strategic step toward final globalization. Preliminary research relative to EU, APEC, NAFTA, AFTA point to the fact that the case for Pareto optimality in the sense that each regional group optimizes its economic welfare without hurting non-member nations is satisfied. Any comment? Has there been any definitive study?*

A. I don't think that there is any definitive way to answer the question scientifically. Obviously, the traditional question of trade creation versus trade diversion remains unanswered since we cannot define either of them clearly, particularly trade creation. We don't really have definite proof either way. I think most of the studies of the European Union do tend to suggest that it has generated more trade creation than trade diversion, and for the world it has therefore been welfare enhancing. At the same time it has obviously had some very negative effects on particular outside countries for particular sectors, notably agriculture, and consequently on the world trading system. The U.S. and others have tried to cope with that through global liberalization negotiations. The success of the Uruguay Round will to some extent remedy the situation in agriculture.

I continue to be concerned about the weakness of Article 24 in the GATT Agreement which tries to square regional arrangements with the global system. Article 24 is very weak. All it says is that regional arrangements should not raise their barriers to outsiders, and that is the one thing we are proposing in APEC. APEC should go further and commit itself to continue reducing its barriers to outsiders, not just commit to raise them. We think that Article 24 should be amended or reinterpreted to include that criterion; then, there will be a firmer handle for the conclusion that regional agreement enhances global as well as regional welfare.

Q. *Is the Asianization of Asia increasingly becoming a reality following NAFTA and its possible implication for Americanization of the Americas?*

A. Well, I think it is a myth. Self-containment in either economic or security terms of Asia or of the Western Hemisphere is not real. The fact points to interdependence, as I have said before. A very strong economic case exists to solidify and even strengthen the trans-Pacific ties. APEC and the Asian-Pacific model stand out as so much more attractive and so much more compelling. Neither an Asia-only grouping nor an American hemispheric grouping will be able to produce the best outcome.

There is one other key point. Some people a few years ago were talking about the world economy; dividing it up into three big blocs centered on Western Europe, the U.S., and Japan. Aside from all the problems, the fact is that no Asian nation wants to be in a bloc led by Japan and the increased likelihood that China, more than Japan or equal to Japan, might lead the East Asian bloc is equally unacceptable to most of them. In addition, we know that the three-player games are very unstable. Asia-Pacific being in some sense the counter poise to Europe, the prospect then would be for the two-player game, the two regions working together to a more stable global system knowing that either could substantially deter and hurt the other's interest if they did not play the ball.

Q. *R.W. Apple, Jr. quotes a prominent German [The New York Times, January 9, 1994]: "We are starting to feel isolated. It used to be Europe and America, the Alantic nations taking on all comers, especially the communist bloc. Now we are afraid, it's you and the Asians, the Pacific nations, who are setting the pace, with us off by ourselves". How do you respond to this European apprehension?*

A. The Europeans do have some fears that both the push and pull factors (we talked about earlier) will cause the U.S. to divert attention to Asia. To the extent the Europeans pursue inward-looking policy and to the extent they cannot get their act together in economic or political terms, the U.S. will, in fact, tend to look more toward Asia where lies the greater economic dynamism. Maybe even greater security risks may lie there.

The Europeans really do not need to have any fear that the United States is turning its back on them. The U.S. obviously will always remain an Atlantic power with deep concerns for Europe, that's historical, that's cultural, and economic as well. What the U.S. is now doing is really a rebalancing of its priorities, turning more to Asia because of its economic dynamism, but always there is potential in security, as we remember that the U.S. has fought three major wars in Asia in the last 50 years - Japan, Korea and Vietnam. So the U.S. is no stranger to an active involvement in Asia. The economic dynamism and the pull of Asia makes it a little clearer now. The U.S. uniquely will remain heavily engaged across both the Atlantic and the Pacific for the foreseeable future. I would really regard it as a more balanced strategy than a turning away from Europe. The Europeans have understandably been used to getting priority treatment from the U.S. in the last 50 years. That probably is going to change to a degree, but it by no means represents a U.S. withdrawal from Europe.

Q. *In the trans-Atlantic relations of the U.S., social, cultural and economic ties have historically been a natural base, as you have stated. In the trans-Pacific relations of the U.S., little can be related to such historical factors and it is purely economics, leaving security aside for the present study. In this situation in the 1990s and beyond, how does economics-based optimization of our trans-Pacific relationship progress best without causing undue concern for Europe and possible economic imbalance of our trans-Atlantic economic relationship?*

A. The U.S. has fought three wars in the last 50 years in Asia and remained heavily involved in the security sense. There are a lot of cultural ties with very large Asian communities within the U.S. While there is obviously a difference it is not quite as sharp as some would like to put it. The operational question remains, of how to avoid any misapprehension that the U.S. is turning its back on Europe. I think part of that is up to the U.S. simply to make clear to the Europeans through deeds as well as words that we are not forgetting about them.

NATO, as it evolves to deal with its new challenges, continues to be a forum for strong U.S.-European interaction. The U.S. certainly continues to be very actively engaged with the Europeans on a range of trade and economic issues. Four of the seven members of the G-7 are European countries, and the U.S. meets with them at the summit every year. It is a heavily European-dominated group. For the trans-Atlantic economic relationship, responsibility must also be shared by the Europeans. They themselves have to be sure that their policies are outward looking, fulfilling their responsibilities. Continued integration of the continent, still absorbing and digesting German unification and the new situation relative to the East Europeans have tremendous challenges for Europe. In the historical perspective, the EU has achieved an unprecedented submergence of sovereignty and integration of economies. In this respect Western Europe is the pioneer for the world. The rest of the world has to first look at what the Europeans confronted and how in many instances they succeeded in trying to work out their cooperative arrangements. They have achieved a lot, even when it looked from time to time as if they were facing setbacks. Thus, while it is up to the U.S. and others outside Europe to make sure that we continue to engage them and avoid any misapprehension on their part about the regional economic arrangements, the Europeans also have to play their part on the global scale and follow a truly outward-looking policy. Or else, they will push others inevitably to arrangements that either exclude or downplay them.

Q. *In my study, limited to economics as it is, reference to defense and security parameters have been left aside. Instead, the focus is on intraregional monetary-fiscal policy coordination for the success of a regional free trade and investment regime. Your comments please.*

A. That is certainly the case historically when the international monetary system has gone awry and the world trade system has been threatened. The most dramatic example is, of course, when the U.S. broke the Bretton Woods fixed-rate system in 1971. Imposition of import surcharges and some pretty aggressive trade threats again followed in 1985. The overvalued dollar continued to plague the U.S. trade imbalance. The U.S. Congress became concerned. The Plaza Initiative of 1987 failed to correct the situation. The Reagan Administration moved for a much tougher trade policy which eventually led to the Super-301 authorizing the U.S. unilateral action to remedy trade imbalances with one or another nation.

So, there is clearly a need for a much better integration between trade and monetary policy. That is one of the reasons I am very pleased that an early step in the evolution of APEC has been the meeting of the finance ministers in Honolulu in March 1994. They did not begin to talk about issues as far-reaching as intra-APEC coordination of monetary policy. Overall, if APEC does develop a meaningful free trade and investment regime, it will be necessary to look at the implications for monetary policy, exchange rates, macroeconomic cooperation and the like, because that is an essential element of a sustainable free trade arrangement.

However, in the short run it has to be remembered that even the ambitious blueprint of our Eminent Persons' Group will not begin the process of trade liberalization for a couple of years. Indeed, it will be a couple of decades before it is completed. This is going to be a slow evolutionary process. We believe at the same time that trade facilitation measures should develop investment codes, standards, dispute settlement mechanisms, and the like. Over time, such cooperative activities will initiate a process for a growing familiarity with each other relative to intra-APEC monetary and macroeconomic issues. It would be some time before either a need for or the possibility of any extensive cooperation on the range of such issues will come to the fore.

We do make a very clear statement that sustaining a free trade regime over time requires a way to deal with trade imbalances and other related phenomena that could adversely affect the maintenance of free trade. We make the point that when those broader imbalances develop, as they eventually will, there is always a risk that countries will react to the symptoms through trade controls rather than going to the root of the imbalances which stem from poor macroeconomic policies, exchange rate imbalances and the like. Therefore, it will be important over time for the APEC finance ministers and the Central Bank governors to develop mechanisms to address the underlying problems in order to avoid disruption in the trade regime through arbitrary policy responses to the symptoms rather than the causes.

Q. I *note with much satisfaction that the issue of monetary policy cooperation is recognized, albeit in the long haul. Vietnam, Laos and Cambodia are expected to become members of the ASEAN Free Trade Area. Will they become members of APEC automatically? How about any new member of NAFTA, following Chile? How about India and other South Asian countries?*

A. I don't think Vietnam and other ASEAN Free Trade Area members will become members of APEC automatically. There is a three-year moratorium on new membership decided in 1993 at the APEC Seattle Summit; thus, no new members will be taken in until 1996-1997.

I don't think that any new membership of APEC will be automatic. For new members from the Americas as they join NAFTA, their APEC membership will not be automatic,either.

However, I think it will be desirable for any new member of subregional agreements - NAFTA or AFTA - to be in APEC to avoid possible inconsistencies between APEC liberalization and the subregional arrangement. On the other hand, some far-reaching questions could be raised. For example, what if Brazil joins NAFTA? Brazil is not on the Pacific. When we talk about Asia-Pacific nations do we require a country in the Americas to border the Pacific? In the Asian case, how do you define the Pacific? How far does it go? So, I think that it will be decided on a case-by-case basis. The EPG simply took advantage of the mandate of the three-year moratorium on new membership and made no recommendation on the issue.

Thus, the issue of new membership can be discussed for India and other South Asian countries and also for countries in the eastern part of South America. How far does APEC get farther away from the Pacific? NAFTA, at least, never put any geographical scope on its membership as the ascension clause to NAFTA does not limit it to North America, or even to the American hemisphere. APEC has not defined its boundaries. This is unlike the European Union which, in the Treaty of Rome, talked only about European countries, albeit they never quite defined what is Europe; they clearly would exclude India or China or the U.S. and the Americas. APEC will have to grapple with that over time. Let me add that I will not overemphasize the importance of the membership issue for the following reason.

APEC will not only liberalize trade within its membership, but will also offer to extend liberalization to non-members. On a global basis, if the EU wanted to make a reciprocal arrangement with APEC it could do it. The same is true for its closer neighbors, India and Brazil. Even if they do not become members, they should therefore be able to avoid any adverse effect on them for APEC liberalization. AFTA countries in Southeast Asia were able to avoid discrimination against most of their trade by doing their free trade agreement with the EU in the early 1970s. One could say in one sense non-members will constitute a second-class membership because they will not have a decision-making participation, but at least it avoids any negative economic effects. In writing the EPG report for the APEC Bogor Summit in November 1994, we were particularly conscious of any possible discriminatory effect of APEC liberalization on non-member developing countries such as Vietnam, India, and Brazil. Thus, specific attention was given to the prospect for extending APEC liberalization to non-members, even if APEC decided not to extend its membership to them.

In terms of the level of development, Brazil or India meet no disability clause for APEC membership. In the case of NAFTA, the U.S. did insist that Mexico has proceeded quite far down the path of liberalizing and deregulating its economy in order to qualify. Now, in the studies at the Institute for International Studies for the economic integration in the American hemisphere, a set of indicators was established to score each of the Latin American countries across seven or eight criteria as to their qualification at this time to join NAFTA. Attention is paid to each country's macroeconomic stability, trade liberalization, investment liberalization, and a whole range of economic variables. Whether it will work the same way in APEC is not yet clear, but certainly no regional economic grouping would want to take a country that has hyper-inflation, or serious trade barriers, albeit non-transparent. Some criteria of qualifications will be required for a country to participate in a regional grouping. Such has always been the case for the EU. Spain, Portugal and Greece were not qualified to be members until each adopted the democratic form of government. APEC will certainly set its own criteria for membership. For APEC, or for NAFTA, certainly the U.S. did not insist on its own brand of democracy.

The guidelines for membership, as and when formulated, must be transparent. For example, as APEC now approaches a decision on adopting an investment code, the first principle is transparency of a country's investment code. An individual member-country can have some barriers, some exceptions from the general APEC liberalization code, but they must be transparent. I think that transparency must be the core of anything that APEC does.

I think that APEC as an institution should concentrate solely on economic issues, certainly at least for a long time. Economics is what is drawing the countries together in one main group. As I said before, there is a security implication in all this because institutionalized economic ties will help solidify the security arrangements, but APEC itself has no need to address security problems directly.

Q. *Is APEC in the 1990s struggling with the same set of issues the EU did in the 1970s?*

A. Well, a lot of the issues are similar. But there is a major difference. In Western Europe, the process of economic integration began with their goal to create a customs union rather than a free trade arrangement. In the Asia-Pacific, the APEC agenda has been, and will continue to be, the free trade arrangement with freedom for the member-countries to conduct their respective trade policies with non-member-countries. The Europeans decided not to do so right from the start. The EU began in the 1970s with a much smaller arrangement of six countries, whereas in the 1990s, APEC started its program with 18. APEC is much bigger in economic terms and much more extensive in its geographical coverage. One of the major motives for the European communities right from the start was to preclude the possibility of France and Germany ever going to war again. In APEC, with the anti-Communist structure of the post-World War II years disintegrated, member-countries share many differences and many similarities as well. I think for a whole host of reasons it would be incorrect to look at the EU, even 20 years ago, as a very precise model of what is going on in APEC. At the same time, APEC's efforts to reduce trade barriers among the group of countries will face some of the same problems that the Europeans faced as they pioneered economic integration, including the non-border measures, competition policies, government subsidies to specific economic activities, government procurement policies, and a whole range of issues.

Member, Eminent Persons' Group. This conversation was taped on August 16, 1994 in Washington, DC, USA.

11 A Conversation with SUHADI MANGKUSUWONDO

Q. *Will you please define in your own words what APEC is?*
A. APEC is a forum for trade liberalization; a forum for promoting a global kind of system by way of inducing as many countries as possible to join the liberalization of the world trading system. Indonesia began by inviting other countries to join in its effort in this regard. APEC is to be distinguished from both the European Union and the North American Free Trade Area.
Q. *There has been some confusion about the two expressions: "free trade area" and "free trade in the area". How do they differ?*
A. The term, "free trade area", is more or less a standard term in order to get provisions for free trade among member-countries, that is, a group of countries moving together towards a free trade arrangement among themselves, fulfilling the sanctions under Article 24 of the General Agreement on Tariffs and Trade . Once you fulfill all the requirements of Article 24, especially with no provision for raising trade barriers against non-members of the group, you have the FTA. Trade liberalization privileges are only available to the members themselves.

The term "free trade in the area" has a special meaning. That is not what we had in mind when we talked about free trade in Indonesia to begin with. The concept of free trade in the area is unique. For the member-countries, it is a move toward free trade among themselves, and at the same time it offers an inducement/encouragement to non-member-countries to do the same. If the APEC member-countries reduce their trade barries, non-APEC countries may be encouraged to reduce theirs. So, the ultimate objective of this free trade in the Asia-Pacific area is to have a response of participation from others as soon as possible without joining as members of APEC. I think that is the main difference between the two concepts - free trade area and free trade in the area.
Q. *Can we be quite sure that it will not add to the confusion between GATT or the WTO regime of a free trade area and APEC with its new term, free trade in the area? Will students of international economics be able to follow the distinction?*
A. For the laymen, I think it is a bit confusing. But for serious students of economics, I think they will see the difference between the free trade area and the new concept free trade in the area.
Q. *To some of us, students of economic regionalization, the happenings in*

Western Europe seem to have acted as the crucial push factor for Asia-Pacific Economic Cooperation. And the pull factor has come from the East-Asian economic miracle. Will you please comment on the impact of Western European economic regionalization on APEC?

A. I think APEC started at one point when people in the Asia-Pacific area became concerned about the possibility of Europe leaning more and more inward. The concern for a possible adverse affect on non-members of EU, especially if the Uruguay Round of GATT negotiations was not finalized, was real. If thc Uruguay Round failed, many people really thought that Europe might or would become even more inward looking. Even when the Uruguay Round was concluded, many in the Asia-Pacific remained convinced that the Asian-Pacific countries should continue to take the lead in continuing the process of trade liberalization.

The Asian-Pacific countries are in the best position to take the initiative without losing the momentum of global trade liberalization, and, therefore, they have moved forward toward the formation of APEC, even though the fact of failure of global negotiations was eliminated. There exists a strong feeling that it is very much in the interest of the Asia-Pacific region itself to keep on pushing towards a more open trading system.

Q. *The East-Asian economic miracle is definitely a pull factor for the new American awareness of Asian economies. If you have to scale the push factor from Western Europe and the pull factor for East Asia, from one to ten, how would you scale that?*

A. I think for Indonesia the pull factor is stronger. People have become so much aware of the benefit that Indonesia has gone ahead for opening its own economy. Statistics clearly point to the fact that trade and investment flow very much within the APEC region including Japan and Australia as well as the United States and Canada. So, people are aware that the policy adopted since the late 1960s of really opening up the economy with the outside world was in the interest of Indonesia. So, my view is that the pull factors were the overriding considerations why the government decided at one point to move ahead and open up. Before Indonesia moved into APEC, the government had been very active in the subregion of ASEAN. Then, based on its experience with ASEAN, the Indonesian government moved to a right arrangement which is APEC.

Q. *I have in my research plotted the dates of Western European and Asian-Pacific economic regionalization for 1957-1994, and it seems to me that the Asian-Pacific initiative has been historically following calendar-wise the Western European initiatives. Will you care to comment on that?*

A. To a certain degree the Western European experiment got a lot of attention from people here in the region. There was a great deal of concern to understand what was happening in Europe. The rapid economic growth of Europe after the formation of the European Economic Community did not escape the attention of the Asia-Pacific economists and policy makers. The benefit that Western European economies obtained from their regional cooperation was very much observable. Now the European Union is an economic reality and its impact must be noted.

Surely that was a factor, but as I have said earlier, other factors played a very important role. The fact remains that this area came out as one of the fastest- growing regions in the world. The European arrangement progressed in parallel. The regional economic pull became the dominant factor. On a scale of one to ten, I would give the Asia-Pacific pull factor six and the European push factor four.

Q. *Do you have a comment on the North American Free Trade Area or its hemispheric expansion in the form of the Free Trade Area of the Americas? How do you view NAFTA within APEC?*

A. I think APEC is based on the realities of ongoing integration of its member-economies and it has quite a strong economic base. This is so because the APEC economic integration that has been progressively manifest over time has been very much based on the market forces, not because of their respective governments' initiative for an economic regionalization. APEC has its own reasons for being in its own form. To facilitate the market-driven integration, as is going on in APEC in the region, is the principal point of consideration to many people in this part of the world. The real challenge is how to ensure that this process of market-driven economic integration can continue. Originally, many people in this region, rather wrongly, looked at APEC as an initiative of the member-governments. Thus, APEC is in substance different from what one sees happening in North America in the form of NAFTA.

Q. *You don't seem to have any reservations when successive U.S. Secretaries of the State state that NAFTA will be a complement to APEC. Any comment?*

A. We will be happy if NAFTA becomes something which is fully consistent with APEC.

Q. *Do you see NAFTA as an attempt to Americanize America vis-à-vis what Professor Yoichi Funabashi referred to as other efforts toward the Asianization of Asia [Foreign Affairs, Winter 1991/1992]?*

A. No, I definitely don't think so. We do not use such a phrase. Maybe he is referring to Japan's perspective.

Q. *NAFTA may now be broadened to include Chile. Chile is becoming a member of APEC. How about other countries in the American hemisphere joining NAFTA and becoming members of APEC?*

A. I think that it will not be desirable to introduce any more discrimination among countries in the region. It will be divisive, too. The idea of extension of APEC membership to all member-countries in NAFTA, as it broadens to include other American hemispheric countries as a group, was discussed at the EPG meeting and finally dropped. APEC's agenda of "open regionalism" cannot really emphasize the preferential character of provisions for trade liberalization in NAFTA. There are others who emphasize the openness of world trade. But the first priority of the APEC regional system on the whole should be geared towards strengthening the global system.

Q. *Do you think that economic regionalization in a broader sense would be more helpful if it follows what I call, a "map-of-the-world" scheme of a region? Should regionalization more faithfully follow the map of the world instead of criss-crossing the Pacific or the Atlantic?*

A. The reason we think that the APEC has its strong economic justification is simply by looking at what actually has happened in the region in the past ten years. Actually, the trans-Pacific trade has been booming and the same is true of trans-Pacific investment flows.

I do not think that the ASEAN Free Trade Area will have a membership barrier. Indeed, the facts show that trans-Pacific trade is increasing without much organized effort by the APEC member- or ASEAN member-governments.

Q. *Do you see NAFTA's membership extending to Korea or Singapore adding to the momentum of Asia-Pacific economic regionalization?*

A. Such an approach will certainly create an element of discrimination in the region. There are already some preferences NAFTA treats as its own. If it adds up to another effort by NAFTA accepting Singapore or South Korea to join its membership, it will just add up to discrimination among the Asia-Pacific countries. I think that it will not be a good idea.

Q. *In the context of sovereign economies of a given region doing some "economic good" together for themselves without doing any "economic harm" to others, do we satisfy the Pareto-optimality condition? Do we really need APEC or any other form of economic regionalization/subregionalization following the success of the Uruguay Round of GATT negotiation and the establishment of the World Trade Organization?*

A. The fact is that the APEC member-economies have become even more intraregionally interdependent. This is happening through the market process. The market took the initiative and this process has been going on, benefiting all APEC member-countries. The process by itself hurts no non-APEC economy. Starting from that situation the question is, should governments of APEC countries step in and create an intragovernment party, or should the

APEC integration process be left to the market? The answer seems to be obvious.

Q. *I very much accept your hypothesis that a natural market-led growth is good. If you were to do an indexing that maximized the economic welfare of each APEC member-nation without hurting anyone not a member of APEC, will that satisfy the Pareto-optimality condition?*

A. This issue is becoming increasingly important. The question has been discussed in the context of the European Union. It seems to be necessary to convince the rest of the world that it is basically optimization of economic welfare of APEC members without diminishing it for others.

The issue has been debated quite vigorously by the EPG itself. Some favor that all liberalization should be unconditionally offered to other countries. For the bigger countries like the U.S., this has been regarded as critically unacceptable because they think such an action will actually do a disservice to the global system. If you offer unconditionally all privileges of intra-APEC trade liberalization to Europe, it will be a disincentive to the EU to open up its market, and that is not in the interest of the global system.

Thus, there is a difference of opinion. Perhaps because of the size of the country or the size of its market, the American position is that if other countries want to have free and open access to the American market, they will have to reciprocate. Other smaller countries, such as Indonesia, do not attach too great an importance to that position. Indonesia's position is that by opening its domestic markets to others, the greatest beneficiary of trade liberalization will have been Indonesians. If other countries enter into our markets, we benefit from it. In turn, the participating foreign countries will eventually realize their own gains and be encouraged to reciprocate privileges of trade liberalization.

Q. *Can APEC, with provisions for the free flow of goods and services, provide for intraregional free flow of factors of production?*

A. At present the discussion is limited to free trade, first to trade in goods, and then to trade in services. No proposal for free movement of factors of production, except perhaps capital, has been considered. Intraregional free movement of labor has not been on the APEC agenda. True that in Western Europe, intra-EU free movement of labor has been provided for. Even in North America, intra-NAFTA work permit provision may be a possibility. APEC has yet to discuss the issue.

Q. *For resolution of disputes in trade and investment, for issues such as environmental protection, will APEC provide for some sort of supranational arbitration/mediation?*

A. For disputes in trade, APEC provides for some type of mediation. There is no provision for binding arbitration. Instead of leaving disputes to bilateral negotiations, multilateral mediation may work better. In areas where mediation does not apply, the principle of competition and the market forces will eventually settle the disputes. Because of interlocking in Japan's domestic economy, it is very difficult for outsiders to compete. China's socialist market system is a special case and no specific recommendation for the principle of competition policy in China has been considered.

In the initial stage the provision for multinational mediation/arbitration should be voluntary. In a specific case, we could agree on having a panel for mediation/arbitration, a panel of three people, one from each country party to the dispute, and at least one coming from a third country. The presence of a member from a third country will foreseeably facilitate the discussions, leading to a resolution of the conflict.

Q. *Will the APEC agenda for free trade include human rights under a multilateral arbitration panel?*

A. APEC deals only with trade issues and human rights are not on its agenda.

Q. *In the EPG report for the APEC Bogor Summit, one reads extensive discussion on standardization of products in trade, harmonization of custom rules, and the rules of origin. Should there be a centralized APEC accreditation authority, or a mutual agreement to accept each other's accreditation system, as in the EU?*

A. Ideally, APEC should try to have harmonized standardization of products traded. In reality, this will take some time. For the interim, the best we can do is to mutually recognize national standards of each other. Malaysia and Indonesia have agreed to recognize the product standards of each other. With the minimum technical requirement we can recognize each other's certificates of accreditation.

Should there be disputes on this score, APEC will have to find a mechanism to settle them. The less-developed economies in APEC need not be handicapped by the hi-tech economies of Japan and the United States. It should be voluntary if an APEC member-country cannot enter into a specific arrangement with another member-country. Following phased adjustments over time, general conformity will be achievable. APEC provides for such flexibility in making related arrangements. The basic question is what should be done to reduce all kinds of man-made obstacles. The simple way for all APEC member-countries is to mutually recognize each other's standards, avoiding double checking or checking at multiple entry-points.

Q. *Can the policy of product standardization/harmonization be made effective, without effective coordination of monetary and fiscal policies within an APEC intaregional macroeconomic core?*

A. As far as Indonesia is concerned we have suffered the adverse effect of currency realignment between the Japanese yen and the U.S. dollar and we have paid a great deal of additional tax because of this currency realignment. Indeed, this is a happening completely outside of Indonesia's domestic policy, decided between one or two or three major trading countries.

I think that the APEC finance ministers will need time to raise the level of their mutual confidence. How to go about coordinating macroeconomic policies remains an open question. It is prudent to move a bit slow, not to rush into doing things which are too difficult for the present. As far as Indonesia is concerned, we are very sure that one area which needs to be looked into is the foreign exchange rate policy. Indonesia must be given an opportunity to be heard if the major currency rates are being considered for changes because Indonesia has a vital interest in the specific issue.

I think that eventually we will be heard. Now of course the APEC agenda has its focus on capital markets, how to encourage the flow of capital for investments. Gradually, APEC will move into more difficult subjects, such as exchange rates.

The EPG Report for the APEC Bogor Summit in 1994 has made its recommendation for regular annual meetings of APEC finance ministers. I don't think that it will receive the top priority. For the present, the issue for APEC's top priority will be agreement on free trade, and then on free flow of capital.

Q. *Vietnam will become a member of ASEAN in 1985. How about the other Southeast Asian countries - Laos, Cambodia, Mayanmar? Will Vietnam become a member of APEC? How about others as they join ASEAN? How about India and other countries in South Asia?*

A. I would say yes, they should. Maybe not immediately, but yes. I am sure that political factors will be an issue. Vietnam is, of course, on the priority list while the others are not.

For India and other South Asian countries, APEC membership is not being discussed, at least not right now. I don't think people are looking at that as something urgent at the moment, maybe down the road that issue will emerge but not now.

Q. *Will APEC provide for a special Development Fund for helping its less-developed members build their infrastructure?*

A. No, we do not think that in the near future APEC should set up funds for that. APEC governments will encourage the private sector in their respective economies to be more active in developing infrastructures. The private sectors in richer member-countries will foreseeably be induced by market forces to invest in building infrastructures in the less-developed member-economies. APEC member-governments could encourage private banks or private financial companies to set up an Industrial Development Bank.

Member, Eminent Persons' Group. This conversation was taped on September 6, 1994 in Jakarta, Indonesia.

12 A Conversation with ZHAO GONG-DA

Q. *The Asia-Pacific Economic Cooperation is different from the European Union, and also from the North American Free Trade Area. Will you please describe in your words what APEC is?*

A. In my view, APEC is a consultative forum for its member-countries. The Eminent Persons' Group works to prepare an agenda for its summit meetings. The EPG submitted two reports. The first report was issued in November 1993 for the APEC Summit in Seattle. Following the mandate by the APEC ministerial meeting in Seattle, EPG drafted the second report for consideration at the APEC Summit in Bogor, Indonesia, November 1994.

The report for the 1994 Summit has substantive proposals for cooperation among APEC member-countries, mainly for free trade and trade-related issues. Trade liberalization is the key issue and it sets up a timetable to that end. The Indonesian ministerial meeting will determine the beginning year and the year of completion for trade liberalization in the APEC region.

For China, we have argued against any uniform set of dates for all countries. We favor that the timetable should be quite flexible. In view of the fact that the APEC member-countries have achieved different stages of economic development, flexibility will facilitate the process of adjustment. To initiate the process for trade liberalization in the year 2000, and complete it by 2020, will provide necessary flexibility. Based on the level of industrialization of their respective economies, APEC member-countries may be placed in three groups: (i) developed and industrialized, (ii) newly industrialized, and (iii) developing. Countries like the United States, Canada, Japan will be in the first group and may complete trade liberalization by 2010, beginning in 2000. Those in the second group may do so by 2015 with the same initial date of 2000. The developing countries in APEC may complete the free trade agenda by 2020, beginning in 2000. A 10-15-20 timetable, with the same beginning date of 2000, will provide enough flexibility. Each country will have the same five-year grace period (1995-1999) to prepare for the initiation of its own trade liberalization program in 2000.

Serving as the EPG member from China, I work independently, not as a representative of the Chinese government. The EPG Report will be finally reviewed by the APEC ministerial meeting at the APEC Summit in Bogor next month. Within China, the EPG draft report is now open to further debate/discussion. Some economists and officials have expressed support for the recommendation that China should complete trade liberalization by the year 2020. Others have criticized it as an impossible goal for China. They argue that China is now engaged in its efforts to perfect and improve its market economy. For China, the process of transition to a market economy will involve adoption of many more new regulations and laws which can be done only over a period of time, a relatively longer period of time. China will need much more time for the coordination of related activities among its different government ministries/departments. In addition, China is still in the process of negotiation with several contracting parties. Ever since 1986, China's efforts have taken more than eight years to make some progress and they are still working on protocol. China needs more time to make preparation for its commitment as an APEC member-country to implement trade liberalization. Be it noted that China accepts the final act of the Uruguay Round and also the free trade agreement of the World Trade Organization.

For APEC to move forward toward trade liberalization, there are two points very, very important for the developing countries in the Asia-Pacific area. First, unconditional MFN should be adopted, and second, developing countries must be given special preferential treatment. China strongly endorses these two points. There is no way to prejudge what will be the outcome of the Bogor Summit in November.

Q. *The APEC objective of free trade and trade liberalization, as you rightly state, is fully acceptable to China. The issue for China's concern is flexibility of timetable in terms of its implementation. If in your judgment China will need more time, do you have a timeframe in your mind?*

A. I cannot state the official position. In my opinion, the APEC Summit in Bogor should give China more time to help China make its preparations. It is difficult to be precise about the timeframe. Basically, it depends upon the pace of China's industrialization. I believe that by 2020 China could be ready. Since the 1970s China's open economic policy, and its opening up of its market to the outside world have made very good progress. I hope that China will move forward more quickly.

Q. *May I ask you two broad questions? In the absence of the two basic happenings - one in Western Europe and another in Eastern Asia - would there be any talk about Asia-Pacific economic cooperation? Was there a push from the Western Europe, which is now known as the European Union?*

A. I think so. However, APEC is quite different from the EU, because APEC is outward looking while EU is very much inward looking. APEC's agenda for trade liberalization will be very much open; it will be open to the APEC member-countries as well as to the countries who are not members of APEC. The concept of open regionalism is key to APEC. I do not know how it will work, or if it will weaken APEC a little.

Let me add that the EU has been a push factor in the sense that the economies, so different one from another, came together and helped mutual economic growth. That was a new experience, and it motivated the countries in East Asia to promote intraregional cooperation, and then APEC is the result.

Similarly, economic development and industrialization in Asia, especially in Eastern Asia, did pull North America to the region and expand its economic initiative in Asia.

Q. *Within the multicontinental economic region, as APEC is, several economic groupings, such as NAFTA, ASEAN, ANZ-CER, have been formed. The World Bank uses the term "China Triangle", consisting of China, Taipei and Hong Kong. How do you think these specific groupings will work within APEC? In Southeast Asia, the ASEAN Free Trade Area has moved to reduce its internal trade barriers - tariff as well as non-tariff - in ten years. In the South Pacific, ANZ-CER sets its own pace and already has accomplished a great deal. In North America, NAFTA will work on its independent timeframe. Will all these subregional groupings go against China's argument for a longer time for implementation of APEC trade liberalization agenda?*

A. I think that all these subregional groups should have good relationships with individual economies within APEC. There should be new openness in terms of trade among APEC member-countries, thus offsetting any possible adverse effect of their separate subregional groupings. It will help promote the prosperity and economic growth of different countries in the Asia-Pacific region.

China hopes that mutual economic cooperation should be secured on the basis of equality, and also the specific nature of benefit to an individual country. From China's perspective, I don't see that these special groupings will be a threat to APEC. As a matter of fact, in North America NAFTA has been in existence in one form or another, even before APEC became an organized forum. The same is true for ASEAN in Southeast Asia and also for ANZ-CER in their subregion.

Q. *Let me press the point. Suppose in December this year, a hemispheric conference of all American economies in South and North Americas is held and the Americas' free trade area is formed. How does it work with APEC? If some East Asian countries, such as South Korea and Singapore become members of the American hemispheric FTA, will it have an impact on APEC?*

A. I cannot comment on what may happen in the North and South Americas. I don't think that China will want to be a member of Americas' hemispheric free trade area, or for that matter of any other grouping discussed earlier. China is China, not a member of any special sub-regional group. China wishes to develop a good economic relationship with all countries.

Economies in Asia, who are members of APEC, should not be interested in their extended membership of NAFTA in North America.

Q. *How do you propose to decide trade disputes in APEC? How do you view the position of big economies in APEC, the United States and Japan? Will China accept mediation of trade disputes within APEC by one or more APEC member-countries?*

A. Mediation may possibly be acceptable, but without abdication of China's sovereign authority. Once China becomes a member of the World Trade Organization, its rules of adjudication could, of course, be applicable. In APEC, there is no provision for binding adjudication of trade disputes.

Q. *Do you accept the proposition that success in trade liberalization among a group of sovereign countries will have to be conditioned by coordination of their monetary-and fiscal policies? How do you view the importance of a stable exchange rate regime?*

A. However important these macroeconomic issues may be, for China, they are not to be discussed at the present time.

Q. *How do you view the question of reciprocity in trade liberalization with non-APEC countries?*

A. If one country wants to reduce its tariff barriers and/or non-tariff barriers, there should be no condition, reciprocity or non-reciprocity. Of course, a final decision in a specific case will be based on terms arrived at by mutual negotiations. The EPG Report didn't touch upon how best to work in a given case. Indeed, that's why we are facing the problem about how to implement what has been described as open regionalism.

For negotiation regarding trade liberalization with a specific conflicting party, China has announced that it will reduce its tariffs by negotiation with the other party, the terms of negotiation being set by mutual agreement. The Ministry of Foreign Economic Relations and Trade [MOFERT] of China will study the related issues and the general principles involved. In its work the MOFERT will be aided by different departments/sectoral units in the Chinese Government, analyzing specific issues.

Member, Eminent Persons' Group. This conversation was taped on October 31, 1994 in Beijing, The People's Republic of China.

13 A Conversation with MITSUO SATO

Q. *How do you view APEC from the vantage position of your office?*
A. I think that the APEC meeting in Indonesia was quite an achievement. Even though the specific program for liberalization of trade and investment is not very clear, I think that they have made an achievement by adopting the declaration that beginning in the year 2000, the APEC member-countries will liberalize trade and investment by 2010, 2015 or 2020, as the case may be for a specific country.
Q. *Do you think that the 18 sovereign member-countries will be able to continue to cooperate towards the 2020 goal?*
A. There will foreseeably be many difficult questions over the years for them to find answers to. In other words, there will be some obstacles and difficulties as they work on the APEC agenda for trade liberalization, but at the same time they have decided to resolve them. The APEC member-countries have made it very clear that they are determined to do the needful. If there is a determination to achieve a goal, any and all obstacles can be overcome. I am quite optimistic.
Q. *Given the fact that some members of APEC are very rich, some are becoming rich, while some others are still poor, does that make a difference adversely impacting the goal?*
A. I agree with you that differences in terms of stages of economic development, or in terms of per capita incomes, among APEC member-countries may pose some difficulties. Insofar as the Asian Development Bank [ADB] is concerned, this institution should be in a position to help APEC member-countries overcome those kinds of difficulties by supporting accelerated economic growth of the developing member-countries in Asia.
Q. *Some of us believe that what is happening in Western Europe, now in the form of the European Union, is acting as a push factor to Asia-Pacific Economic Cooperation. Any comment?*
A. I think that the EU has been a kind of stimulus for the member-countries of APEC to act in concert. The fact that Sweden and several other countries in Europe have recently elected to become members of the EU will act as a further stimulus for APEC. For APEC, to act in concert will ensure the common objective of liberalizing trade and investment by 2020.
Q. *The other factor that has been important is the economic growth in East*

Asia, which we may call the pull factor. How do you view it?
A. I fully agree with you that the high rate of economic growth in Eastern Asia has been a kind of pull factor for APEC. These are very positive factors. Of course, the Asian Development Bank has been in a position to follow that high economic performance in this part of Asia. Indeed, the Bank will be a very important resource institution for APEC in terms of achieving its target for liberalization of trade and investment by the target date of 2020. I think that it is truly important to keep the target date of 2020. Even though it might be actually difficult to implement full trade liberalization by 2020, it is still very important to have the target date, simply because it points to the focus and specificity of the APEC agenda.
Q. *Now let me refer to two specific controversial issues. One writer has noted that the North American Free Trade Area may be a hindrance to APEC. Should there be the same kind of reservation for the success of APEC as the ASEAN Free Trade Area in Southeast Asia progresses?*
A. It's quite a difficult subject. Personally, I do not think that NAFTA in North America or AFTA in Southeast Asia would act as a hindrance to APEC. Independent of these subregional groupings, APEC can work on its agenda for intraregional free trade and investment by 2020. NAFTA and AFTA can work on their respective timeframe for their respective subregional economic cooperation. As long as there will be shared commitment to free trade, there will be no conflict with the APEC agenda.
Q. *Will you make a stronger statement that they may facilitate APEC?*
A. In a sense it may do so. A healthy competition between these subregional arrangements may facilitate the APEC initiative for free trade in the region as a whole. In no case, will they act as constraints to APEC.
Q. *Do you think there is any merit in implied allegation or suggestion, that APEC is a vehicle for the domination by the U.S. dollar and the Japanese yen over the huge market of 18 Asia-Pacific countries?*
A. I reject the suggestion. There is indeed no scenario for any super-currency game. I don't think that the domination of the Japanese yen will act to discourage APEC. In Europe, the domination of the German mark was no constraint for the successful growth of the European Union. In NAFTA, the dominant U.S. dollar is no hindrance. I don't think that the dominance of the U.S. dollar and the Japanese yen would act as a kind of discouragement to the APEC agenda. These are natural developments and as situations unfold there will be many more stronger currencies.
Q. *Will you please comment on the Australia and New Zealand Closer Economic Relations Act?*
A. I have not been much acquainted with the Australia and New Zealand

Closer Economic Relations Act. However, for the same reason as I have stated about NAFTA in North America and AFTA in Southeast Asia, I don't think that a subregional arrangement between Australia and New Zealand would act as a constraint or hindrance to APEC.

Q. *The second controversial point that I would like to discuss with you may relate to the different membership composition of APEC and the Asian Development Bank. There are many member-countries of the ADB, who are not members of APEC. Does that pose any problem in APEC-ADB cooperation?*

A. I don't say that it does not pose a problem. I say that it may be a problem. However, I think that a clear understanding for operational purposes can and will be worked out toward sustained and effective collaboration between APEC and the ADB.

Q. *In the APEC Report prepared by the Eminent Persons' Group, issues, such as human resource development, environment, harmonization of tariff codes, standardization of traded goods and services, rules of origin, have been discussed at some length. Would you care to comment on them?*

A. Pending a fuller review of the EPG Report, I have the impression that there will be a great deal of work for APEC and the ADB for cooperation on many issues of regional interest.

Q. *Exchange rate stabilization is a key step for a free trade regime. Do you think that APEC, as an institution, will be a useful forum to address the issue?*

A. Indeed, the subject of a stable exchange rate is very closely related to trade liberalization, and free flow of trade and investment among the member-countries of APEC. So for that reason it is quite logical that APEC leaders will find it necessary to recognize the importance of exchange rate stabilization. The ADB, as an international bank for development in the Asian region, has no specific role in this regard.

APEC may be a new forum to add input to the discussion which has been going on between Tokyo and Washington on the yen-dollar exchange rate. Indonesia and Malaysia, whose oil exports are in dollar denomination, have expressed their concern for the high appreciation of the yen. We can reasonably expect that APEC will be able to inject a new element into the discussion. It must be noted that exchange rate stabilization is basically an issue for global discussion, and the G-7 Summit may be a more effective forum. In the Asia-Pacific region, APEC will be a forum for at least an exchange of relevant information among its member-countries. A mediation of the question of yen-dollar rate stabilization may follow.

Q. *The EU has made a specific provision for setting up a fund for structural adjustment of its member-economies. Contributions to the fund will come from the richer EU members, and its disbursement will be committed for structural adjustment of the economies of its less affluent members. Do you see in APEC, its developed, industrialized member-countries making a parallel arrangement for its developing, less-industrialized members?*

A. I think that provisions for intra-APEC economic development should be in order. Member-economies up on the development ladder should come to assist others at the bottom of it. Otherwise one cannot expect that APEC can successfully develop the kind of regional organization it envisages.

My personal view is that this is an area where the ADB and APEC can work together. The founding charter of the ADB aims at providing funding support for accelerated economic growth of undeveloped/underdeveloped poor countries in Asia. As in NAFTA and the EU, the most important question for APEC is how to reduce the gaps in terms of per capita income among its member-countries. That is the most critical issue facing any regional economic cooperation.

The ADB, as an international bank for economic development, is reasonably aimed at reducing the income gap among the member-countries of this institution. Much cooperation with APEC in this regard should be the goal.

Q. *Will you discuss the one key issue which you think needs priority attention if APEC is to be successful?*

A. The most important issue facing APEC at this moment is to define APEC itself. Its agenda needs to be specific and clearly stated. The rest will follow. The APEC agenda itself will state the scope of cooperation between APEC and the ADB. I think that APEC will want very much to reduce the income gaps among its member-countries and that programs for collaboration between APEC and the ADB to this end will follow.

If the goal of APEC is liberalization of financial and capital markets in its member-countries, specific provisions for collaboration with the ADB should be helpful because the ADB advises its member-countries regarding its lending programs.

Alternatively, if APEC defines itself as a more technical institution, the ADB will be able to collaborate, drawing upon its accumulated pool of expertise and experience, by way of advising how to finance the infrastructure, telecommunication, human resources and environment in a member-country.

The Asia-Pacific region is the most dynamic part of the world economy and its economic growth is projected to be sustained in the years ahead. Any form of protectionist agenda will hurt this growth process, and as such must be rejected.

To match "regionalism" with "globalism" must be the goal, as the late Dr.

Okita once stated. APEC, as a regional institution, is committed to a free trade regime in the Asia-Pacific and will function within the global free trade regime, as is visualized by the General Agreement on Tariffs and Trade. I think that APEC will be successful. I would like to add that the ADB will have a positive, collaborative role to play.

President, Asian Development Bank. This conversation was taped on November 17, 1994 in Manila, Philippines.

14 A Conversation with LEE TSAO YUAN

Q. *People describe APEC in many different words and everybody is anxious to say it is different from the European Union, the North American Free Trade Area and the ASEAN Free Trade Area. How would you define APEC?*

A. APEC is, of course, an acronym for Asia Pacific Economic Cooperation and I think that very aptly describes what has been happening in the last six years of APEC. To borrow an analogy by Gareth Evans, "APEC is like a three-tiered wedding cake, the first level being that of useful dialogue, the second being that of trade facilitation, where you begin to discuss the terms of harmonization of standards, customs, implementation of tariff data bases, and so on, and the third tier would be one in which I think APEC has just made a political commitment to the whole area of trade liberalization". So APEC to me is a process, it is a process of economic cooperation. I think that the countries of Asia-Pacific are at this point in time in many ways still groping towards finding out what form this economic cooperation will take.

I do think that the APEC Summit in Bogor in November 1994 had actually given APEC a much greater substance in terms of form than ever before. At this summit, the economic leaders of 18 APEC member-nations signed the Declaration and made the political commitment to establish free and open trade and investment by the year 2010/2020. That immediately establishes APEC as the one big region of 18 nations where free trade will be the order in 25 years. I would say APEC is a process, a moving target, and it is very hard to define a moving target; but that is what APEC is right now.

Q. *You suggest that APEC is a process, a moving target, moving towards a well-defined target and you are, of course, right. How does APEC differ from any other regional economic cooperation process, elsewhere in the world?*

A. Yes, the dimension of APEC which now has 18 member-nations across the Asia-Pacific region immediately comes to my mind. It started off with 14 countries while the European Union started with only six countries.

Second, there are many differences as to how APEC evolved historically. The European Union, for example, from the very beginning started as a supranational organization for economic cooperation. It began when as early as the 1950s, an intraregional commission actually took charge of the management of steel and coal in its member-countries. In APEC there is no such concept, whatsoever, of any organized supranational authority.

The APEC secretariat which coordinates functions within APEC is a coordinating mechanism, not a supranational organization. It cannot be compared with EU secretariat in Brussels.

Comparing APEC with NAFTA, NAFTA is very legalistic; it has rules and it has laws. APEC at this point in time is non-binding in all that it does. Even the recently established investment principles are non-binding. APEC is managed by consensus. Regarding the Bogor Declaration, there is a political commitment to a free trade regime by the year 2010/2020. But it is not a binding commitment in the sense that if a member-country were to fail to implement the agreement by 2010/2020, it would be taken to court. There is none of that. The Bogor Declaration provides for the establishment of a dispute mediation service, but again, that would be non-binding. Both in its structure and historical origin, APEC differs from the EU and NAFTA.

Q. *Many researchers have suggested that economic regionalization in Western Europe, now the EU, is a push factor to various forms of economic cooperation arrangements in other regions including APEC. How much did the EU movement contribute as a push factor to APEC?*

A. I would say that in general it was a push factor. However, that has not been discussed very much, not because it is a sensitive issue, but because it has never come to the forefront of awareness. If it is a push factor, it is not an important push factor.

The important push factors, I think, are: first, the Asia-Pacific economic dynamism which is rooted in the private sector and actually needs an intergovernmental organization to provide a framework for its sustained continuation. Second, in recent times the Uruguay Round trade negotiations under GATT became stalled and this caused concern that the world might indeed break up into protectionist trade blocs, the EU in Western Europe being one prime example. Third, there was a political concern. With the end of the Cold War, the United States might pull away from the Asia-Pacific both in terms of security arrangements and economic presence. That, in many ways, would literally spell disaster for the continued economic growth in the Asia-Pacific.

Q. *If there were no European Union movement for the past 30 to 40 years, since the signing of the Treaty of Rome in 1957, would there be an APEC initiative? If Belgium remained Belgium, would there be any need for any informal or formal economic regionalization for Singapore? Let us ignore defense and extra-economic considerations. If by magic the EU is disbanded totally tomorrow morning, will it have any impact on APEC?*

A. Of course, answers to such questions will always remain open to many forms and variations. For Singapore, I would immediately think more of the Association of Southeast Asian Nations, which was formed out of political considerations. It had nothing to do with economic regionalization and the EU.

The political considerations were to maintain peaceful and harmonious relations in Southeast Asia. Historically, there were tensions among the nations in Southeast Asia, and ASEAN was an institutionalized arrangement for political cooperation. Much of ASEAN's success for the past 25 years materialized through the preservation of peaceful and harmonious relations. I do honestly believe that but for ASEAN, we would probably be exposed to more political tensions in Southeast Asia. The fact that the ministers and officials met so often and there were so many dialogues among the principals of the member-nations actually provided for that framework of peace which enabled economic growth in the region to continue.

Q. *May I return to the economic dynamism of the region, which I have called the pull factor of the APEC economic cooperation. If the push factor from outside has been less important, would you say that the pull factor of economic dynamism from within the region became the only factor?*

A. There is an underlying push factor, and I think that underlying push factor is security. The United States has provided for security in this part of the world in many ways since World War II, and if there is going to be a significant withdrawal of the United States' security presence from this part of the world there would be a power vacuum. This could immediately result in a tussle for power in this part of the world, especially with an emerging China, and create a great deal of nervousness among the countries. So if there were any push factor towards the formation of APEC, I would say, that is it.

Having said that, I think that APEC remains strictly an economic organization. There is now actually another organization, the ASEAN Regional Forum, that is beginning to take care of security aspects for the region. These two separate arrangements for economic and security cooperation will work better, better than everything being mixed up together in one organization.

Q. *To paraphrase Professor Charles P. Kindleberger, an international order needs provisions for public good, international public good - one component of which is defense and security and another is trade and investment flows in a stable monetary and fiscal policy regime. How does APEC make arrangements for intraregional provision of public goods, especially a stable monetary-fiscal regime? In the end, does APEC as a provider of intra-regional public goods emerge as a supranational authority?*

A. Not necessarily so. APEC is still too new an order for it to provide for intraregional public goods, especially in terms of monetary-fiscal stability. It is too soon to predict what form APEC is going to take. Now, APEC is a forum where the ministers of its member-countries meet and discuss specific issues. At the summit in Bogor, heads of the 18 member-states met and shared a commitment to a free trade regime.

There is no supranational authority, nor there is a need for a supranational institutional arrangement. APEC operates by consensus, flexible consensus. True, APEC in 1994 is not what it was in 1989. Certainly, it has evolved. But APEC is not yet the provider of the two components of international public goods in the textbook sense.

The heads of member-governments, foreign ministers, finance ministers and various other ministers of member-countries are now involved in the APEC process. The issues for discussion include environment, transportation, telecommunication, human resources, and it goes down the line in terms of many and varied forms of economic cooperation. Incidentally, in terms of public good, I think one public good which would actually have a lot of benefit and spin-offs would be regional infrastructure.

As for the security aspect, the defense principals of the participating countries who are only just beginning to be involved in the ASEAN Regional Forum are doing so at the suggestion of foreign ministries of the member-governments and will probably remain this way at this time.

Q. *Since the Seattle and Bogor Summits in 1993 and 1994, respectively, APEC has attracted much attention. For citizens and academics in the APEC member-countries, the one crucial issue is the public financing of APEC and its institutionalization, involving so many meetings and related activities. How would you explain this fast emerging phenomenon, however modest?*

A. In APEC, the economic leaders of member-governments are definitely involved. They were very much involved in Seattle in 1993, and in Bogor in 1994. The principals of several cabinet departments of its member-countries - foreign affairs, finance, environment, energy, commerce, communication - have become involved in APEC activities.

Q. *Will you speculate that by the year 2000 a supranational authority, involving participation by the member-governments will become a reality? Will APEC eventually add to its agenda defense and security item?*

A. I'm afraid I don't know anything about defense or the Pacific Defense Council. The only regional organization concerned with security matters that I know of is the ARF arrangement. It will not be possible to speculate how APEC will shape up in the future.

Q. *Returning to APEC, a forum for free trade, how would you comment on the role of international price and exchange rate?*

A. I believe that the 1994 Report of the Eminent Persons' Group recommended that the finance ministers should meet more often, working toward better coordination, and being engaged in mutual discussions of macroeconomic and various economic policies. I don't believe that the Report went so far as to say they actually coordinate exchange rate management.

Singapore and Hong Kong, both APEC members, are unique case illustrations of free trade at world market price with their respective currencies fluctuating in the open market. The Hong Kong dollar is linked to the U.S. dollar, and the Singapore dollar actually has been gradually appreciating in terms of the U.S. dollar. It follows that it is actually possible to have free trade - open trade among countries - without managing the exchange rate. Stability of exchange rates would definitely greatly reduce the risk of free trade, but it is possible to have trade without managing exchange rate stability.

Q. *Does the picture change if a member-country - say the United States, Japan or China - has a high rate of inflation, a huge national debt, or a sustained trade imbalance?*

A. Oh certainly, huge macroeconomic imbalances would change the picture. Such macroeconomic imbalances would have to be corrected by huge exchange rate adjustments. I think that it is possible to have free and open trade without managed exchange rate stability. However, if there could be some mechanism to help stabilize exchange rate, that would greatly facilitate trade/investment flows across nations.

In fact, the EPG Report in one of its recommendations underlines the important role of balanced macroeconomic policies promoting stability of exchange rate. However, I believe that it is actually an issue related to, but rather separate from, the issue of trade and investment liberalization. The issue of coordination of macroeconomic policies is really a separate and much larger issue.

Coordination of macroeconomic policies in particular for a long time has been a baffling issue. The G-7 experience in this regard, since the Plaza Accord of September 1985, has not been very successful. Even in the EU itself, its attempts at macroeconomic coordination in terms of containing the parity of exchange rate of its member-countries also broke down at some point in time. True, following the Maastricht Treaty in 1992, the EU set up an institutionalized arrangement. Will it truly work? History has shown that it is actually not easy to have effective macroeconomic coordination. The economic boom in Southeast Asia has been a factor for us to shelve the discussion of the issue.

Q. *Some political scientists have described the North American Free Trade Area as a co-prosperity area in North America. The forthcoming conference of all nations in the North and South Americas (excepting Cuba) in Miami, hosted by the United States, with its agenda for the Americas' free trade area may be viewed by some as a step toward Americanization of America. How do you view it from the perspective of Singapore?*

A. In one sense I think it is a good thing because it would probably serve to be a powerful factor for opening up the South American countries. If there is increased economic growth in North America or in the Americas, it will further expand trade and investment markets for APEC countries.

However, there is at the same time some anxiety for some of our neighbors should the American hemispheric arrangements cause the possibility of investment diversion. Many of the products of this part of the world are exported to America and their free access to the American market is crucial. American investments in Asian countries also play an important role. Will the countries in the American hemisphere within the Americas' FTA become more attractive for American foreign investment?

Basically, I think the regional integration in North America and in the Americas are natural events and will in the long run be good for more trade and investment for all countries. The fact is that NAFTA exists within APEC. In addition, the Australian-New Zealand economic cooperation arrangement and ASEAN continue to function within APEC.

The American hemispheric free trade arrangement in the long run can effectively work with APEC. It, however, did not actually influence the Bogor Declaration in any significant way. One concern in Bogor was if the countries like Malaysia, China and Japan would come aboard there was little concern about what would happen in Latin America.

Indeed, the Miami Conference with its agenda for the Americas' free trade area was scheduled in December 1994 and at the APEC Summit in Bogor in November 1994; it was not an item for consideration. Indeed, it had no impact on the Bogor Declaration. On the other hand, though, it might have had an impact on subsequent APEC Summits. The Bogor Declaration in November targets free trade for APEC by the year 2010 or 2020. If in December, the Miami Declaration proposes free trade for the American hemispheric FTA by 2010 or 2015, discussions within APEC would immediately follow, and the Miami Declaration could be a push factor for APEC to expedite its target date for free trade. If it does, then I see it as a positive push factor for APEC to come up with a blueprint for exactly how it is going to rearrange its 2010/2020 vision at the APEC Summit in Osaka in November 1995.

Q. *Would you comment on the Malaysian initiative for the East Asian Economic Caucus? or for Asianization of APEC by limiting its membership to Asia only including China?*

A. Malaysia has always been very keen on the EAEC. But the EAEC is very much dependent on Japan, and Japan in turn is very much dependent on the United States. Thus, the EAEC at this point is in limbo. It will be too speculative to suggest whether there will be any impact of the Miami Conference on the EAEC initiative.

Yes, Japan's response in this regard has always been positive and open, albeit with no definitive commitment. I think that China is rather favorably disposed to the EAEC; so is Korea, but Japan is the key actor.

Q. *How does Vietnam fit into the APEC scheme of economic regionalization? How about Laos, Cambodia and Mayanmar?*

A. Vietnam has formally applied for membership to ASEAN and I do think that Vietnam will become a member of ASEAN in 1995 and will become a member of the ASEAN Free Trade Area. I believe that Singapore will most likely support Vietnam's membership to APEC, after the three-year moratorium for new members.

The case for Laos and Cambodia will eventually be taken up. The issue of their membership for ASEAN and ASEAN FTA will finally be dependent on how fast the economic reforms in Laos and Cambodia will have been put in place. Myanmar is to be discussed in its own context. None of these countries is in the immediate timeframe as is Vietnam. They are very much in the background.

However, already there are informal talks, discussions at the academic level, with Cambodia and Laos, regarding regional cooperation. The whole purpose of ASEAN is to maintain peaceful relations and harmony in Southeast Asia. It is not a defense arrangement; it is more a foreign policy coordination for all the countries in the specific region.

Q. *How would you distinguish between the two expressions, often confusing: free trade area and free trade in the area?*

A. A free trade area is very much defined as a situation where no trade barriers among countries within the area exist, but for the countries outside the area trade barriers remain the same.

Free trade in the area means free trade among member-countries in the area; there is nothing explicitly said about trade barriers *vis-à -vis* non-member-countries. The expression couples free trade in the area with the EPG concept of open regionalism, which permits extension of concessions regarding trade barriers to member-countries within the area to non-members outside the area. Thus, while barriers towards insiders come down, barriers towards outsiders will also come down, but not necessarily at the same rate. If the barriers towards insiders and outsiders come down at the same rate, then that will be equivalent to trade liberalization on an unconditional basis. Should barriers towards insiders come down at a faster rate than barriers towards outsiders, then a situation of some preferential arrangement will have prevailed. Each individual APEC member-country will have its freedom to independently formulate its own policy; thus, it is not an FTA.

In the framework of open regionalism, individual members agree to actually extend trade liberalization to non-members exactly as they like. Actually, individual members extend their trade liberalization to others on an entirely unconditional basis. In a free trade area there is no understanding regarding how barriers towards outsiders will be treated. The policy will be one of wait and see.

In NAFTA, Mexico has entered into free trade agreements with Canada and the United States and has elected to extend its free trade area agreements to several other Latin American countries. However, all that is on an entirely conditional MFN basis.

Q. *In any form of free trade area, optimization of the movement of final products in trade and investment flows are believed to optimize the economic gains of all member-countries within the area. Would you consider that free mobility of factors of production, especially of labor and human resources, merits consideration?*

A. I would say that labor mobility across the countries within the area is an extremely sensitive topic. Singapore with foreign workers from several ASEAN countries - Malaysia, the Philippines, Indonesia - is facing the issue. Singapore now has a tight labor market. I believe that the issue is being discussed in NAFTA, given the high unit labor cost in the United States. The American debate on illegal immigration relates to this issue. That is one of the reasons NAFTA was established in the first place.

The factor movement in terms of labor would actually be the elimination of non-tariff border barriers, or non-border barriers. The issue is important. However, at the present time, the prime focus centers on tariff barriers, border barriers, non-border barriers, and so on.

It should be noted that at this time within the ASEAN Free Trade Area, there is no agreement or any significant push towards coordinated investment liberalization among its member-countries. However, investment liberalization is occurring on an individual-country basis. Of course, I believe that APEC non-binding investment principles will be operational in the ASEAN countries.

For APEC, the Jakarta Ministerial Statement in 1994 refers to human resource development which is of course different from the labor movement.

Q. *Would you agree that an effective free trade regime will essentially be conditioned by free mobility of both final products in trade and factors of production - human and non-human - in the absence of the heroic assumption that the production functions of the member-economies within the given area are uniformly developed? Would you accept that the EU has made progress?*

A. Yes, I recognize the economics of the argument and also the EU experiments. I think that APEC will address the issues over time. For APEC, it is too soon to broaden its agenda.

Q. *For APEC, the Bogor Declaration has put much emphasis on the two issues - harmonization and product standardization. Any comment?*

A. Harmonization of tariff nomenclature, for instance among the APEC member-countries, will be relatively easy, albeit it may involve a great deal of paperwork. The process of harmonization will begin by assigning a common code number for tariffs on traded goods in different countries within the APEC region. It will help eliminate considerable paperwork and confusion.

Standardization of products traded is a necessary condition for a free trade regime. However, the process will involve a good deal of difficulty. The goal is to reduce/remove tariffs on a specific product, the standard of which will have to be the same in all countries participating in intraregional free trade. Should the standards of a set of products in one country be different from those in the other member-countries, free trade is impeded.

Singapore is totally open, so is Hong Kong. In other APEC countries the subject of standardization will be open to much debate. For pharmaceutical goods and textile products the standards in Indonesia, China, Japan and the United States of America are not expected to be uniform. How to standardize the products across the member-countries is the question that remains to be answered.

One way is for APEC to set up working groups for standards and conformance. APEC could work towards the mutual acceptance of standardization by accredited institutions in each member-country. It will involve mutual recognition of certification of standards by each member-nation.

Q. *How would you deal with unilateral actions, say by the United States under its own law, known as Super-301?*

A. Honestly I don't know. I shall not go into any details of legal/technical issues. The Bogor Declaration provides for APEC mediation and this could be a way to resolve any such unilateral actions by any APEC member-country. I hope that APEC mediation service will get off the ground soon. It will be a good way to resolve such disputes, albeit the recommendation by mediation will be non-binding. It is a good thing if it works, hopefully it will work. In addition, APEC mediation is to be complementary to the formal arbitration process of the World Trade Organization. If mediation will not work, then the dispute may be taken to the WTO, except that the WTO may not cover all the issues.

Q. *Will you comment on the two other issues - human resource development and environment proctection - in the APEC agenda?*

A. Well, the APEC ministerial meetings and designated working groups are working on developing the details of both the programs.

The ministers for environment and for education in the governments of the APEC member-countries will have the responsibility in their respective areas. There are APEC working groups for specific assignments. Members of the working groups will be drawn from related ministries of governments of the member-countries.

For example, in Singapore there are officials in various ministries - foreign affairs, education, industry and trade, and environment - working on APEC-related issues. There are provisions for working group meetings, for meetings of the senior officials, finally, to be followed by ministerial meetings - finance ministers, environmental ministers, education ministers, telecommunication ministers, and so on. The coordination of various working groups occurs along their respective specialized, functional lines.

The cabinet-level ministers of the governments of APEC membercountries will be the people responsible to appoint officials to do the jobs and they will report to their presidents and prime ministers.

Q. *Does it look like a supranational government with 18 presidents?*

A. To me, the difference is that here you have 18 economic leaders of 18 member-countries who sit together and by consensus take decisions on certain issues and make joint political commitments. There is no supranational authority with its command over the assigned intraregional program. For example in the EU, the European Commission decides on trade policy on behalf of all its member-countries who have delegated the authority to the Commission. In APEC, there will still be the 18 economic leaders of the eighteen member-countries to ultimately decide on the trade policies. In that sense, I think APEC is not a supranational authority. I think there is a very great difference between APEC and EU.

Q. *Finally, based on your work on APEC for some years, what would you say have been your disappointments?*

A. I am really very happy that most of the recommendations of the EPG Report were actually affirmed by the summit leaders. Let me respond to your question as to the three specific areas in which I would like APEC to make further progress.

First, it is crucial that the private sector business in APEC countries takes more initiative in its participation in the APEC agenda for free trade. At the conference sponsored by the Pacific Economic Cooperation Council in Jakarta, November 13, 1994, I discussed the issue of institutionalization of APEC and argued that what is called for is greater participation of the private sector. Trade liberalization benefits the business sector and the leadership for trade liberalization must belong to them.

Second, APEC must beef up its analytical abilities. Its core agenda of free trade definitely relates to many and varied issues which are complex and technical. The need for intensive research is obvious.

Third and finally, the issue of macroeconomic coordination, to which you have made much reference, remains to be studied. In the long run, free trade policy cannot be sustained in the absence of some degree of macroeconomic coordination.

Member, Eminent Persons' Group. This conversation was taped on November 29, 1994 in Singapore.

15 A Conversation with The Honorable NEVILLE WRAN

Q. *People have been trying to describe APEC by saying what it is not - neither EU, nor NAFTA. One of your fellow EPG members has called it a moving target and thus hard to define. How would you define APEC?*

A. The terminology which first defines APEC is economic regionalization based upon the concept of voluntary association with its focus upon free trade in the region. It is a term one will see frequently in the first EPG Report and occasionally in the second EPG Report. Its structure is flexible and with no compulsory overtones in relation to specific objectives or decisions. The purpose of APEC is to facilitate trade between its 18 member-countries.

Q. *How would you distinguish between the two expressions - free trade area and free trade in the area?*

A. In my view, a free trade area connotes an association of member-countries at the expense of non-members, with free trade within the defined region or among the defined countries, but with sanctions and non-extension of benefits to non-member countries.

Free trade in an area means that among the member-nations in the specific area there will be an absence of impediments, direct and indirect, to free trade. Then, there is a capacity for member-nations to extend to non-member-nations the benefits which are available to the members in the area. Indeed, the steps for trade liberalization, as defined within the APEC region, should become the norm globally. In other words, no country is prevented from participating in the free trade provision provided there is some reciprocation.

Q. *Could Australia, then, give some non-APEC countries bilateral or trilateral trade benefits? Could Australia do something to non-APEC countries without reciprocation?*

A. Yes, but it will not be cheaper, if it did. This is no theoretical game. APEC is an association of nations engaged in trade and its purpose is the promotion of trade for the promotion of economic benefits to all member-countries. It is out there in the cold hard world where they all want to see a positive result. What will be the positive benefit to Australia for it to make such a gesture? Trade benefits are not going to be extended to non-member-countries who do not give something back. This is all about improving one's trade position. If APEC doesn't improve the trade position of its member-nations, then they will get out of APEC.

Q. *You seem to suggest that the two concepts - free trade area and free trade in the area - are almost the same.*

A. No, they are not. With APEC there is a degree of flexibility which doesn't exist with the fortress Europe. One of the strengths of APEC ultimately will be the quality of flexibility. APEC will be able to make decisions and to pursue courses of action without the agreement of every member of APEC. There will be those APEC members who don't want to participate and stay on the sideline. But obviously, if the course of action decided upon by the majority is beneficial to that majority, then those who chose to be left out will soon want to come in.

Free trade arrangements either regional or subregional is one of the unique qualities at the present position. The Asian nations in particular are keen not to see institutionalization of APEC with a centralized administrative infrastructure. APEC has set the goals for trade liberalization and the principles for trade facilitation. Let the member-nations individually work it out themselves. There is no need for a central bureaucracy endeavoring to administer the APEC free trade regime.

Q. *How will you view the North American Free Trade Area and the recent conference in Miami of all states in the North and South Americas (except Cuba), hosted by the United States (call it the Miami Initiative) with its projected agenda for a hemispheric free trade area of the Americas? How does it relate to APEC? How do all these programs for region-specific free trade areas relate to the World Trade Organization, following the GATT Agreement?*

A. Honestly speaking, the Miami Initiative came like a bolt from the blue. I'm a bit surprised, and the timing of it, I think, is unfortunate. I also find it difficult to reconcile the fact that four members of North Americas' free trade area - Canada, the U.S., Mexico, Chile - are concurrently members of APEC. How will the differences between the laws governing trade in the two regions be reconciled for those four members of NAFTA and the remaining members of APEC?

There has always been in the minds of some countries a suspicion that the U.S. initiative for APEC is not quite clear. Now, there seems to be evolving a larger and more comprehensive vehicle, which would make it, from one point of view, all the more easier to absorb APEC into what is almost a total American initiative. I'm leaving aside whether that's a good thing or a bad thing. I do know that many Asian countries do have a suspicion that the U.S. objectives are not as clear as the U.S. expresses.

Naturally, there has been some discussion between various members, and one of the tasks which has been given to the EPG by the summit leaders at Bogor is to look at APEC in the context of other regional arrangements. The emerging FTAA, the hemispheric free trade area of the Americas, may be a topic for discussion at the first EPG meeting after Bogor. I think with some difficulty and some degree of confusion that the first thing will be to ascertain how these regional/subregional organizations will relate to each other. APEC has declared that it will be GATT/WTO consistent, and in terms of trade liberalization, APEC's objectives will foreseeably be to act just a little bit ahead of GATT/WTO, or, these regional bodies are not needed. Pushing the limits of GATT/WTO further and further until eventually we do have global free trade should be APEC's agenda. How will FTAA be GATT/WTO consistent?

I think that is somewhat idealistic and the world being what it is, nations being what they are, and the state of commerce and industry being what it is, there is more than an element of idealism about it. Nevertheless, the limits can be pushed further and further if there is a genuine commitment from a sufficient number of nations. Because it's hard to achieve, there is no reason not to try to achieve it.

Q. *Let us return to the APEC Bogor Summit and its agenda for a free trade regime by 2020. How do we get to it?*

A. No one has specified how they will get to the 2020 objectives. Some member-nations will get there quicker than others, and some may be slower than others. The state of the economy will dictate the pace for the specific member. I do expect, however, that the majority of APEC members will fulfill the trade liberalization, some possibly under peer pressure. No individual member in the group will prefer to be left behind.

Not that it will just become fashionable. Trade will move to those whose policy of trade liberalization would make it easier to do trade with. If a member-nation is not in it, it will be out of it, and the net result will be its loss of trade and economic gains that follow. The real pressure for one nation will be its loss of benefits, and it will maximize its effort to minimize the loss.

Q. *Let us return to Europe for a minute. If economic regionalization in Western Europe were not a reality, would there be any momentum for any kind of economic regionalization in the Asia-Pacific?*

A. The movement for economic regionalization in the Asia-Pacific would become real for reasons of its own. However, I don't pretend that the Western European initiatives, now the European Union, did not have some effect upon the pace of the movement. First, in this region, we had what I call a subregional arrangement, like ANZ-CER. All trade barriers between Australia and New Zealand have been removed. It may be added that there is informal coordination of monetary and fiscal policies, with much emphasis on the word informal.

Q. *I gather that ANZ-CER follows the European Union, more or less. What do you really mean when you state so forcefully that the EU makes it the fortress Europe?*

A. To me, it is laughable to suggest that it is not a fortress Europe. In relation to agricultural products, there is, as we all know, a high level of protection. While that sort of impediment may not be obvious in relation to other products it is still there. Of course, the EU's trade with other parts of the world is increasing, just as the world demand for traded goods is increasing. Merely because we are members of APEC does not mean we don't seek to trade with other nations, we very much do. To me, it is quite evident that Europe has protected barriers to bolster domestic activity among the members of the EU, and at the same time to make it impossible for non-members to trade in certain products.

Q. *My research shows that the initiative for the APEC follows a time path of economic regionalization in Western Europe ever since the signing of the Treaty of Rome in 1957, and its subsequent landmarks - the Single European Act of 1985 and the Maastricht Treaty of 1992. Is APEC trying to outdo or match the EU?*

A. Outdo, perhaps; match, no. The course of APEC action is quite the reverse. By a process of trade liberalization distinct from one of trade protection, APEC is endeavoring to promote trade within the Asia-Pacific, and also with the countries who trade with the Asia-Pacific. I see no real parallels between the two.

Q. *As Americanization of America by forming a hemispheric free trade area is increasingly coming to be a fact, albeit not realized, the concept of Asianization of Asia also has recently become a subject, discussed especially by political scientists. The Europeanization of Europe following the Single European Act of 1985 is on record. Any comment?*

A. Let Americans have their own (hemispheric) agenda. For APEC, as I mentioned earlier, we must look at how effectively its subregional arrangements - the ASEAN free trade arrangement, ANZ-CER arrangement and NAFTA - stand together with the overall APEC agenda. The impact on the economies of the APEC member-countries will be the key issue and this will need to be worked out over a period of time. Let's face it, we never had an organization like APEC before.

If Asianization of Asia means that all Asian countries should be lumped together, the reality does not support it. Let the economies of Asia, so disparate in their stages of development, evolve into a state of mutual understanding. What I detect by talking to Asian leaders and economists is that they first of all place the success of their respective economies squarely on the fact that they have market economies. They also point to the fact that their respective governments became a force in support of free enterprise. Industrialization in East and Southeast Asia became a reality. Being practical peoples, as they are, I think that they will continue to adhere to the precepts of free enterprise market economic systems.

In addition, Asianization of Asia in terms of relationships in both trade and security purposes will encourage isolationism. For a huge economy like the U.S., if the U.S. built a fence around it, it can still be self-sustaining and self-supporting. For most of the Asian countries in APEC, the size of their economies is quite small. Then, there are economies of Japan at one end, and of the People's Republic of China at the other end. Natural endowments of these economies also are very different. Given the cultural differences among its diverse peoples, Asia is a mixed bag; their histories are also different.

Q. *Let us go back to your opening remarks stating that APEC does not want to institutionalize with a centralized authority. My one-day visit to the APEC Secretariat in Singapore makes me think otherwise. I venture to suggest that APEC is already a well-organized supranational institution, presided over by an 18-member presidium, aided by 18 ambassadors; one designated by each member-country with the exalted title of Eminent Person; ranking officials at every member-nation's capital, including Canberra and Washington, DC, and a host of operational committees and councils - working groups.*

A. One of the things we have always been good at is getting people to work for nothing, in a sense. But compared with other international/multinational organizations, APEC is a lean machine and has aborted all the trappings of authority, breaking away from the basis of any supranational government-type relationship. Naturally, there are members of each government working on APEC assignments, but once again I emphasize that it is lean, very lean.

Q. *In your APEC Bogor Summit Declaration a brief paragraph refers to macroeconomic coordination. Will you please elaborate?*

A. At least at the beginning the task should be to identify areas of macroeconomic reform, areas which can be examined without any loss of sovereignty for the member-nations. No nation, no country is giving up its sovereign rights to have its macroeconomic policies determined by its respective national authorities.

There are specific areas, such as human resources, infrastructure, energy, transportation and pure water supplies where a common, united intra-APEC involvement may be examined. Indeed, the richer APEC member-nations may well help arrange a regional program, all through private banks or other development banks. The goal must be to devise common objectives which can be worked out without compromising the sovereignty of any member-nation.

For issues such as inflation, interest rate, and taxation, APEC can be a forum for discussion and exchange of views only. I think that APEC can more successfully work on developing an intraregional common policy for investment flows, which will be a much more achievable goal.

Q. *Are you satisfied with the progress since the Bogor Summit? What is your biggest concern?*

A. APEC was founded in 1989, and in five years its achievement has been great. Not only its progress, but the will to progress for the member-nations has really been good. Two years ago, the picture looked rather bleak. So it is both a surprise and a sense of satisfaction to see what has occurred. It speaks volumes for the sophistication of the current leaders, who carried the battle firmly for the success of the Bogor Summit and who will be remembered for this achievement.

Q. *Will you please close by stating one issue you would work hard to oppose at the APEC Osaka Summit in 1995?*

A. I'm a positive thinker, not a negative guy. I would oppose any attempt for significant growth for APEC bureaucracy. It will send wrong signals. The flexibility which I mentioned in the beginning is critical. In 1994, at Bogor we observed a high degree of agreement and support among the summit leaders. However, in a forum like APEC there must be flexibility to accommodate possible reservations as to specific issues on the part of some leaders.

Q. *Will you object if the United States proposed that any and all members of the Free Trade Area of the Americas (FTAA) should automatically become APEC members, as was the case for Chile?*

A. I don't think it would be a bad thing. However, I do think it is a big mouthful to swallow, too soon and too fast. Many countries will argue that we should have more experience working with a little APEC before we move on to a big APEC. Let the process of evolution work itself out in a measured course. Too many strides at once are likely not to evolve correctly and ruptured relationships can occur. I think APEC needs time to keep going forward at a steady, rounded, rapid pace.

Let me add that I would oppose APEC being any identity as an instrument to solve non-trade issues, such as human rights or industrial relations. APEC must limit its agenda to trade issues. Defense may be another issue, because an intraregional security is a rewarding spin-off. It must, however, be emphasized that defense is not an objective for APEC.

Member, Eminent Persons' Group. This conversation was taped on December 5, 1994 in Sydney, Australia.

16 A Conversation with NARONGCHAI AKRASANEE

Q. *I would appreciate it if you would define APEC.*
A. A lot of people think APEC is going to be a trade forum, trade and investment forum - a forum spending most of its time in the development of trade and investment.
Q. *How does it relate to the Miami initiative - a conference in Miami in December 1994 of all nations of the North and South Americas (except Cuba), hosted by the United States, proposing a free trade area of the Americas?*
A. The Miami initiative is a call for another free (trade) forum. I believe that the U.S. is determined to open up trade around the world and will use every means possible, unilateral, bilateral, regional and multilateral. APEC is a forum whereby the U.S. can be active in opening trade and further the same objective.
Q. *I want to bring to your attention the concern of some economists from other parts of the world, a concern that this Americanization of America may be a matter of concern to the APEC initiative.*
A. I don't think so. APEC is a forum of (sovereign) members sharing the goal about the opening up of intra-APEC trade. All APEC nations may not be ready to the same degree, but certainly the fact that the 18 countries are signatories to the APEC Agreement must mean that they subscribe to the same common goal.
Q. *You do not seem to suggest that the Miami Initiative may encourage an Asian hemispheric initiative - Asianization of Asia.*
A. No, I don't think so. I think that the U.S. will respond appropriately. The U.S. will play a very dominant role in America's opening of trade/investment. America is a most powerful country and it has a role in the opening up of trade and investment regionally as well as globally; it has the ability to lead the Pacific economies and others to come together in a joint endeavor. The proximity of the Americas - countries in North America and in Latin America - will have to be recognized. As far as APEC is concerned, the U.S. knows that Asia presents a very big economic market for trade and investment and the Asia-Pacific market impacts in many ways upon the U.S. economy.

The U.S. will continue to be an active member of APEC. I also believe that many of the APEC countries see the importance of the U.S.; therefore, the idea of Asianization of Asia will not be relevant. Of course, trade among Asian nations will continue to grow, but it will not hinder the development of APEC, nor will the FTAA, as and when it develops, hinder APEC.

APEC is not yet a free trade area, but it may be one in the future. It will be an open area for trade and investment, albeit the degree of openness may vary for an individual member for a given time. APEC is definitely going to be very active.

Q. *Should members of the Free Trade Area of the Americas become members of APEC following APEC's acceptance of all NAFTA members into its membership?*

A. There are two ways of handling the situation. First, to establish a linkage between APEC-free trade area and free trade area of the Americas, which can be done without merging membership of the two regional groups. Second, a specific provision for the free flow of services between the two regional groups will preempt the need for APEC countries to become members of the Americas' hemispheric free trade area.

Q. *Vietnam will be a member of ASEAN very soon (in 1995), others in Southeast Asia - Laos, Cambodia and Mayanmar - may follow. Will the ASEAN propose to admit its new members to APEC membership?*

A. Possibly, but not too soon.

Q. *At the APEC Osaka Summit in 1995, South Korea may propose that North Korea be admitted to APEC membership. Any comment?*

A. That is a surprise to me. I do not think that it will be realistic to expect the addition of North Korea to APEC before the summit in Osaka in 1995.

Q. *Since the APEC Summit in Bogor in 1994 there has been a minor/major difference of opinion, especially with respect to "reciprocity" in free trade. One initiative is referred to as the Japan-Indonesia-Australia approach, as opposed to the other - the Washington approach. What will be Thailand's position?*

A. For Thailand, I don't know. Personally, I prefer no reciprocity. Thailand is already unilaterally demolishing its trade barriers and eliminating all other non-trade barriers. Free trade is good for Thailand. It has no reason to sit back waiting for reciprocity.

Q. *APEC is within the GATT framework and APEC's operations will have to be consistent with the trade regime of the World Trade Organization. If so, why do we need APEC?*

A. We aren't sure. There is a general assumption that GATT or its successor organization, the WTO, is not going to go very far.

Q. *Could you elaborate on the essential contributions of APEC?*

A. Members of APEC, the majority of them, I am sure, see the benefit of free trade and investment. APEC members have opened up markets for trade and investment. Thailand has unilaterally done a great deal and many other countries are willing to do so.

Q. *If so, will APEC as an intraregional institution grow into something more than what it is? What will it be?*

A. It will grow beyond what it is now. ASEAN is a smaller forum. By using this forum itself, its member-nations can actually initiate programs for development for them, and that is what they are doing. The APEC member-countries are at present looking solely for free trade and investment. Some APEC members want others to keep trade and investment open, while they themselves are reluctant about the opening up of trade/investment. APEC can be effective in getting all its member-countries to be more open about trade and investment.

Q. *Are you suggesting then APEC will work as a political or moral force for liberalizing intraregional trade/investment?*

A. APEC is somewhat of a political force. But APEC is primarily an economic force. APEC member-countries don't want to lose the American market and want to continue to trade with America, especially with the U.S. Its huge market is an essential component for Asian partners to be attracted to trans-Pacific economic cooperation.

Q. *Given the high growth rate of several Asian economies, America's interest in Asia will grow. Do you accept the hypothesis of mutual gains?*

A. Yes. We have a common interest here. APEC members share a common philosophy, a common ideology, and a common policy for free and open markets, albeit in varying degrees. The U.S. is the most open economy.

Q. *Some of your fellow EPGs have drawn my attention to the defense and security contents of APEC within the APEC economic umbrella. What do you think about that?*

A. Historically, some people have been convinced of that. Some will point to the so-called implication of the make-up benefit of APEC by way of having American security presence in the Asia-Pacific. There cannot be any generalization of this view. America is not at war with Asia and there is hardly any threat to security.

Q. *In your view, from Thailand's perspective, security issues are not dominant, economic issues are.*

A. In Thailand, there are people who subscribe to diverse views on this score. Some politically oriented thinkers focus on APEC's security parameters. They are not the dominant group. Most others have economics orientation, and their concern for free trade and investment relates to the economic development of Thailand. Economics is the dominant issue. There exists no so-called national view. I am sure that the same is the situation in other countries.

Q. *Coming back to the reciprocity issue, you seem to be saying that you support the Japan-Indonesia-Australia approach, as opposed to the Washington approach. Do you see a compromise one way or another?*

A. APEC is committed to consensus-based decision making, not to a rule of the majority vote.

Q. *A growing view in the United States favors reciprocity, simply because it is fair economics.*

A. Reciprocity on an individual-country basis is not feasible. A common decision for all APEC members will have to be worked out.

Q. *Some research, including my own research, shows that the momentum for APEC - an economic regionalization - comes from the economic regionalization in Western Europe. Do you think that in the absence of economic regionalization in Western Europe, APEC would not be formed?*

A. I don't know enough about the cause-and-effect relationship, nor do I have enough political evidence. In my view APEC is a regional arrangement for the development of trade by moving towards more open trade. Member-nations, relying on export more and more so, must realize that eventually they too will have to open up their imports. One nation cannot just continue to export without allowing inflow of imports. True, some nations may not be able to completely open their economy all at once. They may begin by making some free trade agreements among their neighboring countries, only as an interim arrangement toward a more comprehensive open economic policy in the future.

Thus, Thailand now joins the ASEAN Free Trade Area. As we work with AFTA we also work on the APEC free trade agenda. We hope to work on APEC with greater ease, as our lateral free trade experience in Southeast Asia will have given us an experience. Thailand may opt to follow its timetable to fit its domestic economic priorities.

I don't think that APEC will have the scope of European regionalization as in the European Union. World trade is growing fast, and its globalization through the WTO will help all countries. Let us make it easy to sell things and to export, and people in all countries will love it.

Q. *The initiative in Western Europe first started soon after the Treaty of Rome was signed in 1957 and became effective January 1, 1958. It was followed in the 1960s by a parallel initiative in the Asia-Pacific, which eventually became APEC in 1989. Any comment?*

A. I am not familiar with this history. The Association of Southeast Asian Nations, of which Thailand is a founder-member, initiated the ASEAN Free Trade Area (AFTA), which then became a part of APEC. It must have had something to do with the Western European events - a process of learning and a source of inspiration. However, the organization of APEC could not be a direct outcome of European regionalization.

Q. *As of January 1, 1995 three more nations will join the 12-nation group of the EU. Will you ignore this as a non-event for APEC?*

A. No, this is not to be ignored. We want APEC to be a powerful political force for economic purposes. The European Union is a very important market for APEC, and vice versa. We do not know how the strong financial union of the EU will affect its trade with the rest of the world.

Q. *One argument forcefully advanced by economists at the Australian National University is that we cannot press for reciprocity because if APEC gives free trade concessions to China, its automatic extension to some other Asian countries, for example, Sri Lanka, India or Mayanmar, will be fair and consistent with the APEC free trade agenda. Is that any valid argument?*

A. I agree, yes.

Q. *Will the nations in Southeast Asia, now not APEC members, and others in South Asia eventually become members of APEC?*

A. Here are two separate issues. First, APEC is an association of like-minded peoples allowing certain member-countries to have access to the regional forum for mutual economic gains. Second, countries in Southeast and South Asia, and still others in Africa and Latin America, are not members of the APEC regional forum. Not much interest exists for their membership.

Q. *Following the APEC Bogor Declaration, harmonization and standardization are prominent items in the APEC agenda. How do you view this from Thailand's perspective?*

A. These issues are important for trade liberalization and are thus related to GATT, now WTO. Some believe that the WTO can be more effective in regard to these issues as they relate to global free trade. There are others who feel that APEC can be more effective in the Asia-Pacific region.

Thailand favors standardization and harmonization, not just for the APEC region, but for world trade. Certainly, Thailand has a long way to go if it follows the GATT/WTO system. Thailand will have to standarize commodity classifications much faster.

Harmonization and standardization of traded products aid open trade and merit support. However, implementation of the program will have to be done by government officials who will prefer to set up their working schedule.

Q. *Can Thailand make a contribution to the APEC agenda for standardization/harmonization of products?*

A. I really don't know. When we import a product to Thailand, say a pharmaceutical product, the Food and Drug Administration [FDA] of Thailand must approve of it. The FDA in Thailand certainly has its own independent standard, and very often that is viewed as an obstacle to import - a trade barrier against imports of the specific product. The Thai business people, however, like it very much as they will face less competition from imports. It is an open question as to whether it is to the advantage of Thailand. APEC is trying to harmonize/standardize products.

Thailand tests imports of Australian meat, of Malaysian meat; it tests pharmaceutical tablets for birth control imported from France which have been tested, tested and tested. Thailand does it because other countries test imports of foreign goods. The issue of product harmonization and standardization has been on the agenda of both ASEAN and APEC. The uniformity of classifications of traded products relates to trade liberalization. The officials designated to do the job will, of course, run into many problems.

Q. *Should APEC institute a common accreditation system? Or, should each member-country set up its independent code, watching each other?*

A. I think that Thailand will computerize the relevant information. Computers in member-countries may exchange information and thus electronically expedite intra-APEC trade flows. If APEC members agree, a twofold system may evolve - an individual country-based accreditation as well as a common APEC-based accreditation.

Q. *How about the three Es - environment, energy and employment - as they may be priority items for the APEC Osaka Summit, 1995?*

A. I think the leaders at the APEC Osaka Summit will make free trade arrangements the centerpiece of their agenda. The other items inclusive of the three Es will just be mentioned in passing. I don't think that the APEC Summit will be specific about environment in a member-country, say in Thailand. The global environmental conference in Rio de Janeiro was the proper forum for the subject. As for energy, the Osaka Summit in 1995, from the Thai perspective, will have little to discuss. On employment also, the summit discussion may be limited to the potential for job creation by trade liberalization.

Q. *Will there be any argument on prison labor and/or child labor?*

A. Impossible - futile - futile: having APEC pushed from Washington or any other member-country's capital will be futile.

Q. *How about the establishment of a development corporation to help the economically less-developed APEC members catch up with the leaders in terms of technology and production efficiency? The European Union has allocated funds to help intraregional structural imbalances in the less-affluent member-economies.*

A. Less-developed APEC members will always put emphasis on the availability of funds to finance technology transfer, which should be determined by market forces. A development corporation cannot be expected to produce the best result. The EU is a completely different case. Each EU member has to open up right away its intra-Union trade 100 per cent. In APEC, provisions for a phased program for trade liberalization exist and each member-nation will have its timetable, so that there will be room for a levelling-up of intra-APEC economic standards. Approaches suitable for an APEC program will be different from those in EU.

The Asian Development Bank should be a source of funds for this purpose. However, most available ADB funds are project specific. Any additional fund may support APEC-related projects, subject of course to intra-APEC political debates.

Q. *Do you suggest that APEC is a political force?*

A. A program for trade liberalization among APEC members must be a political force.

Q. *That certainly is a strong statement. I spent a day at the APEC Secretariat in Singapore and the establishment is truly an off-budget aparatus, with minor exceptions for a few junior staff positions. All ranking employees are paid by their respective governments through preapproved budgetary provisions of specific departments/agencies of the respective member-country governments. In the capital of each APEC member-country, including Bangkok, I have had occasions to meet with public officials in various government departments/agencies with APEC-related assignments. Then the eminent persons, as designated by the government of each member-country, serve as de facto ambassadors to APEC for their respective countries, albeit honorary.*

A. Very obviously - there is no question that APEC has a political presence with a bureaucracy working for it in Singapore and at every member-nation's capital. Eventually it will become bigger and bigger. If, in 1994, the APEC Secretariat has only a dozen ranking officers, by 1996, I predict the number will rise, albeit I cannot predict an exact figure. The APEC government structure is in the process of emerging and is programed to emerge.

APEC is a multicountry program - an international agreement of sovereign nations with a political dimension, and without a central organization, it cannot get anything done. Eventually the off-budget Secretariat will be budgeted up front.

Following the successful adjournment of the APEC Bogor Summit in November 1994, EPGs offered to be relieved of their duties. However, at the request of their respective governments, they agreed to continue to serve as EPGs.

Q. *Would you like to see headquarters, as one of your fellow EPG members suggested, spread across the capitals of APEC member-nations, each with a specific function, say environment in Ottawa, energy in Bangkok?*

A. APEC will have to have a central headquarters, and Singapore is the most suitable place. APEC will have its functional committees in various national capitals. Thailand has learned from the institutional growth of ASEAN.

Beginning with a modest staff, over time ASEAN has grown to a supranational organization with a large secretariat and a fairly large budget.

Each APEC member-country would naturally like to host a functional committee which will be served by a ministry or a group of ministries of the government of the specific host country. I must hasten to add that we in APEC don't want to create a Brussels-type centralized institution as the EU has done. It will be good to remember that Brussels came into existence over a long period of time.

Member, Eminent Persons' Group. This conversation was taped on December 13, 1994 in Bangkok, Thailand.

17 A Conversation with Dato NOORDIN SOPIEE

Q. *Let us begin by referring to the Miami Initiative, that is, the Conference of all hemispheric states in North and South America (except Cuba) in Miami, December 1994, and its impact, if any, on APEC.*

A. Let me first be on record that my responses must be considered completely personal, in no way that of the government of Malaysia. The Miami initiative is quite a natural event. There are so many regional organizations - the Organization of Economic Cooperation and Development, the European Union in Western Europe, others in Central Europe, in Eastern Europe. Just as globalism is real, so is nationalism, and also regionalism. These are natural manifestations of people and countries who for political, economic or other reasons are trying to join together to better the economic conditions of their peoples. It is very natural for this to happen. In fact, in historical terms it is a natural manifestation of something that started with the Monroe Doctrine in the nineteenth century. Some people get very upset by it for various reasons, of course, understandable reasons.

Q. *Does the Miami Initiative relate to your 1992 initiative? Does it now encourage you to convene another Pan-Asian economic cooperation convention, as you did in 1992?*

A. I think that it doesn't encourage us, nor does it discourage us to do what should be done. An Asian initiative will be considered a natural course of events. I think that it is natural for Asia to learn to be close to the West and to other parts of the world - to Africa and Latin America. At the same time, it is also natural for Asians to get to know each other better - to rediscover themselves - especially since we have now come to a new phase in world history when for the first time in 500 years some Asians have discovered the worth of Asian economies. For the first time in 500 years a large number of Asians are saying that Asians are not inferior, that Asians have ways of doing things in their own ways, and that their ways of doing things may be pretty good for them. Asian nations should get closer to each other and work closer with each other, just as they work closer with Europe, with North America and so on. This Asianization of Asia and the rediscovery of Asia and the coming together of Asia are only natural, very natural.

We hope that people elsewhere will not get so worked up when we propose to do what they do. For some strange reason not only do they fail to appreciate an Asian initiative, but also they express resentment. Indeed, the phenomenon is worthy of academic analysis. We in East Asia have been extremely outraged that any effort on our part to meet at an international forum of Asian nations to discuss whatever we want to discuss is open to criticism. There's a sort of *verboten* sign that says "this is forbidden to you". Every time we mention East Asia economic cooperation involving East Asian economies, not including Australia and New Zealand, Canada, the United States, or for that matter, the United Kingdom or Germany, there is a strong resentment. When the Europeans formed the European Union, excluding any and all economies that do not belong to Western Europe, there was no cry against the exclusion of all non-Europeans. The EU does not include the United States, Canada, Japan, Australia and New Zealand. It does not include even the Solomon Islands. Surely, this is not inappropriate as they are not part of Europe. Thus, the non-inclusion of economies that are not part of East Asia in an East Asia initiative is surely equally appropriate. Europeanization of Europe is accepted, why not the Asianization of Asia?

Q. *One way is to take a map-of-the-world view of the Americas, of Europe, of Asia. For those of us who elect to take a map-of-the-world view of APEC, it must be no less natural. Do you appreciate this APEC view of economic regionalization as it is evolving?*

A. We must make sure that APEC succeeds in creating this Pacific community and this effective economic entity. We hope that the United Nations can do much more for the global community. However, I do think it is also legitimate that East Asians get together at a forum of their own. I also think that we shall see alternative approaches involving the South Asian nations and South Africa. Let us welcome many and varied expressions of the natural course of evolution of the historic process of economic regionalization.

Q. *Returning to Europe, it is noted that the European initiative for economic regionalization, now in the form of the EU, had an impact on the APEC initiative in the Asia-Pacific, albeit with a time lag. I note that there is a great deal of consensus that APEC cannot be a replica of the EU. We don't want to replicate Europe in Asia but will you accept the point that European economic regionalization has been the intellectual force responsible for economic regionalization in the Asia-Pacific?*

A. Well, actually - what the European Union and the European process have done in Europe have had much impact on Asia-Pacific Economic Cooperation.

Member, Eminent Persons' Group. This conversation was taped on December 16, 1994 in Kuala Lumpur, Malaysia.

18 A Conversation with HEINZ W. ARNDT

Q. *Asia-Pacific Economic Cooperation held two successive annual summits at Seattle in 1993 and Bogor, Indonesia in 1994 with great success and with much world attention. How do you view the Miami Initiative of the United States of America, hosting a conference of all states of North and South Americas (except Cuba) and the proposal for the hemispheric free trade area of the Americas? and its impact on APEC?*

A. I welcome the general approach. I welcome an arrangement which will help focus on non-discriminatory trade liberalization. Each country is encouraged to liberalize trade independently of reciprocal or discriminatory arrangements. We have been anxious to avoid APEC becoming a discriminatory trade bloc or a free trade area. I am unhappy about suggestions that APEC should be linked to the North American Free Trade Area.

The problem came to the fore in the second report of the Eminent Persons' Group when Fred Bergsten, the U.S. member of the group, inserted into the draft a formula which seems to sugges t that there should be non-discriminatory trade liberalization within APEC, but it could be discriminatory for outsiders. Towards non-member-countries, APEC members would have the option of offering liberalization on a reciprocal basis. This has been the center of the argument. I think Bergsten feared that if he gave too much away, the Uruguay Round ratification might be in danger, or, there would be a general backlash in the United States. For APEC, the concern was to confirm a resolution to liberalize trade unilaterally. In my view, Indonesia and other Southeast Asian countries would go along with this. APEC's chief purpose must be to avoid the breaking-up of the world trading system into self-contained blocs. In particular, a continuing confrontation on trade between the United States and Japan is most unwelcome. All along we have argued that the main purpose of APEC is to bring the United States and Japan under a single umbrella. APEC will help engage the two in a dialogue without the risk that each will form its own bloc.

From that point of view the Miami Conference is an extension of NAFTA. It extends the coverage of discriminatory free trade arrangements to the American hemisphere, albeit without Cuba. It is possible that the trade creation effect in this huge American market will outweigh the trade diversion effect in this case, and that is all to the good. In principle, we don't like the idea of discriminatory arrangements.

We are fully aware of the argument, forcefully made by some, that the US cannot afford to open its market without reciprocal concessions, particularly from the Europeans. They are worried about the free-rider problems.

Q. *Since the APEC Summit in Bogor accepted NAFTA in North America in its present form, it follows that in principle, there should be no problem in having a larger free trade area of the Americas within APEC. APEC has accepted NAFTA member-countries as its members plus Chile. Your comment please.*

A. It depends on what one means by a free trade area. Do you mean the one that confines trade liberalization to its members? The United States has to make up its mind whether its commitment to APEC can be reconciled with its American hemispheric arrangement. Trade liberalization within NAFTA or in the hemispheric context will conflict with the APEC policy for free trade, and the membership of the two sets of regional organizations will be different.

Q. *Should North Korea become a member of APEC? Should Vietnam and Southeast Asian countries now outside ASEAN become members of APEC as they become members of ASEAN? How would you define the issue of APEC membership?*

A. I think that is a good question. I have all along been cautious about indefinite extension of APEC membership. I have my memories of ECAFE and ESCAP, especially when the organization became too large, with its ever-larger membership and an ever-larger bureaucracy and politicization. I would like to avoid rigid institutionalization of APEC.

From that point of view, I would prefer to see ASEAN not going out to recruit more members. When I was in Singapore the other day this question came up, and I said, "Why do you have to have Vietnam and Myanmar in ASEAN?". They said it is simply a symbolic issue. The Association of Southeast Asian Nations cannot really exclude any Southeast Asian nation, and Vietnam, Cambodia, Laos, and Myanamar think of themselves as Southeast Asian. That seems to me an acceptable argument, but I don't see why it should be extended beyond Southeast Asia to any countries in America, to Russia or to wherever.

The issue really relates to the concept of APEC. If APEC is nothing more than an association of countries which individually pledge themselves to liberalize their trade and cooperate in all sorts of dialogues about harmonization of standards and investment codes, then it really doesn't matter how many nations are its members. It only becomes a problem if APEC is institutionalized with its Secretariat, with more and more member-countries sending their public servants to serve there, more and more prime ministers and other ministers meeting all the time - that's the sort of thing I would like to avoid.

Returning to the Miami Conference, it seems to me that any increase in U.S.

emphasis on the Americas' hemispheric free trade area arrangements is bound to encourage parallel moves elsewhere in the world. There is always a danger that the Japanese or others will say if that is the way the Americans play the game, well we will play it too. That is why I am very unhappy about the principle about the American emphasis on discriminatory free trade area arrangements in North America or in the American hemisphere. Even if one concedes that the trade creation effects may possibly outweigh the trade diversion effects in this case, I think there is a danger of self-contained blocs with discriminatory arrangements.

Q. *Expansion of ASEAN membership in Southeast Asia fits into the description of what I have called a map-of-the-world view of a region. The EU in Western Europe is also following the map. A map-of-the-world view of an economic regionalization plan covers all nations who belong to the region. Does that argument have any merit?*

A. As I said before, if all that APEC membership means is an association of countries pledging themselves to the common objective of non-discriminatory trade liberalization within the GATT framework of a global free trade system following the Uruguay Round of trade neogotiations, the issue of expanded membership in an APEC regional group is simple. The problem only arrives once institutionalization or substantial institutionalization of APEC takes place. Dialogue probably works better among regional neighbors who understand each other. I wouldn't want to invite Mauritania, Mali, Kenya or Albania to become members of APEC. But within the Asia-Pacific region the issue should certainly remain open.

Q. *The Australia-New Zealand Closer Economic Relations Act presents a unique case of economic regionalization in the South Pacific and it is very much integrated. Is this EU without union, without Brussels?*

A. Peter Lloyd has written a great deal on ANZ-CER. I understand it has gone a long way toward complete removal not only of border but also of non-border trade barriers.

Most non-border obstacles to trade relate to the notion that ANZ-CER could be in some way linked with ASEAN or some other free trade area. This is based on false grounds because the exemption of the LDCs from the GATT ban on free trade areas does not apply to developed countries. Therefore, the ANZ-CER could not get consistently linked with ASEAN or with any other free trade area, as I understand it.

Also, there is very little in the way of external trade barriers in ANZ-CER compared with the degree of protectionism that the European Union has towards non-members of EU. Australia and New Zealand have liberalized trade. There are, of course, a few barriers, but effective restrictions for New

Zealand trade has come down remarkably. Although it is technically discriminatory against outsiders, in reality the degree of discrimination is very small and it is expected to be further dismantled. So, from that point of view, it is a case of less-objectionable discriminatory trade arrangements.

Q. *I have argued that monetary-fiscal policy coordination is a key to the success of an effective free trade regime. How does it work in the context of ANZ-CER?*

A. To the best of my understanding, the monetary-fiscal policy of New Zealand very much follows the standard textbook lines. Indeed, the New Zealanders have been more adventurous, for example, keeping the inflation rate down to 2 per cent is very much the core of its monetary policy. If inflation goes over 2 per cent, the governor of the central bank is dismissed. This puts enormous pressure on him to pursue very rigorously anti-inflationary money management policy. They have greatly liberalized trade and the domestic market.

In all sorts of ways, they have carried out reforms which in Australia have been politically impracticable because the government in Australia is very much subject to pressure by the Australian trade unions. The unions are much weaker in New Zealand. I think there is a difference. Even though they might be on the telephone to each other, I don't think they would come out with the same conclusion.

Q. *How do you respond to the concept of a GATT-consistent free trade area or an economic union?*

A. I believe that APEC is defined in the EPG Report (not the Bergsten version) as consistent in a way with the GATT arrangement and the WTO, following the Uruguay Round negotiations. I think, neither AFTA in Southeast Asia, nor NAFTA in North America would be in that position. It is because GATT allows discriminatory arrangements if they are a part of a move towards a common market.

Q. *Let us return to macroeconomic coordination. If we have a disciplined government as in New Zealand, firmly committed to 2 per cent inflation rate a year, or 3 per cent, with 3 per cent annual growth, leaving the rest of all economic activities to microeconomic actors - households, corporate firms and businessmen - it would indeed be a better and stable economic framework. Would you reject that because it involves greater institutionalization?*

A. First of all, the notion that governments leave decisions to microeconomic actors - households and business firms - is grotesquely unrealistic. Governments all over the world have thousands of pages of regulations which regulate and interfere with microeconomic decision making at the business or household levels. They are responsible for hundreds of regulations for all sorts of purposes - environmental, social order, safety, health and so on.

In Australia we have innumerable commissions controlling business behavior. Individually looked at, much of it is supportable, and the causes are laudable. Taken together, there is an absolutely enormous bureaucratic regulation of the economy.

During the last ten years, it was in some degree deregulated. Freeing businesses from border control by import restrictions and foreign exchange control and banking legislation were valuable accomplishments. Interest rates have also been freed. But it is unrealistic to think of micro decisions being left wholly to individual actors. Governments regulate much of their activity.

In general, there is a case for macroeconomic coordination. Leaving that aside, there is a case for member-countries of APEC to pay attention to microeconomic coordination. The issue resolves essentially into whether a member-country should try to eliminate imbalances by domestic policy measures and coordinated fiscal-monetary policy, or should leave it to the market to ensure necessary adjustments. If each member-country runs its own monetary-fiscal policy, then the case for flexible exchange rates will prevail.

On the other hand, if you have a situation where a flexible exchange rate won't overcome the problem of macroeconomic imbalances, then you move towards the EU-type approach of trying to get countries to coordinate their macroeconomic policies and to have a single currency. This would completely eliminate the flexible exchange rate adjustment mechanism. In Western Europe, several countries which have strong trade unions and all sorts of obstacles to growth, failed to maintain their currency rate to the European Currency Unit, which is tied to the Deutschmark. In 1992, Britain, Italy and France delinked their respective currencies from the ECU. The problem may be the same in any other regional common currency arrangement. In addition, there are political obstacles for sovereign member-countries in a regional grouping, each proud of its independent currency.

Q. *I accept that. I do not advocate any form of replication of the European Monetary System or currency integration in APEC. How about an APEC program toward developing a common intra-APEC agenda for environment, energy, harmonization and standardization of products, rules of origin. The APEC Secretariat in Singapore is ready to compile and publish customs rules of all 18 member-countries so that their harmonization will become possible.*

A. The APEC Secretariat in Singapore is working on the harmonization of standards. Harmonization of customs procedures will involve different regulations at the micro level developed by governments in different member-countries and will facilitate intra-APEC free trade. It has nothing to do with macroeconomic policy coordination. Therefore, the standardization of rules governing resource allocation is quite distinct from and different from the issues which are involved in macroeconomic, fiscal and monetary policy, and exchange rate policy. Let APEC move quite far in their various programs towards eliminating non-border obstacles and resistances to trade, arising from these different regulations of one kind or another, of course, without prejudice towards one or another member-country.

Q. *Will environmental policy coordination by APEC with its diverse membership involve a good deal of activity with much impact on monetary and fiscal policies of various governments? Will it be the same for energy policy coordination for APEC?*

A. APEC coordination of environmental and energy policies will have nothing to do with macroeconomics. Let each government decide its program for environmental protection. That is a decision of resource allocation. Pareto optimality is not the only criterion for microeconomic resource allocation.

Environmental conservation is a constraint. It is the same as control of the pharmaceutical industry because certain drugs are prohibited. It all concerns microeconomics, not macroeconomics. Macroeconomics is concerned with the level of national income, money supply and exchange rates. Where macroeconomic and microeconomic decisions begin to overlap is in budget policy.

Q. *How about the APEC Summit in Bogor calling for regular meetings of finance ministers of its member-countries?*

A. It is my impression that no member-country in APEC is enthusiastic about monetary-fiscal policy coordination as the EU is doing in Brussels. I don't really think that macroeconomic coordination is a very important issue for promotion and facilitation of trade. Let us take the case of Australia's trade with Japan. Japan buys Australian primary products: wool, fuel, food and so on, and Australia imports machinery and equipment from Japan. There is a bilateral trade imbalance. The triangular balance of payments of Japan with Australia, the U.S. with Japan and the U.S. with Australia presents a different picture. The overall global balance is the issue. The capital accounts of each country will also have to be taken into consideration. If any country, in a balance of payments crisis, unilaterally impose exchange control, then, of course, it would seriously hamper trade. It is unlikely that Australia or the United States would get into that sort of situation.

In certain situations, such as a very high rate of inflation, things can go wrong. Equally, if a member-government adopts a budgetary policy which results in a very large budget deficit, there will certainly be a problem. Such specific cases will cause exchange rate imbalances and hurt trade. If a member-country has a high unemployment rate, its policy of free trade may be derailed. The political pressure from protectionist demands at home will halt trade liberalization, even though to blame trade liberalization for unemployment is totally wrong economics.

Each country should try and aim at internal balance - full employment without inflation - and must avoid either a high rate of unemployment or underemployment and inflation. Any severe departure from internal balance in either direction is liable to hinder trade. I hope that at the APEC finance ministers' meetings, each of them would support domestic macroeconomic policies which would have the goal of full employment without inflation.

Q. *Will you support specific members being excused from APEC membership, at least for a period, if they could not adopt the macroeconomic goals as you state. The EU has a provision for such leave of absence from its membership.*

A. That is not the way I look at it at all. APEC should have no conditional membership. Any country is welcome to join APEC only if they accept the objectives.

Q. *Australia has developed successful economic dialogues with Japan, the United States, and also with China. The Australian leadership is firmly established to enhance its economic ties with Southeast Asia. How about India and other South Asian countries?*

A. Ross Garnaut, particularly, has been very optimistic about the opening in India. The Australian National University has already decided to set up the South Asian Economic Research Unit. There are trade development opportunities for Australia in India and other South Asian countries. Ross Garnaut argues that the world economies will benefit if the South Asian economy becomes less inward-looking. In his view, China took off like this, and India will take off ten years later in the same way. Personally, I am not quite sure of this.

Professor of Economics (Emeritus), The Australian National University. This conversation was taped on December 8, 1994 in Canberra, Australia.

19 A Conversation with ROSS GARNAUT

Q. *I would like to make use of our limited time for a discussion on the Miami Initiative - the recent conference of all nations in the North and South Americas (except Cuba), hosted by the United States in Miami, with an agenda for the Americas' hemispheric free trade area. It comes soon after the APEC Summit in Bogor, Indonesia in November 1994. How do you think it is going to impact on Asia-Pacific Economic Cooperation?*
A. Well, I see the economic regional game in the Americas as a "little league" and in the Asian-Pacific as a "big league" - all in the World Series. The game here is the big league because the world's strongest and dynamic regions, especially in the twenty-first century, are going to be in the Asian-Pacific region. The United States is in the process of making a decision whether it is a player in the little league or the big league in the World Series. There is some feeling within the United States at the moment that economic integration with Latin America is more comfortable than with East Asia - there is less competitive threat, less competitive pressure, and with Latin America there is less political disagreement and fewer differences of political values within the United States.

There is no reason in principle why there should be a conflict between the two paradigms - U.S. integration along the Americas and U.S. integration across the Pacific - especially if the guiding idea of Asia-Pacific Economic Cooperation is open regionalism. Economic regionalism as in the North American Free Trade Area in North America is not "open" as is always the case for a free trade area. The idea of the Americas' hemispheric free trade area at the moment may also be one of closed regionalism. FTAs negotiate internal free trade within the region while maintaining barriers against the rest of the world. The European Union is a case of closed regionalism, as is NAFTA.

Following the Miami Initiative, the United States' policy will probably be to extend the same idea throughout the American hemisphere. If that happens, all the countries in the North and South Americas will in effect enter NAFTA. It must be noted there is some kind of thought current about open regionalism in Latin America. Chile, for example, has committed itself to unilateral trade liberalization and thus demonstrates a clear understanding of the idea of open regionalism. If open regionalism is the guiding idea of APEC, then following the Bogor Declaration (as I argued in my presentation before the Bogor

Summit), each APEC country must set about attaining the goal of reaching free trade by the year 2020. No advance attempt to negotiate schedules of movement swiftly to free trade, as one will need in the case of discriminatory trade liberalization, will be in order.

The open regionalism route without any discrimination does not need to meet the conditions of Article 24. Each APEC member-country can get on with its job of trade liberalization as per the target date of the Bogor Declaration, that is, the year 2020. Some of the APEC member-countries can be members of other free trade areas that do discriminate against non-member-countries. That certainly introduces a bit of a problem of rules of origin, but the existence of APEC itself does not get any more complicated. So as long as APEC countries strictly accept the idea of open regionalism in developing their free trade agenda, there is no conflict. On the other hand, if the United States was entering into a Pan-American free trade area extending NAFTA to one country, then another, then another in the American hemisphere to negotiate any such extensions, APEC member-countries must get involved together. Japan, China, Indonesia and Australia would have to take a close interest in the details to be negotiated between the United States and Brazil. At the same time, if the U.S. is seeking to set up a free trade area in the Asia-Pacific, as per Article 24 of GATT/WTO, there would be all sorts of conflicts.

Q. *Suppose in the APEC Summit in Osaka in 1995 or in Manila in 1996, the United States proposes that all the American hemispheric FTA member-countries be admitted to APEC membership. How would Australia vote? How would you advise Australia to vote?*

A. That would only be a problem if the basic idea of economic regionalism, upon which the Bogor Declaration was moved forward, had not been clarified before that time. It would be a very big problem if there was still dispute about whether APEC trade liberalization was going to be discrimatory under Article 24 of the GATT/World Trade Organization, or whether it was to be genuinely open with each member-country committing itself to be a free trade country by the year 2020. If this issue remained open, then bringing in all of the Latin American countries that were already committed towards discriminatory free trade areas in the Americas' FTA would be incompatible with the idea of open regionalism - an idea dominant in the Western Pacific which would increase the scope of discriminatory regionalism. On the other hand, if in the next few months it becomes clear that the guiding idea for implementation of the Bogor Declaration is open regionalism with full non-discrimination and no attempt to negotiate the Article 24 agreement, and if the Latin American countries would have accepted that along with North America, then it could be quite helpful towards liberalization of global trade.

But I guess it is not likely that those two things could happen so soon. It is possible that the resolution in favor of geniune open regionalism in APEC and the United States' plan to bring all countries of the Americas in APEC, will be two parallel developments. The extension of NAFTA-type arrangements throughout the Americas alongside the implementation of the Bogor Declaration consistently with the Western Pacific ideas of open regionalism can, however, progress at the same time.

Q. *The process of Americanization of America, which according to some began with NAFTA in 1994, may be accelerated by the Miami Initiative, as has been suggested by some political scientists. How do you see it?*

A. That is certainly a possibility. If discriminatory, NAFTA-style regionalism is the guiding idea of Pan-American free trade integration as it probably will be, and if the development of the new Americas' hemispheric free trade area adds to discrimination against Asian countries and Western Pacific countries, then there is no doubt that it will add to Pan-Asian political sentiment. Indeed, it has grown quite a lot over the past couple of years.

It was motivated first by some very clumsy handling by the new Clinton administration of trans-Pacific relations tensions with regard to issues such as ozone and the environment, labor and human resources, and its link to the free trade regime. The tensions with China, especially with respect to decoupling of human rights issues from trade arrangments, created much pressure. The continued tensions with Japan regarding trade arrangement of various kinds may have fueled the growth of Pan-Asian sentiment. Through 1994, the U.S. administration has become much more adept at handling the situations. I think that it managed relations with Japan, China and ASEAN much better and that has been helpful. I think that it was a big factor for the East Asian Economic Caucus to consider, leading up to the Bogor Declaration.

A great deal of communication among the influential persons in the United States and in ASEAN countries, especially Indonesia and Malaysa, also in Japan and China, successfully followed. Without there being a formal East Asian economic caucus, those communications were important in shaping the Bogor Declaration and the compromises (and in ways some very crude compromises) that became part of the EPG Report.

The report was unanimously adopted by the heads of the 18 member-countries at the APEC Summit in Bogor, November 1994. No wonder the Bogor Summit was a great success!

Q. *What shouldAustralia's role be in this discussion? What will Australia's position be in case this debate becomes divisive?*

A. I think that Australia's credentials in this discussion are derived from the fact that Australia has been extensively involved in developing and strengthening its economic relationships with the East Asian countries - Japan, Southeast Asia and China. As such, Australia will foreseeably be able to play a positive and cohesive role.

Professor of Economics, The Australian National University. This conversation was taped on December 6, 1994 in Canberra, Australia.

20 A Conversation with PETER DRYSDALE

Q. *Do you think that the Miami Initiative, that is, the conference in Miami of all nations in the North and South Americas (excepting Cuba), hosted by the United States, and the proposal for the Americas' hemispheric free trade area, will have an impact on APEC?*

A. I think that the Miami Initiative of December 1994 is a continuation of the United States' policy of encouraging economic liberalization in North America, and of broadening it towards the American hemisphere. The political objectives of the United States in the Americas is consistent with that. It is important in that context, but I do not think that it will have a powerful impact on what is going on in the Asia-Pacific, especially in the context of APEC. If anything, it is reinforcing the agenda of trade liberalization, adopted at the APEC Summit at Bogor in November 1994.

The Miami Conference points to, some might argue, an economic initiative that would lead to a redirection of North American attention to the creation of a broader hemispheric American free trade area. I think that is most unlikely. First of all, in the Americas, especially in Latin America, there are a number of countries not automatically fitting into the same framework of commitment to liberalization that there was in Mexico when it became a member of the North American Free Trade Area. Even in Chile, the most likely candidate to join NAFTA, there are serious reservations about formal membership in NAFTA. The reservations incidentally have to do with the constraints that membership of NAFTA would put on Chile in terms of its dealings with other countries. The constraints include how to deal with rules of origin with respect to investments in Chile and other matters as well. Of course from the United States' perspective there are constraints, too. It is unlikely that the United State' Congress would readily and immediately take on a significant extension of NAFTA. From the viewpoint of political feasibility, the stream of thinking that suggests that the Miami Initiative signals the beginning of a giant hemispheric American free trade area which would conflict with the Asia-Pacific Economic Cooperation fails to convince me.

On the other hand, the Miami Initiative is important from the perspective of encouraging the thrust of liberalization in the Americas, and that is quite consistent with what people are trying to do in Asia-Pacific. As I said at the beginning, the two initiatives can be mutually reinforcing. Indeed, one hopes that the commitments made in Bogor, a few weeks ago in November, to liberalize trade and investment flows in Asia-Pacific will reinforce the interest in liberalization in the Americas as well, and set the context in which NAFTA will develop in the longer term. I hope that the efforts in Asia-Pacific and in the Americas will complement each other in a similar context to that in which the European Community developed in the 1960s and 1970s; one in which there was a more general effort at global liberalization alongside the efforts in Western Europe toward intraregional liberalization.

Q. *Others do not share your more positive view of the Miami Initiative and express concern that it has been ill-timed and may encourage misunderstanding in the Asia-Pacific, even give a boost to the Malaysian initiative for the East Asian Economic Caucus. Any comment?*

A. I can understand that politically there are sensitivities about the Miami Initiative alongside what is going on in Asia-Pacific. A close evaluation of the substantive issues involved is in order. I think that there is a very realistic view in the capitals of East Asia about what Miami involves, and in my view there is nothing that will challenge the efforts in Asia-Pacific in any significant way. I think from the viewpoint of the U.S. interest in the Americas, it is important for the United States to continue to work in support of liberalization in the Americas and the Miami conference is a step in that process. There is no reason to be unduly nervous. A consistent undertaking for economic liberalization must be the goal for all member-countries in APEC, and also for all other non-APEC countries in the Americas.

Q. *How would you reconcile between the two views - Australia, Japan and Indonesia on one side, and the United States on the other side - regarding open regionalism and APEC free trade agenda only with reciprocity?*

A. Whether it is in Australia, Indonesia, Japan or North America, people have characterized a particular approach in many different ways. Is there a North American approach as such? Indeed, there are many streams of thinking in North America about this issue, even within the U.S. administration. It is the first false assumption that people in other countries make about what the American approach toward a specific issue is. I just attended a meeting in Tokyo in which the American Embassy representative denied what some have described as the North American approach. The importance of moving towards a free trade regime in the Asia-Pacific area is what is accepted. Certainly officials in North America do not see there being any fixed position as to its operational details. To begin with, a quick generalization of the American approach as to regional economic integration in the Asia-Pacific is not helpful. I would not like to characterize one particular approach as being the North American approach, or one particular approach as being an Australian approach or a Japanese approach. It is more complicated than that. However, there are different approaches, so let me distinguish between the two approaches that I think you have indicated.

One approach indeed reinforces what has been going on, at least in the Western Pacific. It permits negotiations for trade liberalization supported by unilateral reduction of trade barriers, tariff and other non-tariff measures on an open basis or on a multilateral basis. An alternative approach favors the creation of a specific "reciprocity" condition in a free trade area. I think the latter approach would be disastrous for Asia-Pacific Economic Cooperation for both economic and political reasons.

The approach based on specific reciprocity cannot be successful because of the limitations it will impose on overall trade development. A free trade area with reciprocity will not be consistent with its commitments to GATT/World Trade Organization, especially Article 24, at least not in the foreseeable future. The idea that the People's Republic of China could commit within the next 10 to 15 years to obligations under the WTO charter, consistent with Article 24, in a free trade arrangement with the United States, Australia or Japan is very unrealistic. By implication, China would have to be excluded from this arrangement in some way. China would have to become an outsider in its own region and China is not the only country involved. On the other side, as I said in respect of the United States and Latin America, the same applies to the United States and East Asia. Is it possible in this timeframe to think of the U.S. Congress voting for a free trade area even with Japan? So there is a feasibility problem. In terms of fulfillment, the reciprocity approach is neither feasible nor sensible.

I also think of the broader Asia-Pacific geographic region as more important. Of course, if we think about the nature of the region and its relationship with its partners within APEC and outside APEC, we have to think about India. India is committing to a significant process of liberalization. India is on the edge of the region, and I believe that the APEC policy should be to encourage its member-countries to engage more and more with India and other countries on the edge. No wrong signal should be sent to India. Setting up a free trade area in the Asia-Pacific exclusive of India will not be helpful toward promoting broader regional trade development. I say resoundingly "no" to any arrangement for trade liberalization conditional on reciprocity.

Even Russia, based on the principles of commitment to a free system with all the difficulties involved and its consequent political effects, is looking more and more to East Asia. The events in Russia and its emerging economic ties with China in the last couple of years have been spectacular. One must note also the growing trade and economic association between Korea and the Russian republics. In the next ten years huge economic potential in the development of gas and energy supplies from Siberia supplying Korea, China and Japan could become a reality. Russia will need to integrate with East Asia.

A reciprocity approach that limits trade concessions to APEC member-countries only will keep out very big economies on the edge of East Asia, especially at this particular time in world history. I think it would be damaging to the economic interests of Asia-Pacific countries. It will also hurt the political interests of APEC member-countries.

The approach which recommends itself for the Asia-Pacific economies is to press ahead with commitment first of all to trade liberalization over the next several years in the context of open regionalism, at once fulfilling all commitments under the Uruguay Round trade negotiations and the WTO charter, and then through that process to accelerate those commitments to countries on the edge of the Asia-Pacific region without reciprocity.

The United States and Japan will be expected to play their specific roles. For Japan to take a lead in pushing ahead a bit further will be helpful, especially with the deregulation of areas that were not negotiated within the Bogor Declaration. Then, in four or five years' time when they have implemented the first round of liberalization, it should be possible to form an Asia-Pacific coalition within the WTO to push forward with a new round of negotiations, a very different round, relevant to the time, and of course, supportive of the WTO multilateral system.

In my view, there is a way forward which does not need to limit choices to the two specific approaches. APEC needs to press ahead with priority attached to the multilateral system because that priority is so important to the East Asian economies; especially if one is coming from behind, still at the early stage of economic takeoff. The principal problem for newly developing countries entering world markets in a big way for the first time is the one of their being discriminated against as new entrants to the market. Protection against the principle of non-discrimination is a priority for all of these countries in this part of the world.

Q. *To many, the biggest problem is clarifying what APEC stands for. How do you view APEC?*

A. In my view APEC is an open forum, a forum of its member-countries open towards non-members. However, APEC provides a necessary forum because we need collective presence in the international political process to support specific initiatives. The Allies did so to support the Atlantic Charter during the war years, and again for the important work of recovery and reconstruction after the war. We need APEC for the Asia-Pacific countries like we needed the Atlantic Charter at that time.

The Atlantic Charter in its principles was open even for the so-called vanquished countries. In fact, that is why Australia got into a close economic relationship with Japan - because of our commitments during the wartime to accede to U.S. pressures to treat Japan equally after the war, as we would treat the United States or Great Britain. These international associations do play their role. They have political importance as coalitions have political importance within a nation. They provide a political confidence in doing the right thing with respect to economic policy. So my view is that it is naive to think that political associations of the kind that APEC represents are not important. They provide a critical reference point in getting the policy directions right and encouraging all the efforts that have to be made at the various levels of government and business to get things moved in the right direction.

Q. *Can any government really do whatever the international or a multinational coalition's directives require it to do without looking at employment, inflation and economic growth at home?*

A. Of course, the APEC Declaration as a reference point of a multinational coalition will have different impacts on the domestic political economy of member-nations. The process works and reinforces the commitments as various member-countries successfully take up management of an agenda jointly agreed upon. The Bogor Declaration was kicked off and became deeply entrenched in Australia. It is important as a reference point. People keep reminding the prime minister that a commitment to fully liberalize trade in the year 2010 has been affirmed and that there are still some problems to resolve. The Bogor Declaration will provide discipline in the political process, and certainly if the Australians keep arguing within that framework, it will keep the pressure on to achieve what Australia has promised to achieve. The process should work in the same way in other countries.

What about Japan? Japan has a huge problem of economic liberalization, which is important nationally as well as internationally. In 1995, Japan is in the chair managing APEC. To liberalize its economy will involve a huge political pressure in Japan. Indonesia has made a commitment for liberalization and its political process will be pressed to act accordingly. It does make a difference to have China on board and in China the process of economic liberalization will have to be worked out. It makes China less liable to retreat from the reform process. Earlier in 1994, China was inclined to halt the process. Now that APEC members are reasserting that China must remain a part of this process, it reinforces China's commitment, and also provides a basis for China's accommodation within the WTO.

I think it is naive to think that these reference points do not have importance. The leaders of APEC member-countries came to the Summit in Bogor with a commitment; they affirmed the process seriously. It followed a lot of argument and deep discussion within their respective governments about what it all meant and how it should be approached. I believe that they adopted the Bogor Declaration in good faith. The debates and discussions that will follow the summit in each of their countries will be influenced by it.

The process will move forward. It will not be perfect. At times, it will be messy. From time to time, there will be an inclination to retreat, to go back. Of course, following the initiation of the process and its goals, the provision for a periodic review mechanism will have to be instituted. Sometimes it will work more quickly, sometimes more slowly.

Q. *The Bogor Declaration has placed much focus on issues such as standardization and harmonization, rules of origin, human resource development, environment. It has given much less attention to macroeconomic coordination. Would you have some specific comments? In most national capitals of various APEC member-countries, including Beijing and Canberra, in the course of my study tour over the past several weeks I have had occasions to discuss APEC with government officials with APEC assignments. These officials come from the ministries of energy, environment, education, human resources and treasury/finance of their respective governments. I also had meetings with ranking officials at the APEC Secretariat in Singapore, working on diverse assignments. Their jobs are off-budget, as they are paid by their respective home governments, not from an APEC budget.*

A. I think it all takes place in the way you define, not in the old-fashioned sense of coordination of macroeconomic policy, financial policy, monetary policy, fiscal policy and so on. The focus immediately is on microeconomic goals of liberalization. The probability is that there will eventually be more attention given to macroeconomic issues. The international monetary system has changed in a way that requires less-centralized institutional management. In addition to the U.S. dollar and the Japanese yen, other currencies of APEC member-countries will become more and more important in transactions.

I think in that sense (that you just described), there will be more policy coordination on a macro level. That is why in the Bogor Declaration, the finance ministers, for example, were encouraged to get together. Particularly in respect to financial matters, there will be a great deal more interest in the way policies are developed and coordinated within APEC. The Japanese administration will resist it to some extent because they are rather conservative about financial market changes. Developments in the financial market in Japan and the role of Japanese financial institutions will eventually encourage a stronger interest from Japan in these affairs.

I think that the degree of policy coordination and harmonization will progress over time. However, it is going to be a steady process, not imposed from above by a supranational authority, formally constituted by APEC member-countries, but developed by consent among member-countries. Coordination of policies will come by itself, through consultation, and the member-countries will settle on common approaches, independent of any direction from a centralized authority. I think some coordination is happening and it will continue to happen.

In a sense, the process of coordination is working much more on the trade policy front. Despite the tensions about particular approaches in recent years, the process of APEC development thus far has been one in which there has been a steady convergence on policy priorities. By and large, the consensus has been built around the open multilateral system. Successful industrialization efforts of the East Asian newly developing countries recommend the priority attached to open multilateral trade liberalization. In the Pacific, there is little support for an old-fashioned free trade area; there is strong support for open regionalism.

For the APEC Secretariat in Singapore, its present scale and form of operation will be acceptable. If it develops in Singapore, it would not be so much of a problem. If it were in Japan, there would be all sorts of anxiety. If it were in the United States or in China, it would be difficult. The APEC Secretariat will certainly play its role. First of all, it should be multi-centered in terms of carrying particular policy interests. A centralized attempt to manage all policy interests will be disastrous. In its present form, the officials consult member-countries and initiate the process of policy development. Countries with a big interest in minerals, countries with an interest in telecommunications, countries with concern in macroeconomic policy coordination or whatever, are free to take initiatives in policy development and assist the evolution of policy convergence.

It is important to note that the structure of the economies in the Pacific is quite different from that of economies in Western Europe, political asymmetries and economic asymmetries are large. The European Union has more coordination and a more centralized secretariat. The situation in the Pacific, on the other hand, recommends more open economic cooperation and small headquarters.

Q. *Do you see that in the APEC process the big countries with its superior economic power will dominate the smaller partners?*

A. I think the evidence so far suggests that is unlikely. APEC member-countries, big and small, have been pretty sensible. This has been so because of the three key principles of the Asia-Pacific economic cooperation. First, the APEC process has to be a step by step approach. Second, the process has to be open. This concept of openness is crucial. It relates to the economic and diplomatic importance of openness within the region and towards the rest of the world. The openness is the centerpiece of the approach to all trade and economic policy discussions. Third and finally, the APEC process must involve equality and, of course, equality in this case means giving equal importance to the smaller partners and the larger partners in the management of the process.

These three key principles require working by consensus and preempt domination by the big partners. That is why it is so important to keep smaller partners on board in the process. Malaysia is particularly important in this context. Prime Minister Mahathir of Malaysia, I think, has a lot on his side in this respect. So I say that the principle of equality has to be respected and has to govern the whole APEC process.

Q. *How about telling me what specific two or three things you would like APEC to do in the near future? What has been the worst disappointment so far for you, if any?*

A. The first thing is that the momentum has to be maintained if the whole process is to be credible. If Japan's relevance to the process is to be credible, the Osaka Summit in 1995 which Japan will chair must build upon the momentum of the Bogor Summit in 1994. So that means new steps have to be taken towards implementation of the three dimensions of the APEC process.

The first dimension of the APEC process is technical cooperation, in reality, development cooperation. The North Americans do not like to call it development cooperation because development cooperation sounds like foreign aid, which it is to some extent. It is fundamental for this region that the development and technical cooperation aspect involves enhancing the transfer of capacities within the region, of non-human physical resources, and of human resources and human capital. Second, in my view, the trade facilitation agenda is in the longer term a much more important dimension than the trade liberalization agenda, especially for the newly developing countries in the region, more so for some other countries which are coming from further behind, like China and even Indonesia. Third, there is the trade liberalization agenda. Those three dimensions are linked together; they have to be related together. There has to be progress on all three fronts simultaneously. Credible advances will have to be distinguished from the bold vision. As to how to deliver some concrete achievements, given the APEC vision, there are a number of ways. First of all, Japan will have to indicate its sincerity by independently declaring some accelerated commitments to deregulation and liberalization. Secondly, I think all APEC members, especially those who have been involved in the Uruguay Round actively as well as those who have not had to declare and document their commitment to liberalization under the Round, must seek to identify areas where they can accelerate the process of liberalization. If the United States can implement the Round by the year 2000, it will be a big step forward. Indeed, it will make a lot of difference.

Beyond that, the APEC Summit in Osaka in 1995 could set up a process whereby APEC members can independently monitor their progress towards liberalization commitments. Australia has a process through its Industry Commission which measures as accurately as possible progress on liberalization and deregulation. Each APEC country should commit to some such process and monitor each other as to the record of mutual accomplishments. Member-countries should compare notes and then as I said, the three key dimensions will have to be woven together. That sets the stage for the formation of an APEC coalition within the multilateral system. The trade liberalization measures can be undertaken consistently with the APEC commitments; consistently with our unilateral liberalization without discriminating against anyone inside or outside the APEC membership region. Later on towards the end of this decade when the time is appropriate, then we can start to think about laying this on the table and have an Asia-Pacific Round within the WTO.

We are still in the process of community building. I think that the Japanese should be looking towards having some collective development cooperation initiative of importance to the region. Maybe it will have to do with analyzing environmental issues which flow from East Asian industrialization. Some commitment to a collective development cooperation initiative would be a sensible companion to the Osaka Summit agenda.

I think the Japanese can do that because the consensus points in that direction. If they do these things, they will have done a marvelous job. So I wish them lots of luck. I think there is a lot of goodwill and a lot support for developments in this direction. I am very positive about the nature of the commitments of the Japanese administration to the Bogor Declaration.

I do not have any major problem and I have no disappointment so far.

Professor of Economics, Australia-Japan Research Center, The Australian National University. This conversation was taped on December 9, 1994 in Canberra, Australia.

21 A Conversation with MOHAMED ARIFF

Q. *The APEC Bogor Summit in 1994 was a great success. How would you describe APEC in your own way?*

A. APEC had its turning point in Seattle in 1993. For the first time at Seattle, the meeting of the Heads of APEC member-countries was called a summit. Now the annual APEC summit appears to have become an institution. Four more annual summits - Osaka, Canada, Manila, Kuala Lumpur - in 1996, 1997, 1998 and 1999, respectively, have been scheduled. APEC is no longer a loosely structured informal grouping. It is now a formally structured institution, a formal intraregional organization.

In the past, APEC was considered simply a forum where issues of common interest were discussed and its decisions were not binding. Since Seattle, 1993 at annual APEC summits, participation by the Heads of its member-states has contributed to its much higher institutional visibility.

Personally, I'm all for APEC. The gravity of the world economy has been shifting from the Atlantic to the Pacific. The Pacific Basin has become the new dynamo of the world economy and all projections point to the fact that it will continue to be the center of growth in the twenty-first century. Clearly, U.S. economic activities within the Pacific continue to grow and have become a dominant share of its overall international trade and investment.

In that sense, APEC is simply a response to the market trends. The pace is being set by the market forces, not by the politicians. APEC, as a formal institutional forum, could facilitate the process. Governments of the APEC member-countries can expedite this process by initiating speedy disbanding of all barriers to intra-APEC trade flows. The business corporations in its member-countries could interact much more freely and the market forces could further invigorate continued economic growth of the region.

The proposal for an APEC free trade area, however, bothers me, because it goes oddly against the trend, especially in East Asia. East Asian economies are growing and they have benefited immensely from the globally open economic system. It is in their interest to make sure that the world economy is in no way divided into regional trade areas or trade blocs. Now to the extent APEC strengthens the global free trade system within GATT, now the WTO, it must be welcome.

In fact, APEC has already done something positive in this regard. I also think that the APEC Seattle Summit in 1993 very much contributed to a successful conclusion of the Uruguay Round of GATT negotiations. The World Trade Organization is the outcome.

Thus, APEC was very useful for the world trade system and we do hope that the APEC member-countries will now set an example for other countries in the world by expediting trade liberalization, maybe ahead of the WTO schedule. Rather than trying to create a free trade area of APEC, which I think is discriminatory, APEC should be a forceful forum for prompting global free trade.

I am not really sure what convinced the United States to propose the APEC free trade area. Many in East Asia suggest that the whole scheme is being sort of engineered by the United States; that the United States is using APEC for its self-interest; that the United States will have APEC as a leverage in its tug of war with the Western European economic community, the European Union. The EU is growing in strength not only in terms of an increasing number of members but also by deepening its integration process. In the event of an economic war between the United States and Western Europe, APEC will have to be a party to the confrontation.

The chances are that the United States will not be able to endure that kind of strife because the EU is quite powerful in terms of market size and economic productivity. In fact, Western Europe is a very important market for East Asian exports. Needless to add, East Asia enjoys an export market in the United States with its share of the market increasing. True, America is opening up in a big way.

In APEC, there is much talk of open regionalism, but do we really know exactly what it means? Does open regionalism mean that APEC will be really open in every sense of the word, with its membership open to every nation and privileges of APEC membership fairly extended to all? APEC membership is confined at the moment to 18 countries, could possibly increase to 22 to include all the preexisting countries (Vietnam, Laos, Cambodia and Mayanmar) in Southeast Asia.

The only way that APEC would be considered open is by allowing other countries to enjoy APEC privileges on a non-reciprocity basis. Arguments in support of my objection to the reciprocity approach are: first, reciprocity will be inconsistent with the goal of global free trade; second, it will hold the rest of the world at ransom, as it will deny access to intra-APEC free trade arrangements to any non-member-country which will not be able to reciprocate. Indeed, it is in the interest of APEC countries to open up their markets without reciprocity. Let non-APEC countries gain from APEC free trade action, and APEC countries will also gain from it.

Nonetheless, it must be noted that APEC has set up a timetable for intra-

APEC free trade by 2020. It is a quarter of a century - 25 years from 1994 - and within this time period, there will be several rounds of negotiations. It is just for political consumption that the timetable is so far away. Does it really matter in practical terms? The APEC Bogor Declaration also provides for a phased trade liberalization over 10-15-20 years, depending on the state of economic development of a member-country. I believe that a much more closely spaced timetable would be preferred. Indeed, the developed industrialized countries should have liberalized their trade forthwith without waiting for ten years until 2010. Why should it take 15 years for other APEC members who are newly industrialized and/or newly industrializing? I would hope for a much faster pace.

The work on harmonization and standardization of products traded and the rules of origin, as proposed in the APEC Bogor Declaration, will be a challenge, involving much paperwork for the bureaucracy. It may create a supranational bureaucracy which may act as a new barrier, too, since the private sector may resent the transaction cost of trade.

Q. *My own research shows that the APEC movement was not initiated by the United States, and that it was initiated by Japan and Australia in the 1960s. The United States joined about a decade later. I think that one important factor to take into consideration was what I call the push factor: economic regionalization in Western Europe, now the European Union. There is a natural process of economic regionalization. Any comment?*

A. I tend to disagree with you if you suggest that APEC is not a forum that the United States wanted. Historically, the process of economic regionalization in the Asia-Pacific might have begun much earlier, ten years ago, but it got its momentum only when the United States joined it and assumed leadership. Asia-Pacific economic cooperation with membership of economies in East Asia, Japan, Australia and New Zealand and United States and Canada was the initial design, and the United States in fact was its leader.

The United States joined APEC because it sees APEC as an important market and its APEC membership was in its economic self-interest. In addition, the United States found APEC to be a countereconomic grouping *vis-à-vis* the emergence of the EU in Western Europe. The Euro-centric economic regionalization was a challenge, as America perceived it. There is no need to replicate the EU in the Asia-Pacific region. I believe that economic integration was not the goal of what is going on in Western Europe. It is the end product. A lot of common history and common vision initiated the Western European initiative.

I am afraid that Western Europe as it continues to progress in its integration is going to miss its market share - trade and investment - in this part of the world. Any concept of a fortress Europe will cost Europe a great deal. APEC must target for the global free trade regime and design its program accordingly. APEC's open economic regionalism must be a motivation and challenge to the EU to pursue the same goal.

Q. *I don't believe that Europe will become a fortress, nor do I think that APEC is working to become one. Both the EU and APEC have a commitment to work within the WTO-consistent regime of global free trade. There is a growing recognition that traditional sovereign state-based national economies provide only a limited framework and as economies deepen by way of industrialization, they seek to widen activities in markets in the region. Will you consider economic regionalization is a natural process of interlinking of the forces of deepening and widening of economic dynamics?*

A. Okay, I got it. I need to make a distinction between regionalism and regionalization. Regionalization of independent national economies for interlinking of such processes will result in increased efficiency in production and add to economic welfare. Resources can flow more freely within the region and thus its member-economies become internationally competitive - much more competitive than before.

If APEC provides for this, it will be fine. APEC will have to make sure that the group does not really put up barriers against the rest of the world. Its agenda to liberalize trade must be very definitive. On the other hand, regionalism as such may involve closing the market to other countries who are not members of the regional group. Regionalism is an exercise in limiting free trade and must be rejected.

If APEC gives concessions to its members without erecting new barriers against the rest of the world, it is still discrimination even though no formal trade barriers will have been created. To the extent that APEC will limit its concessions to its members, the non-members will have a disadvantage. One option is to extend intra-APEC concessions to all non-members without reciprocity. Or, APEC will have one agenda for its membership and another for the rest of the world. I strongly favor the case for open regionalism.

Regionalism to me has a special connotation. Could the two concepts be compatible? To some extent Article 24 is being flaunted by America even when no regional grouping has been really subjected to the severe test of Article 24. Only in the case of open regionalism will there be compatibility.

Q. *Returning to the APEC Bogor Declaration, standardization of products traded and harmonization of tariff codes are the two issues the officials are working on in the national capitals of various APEC member-states. Will you add any more to what you briefly referred to on this score in your opening remarks?*

A. Let me begin with standardization. Standardization means that you are going to apply one kind of product standard for every APEC member-country. First, the process must provide for varying stages of economic development of member-countries. Then there will be a host of other issues. For example, a common environmental standard for all countries will be unfair. Imposing one standard for a very diverse group of economies will send the wrong message. each member-nation has its own priorities and standardization will have to be tailored to the same.

Harmonization is probably much more acceptable, at least for the political economic agenda.

Q. *The agenda of the APEC Osaka Summit in 1995 may have more focus on environment, energy and employment - the three Es. Will you please comment on the same?*

A. These are three important issues. Because of the happenings in the Middle East, energy is a crucial factor. It is one area where APEC could make a contribution. Availability of energy reserve in several APEC member-countries is well known and its exploration will help intraregional economic growth.

Employment for the present is an issue of concern for many countries with relatively high rates of unemployment, including Malaysia, Japan, Taiwan, Singapore, Korea as well as the United States. Special notice should be taken of the fact that there are large pockets of unemployment in richer economies. An APEC program to make optimum economic use of all available human resources will be good for all its member-countries.

An aspect of the issue relates to illegal immigration, as a result of labor movement from less-industrialized APEC member-countries with higher unemployment to others with relative labor shortage. Such labor flows create more problems than they solve. The issue has been responsible for unhelpful political debates in the Philippines, and also in Indonesia. It will be good if APEC develops a plan for intra-APEC flow of labor in a very orderly fashion for the mutual benefit of all APEC members.

Environment is equally important, too. APEC efforts to focus on the importance of environment and the environmental consequences of economic development must be welcome. Forest fires in one country quickly spread to its neighboring country and both economies suffer losses. Developing countries in this part of the world are beginning to appreciate the importance of environmental conservation - the quality of environment they are living in, the quality of air they are breathing, the quality of water they drink. However, the pressing demand for more immediate needs often limits the scope of substantive action in this regard. I think this clearly is an area where concerted

APEC initiative will be welcome.

Q. *Will you comment on the APEC Bogor Declaration urging the finance ministers of member-countries to convene regular meetings to help develop programs for macroeconomic coordination.*

A. The issue is important, but the task will be difficult. As APEC initiative progresses to more and more intraregional economic integration, the issues of macroeconomic coordination will increasingly receive more attention, with or without the meetings of the finance ministers.

APEC leadership in this regard will be useful only if the guidelines, as they may develop, will have carefully factored in the priorities of its member-countries at varying levels of economic development. We in Malaysia wonder if Japan and the United States, the two leading APEC members, will assume the responsibility that should be theirs. The domestic political considerations in the two countries may be limiting factors. Macroeconomic coordination may prove to be too difficult a task.

Professor of Economics, The University of Malaya. This conversation was taped on December 15, 1994 in Kuala Lumpur, Malaysia.

PART III

APEC: Organization and Agenda

22 APEC Organization

EMINENT PERSONS' GROUP (EPG)

In Part II, I have shared with the readers my extended conversations with the "Eminent Persons" of South Korea, the United States of America, Indonesia, the People's Republic of China, Singapore, Australia, Thailand and Malaysia. Earlier in 1994, I also had an occasion to exchange views on APEC with the EPG member of Japan (Yamazawa, 1994). I remain pointedly advised by each eminent person I have spoken with that he/she acts not as an official of the government of the specific member-country, but as a non-official advisor. In a different context, they would have been designated their home country's Ambassador to APEC. Or, the designation Advisor Plenipotentiary may appropriately describe the office. An international organization of 18 sovereign nation-state-based economies with a combined gross national product of U.S.$ 13.2 trillion in 1993, 56 per cent of the world's total GNP, and 46 per cent of the world's total merchandise trade, would certainly warrant a standing appointment of a group of high ranking advisors.

In 1992, APEC foreign ministers at their meeting in Bangkok, Thailand voted to set up an *independent, non-governmental* Eminent Persons' Group, with one eminent person from each member-country. Professional/scholarly eminence became the basis for an individual member's designation. These eminent persons, so appointed, resolutely maintained their independent, non-governmental status.

The EPG's assignment was to develop an agenda for APEC, and they completed their task by developing, *A Vision for APEC: Towards an Asia-Pacific Economic Community* (APEC, 1993). The tenure of the group was renewed and the EPG was asked to continue its work toward developing an APEC program and the EPG Report, *Achieving the APEC Vision: Free and Open Trade in the Asia-Pacific Region* (APEC, 1994). This report became the core of the 1994 Bogor Declaration at the Leaders' Summit. In 1995, APEC economic leaders at Bogor persuaded the group to further continue their work in 1995 for formulating recommendations toward accelerating intraregional cooperation. A careful review of the interrelationships between APEC and the subregional trade groups within APEC became a part of their 1995 assignment. The EPG report, *Implementing the APEC Vision* (APEC, 1995a) was ready for the Osaka Summit, November 1995; technically, the EPG then ceased to be functional.

THE LEADERS' SUMMIT: THE MINISTERIAL MEETINGS

Since its founding in 1989, the APEC organization has foreseeably evolved to its present pyramidal structure, with the taxpayers of the 18 APEC member-economies providing its base (see Table 22.1). It is important to note that APEC operates by *consensus*. In 1991, APEC members' commitment to the operational guideline of "open dialogue with equal respect for the views of all participants" was reaffirmed (APEC, 1991, 1995c, 1996).

The Leaders' Summit most certainly sits at the top of the pyramid. The summit was instituted in Seattle in 1993 with the President of the United States as the host, and heads of the member-economies attending. Next came annual summits in Bogor, Indonesia 1994, and Osaka, Japan 1995; to be followed by the Philippines in 1996, Canada in 1997, Malaysia in 1998 and New Zealand in 1999. Indeed, annual Leaders' Summits have become a very important feature of the APEC organization, giving the community intra-regional political empowerment with highest visibility.

The cabinet-level meetings of the foreign ministers of APEC member-countries, especially at their first meeting in Canberra, Australia in 1989, became the first step in APEC becoming institutionalized. Subsequently, their annual meetings were held in Singapore (1990); Seoul (1991); and Bangkok (1992). Since 1993, the foreign ministers have had their meetings along with, the annual Leaders' Summits and will foreseeably meet during the Leaders' Summits in the years ahead, as scheduled 1996-99.

The APEC Bogor Declaration made specific reference to finance ministers' annual meetings - they first met in Honolulu, March 1994, and then in Bali, April 1995. In addition, meetings of cabinet-level ministers of related programs - finance, trade, telecommunication and information, education, environment, human resource development, energy - have become a part of the APEC organization.

The Senior Officials' Meeting (SOM) features next in the APEC organization. These senior officials come from various government departments of the APEC member-countries. Their participation and the number of times they meet a year will vary very much, depending on the nature of the specific assignments.

For its efficient functioning, APEC established the Budget and Administrative Committee (BAC) in 1993. The BAC holds two regular meetings a year, and certainly fills a gap in the APEC organizational structure. In addition to the regular budgetary administrative duties, consideration of the formula for APEC members' contribution to the APEC Central Fund is a

Table 22.1 APEC organization

Leaders' Summit
Foreign Ministers' Meetings
Ministerial meetings
- Finance ministers
- Trade ministers
- Environment ministers
- Commerce and industry ministers
- Energy ministers
Senior Officials' Meetings (SOM)
Budget and Administrative Committee (BAC)
Economic Committee
Committee on Trade and Investment (CTI)
- Subcommittee on Standards and Conformance
- Subcommittee on Customs Procedures
Policy Level Group on Small and Medium Enterprises (PLG-SME)
Working Groups (ten as of 1996):
- Trade and Investment Data Review
- Trade Promotion
- Industrial Science and Technology
- Human Resource Development
- Regional Energy Cooperation
- Marine Resource Cooperation
- Telecommunication
- Transportation
- Tourism
- Fisheries
Secretariat
Eminent Persons' Group
Pacific Business Forum/ APEC Business Advisory Council

Source: Compilation based on APEC (1995c, 1996).

charge of the committee.

In 1993, following their Declaration on Trade and Investment Framework, APEC ministers constituted the Committee on Trade and Investment (CTI) to facilitate intraregional flow of trade in goods and services, investment, technology, and help create an APEC perspective on trade and investment liberalization in the region. In 1994, APEC ministers appointed two subcommittees under the CTI, (i) Subcommittee on Standards and Conformance, and (ii) Subcommittee on Customs Procedures; the former working on "simplification and harmonization" of customs rules of APEC member-countries, and the latter on four specific areas: (a) conformance of APEC members' standards with international standards, (b) cooperation with specialist regional bodies, (c) intra-APEC mutual conformance of standards, and (d) developing an APEC regional technical infrastructure (APEC, 1995a, 1995b, 1995c).

The CTI is a key APEC program and is responsible for the implementation of the Osaka Action Agenda, as outlined at the Leaders' Summit in 1995. Its work will encompass issues such as: Trade Policy Dialogue, Tariff Database, Tariffs, Non-tariff Measures, Services, Deregulation, Dispute Mediation, Uruguay Round Implementation, Investment, Customs Procedures, Standards and Conformance, Mobility of Business People, Intellectual Property Rights, Competition Policy, Government Procurement and Rules of Origin (APEC, 1996). In 1995, following the Joint Ministerial Statement in Jakarta in 1994, APEC established the Economic Committee to help promote the broad-based intra-APEC economic cooperation by analyzing the trend and cross-section key economic indicators of member-countries. The committee's 1996 work plan will cover specific issues - economic instruments for environmental protection, intraregional migration, information society, and cost and productivity trends.

In October 1994, the SME ministers of APEC member-countries met in Osaka and recommended the establishment of the Policy Level Group on Small and Medium Enterprises (PLG-SME). The PLG-SME was thus constituted in 1995 to attend to the specific needs of intra-APEC development of small and medium-scale enterprises. Indeed, the 1994 Bogor Declaration prioritized the program for its relevance to the overall economic development of the region. The APEC Center for Technology Exchange and Training for Small and Medium Enterprises was scheduled to be set up in the Philippines in September 1996.

The working groups come next in the APEC organization. As of 1995, ten working groups on ten specific subject areas are: (i) trade and investment data review, (ii) trade promotion, (iii) industrial science and technology, (iv) human resource development, (v) regional energy cooperation, (vi) marine resource cooperation, (vii) telecommunications, (viii) transportation, (ix) tourism, and

(x) fisheries. The working groups consist of officials/specialists, with due representation of APEC member-countries (APEC, 1991, 1993, 1994, 1995a, 1995b, 1995c, 1996).

A special mention of the Working Group for Human Resource Development, established in 1990, follows. This group which manages as many as 70 projects in 1996, has four subgroups: (i) the Business Management Network for executive education with special focus on management of changing economic structures in newly industrialized/industrializing economies in the APEC region; (ii) the Industrial Technology Network for studying skill gaps relative to technical and professional standards; (iii) the Education Forum which has its focus on developing programs to enable the education systems in APEC countries to cope with the demand for manpower in the changing labor markets; and (iv) the Economic Development Management Network, which studies the regional labor market and the utilization of all available human resources for economic development. The Working Group on Human Resource Development (HRD) subscribes to a threefold, interactive thematic agenda: (a) HRD for small and medium enterprises, (b) HRD for sustainable development, and (c) lifelong learning.

SECRETARIAT

At the ministerial meeting in Bangkok in 1992, APEC ministers resolved to set up a permanent secretariat in Singapore. Approval of the budget to support the secretariat and the work programs of APEC's policy-based groups and its ten working groups followed.

In February 1993, the APEC Secretariat was established in Singapore, headed by an executive director and a deputy executive director and several program directors. The executive director is selected from the member-economy, holding the APEC chair (the host country for the year's APEC Leaders' Summit) and serves for one year. The deputy executive director is appointed by the member-economy designated to assume the chair (the summit host) in the following year, and succeeds the executive director.

Singapore is widely thought to be the optimal location of the APEC Secretariat. Not Tokyo, or Beijing, or Ottawa, or Washington, DC appears to be on the preferred list. Establishment of specific functional offices in other member-countries seem to be widely welcome.

SINGAPORE, NO BRUSSELS: A FALSE DEBATE

Several EPG members (see Part II) forcefully argued in support of the present relatively modest-sized Singapore Secretariat. They would very much resent an expensive high-budget APEC Secretariat, lest it should replicate the European Union's Secretariat in Brussels. The EPG Report (APEC, 1993) added the words of caution by emphasizing the "efficiency" aspect of the Secretariat, and by warning against its burgeoning into "an embracing bureaucracy" as in the OECD or the EU. However, several EPG members candidly shared their views with me that the APEC Secretariat and its budget will grow rapidly. They point out that such has been the experience of most international organizations, including ASEAN, and that it will be no different for APEC.

It is important to note that many of the ranking officers at the APEC Secretariat continue to belong to the budget of their respective home governments. These off-budget services make the formal APEC budget appear deceptively too small, which fails to reveal the fuller and truer picture in this regard.

It is further to be noted that at the national government level of each APEC member-country there are officials who have APEC-related assignments. These officials belong to various ministries of the member-governments - foreign affairs, economic affairs, finance/treasury, trade/commerce/industry, education and environment. In July-December 1994, I had personal conferences with distinguished public officials in several APEC capitals; namely Jakarta, Beijing, Sydney, Bangkok and Kuala Lumpur. Their APEC-related assignments invariably constitute a part of their regular work load, paid for by the regular budget of their home government. In Seoul, Tokyo, Ottawa and Washington, DC, the picture is the same; thus, the comprehensive accounting of the APEC budget remains to be undertaken.

There cannot be a predefined dimension of the budget and/or number of employees which will be optimum for the APEC Secretariat. The issue is cost-effective delivery of service, given the APEC action agenda for its 2.16 billion people in its 18 member-countries, (United Nations, 1996; APEC, 1996).

An economic profile of APEC member-economies in terms of population and gross national product in 1995 is presented in Table 22.2. Two of the world's richest economies - the United States and Japan - and three of the world's most populous countries - the People's Republic of China, the United States of America and Indonesia are members of the group. In terms of per capita GNP, Japan and the United States lead with Singapore and Hong Kong closely following. Figures for Canada, Australia, Brunei Darussalam and New Zealand in 1995 range between US$14,340 and US$19,380. The People's Republic of China, Indonesia, the Philippines and Papua New Guinea remain at the lower end.

Table 22.3 presents a trade profile of APEC economies in terms of merchandise trade - export and import - in 1995 US dollars and their shares in the GNP of the member-economies. The share may be viewed as the individual economy's openness to the world economy.

APEC, an intraregional organization of 18 sovereign nation-state-based economies with a combined gross national product of US$15.6 trillion in 1995, and better than 50 per cent of the world's total merchandise trade is indeed a much larger economic community, or call it an economic "family", and must exercise its right to have a secretariat which will be able to efficiently deliver the services as per its well-specified assignment.

It is a false debate whether the APEC Secretariat in Singapore will become a replica of the EU Secretariat at Brussels. What is crucial is to recognize that APEC is "a critical first step in the process of filling the intergovernmental institutional vacuum in the region" (APEC, 1993).

PACIFIC BUSINESS FORUM/APEC BUSINESS ADVISORY COUNCIL

The Pacific Business Forum (PBF) is a non-government forum. To help identify issues, APEC should address the issue of facilitating intraregional liberalization of trade and investment flows. At the Blake Island meeting in November 1993, APEC economic leaders resolved to set up the PBF with two representatives from each member-country - one from a large business and one from a small business.

The PBF became operational in June 1994 and submitted its report, *A Business Blueprint for APEC: Strategies for Growth and Common Prosperity* for the Bogor Leaders' Summit in November 1994. The report was well received and the PBF was invited to continue its activities. Indeed, this private business forum provides a unique mechanism for relating APEC's official activities to the revealed preferences of the leaders of the free market.

In November 1995 at the Osaka Leaders' Summit, the Osaka Action Agenda was adopted. Implementation of the agenda would warrant receiving much advice from the business sector and its specific priorities. APEC ministers elected to broaden the Forum's scope by establishing the APEC Business Advisory Council (ABAC) with a panel of three members from each member-country. The ABAC will work on how best to deepen "the sense of community" in the Asia-Pacific region and will report to APEC ministers.

Table 22.2 An economic profile of APEC member-economies

	Population Millions 1995	GNP US$ Millions 1995	GNP per capita US$ 1995
Australia	18.05	337,909	18,720
Brunei Darussalam	0.28	4,996	17,039
Canada	29.61	573,695	19,380
Chile	14.22	59,151	4,160
PRC	1,200.24	744,890	620
Hong Kong	6.19	142,332	22,990
Indonesia	193.28	190,105	980
Japan	125.21	4,963,587	39,640
Korea	44.85	435,137	9,700
Malaysia	20.14	78,321	3,890
Mexico	91.83	304,596	3,320
New Zealand	3.60	51,655	14,340
Papua New Gunea	4.30	4,976	1,160
Philippines	68.59	71,865	1,050
Singapore	2.99	79,831	26,730
Taipei	21.30	258,347	12,439
Thailand	58.24	159,630	2,740
U.S.A	263.12	7,100,007	26,980
Total	2,166.04	15,561,030	

Sources: *World Development Report*, 1996 World Bank, *World Bank Atlas*, 1997 for computing GNP per capita, *Brunei Darussalam Key Indicators 1995/1996*, *Statistical Data Book*, 1996, Chinese Taipei, APEC Secretariat Compilation.
Note: Hong Kong and Brunei GDP, GNP for all others.

Table 22.3 Trade profile of APEC member-economies

	Merchandise Trade, 1995 in US $ Billions			
	Export (X)	Import (M)	X + M /GNP	
Australia	53.1	61.3	114.4/338,0	< 1
Brunei Darussalam	2.4	2.1	4.5/5,0	< 1
Canada	192.2	168.4	360.6/573,7	< 1
Chile	16.0	15.9	31.9/59,2	< 1
PRC	148.8	132.1	280.9/744,9	< 1
Hong Kong	173.9	196.1	370.0/142,3	> 1
Indonesia	45.4	40.9	86.3/190,1	< 1
Japan	443.1	336.0	779.1/4,963,6	< 1
Korea	125.1	135.1	260.2/435,1	< 1
Malaysia	74.0	77.7	151.7/78,3	> 1
Mexico	79.7	72.9	152.6/304,6	< 1
New Zealand	13.7	13.9	27.6/51,7	< 1
Papua New Gunea	2.6	1.4	4.0/5,0	< 1
Philippines	17.5	28.2	45.7/71,9	< 1
Singapore	118.3	124.5	242.8/79,8	> 1
Taipei	111.7	103.6	215.3/258,4	< 1
Thailand	56.5	70.9	127.4/159,6	< 1
U.S.A	583.9	771.3	1,355.2/7,100	< 1

Sources: *World Development Report*, 1996 World Bank, *World Bank Atlas*, 1997 for computing GNP per capita, *Brunei Darussalam Key Indicators 1995/1996*, *Statistical Data Book*, 1996, Chinese *Taipei, APEC Secretariat Compilation.*
Note: Hong Kong and Brunei GDP, GNP for all others.

23 APEC Vision: Action Agenda/Action Plan

APEC VISION

The creation of a true economic community in the Asia-Pacific region has been at the core of APEC vision. The pronouncement was loud and clear that the Asia-Pacific Community would *not* seek to replicate the EU by way of establishing "a single internal market" with an agenda for a common currency. The Community would seek to optimize economic gains for all member-countries by an active intraregional trade liberalization program, reiterating its commitment to global trade liberalization under GATT and WTO. The vision was for a "market-driven" Asia-Pacific regional integration. To this end, the APEC EPG Report (APEC, 1993) stated that the Asia-Pacific region should develop with focus on:

- an investment code,
- a dispute settlement process,
- a greater coordination of macroeconomic policies,
- cooperation on competition policy,
- harmonization of product standards, customs laws,
- environmental cooperation, and
- a trade and investment framework with proper "rules of origin".

The APEC Leaders' Summit in 1994 (APEC, 1994) went on to further streamline the APEC vision "on the basis of equal partnership, shared responsibility, mutual respect, common interest and common benefit". There was a reaffirmation of the position that APEC will not be "a single internal market" as is the case in the EU, and that APEC's goal would be a GATT/WTO-consistent *comprehensive free trade* regime in the region with the provision for "flexible implementation", given the varying levels of economic development of its member-economies. Following the 1994 Summit, the Bogor Declaration set a two-stage timetable for free and open trade and investment in the Asia-Pacific; (i) 2010 in the case of industrialized economies and (ii) 2020 in the case of developing economies. An individual member retained its freedom to voluntarily implement the program anytime sooner.

The relationship between APEC and the subregional groupings within the region - Free Trade Areas in Southeast Asia, North America and South Pacific

- AFTA, NAFTA and ANZ-CER (see Part IV) - was noted to be an issue to be addressed.

AN APEC ACTION AGENDA/ACTION PLAN

At the Osaka Leaders' Summit in 1995, the emphasis was clearly on an action agenda. At the two summits in Seattle (US) and Bogor (Indonesia) in 1993 and 1994, respectively, the APEC *vision* was outlined, while at the summit in Osaka (Japan) in 1995 the APEC *action agenda* was prioritized (Bergsten, 1995, 1996). The challenge to translate vision into a reality was APEC's.

Four key questions warranting immediate attention of the Leaders' Summit were (APEC, 1995b, pp. 151-75):

1. *Trade*: Implementation of APEC's GATT/WTO-consistent trade liberalization program within its framework of open regionalism must be accelerated.
2. *Investment*: APEC members must further strengthen the *nonbinding* investment code, agreed in 1994.
3. *Subregional trade arrangements*: The interrelationship between APEC and the three subregional trade arrangements within the region - ASEAN Free Trade Area (AFTA), Australia-New Zealand Close Economic Relations Trade Area (ANZCERTA) and North American Free Trade Area (NAFTA) - must be optimally harnessed toward overall agenda of trade liberalization for the region. Let the APEC policy of open regionalism relate to that of open subregionalism.
4. *Macroeconomic policy*: Adoption of a program for deepening intra-APEC cooperation on monetary and macroeconomic issues to support its free and liberal trade and investment agenda was very much in order.

Finally, "another vital area" for intra-APEC cooperation "to fill the gaps in technology, management, and planning and administration among its diverse members" and also in the intraregional infrastructure, came to the focus at the summit. The emphasis was clearly on "empowerment of all participants in the cooperation process", rejecting the conventional donor-recipient cooperation framework. Japan, chair and host of the 1995 Summit, proudly presented the proposal entitled "Partners for Progress" which moved toward narrowing the economic disparities between APEC member-economies in their shared commitment to an agenda for intraregional trade and investment liberalization.

The summit received the ten-point program of Osaka *deliverables*, as developed by the Pacific Business Forum (PBF). The ten items included were:

(1) acceleration of trade liberalization and facilitation beyond the Uruguay Round through simultaneously deepening and broadening APEC action agenda, (2) strengthening the APEC non-binding investment code by the 1996 Summit in the Philippines, (3) facilitation of business travel/residency visas, (4) customs harmonization, (5) standards and conformance, (6) protection of intellectual property rights by adequate enforcement of the existing laws by the APEC member-countries, (7) institution of the office of trade and investment *ombudsman* to mediate intra-APEC disputes, (8) infrastructure development, (9) support for small and medium enterprises by establishing special programs inclusive of the APEC Center for Technology Exchange and Training in the Philippines in 1996, and (10) human resource development.

The Osaka Statement which followed delivered the road map to APEC's 2010/2020 vision by specifying an "action agenda", drawing extensively on "the Osaka *deliverables*". The action agenda was fully in conformity with APEC's commitment to the three major policy planks: (i) liberalization, (ii) facilitation, and (iii) development cooperation. The action agenda in its two parts covered (a) liberalization as well as facilitation of trade and investment, and (b) economic and technical cooperation. Given "the marked regional trend toward economic reform and liberalization", the approach would be to combine "unilateral actions, collective actions and multilateral actions.".

Matching the action agenda is the *action plan* with the stipulation for annual review of overall progress. For trade and investment liberalization and facilitation, the APEC member-economies must be able to make "deliveries" by taking concrete actions in 15 specified areas: (i) tariffs, (ii) non-tariff measures, (iii) services, (iv) investment, (v) standards and conformance, (vi) customs procedures, (vii) intellectual property rights, (viii) competition policy, (ix) governmen t procurement, (x) deregulation, (xi) rules of origin, (xii) dispute mediation, (xiii) mobility of business people, (xiv) implementation of Uruguay Round agreements, and (xv) information gathering and processing.

For economic and technical cooperatión, the specific action areas noted are: (i) human resource development, (ii) industrial science and technology, (iii) small and medium enterprises, (iv) economic infrastructure, (v) energy, (vi) transportation, (vii) telecommunications and information, (viii) tourism, (ix) trade and investment data, (x) trade promotion, (xi) marine resource conservation, (xii) fisheries, and (xiii) agricultural technology.

The Osaka Statement, with its action agenda and action plan, certainly deepened APEC's commitment to intra-regional cooperation and its progressive evolution as an Asia-Pacific Economic Community.

APEC: BOGOR TO OSAKA: ISSUES AND ANSWERS

As the crucial *first steps* toward trade liberalization and facilitation, the APEC CTI and its two subcommittees - one on customs procedures and another on standards and conformance - have to their credit notable accomplishments. Over the year between the summits in Bogor 1994 and Osaka 1995, they have produced their reports on harmonization of customs laws of the 18 member-economies and also on harmonization and conformance of product standards.

The Osaka Statement notes with much commendation that since the Bogor Declaration, various APEC working groups have initiated their activities as per terms of appointment of their respective groups.

An evaluation of the APEC Action Agenda/Action Plan, in the context of recorded conversations with several APEC EPG members and APEC scholars (see Part II) is in order.

First, there is a pronounced emphasis to distinguish APEC from the EU. APEC is no attempt to *replicate* the EU, they affirm and reaffirm at every ministerial meeting, and at every summit. The EPGs and scholars, as we have reported, have invariably and emphatically warned against any and all misunderstanding, should one become a victim to non-appreciation of the difference between APEC and the EU. Indeed, there has been no suggestion to photocopy or replicate the Western European model of economic regionalization in the Asia-Pacific. Is there truly a core issue of intraregional economic cooperation, especially with a map-of-the-world view of a region in the Asia-Pacific?

Second, terms such as, "free trade area", "free trade in the area", "regionalism" and "open regionalism" appear too frequently in all APEC discussions and its publications. Does that add to the confusion? APEC has elected to opt for "free trade in the area", not for a "free trade area". Its choice is for "open regionalism", not "inward-looking" regionalism. EPGs and scholars have had conversations and have placed added emphasis on this. Some of them strongly argue for sharing APEC trade liberalization and facilitation provisions to non-member economies in the region. Some EPG members, however, argue that in reality it may not work effectively. Some other EPGs forcefully argue that the debate truly centers on open regionalism with or without reciprocity. Could APEC achieve the same goal if it were a free trade area, an area of free trade, without raising *new trade barriers to non-members* by progressively broadening its membership to economies belonging to the map of the region?

Third, APEC members seem to share much concern to assure each other of the sovereignty of each individual member-state. An agreement-specific, intraregional and/or international cooperation among sovereign nation-state-based economies does not involve any compromise of an individual member-state's sovereignty. Such has been the verdict of the highest courts of law in several countries (the United Kingdom, Germany) in the context of the European Union. Does the right to withdraw from APEC membership protect a member-country's core sovereign authority?

Fourth, APEC's commitment to a GATT/WTO-consistent agenda and action plan is equally as good as the EU's commitment to subscribe to the WTO codes of global trade liberalization and facilitation. Let the EU elect only *one* person to represent the 15-member Union at the WTO, to be joined by 18 fellow-members, each representing one of the 18 APEC sovereign member-economies. It will have little economic implication. The world has witnessed that the disintegration of the former Soviet Union, and also of some other East European countries, has recently added to the WTO membership. The rest of the world must accept the politics of the situation and the consequence of redrawing the map of the world.

Independent of such essentially extraeconomic happenings, we believe that regionalism and globalism can and must work together if the goal is achieving the Pareto optimality condition. Is there a paradigm of what is referred to as inward-looking closed regionalism? We have argued that neither the EU nor APEC presents a fortress model.

Fifth, APEC's choice for free trade in the area now begs to be reconciled with the three free trade areas in North America, Southeast Asia and the South Pacific, all within the APEC region. APEC's action agenda recommending a plan for open subregionalism may offer an option.

Sixth, given the diverse levels of economic development and markedly varying degrees of market reform and economic liberalization among its membership, APEC has very rightly elected to accept its challenges in four major areas:

1. *Structural divergences of APEC member-economies*: intraregional infrastructure development is a key issue toward trade and investment liberalization and facilitation, as noted in the 1994 Bogor Declaration. Partners for Progress (PFP) presents an action agenda by setting *target areas with focus on mutual assistance outside the traditional aid-giving and aid-receiving relationships.* The 1996 Osaka Statement attends to the economic merits of developing intra-APEC infrastructure toward its trade and investment liberalization and facilitation agenda.
2. *Macroeconomic policy coordination*: the issue of a supranational, intraregional macroeconomic core has been the subject of much debate (APEC, 1993, 1994, 1995a, 1995b; Arndt, 1993; Bergsten, 1995, 1996; Dutta, 1994a

and 1994b; Hufbauer, 1995; Yamazawa, 1994; Yoo and Sung 1994). Both the Bogor Declaration and the Osaka Statement, following the Leaders' Summits in 1994 and 1996, respectively, have addressed the issue. Indeed, without effective coordination of monetary-fiscal policies, action agenda for trade and investment liberalization and facilitation may fail to work. Failure to optimally manage monetary and fiscal policies by an APEC member-economy may cause serious dislocations and its free transmission to all other economies in the intra-regional group may follow. True, macroeconomic policy coordination has been a challenging task in the context of a national economy. It will not be less so in the context of a group of sovereign nation-state based economies.

Is there a choice? It is to be appreciated that much of the APEC initiative is based on high performance of the newly industrialized/industrializing economies in the region, and was conditioned by the intraregional macroeconomic stability very much anchored to the value of the U.S. dollar. Some EPGs (see Part II) have referred to the defense and security parameter that the United States has historically provided to the region. The Asia-Pacific strategic security alliances became a platform for the strategic economic regionalization. The macroeconomic stability was indeed a necessary condition. The scenario changed, and the United States was unable to unilaterally satisfy the necessary condition. The burden was too much for the U.S. dollar.

The APEC initiative emerged to fill up the vacuum. The need for intraregional supranational macroeconomic policy coordination is all the more pressing and can be ignored only with serious consequences. One view is to continue to talk about the subject until a consensus emerges. Following the 1994 Bogor Declaration, the annual finance ministers' meetings were a welcome initiative. The APEC action agenda in this regard need not be to replicate the EU and plan for an APEC central bank with an APEC currency.

3. *Mediation of intra-APEC trade disputes*: unilateral actions to settle trade disputes, including the U.S. Super-301, is very much cost-ineffective. The bilateral negotiations are no less so. In the absence of an intraregional dispute mediation mechanism, APEC trade and investment liberalization and facilitation agenda cannot progress. Should APEC members bypass APEC and take their grievances to the WTO? Will the WTO's dispute settlement mechanism help or hurt the APEC initiative? The 1995 Osaka Statement and the 1994 Bogor Declaration may have initiated some necessary steps in this regard. A more positive action plan is in order.

4. *Harmonization of customs laws and product standards*: the issues have received priority attention. The Declaration on APEC Standards and Conformance framework is in place. Customs laws and procedures of the 18

member-countries must be standardized and efforts toward this end are in progress. The issues involve many legal and bureaucratic challenges, and often face the question of political expediency.

Could intra-APEC harmonization of product standards be an easier task by mutual acceptance of the product standard of each other? Should each APEC member-country have its own sector-specific institutions for standardization of its diverse products and services, their mutual accreditation could facilitate the work. The option for instituting an intra-APEC body for the job will hardly be practical.

Implementation of the agenda to harmonize product standards, which has been straightforwardly adopted, continues to be baffling. The issue of *transparency,* involving "availability of and access to standards and conformance information in each APEC economy" and intra-APEC "exchange of such information" possibly with a computer network, remains to be addressed. Cooperation with specialist regional bodies such as the Asia-Pacific Laboratory Accreditation Cooperation, the Asia-Pacific Legal Metrology Forum, the Asia-Pacific Metrology Program, the Pacific Accreditation Cooperation and the Pacific Area Standards Congress may be helpful (APEC, 1995b).

APEC's subscribing to the WTO guidelines (the Agreement on Technical Barriers to Trade and the Agreement on the Application of Sanitary and Phytosanitary Measures) is on record. Beginning with 1996, much work remains to be done and the progress reports are due in 2000 and 2005.

Seventh and finally, APEC has elected not to address the issue of intra-regional factor mobility, especially labor. Several EPG members (see Part II) have noted the significance of the issue, but the issue is not on APEC's action agenda. The issue of illegal immigration has been important not only in the advanced, mature industrialized economies (the United States, Canada, Japan, Australia and New Zealand) but also in several newly industrialized and industrializing economies in Asia (South Korea, Hong Kong, Singapore, Malaysia and Thailand). As an economy progressively industrializes, its demand for aggregate stock of labor exceeds aggregate supply and provides a benchmark - the year of migration transition - for inflows of immigrant labor (Freeman and Mo, 1996). Given the intra-APEC agenda for the free flow of physical capital input as the profit-maximizing norm of its free market member-economies, can intraregional free flow of labor input be far behind?

24 APEC and Trade

BEYOND TRADE

I have argued (see Part I) that two sets of forces, governed by push-and-pull factors, the former from Europe and the latter from Asia, have contributed to progressive institutionalization of APEC. Economic regionalization in Western Europe acted as the push factor. The European Union continues to experiment with its model of deep economic integration with much success and presents a challenge to the rest of the world.

In Part II, I have presented my conversations with several members of APEC's EPG and independent scholars in various APEC member-countries, with each of whom I pressed the argument. In general, a consensus exists that the live experiment in Western Europe has certainly been a model to learn from, an educational process. It has had some impact on the happenings in the Asia-Pacific.

Some eminent persons have argued that the APEC Summit in 1993 had its impact on the EU, persuading the Europeans to accept the Uruguay Round of the GATT Agreement after six years of strenuous negotiations. Still others have forcefully argued that the EU, rooted to the concept of fortress Europe, could hardly have an impact on APEC and its commitment to free trade in the area. The EU does not present a fortress regional model, I continue to argue.

Some other eminent persons point out that the historical fact of the security and defense umbrella provided by the United States in the Asia-Pacific region has been more of a push factor. An absence of this key international public good would very much act as a destabilizing force. The shared agenda for the continued provision of such precious extraeconomic services has been more of a compelling argument for the APEC intraregional economic cooperation, they add.

I maintain that if the EU's paradigm of economic regionalization failed to materialize, the presence of pull factors in the Asia-Pacific region in terms of high economic growth and a superior performance regarding international trade and investment flows, in and of themselves, would not warrant the formation of APEC. If the 15 sovereign nations in Western Europe continued to behave as independent economic entities in their respective international economic relationships, as they did in the pre-EU regime, the rest of the world would hardly press its search for some mode of economic regionalization. The search for an alternative mode, be it a customs union, an economic community, a free trade area, or a trade preference group, became compelling.

The EU, a unique model of economic regionalization, as it is, has pushed the rest of the world to develop its articulate search for some form of intraregional economic grouping. Acceptance of the twofold agenda of regionalism and globalism and firm commitment to GATT/WTO-consistent economic regionalization has become the cornerstone of the framework of international economics in the 1990s and beyond.

TRADE 1970-1989: ASIA'S NEWLY INDUSTRIALIZED/ INDUSTRIALIZING ECONOMIES

If the pull factors in and of themselves were considered inadequate, the push factors alone also would fail to present necessary and sufficient conditions for economic regionalization. Thus, many and varied attempts to constitute one or another form of intraregional economic grouping of sovereign national economies in recent decades have failed to produce adequate results. In most cases pull factors were absent, and/or limited, and thus were unable to reinforce the push factors from the Western European experiment.

The notable exception has been the case of the Asia-Pacific. The pull factors became manifest in the flow of trade. I have argued (see Part I) that these trade flows very much became determined by the agenda for accelerated economic development by a policy of importation of capital goods and their adaptation to the labor-intensive, agriculture-dominant, indigenous Asian economies. The industrialization of the selected Asian economies followed. Only by their successful programs of adaptive innovation were they able to pay for their imports by exporting their new products, which were competitive in the world market in terms of both cost and quality.

Thus, trade among themselves reinforced Asia-Pacific intraregional economic cooperation. Of course, it very much facilitated the regional buyers-sellers meeting. It became evident that mutual economic gains would be optimized by freer engagement in trade in the region, given the Pareto-optimality condition. I have discussed (see Part I) that, as early as the late 1960s, a few years after the Treaty of Rome became operational on January 1, 1958, the first initiative came from Australia, New Zealand, Japan, Canada and the United States. The five competitively advanced industrialized economies in the region joined their efforts, and the group of five led the non-official cooperative effort, the Organization for Pacific Trade and Development (OPTAD). The OPTAD initiative progressively became a much broader Pacific regional economic cooperation forum. This non-official umbrella in the Asia-Pacific ushered in the intraregional leadership which was able and willing to institute a strong economic base toward facilitating Asia-Pacific trade and investment liberalization and industrialization. In 1989, APEC was officially founded.

The period of 1970-89 and the story of Asia's NIEs over the 20-year period are of much relevance to the present study. In the 1960s, these economies adopted open economic policies by way of switching from their respective import-substitution regimes to one of export-led growth. Taiwan (Taipei) took the lead in 1963; while South Korea changed its economic policy in 1968. Hong Kong, of course, was always an open economy. In Southeast Asia, ASEAN was formed in 1967 with Thailand, Malaysia, Singapore, Indonesia and the Philippines as its five original members. It became an important date for the ASEAN member-economies both for its intraregional strategic and economic cooperation. Thailand always had an open economic policy. Malaysia, Singapore and Indonesia adopted the new policy in 1960s. Only the Philippines continued its old import-substitution policy until the late 1980s. Thus, we have elected to analyze the trade flows for the 20-year period, beginning with 1970 when the open economic policy, in general, became the rule for the specific Asian economies, and 1989 when APEC was institutionalized.

The trade-flow patterns of selected economies in East and Southeast Asia, Asia's newly industrialized/industrializing economies, presented here, point to the pull factors and its progressive reinforcement of the process of Asia-Pacific economic cooperation. Based on trade data, total exports and total imports in billions of U.S. dollars for 1970-87 (for Taiwan, 1970-88), Figures 24.1-8 present the changing trade profiles of Korea, Taiwan, Hong Kong, Singapore, Thailand, the Philippines, Indonesia and Malaysia, respectively. Trade destinations of each economy are presented in two panels; in the top panel, the total of each selected economy's trade, export as well as imports, is shown in terms of five-fold market destinations: (i) the United States (U.S.), (ii) Japan, (iii) Australia and New Zealand (ANZ), (iv) Asia-4 (South Korea, Taiwan, Hong Kong, Singapore, Thailand, Malaysia, the Philippines, Indonesia, China, India, Pakistan, Bangladesh, Sri Lanka, and (v) rest of the world (ROW). In the bottom panel, we present each economy's market for both exports and imports for Asia's newly industrialized/industrializing economies - (a) South Korea, Taiwan and Hong Kong (NIEs), (b) Singapore, Thailand, Malaysia, the Philippines, Indonesia (ASEAN-5), (c) China (excepting South Korea and Taiwan), and also for (d) India, Pakistan, Bangladesh and Sri Lanka (SAARC-4). (See appendix pp. 75-76 for explanations regarding data.)

Over the time period, the pattern of overall growth of both exports and imports is noted. One notable exception is the case of the Philippines (Figure 24.6). Indonesia and Malaysia have experienced uneven courses, but each has upheld its trend growth (Figure 24.7). A review of the top panels of the fivefold market destinations, in general, points to the fact that each economy has broadly diversified their market destinations to the U.S., Japan, ANZ, Asia-4 and ROW.

Returning to the bottom panels we study the growth of export-import markets of the selected economies in terms of their intra-trade. For Korea, Taiwan and Hong Kong, their three-economy intra-trade has grown, and so have their respective markets in Southeast Asia (ASEAN-5), with its newer market marginally widening out to South Asia (SAARC-4). From the bottom panels of Hong Kong, Singapore, Thailand, the Philippines, Indonesia and Malaysia, one notes the growth pattern of each economy's trade with China. Each has experienced a market expansion within the Southeast group and also with the newly industrialized group (NIEs); trade with South Asia is relatively small, albeit growing, excepting Thailand and Indonesia whose respective trade with South Asia (SAARC-4) is more visible.

Based on data presented in the tables a review of percentage distributions of trade, export as well as import, for 1970-89, for each of the above economies is revealing. In general, trade for the seven countries under review is predominantly with the APEC member-economies; the exception is Singapore. Their intra-APEC trade shares for both exports and imports range from two-thirds to four-fifths.

For Korea (Table 24.1A), both for its exports and imports, the dependence on both the U.S. and Japan shows a declining trend. On the other hand its trade share, for both exports and imports - with ANZ, Asia-4 inclusive of NIEs, Southeast Asia (ASEAN-5), South Asia (SAARC-4), (China not included), and also with the ROW show a growth trend.

For Taiwan (Tables 24.1B), its trade share distributions show a different profile. For both exports and imports, its dependence on both the U.S., Japan, ASIA-4, and ROW continue to be at the same level, albeit with region-specific fluctuations in selected years. Taiwan's trade with ANZ has followed a different time path, its export share steadily increasing while its import share is generally declining.

For Hong Kong (Tables 24.1C), for both exports and imports, its trade shares with each region - the U.S., Japan, ANZ, and ROW - has steadily declined, except the phenomenal increase in its trade shares with Asia-4, which includes data of its trade with mainland China. With China, its export share has risen to 25.7 per cent in 1989 from 0.4 per cent in 1979, while the import share rose from 16.1 per cent in 1970 to 34.9 per cent in 1989.

For Singapore (Tables 24.1D), its trade share with the U.S., for both exports and imports, shows a rising trend; with Japan, its shares remain relatively stable at about 10 per cent for exports and 20 per cent for imports; with ANZ, its trade shares for exports hold at about 4 per cent while for imports the share steadily declines from a high of 5.1 per cent in 1970 to a low of 1.9 per cent in 1989. Singapore's trade shares with ASIA-4, inclusive of China, NIEs, ASEAN-5 and SAARC-4 for both exports and imports, fluctuate around the high 20 per cent range. For the ROW, its export and import shares seem to have settled around 30 per cent in late 1980s. The trend appears to be one of increase in Singapore's intra-APEC trade and a trend decline in its extra-APEC trade share.

For Thailand (Tables 24.1E), for exports its trade share with the U.S. shows a strong rising trend, while with Japan the trend is reversed by steadily declining from 26.6 per cent in 1970 to 16.5 per cent in 1989. Thailand has rising export trade shares with ANZ, China and South Asia (SAARC-4), with its intra-ASEAN share (ASEAN-5) declining. For imports, its shares with the U.S., Japan and ANZ remain stable with minor fluctuations; Japan's share being uniformly much higher than that of the U.S. in most years. Its import trade shares with ASIA-4 has phenomenally risen from a low of 8.4 per cent in 1970 to a high of 24.6 per cent in 1989. The pattern holds for each subregion in Asia-4: namely, China, newly industrialized economies (NIEs), Southeast Asia (ASEAN-5) and South Asia (SAARC-4). For both exports and imports, Thailand records good trade shares with South Asia.

For the Philippines (Tables 24.1F), the economy's overall performance has been quite uneven, pointing to its relative non-competitive position *vis-à-vis* its Southeast Asian neighbors. The economy's trade dependence on the U.S. and Japan for both export and import shares remains predominant. Next, its export and import trade shares with ANZ, NIEs and ASEAN-5 show an upward trend. The market-share of the Philippines in China is beginning to be explored.

For Indonesia (Tables 24.1G), for both exports and imports, the U.S. and Japan remain dominant partners, together taking 50 per cent of the trade shares, Japan taking a more leading role. Indonesia's trade share with ANZ, the close South Pacific neighbor, is important, increasing rather consistently in imports, and quite irregularly fluctuating in exports. About 10 to 20 per cent of its exports and about a third of its imports relate to the rest of the world market (ROW).

For Malaysia (Tables 24.1H), its trade shares present a profile of its own. The U.S. and Japan are important partners in trade. Malaysia's major trade shares for both exports and imports are with the Asia-4, which includes China, NIEs, ASEAN-5, and SAARC-4. Its trade shares with both China and South Asia are to be noted. Malaysia's intra-ASEAN trade shares are competitively high. Malaysia has increasingly become a trading partner of APEC member-economies of both shores of the Pacific, with an extended outreach to South Asia.

TRADE PROPELS ECONOMIC REGIONALIZATION

Industrialization and economic development has been paid for by trade. Partners in trade look for developing a vehicle toward sustaining the mutual economic gains, and thus offer to cooperate on liberalization of trade barriers, tariffs and non-tariffs, harmonization of customs laws, standardization of tradables - goods as well as services, liberalization and facilitation of investment flows to support and enhance the economic potentials of the economies in trading partnership, mediation of trade disputes, and cooperation on intraregional human resource development by optimal management of health-care delivery, education and training, and environmental resources. They also begin to appreciate that intra-regional coordination of monetary-fiscal policies alone can help control inflation and adventurous public programs by heavy borrowing in a partner country, and thus effectively optimize economic gains of micro actors - households and business - in all member-economies. Thus, trade propels the engine of intraregional economic cooperation.

Eighteen member-economies of APEC are empowered with economic pull factors, each in its own way, which very much reinforce their common goal for economic cooperation on fundamental economic rationale. They recognize that together they can further broaden the scope for optimization of their economic gains by joining the membership of an intraregional institution for economic cooperation. This is their way to sustain economic growth of the member-economies and add to their trade and investment potential.

Figure 24.1 (A) Korea: exports and imports

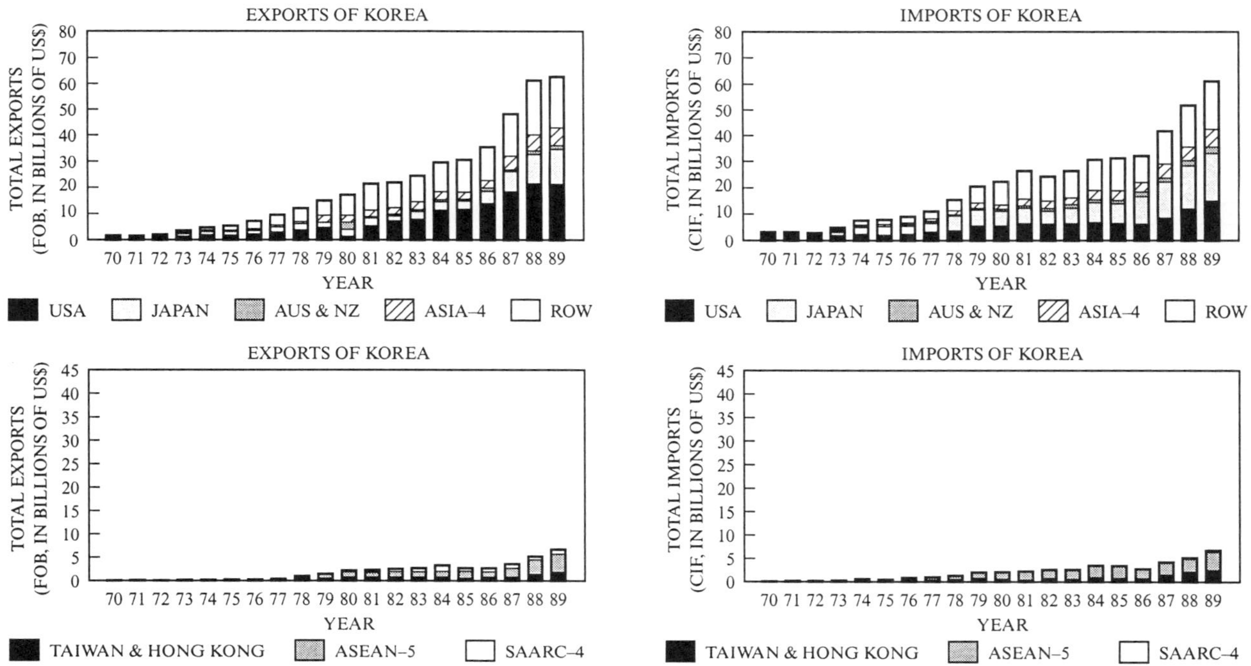

Source: see Appendix, Chapter 6

Figure 24.1 (B) Taiwan: exports and imports

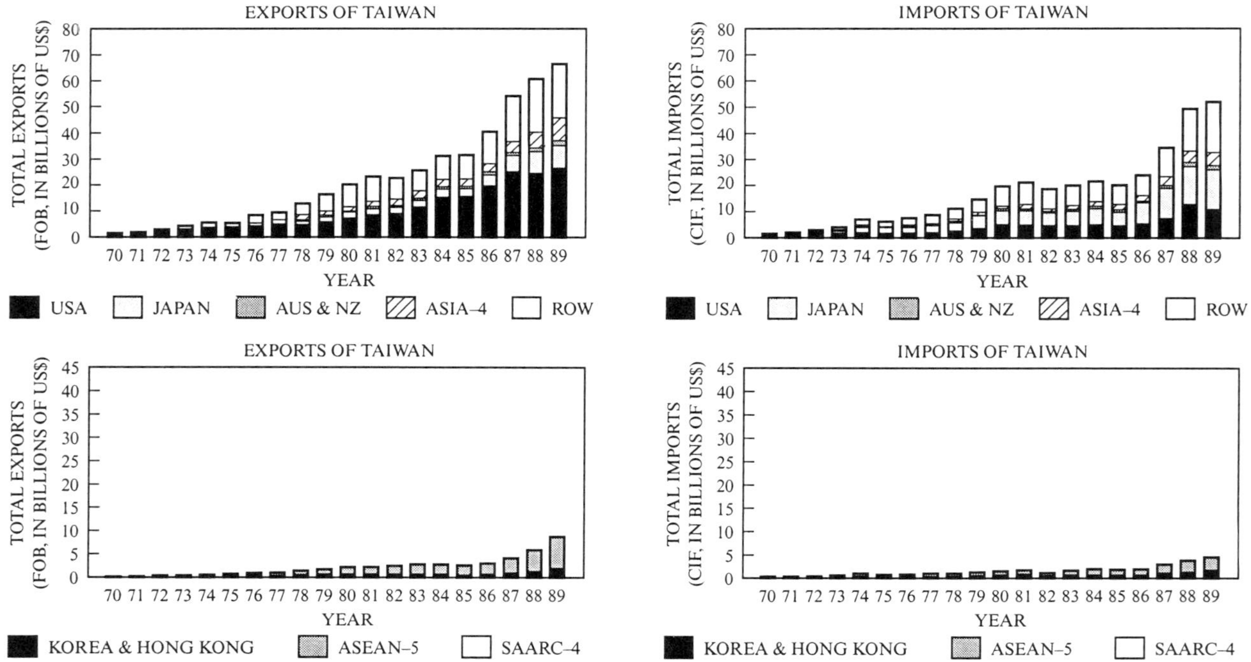

Source: see Appendix, Chapter 6

Figure 24.1 (C) Hong Kong: exports and imports

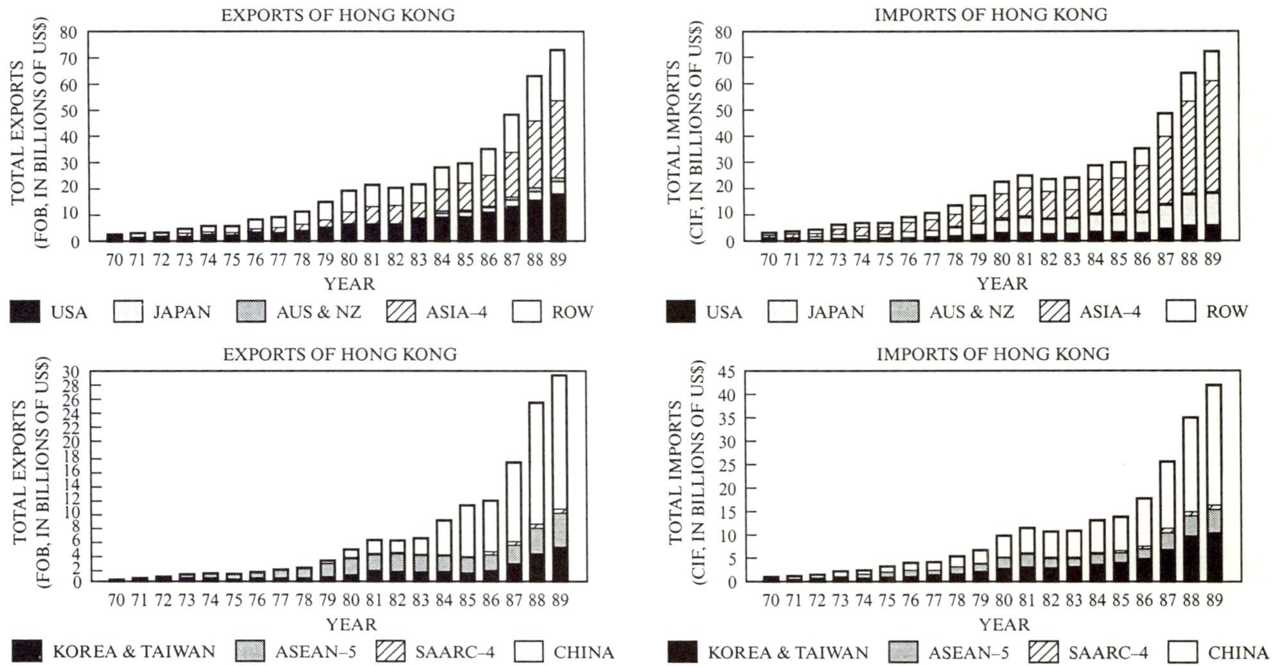

Source: see Appendix, Chapter 6

Figure 24.1 (D) Singapore: exports and imports

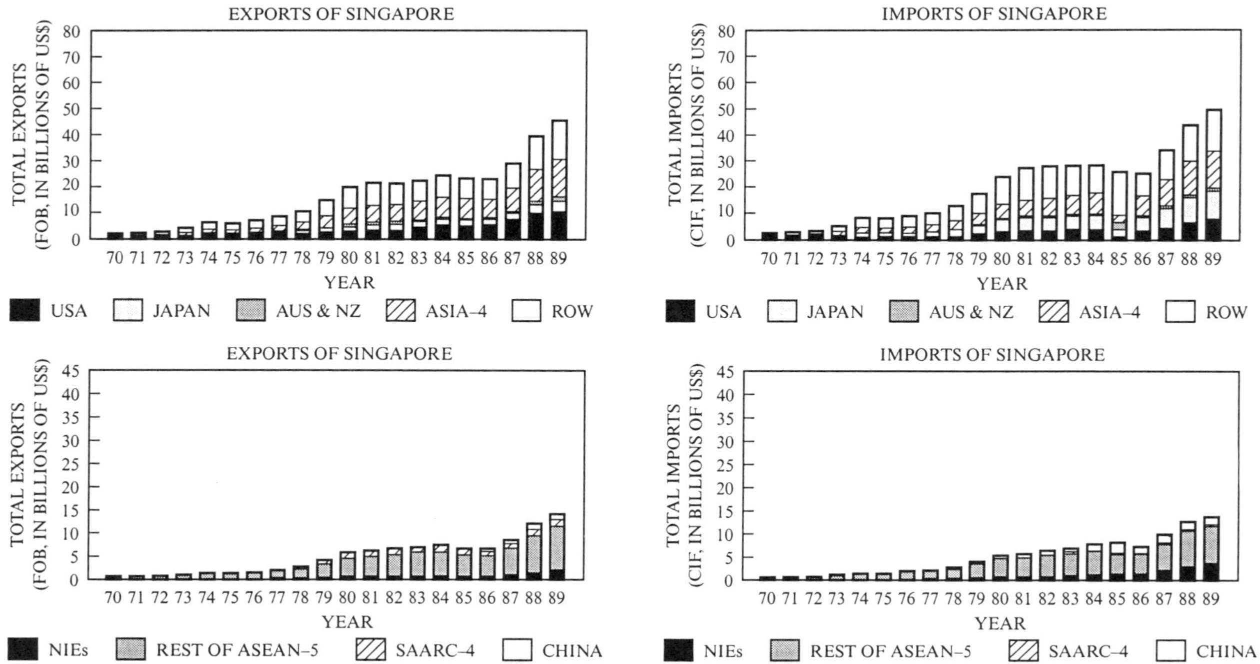

Source: see Appendix, Chapter 6

Figure 24.1 (E) Thailand: exports and imports

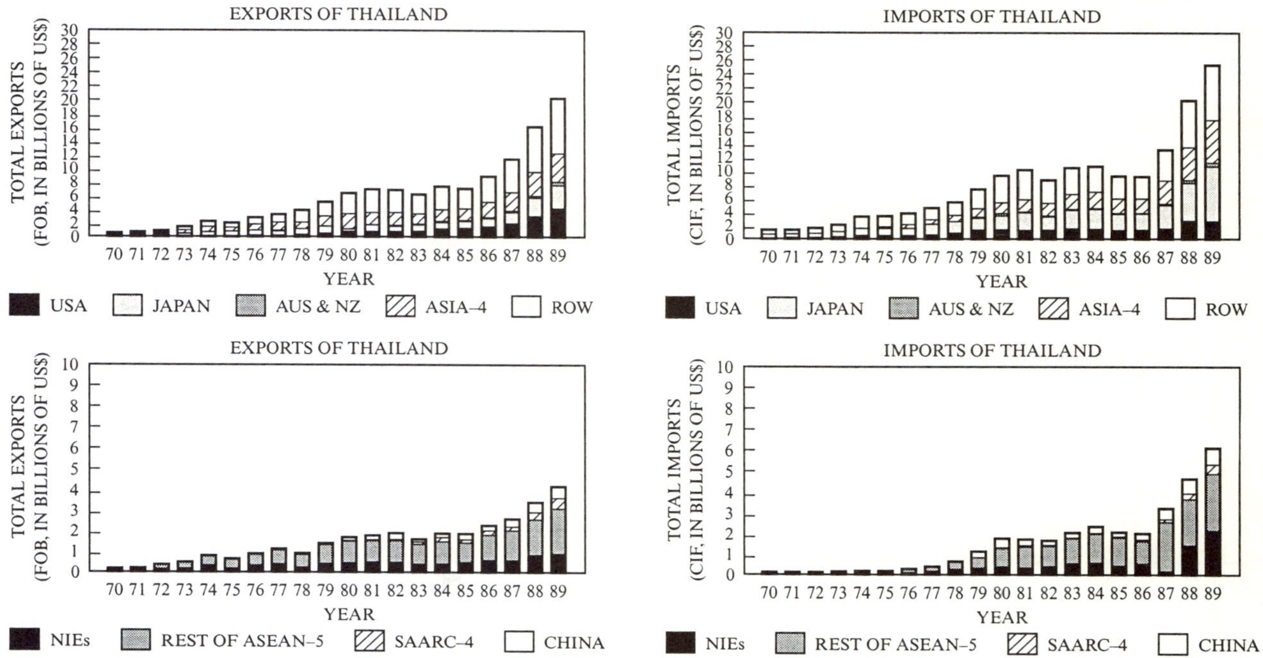

Source: see Appendix, Chapter 6

Figure 24.1 (F) Philippines: exports and imports

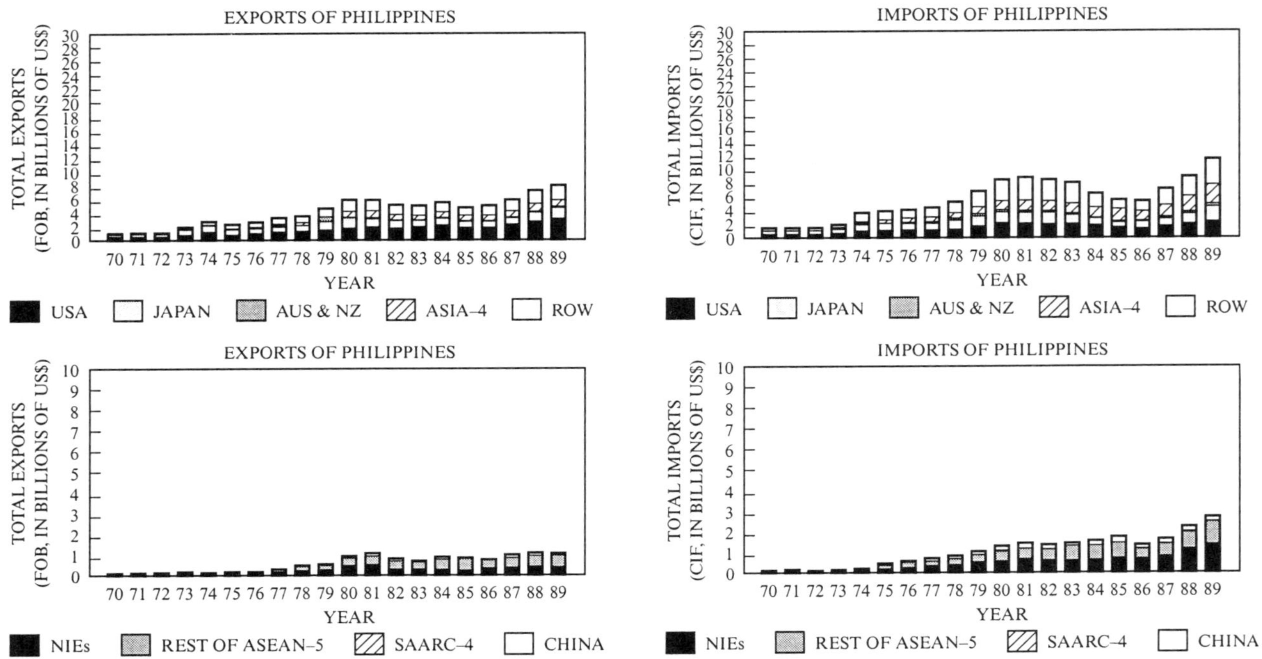

Source: see Appendix, Chapter 6

Figure 24.1 (G) Indonesia: exports and imports

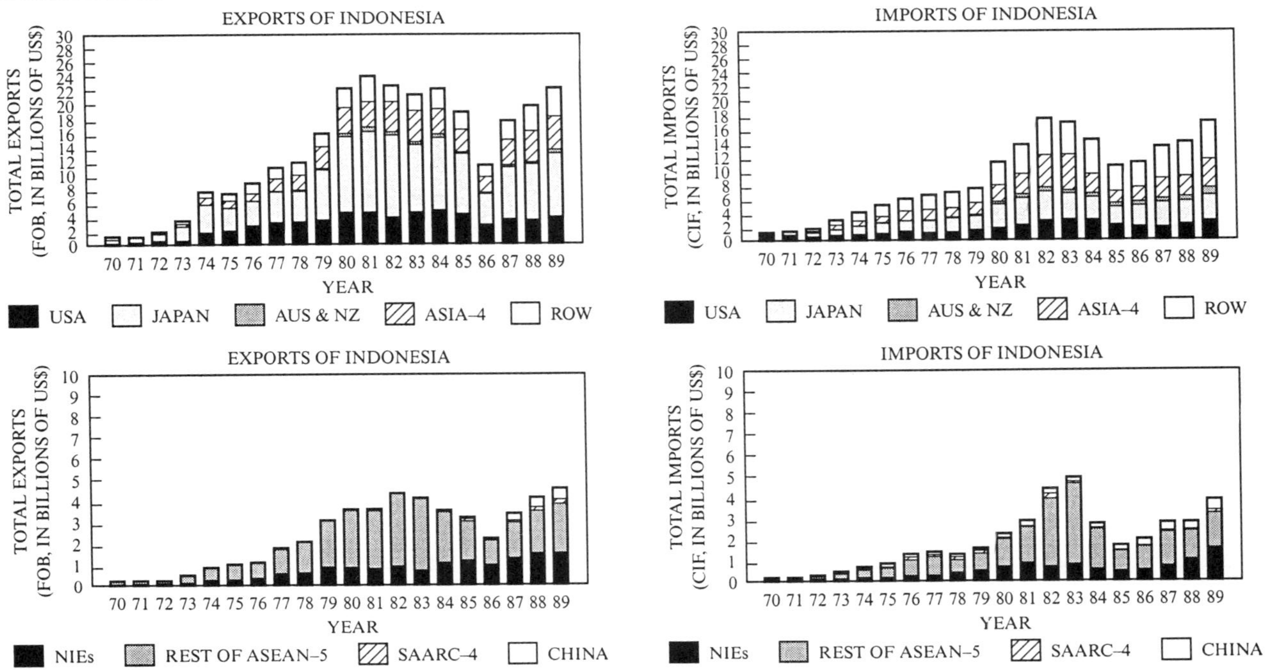

Source: see Appendix, Chapter 6

Figure 24.1 (H) Malaysia: exports and imports

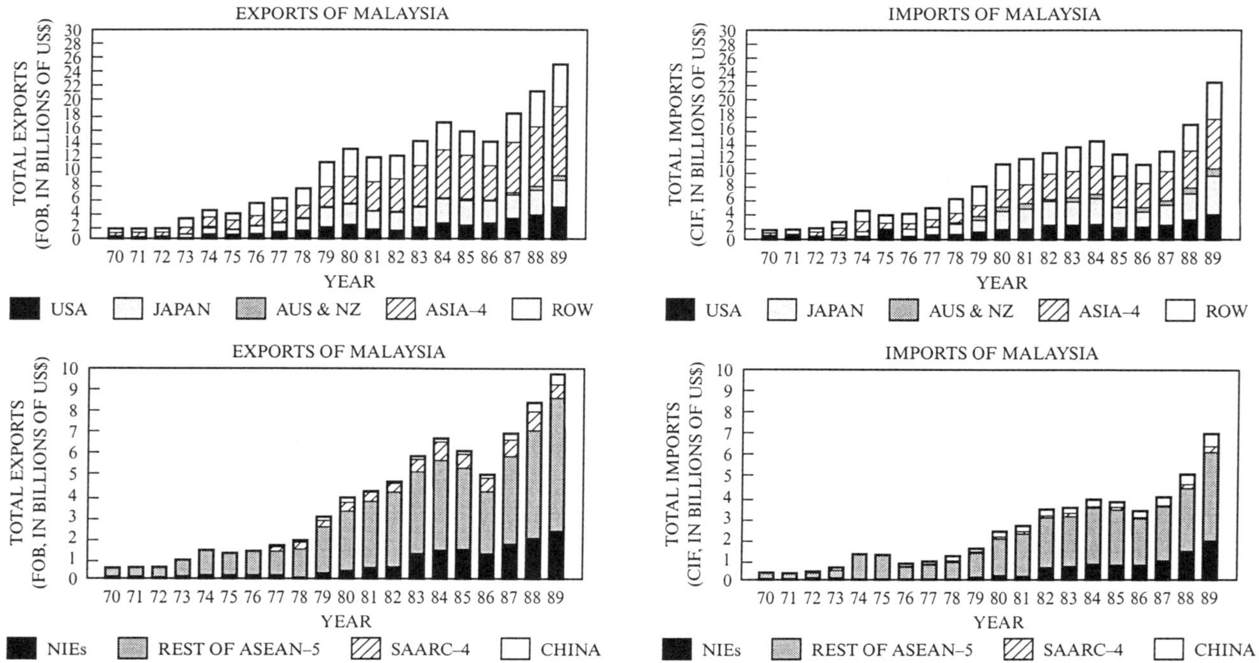

Source: see Appendix, Chapter 6

25 Challenges for APEC

In the absence of a supranational macroeconomic core for an intraregional economic community, especially for APEC, challenges will be overwhelming. We refer to five key issues.

First, we must draw upon the specific Asia-Pacific economic experience. A thorough appreciation of the paradigm of adaptive innovation, as discussed earlier (see Part I), is in order. These APEC member-economies became successful by importing alien technology and paying for them by exporting their end-products to the world market. Thus, the intraregional trade and investment flows have grown, as was expected. It follows that the CAB becomes a key parameter. APEC member-economies watch it all too carefully.

Can APEC maintain a policy of rational vigil for intraregional welfare? If not, mutual bashing of APEC membership will result. On the other hand, any form of unilateral punitive action, such as the U.S. Super-301, to correct a situation of perceived unfair competition, can only be counterproductive (Lipsey, 1992).

Second, complex issues, such as human rights and nuclear proliferation, can and must be discussed and that can be done best at the regional forum before they are taken to the global forum. Binational diplomatic confrontations cannot be helpful for multilateral economic cooperation. If human rights is an issue for sustained economic cooperation, it should be so for member-economies in APEC, until, of course, the one global macro core is effectively operational. The intraregional consensus can help as a building block for the global agenda. Broadening the forum to all APEC members and making the penalty, if any, an all APEC penalty will have its optimum impact. There are multilateral views of human rights, democracy and pluralism and a multilateral institutional arrangement may address these issues. The argument is equally valid for issues such as drug traffic and trades in crime.

Third, environment is an issue which can never be optimally dealt with in the sovereign national context. Externalities span across political borders of sovereign nation-states. Let there be a supranational, intraregional, coordinated environmental policy for APEC and let them deal with the issues of environment for all members of the region.

Acid rain and Mexican environmental pollution can indeed be a subject for the North American joint venture. Given the global parameters of environment, the regional arrangements must be supplemented by a global agenda.

Fourth, an APEC agenda for an intraregional economic cooperation must pay a great deal of attention to the relative economic standing of its member-nations. Most Asia-Pacific economies in APEC are at varying stages of economic development and industrialization.

In this study we have referred to two groups of APEC members: first, the five richer and advanced industrialized members - the U.S., Canada, Japan, Australia and New Zealand - who began with the OPTAD regime, and second, the 13 others with varying stages of industrialization and economic affluence.

Several economies in Southeast Asia and seven economies of South Asia in the South Asian Association for Regional Cooperation (SAARC) are not yet members of APEC, albeit referred to in the present study as we take a "big tent", map-of-the-world view of Asia.

The 1995 APEC Summit in Osaka has carefully considered the "Partnership for Program" as discussed earlier. An intraregional institutional arrangement for structural adjustment of the weaker/poorer member-economies, following the provisions in this regard in the Maastricht Treaty of the EU merits attention. Portugal, Spain, Ireland and Greece stand to gain from the provisions to which the richer EU members have made a commitment. Or, the divide between the rich and the poor may eventually hurt the intraregional economic cooperation.

Finally, failure to coordinate monetary-and-fiscal policies of intraregional member-economies may be a serious blow. If one member-nation, especially one in the process of accelerated industrialization, pursues a wrong policy it must be of concern to all member-economies in the regional compact.

A supply of too much money, unmatched by real economic growth and the threat of inflation, must be of concern. A close watch on the money supply to GDP ratio is important. Too much borrowing and an adverse ratio of public debt to GDP needs monitoring. However, a cooperative, multilateral intraregional policy coordination alone can help correct imbalances in a member-economy. Or, acts of retaliation must result in the disintregration of APEC. The recurrence of serious inflationary pressures in China has been a point of concern, and the failure of macroeconomic policies in Mexico in 1995 indeed became a challenge to NAFTA. There are important lessons to learn.

The list of five issues cannot be viewed as exhaustive. The issues point to the recognition of the case for a gravity model based on a supranational, multilateral, macroeconomic core. In its absence, the location in its common geographical space will prove to be too inadequate to promote and sustain economic cooperation of sovereign member-nations belonging to the Asia-Pacific region. Comparative advantages explained to cost of transportation, be it by land, water or air, may not be enough to provide an optimum base for APEC. An economic space remains to be mapped onto the geographic space.

PART IV

Geo-economics and Intra-APEC Subregional Economic Cooperation

26 Intra-APEC Geo-economics

GEO-ECONOMICS AND THE LINK

Geo-economics provides the practical and effective linkage between a sovereign nation-state economy and the one-world international economic regime. It is an intermediate step in the right direction. The global order of a free and perfectly competitive market economy certainly remains the ideal, but it continues to elude us. Given the necessary and sufficient conditions, the global order will foreseeably become real. Until then, the next best option is a marriage between regionalism and globalism, and thus, geo-economics has become the order of the day. Sharing economic fortunes of a given economy with its neighboring economies will add to the economic gains of all in the region without subtracting anything from others not belonging to the map of the region. Geo-economics thus satisfies the Pareto optimality condition.

We have discussed (see Part I) that in recent time, geo-economics has become the core of economic regionalization in its different manifestations in different regions of the globe. I have argued that a map-of-the-world view of a region should be the optimum base for all such economic regional groupings. The neighboring sovereign economies reach out to each other and *elect voluntarily* to join together to broaden their common economic base with a shared agenda towards optimization of economic gains of all micro units - households and businesses - in all sovereign member-countries in the group.

The EU in the map-of-the-world view of Western Europe with its agenda for free trade in goods and service, free mobility of factor inputs both capital and labor, and a common macroeconomic core with coordinated monetary-fiscal policies, uniquely fits the bill of geo-economics in action.

Returning to the Asia-Pacific, geo-economics in action is very much manifest in the form of FTAs, in Southeast Asia, South Pacific and North America. Parallel efforts are in progress in South Asia. In Central Asia, the Golden Triangle of China-Hong Kong-Taiwan (Taipei) is real, albeit the Triangle is not an entity with a well-defined agenda, as in an FTA or in an economic community.

In Northeast Asia, the debate on a geo-economic grouping remains inconclusive. The East Asian Economic Caucus (EAEC), a proposal favored by Malaysia, an APEC member, has not captured broad support.

The FTAs have a limited agenda for liberalization and facilitation of trade and investment flows among its member-economies, without raising any barriers to non-member economies.

APEC is not a replica of the EU, nor is it an FTA. APEC's 18 sovereign economies share a common agenda for trade and investment liberalization and facilitation, not in the framework of a free trade area. Its goal is "free trade *in the area*", "open regionalism" not regionalism as in a typical FTA, as we have discussed earlier (see Parts II and III).

In what follows, we shall limit our discussions to an exposition of the two specific issues of immediate relevance to APEC.

First, reconciliation of the three region-specific FTAs of APEC member-economies - AFTA in Southeast Asia, ANZ-CER in South Pacific, and NAFTA in North America - is a priority. Indeed, the APEC Summit in Osaka in 1995 reviewed the specific issue. These FTAs can be viewed as articulate expressions of subregionalization on the vast and colorful canvas of APEC regionalization, based on the-map-of-the-world view of the Lake Pacific region. The Osaka recommendation is to make these FTAs accept the code of open subregionalism within the framework of APEC's open regionalism.

Second, the subject of geo-economic grouping or subgrouping merits a further review because of two recent initiatives in each, of which selected APEC member-economies have been actors. One of the initiatives I refer to as the Miami Initiative (see Parts I and II), and the second one relates to the Indian Ocean Grouping Initiative (see Parts I and IV).

In December 1994, the United States, a prime leader in APEC, hosted the conference of all American sovereign economies (excepting Cuba) in Miami, and the American hemispheric agenda towards forming the FTAA was set in progress.

The Indian Ocean Group Initiative has been joined by several other APEC member-economies - Australia and New Zealand in the South Pacific, and Singapore, Thailand, and others in Southeast Asia.

The APEC initiative must address the issue. Is the Lake Pacific an effective, viable economic region of the world map? To the extent that the two above initiatives point to an uneasiness in defining the map of the economic region of APEC, APEC leaders must deal with them forthwith. I have argued that an effective economic regionalization must develop a shared macroeconomic agenda towards coordinating monetary-fiscal policies (see Parts I and III). Of course, this can be done without replicating the EU model of one currency, Ecu or Euro by January 1, 1999, and one central bank or one EMI, as instituted on January 1, 1995 in Frankfurt. A typical free trade area or an adaptation of it as a model of free trade in the area is not likely to fulfill the necessary and sufficient condition for effective economic regionalization within APEC. Privileges of a free trade regime must be conditioned by the common code of macroeconomic discipline imposed by supranational, multilateral, intraregional monetary-fiscal policy management.

THE NORTHEAST ASIA

In several subregions within APEC, specific geo-economic groupings have successfully emerged over the past several decades and we shall review them in the chapters that follow. The fact that Northeast Asia remains an exception with no subregional economic compact of its own is the subject of attention.

Northeast Asia is one of the most dynamic geo-economic entities. Japan, South Korea and Taiwan (Taipei) belong to this map-of-the-world regional space and they most certainly are the most eminent performers in Asia's economic miracle. During the Cold War years, a Northeast Asian Security Compact of these sovereign nation-states, along with the United States and other allies, would be a different story.

The Northeast Asian subregional economic grouping has been an item on the agenda (Yoo and Lee, 1994). One reads the geo-economic map of Northeast Asia, including Japan, North Korea, South Korea, Mongolia, China, Taiwan (Taipei), Hong Kong, plus the eastern provinces of Russia. The Russian leaders have expressed much interest in economic cooperation with APEC and with the Northeast Asian economies. Reportedly, Russia has designated Nakhodka, Vladivostok and the Sakhalin Island as a free economic region for promoting inflow of investment from the richer, neighboring economies in Northeast Asia. Yoo and Lee (1994, Introduction, p. 9) state that the formation of the Northeast Asian economic bloc will bring each economy (of the subregional map) both opportunities and threats. In terms of industrial structures and natural resources (endowments), countries in (Northeast Asia) have a highly complementary relationship, and the growth potential is very high. In contrast, differences in political systems and economic capacity and historical peculiarities among countries in the region may act as *obstacles* to economic cooperation, the authors add.

Indeed, for Northeast Asia, extra-economic considerations seem to have been too baffling. Too many questions continue to beg answers. How will the political relationship between North and South Korea be resolved? How does one develop an agenda for the Korean reunification? How will the often referred to emerging subregional compact of the Golden Triangle of China - Mainland, Hong Kong and Taiwan (Taipei) - unfold? Will the eastern areas of Russia be allowed to join the Northeast Asian economic group with necessary decision-making autonomy? Will Japan elect to opt for the Northeast Asian economic cooperation regime? Or, will she opt for continued sharing with the United States of the leadership role in APEC?

It is instructive to note that in both APEC and the three FTAs within it - AFTA, ANZ-CER and NAFTA - the contracting parties are invariably sovereign economies. The seven member-economies of SAARC in South Asia and the 47 Indian Ocean littoral (some landlocked) economies in a possible Indian Ocean grouping are all sovereign nation-states. Any proposal for a Northeast Asia subregional economic compact must squarely face the issue of how to entertain membership of select areas of the sovereign economy of Russia. For China, with its vast geographical spread over the Asian continental landmass, only the select provinces in Northeast Asia would be plausible candidates for the subregional economic grouping. In both cases, the formation and functioning of an FTA in Northeast Asia would pose an economic challenge with the institution of a Northeast Asia group and an FTA with Japan, South Korea and Taiwan. Whether it would yield the desired economic result, remains an open question.

THE AMERICAN HEMISPHERIC FTA AND THE INDIAN OCEAN GROUPING

Further to my earlier discussions (see Part I) regarding the two above initiatives, it is crucial to emphasize their impact on APEC. In the course of my conversation with members of EPG-APEC (see Part II), the specific issue of the Miami Initiative and eventual establishment of an FTAA came up for review as our discussions dealt with Asianization of Asia *vis-à-vis* Americanization of the Americas. The response was very much universally in support of progressive strengthening of APEC. Indeed, the economic contents of any such regrouping of APEC member-economies into the two trans-Pacific camps - one in the Americas and another in Asia - would be less attractive and thus marginalize possible economic gains. The economic pull factors of APEC member-economies that promoted trade on both shores of the Pacific would be absent.

It must be added that several EPGs welcomed the Miami Initiative. They saw the FTAA as a progressive extension of the U.S. leadership to further liberalize and facilitate American hemispheric intercontinental free trade, and thus promote the WTO agenda for global free trade. The move would facilitate the APEC agenda to that end. Some EPGs, of course, expressed reservations. Some others took a forward-looking view and were willing to see a much larger APEC compact, including Brazil in South America and India in South Asia. An economic regionalization of all the sovereign economies on the map of Asia and the American hemisphere would certainly remain a remote possibility. Some economists from Western Europe have shared their concern regarding the U.S. moving latitudinally toward Asia or longitudinally toward the American hemisphere (see Parts I and II).

The Indian Ocean Initiative, following the inter-governmental meeting at Mauritius, is at its very early stage. The non-official efforts of concerned scholars at the two recent conferences - one at Perth, Australia , June 1995, and another in New Delhi, India, December 1995 are expected to complement the movement. However, too many questions remain to be answered.

We have noted above that the American hemispheric initiative, beginning with the Miami conference in 1994, has been led by the U.S., a leader in APEC; and the Indian Ocean Initiative in 1995 has been joined by several APEC member-economies in South Pacific and Southeast Asia. Much more is yet to come and APEC must continue to face the challenge.

27 The Association of Southeast Asian Nations (ASEAN)

ASEAN is a most successful expression of bringing together several (five in 1967, seven in 1995), sovereign nation-states in Southeast Asia to a shared commitment to a jointly defined intraregional agenda. Specific contributing factors to the ASEAN success story merit careful evaluation.

First, ASEAN, since its founding in 1967 with Indonesia, Malaysia, the Philippines, Singapore and Thailand, has experienced a history of evolution in intra-regional cooperation for a long period. A commitment to a common regional security and defense arrangement over the past many years helped in the effective promotion of a broader political framework of mutual appreciation of each other's concern. The phased progression of ASEAN regionalization by a series of Declarations helped to develop a mutual understanding among the leaders of the five sovereign member-states and cemented the intraregional bond.

The process was never threatened by the dictum of the majority rule, and sovereignty of each member-state was respected. Member-countries carefully noted the limitations of any form of super-power game and related to each other accordingly. The so-called "ASEAN way" or "ASEAN consensus" became the mode of operation and sustained the ASEAN togetherness. A commitment to flexibility for both intraregional and interregional accommodation has been at the core of ASEAN success. As Brunei and Vietnam became members of ASEAN in 1985 and 1995, respectively, the new sovereign member-countries fully appreciated and accepted the institution and its way of operation. Thus, the Southeast Asian experiment in intraregional economic cooperation presents a unique learning experience.

Second, ASEAN member-economies uniformly adopted the open economic policy, encouraging free flow of trade and investment. The rest of the world convincingly noted that there never was an attempt to form a "fortress" Southeast Asia. The rules of free enterprise market economy in general became the norm. The private corporate sectors in member-countries responded to the market intiative with vigor. In addition to mutual security, the intraregional economic cooperation presented a framework of a widened market for profit maximization for microeconomic actors in each member-economy. ASEAN member-governments facilitated the process and effectively reinforced the process of economic regionalization. Each member-country independently managed its monetary-fiscal policy to that end, albeit with varying degrees of success.

EVOLUTION OF ASEAN

Institutionalization of the Southeast Asian subregional forum evolved through a series of Declarations, in 1967, 1971, 1976 and 1987, respectively. In 1967, ASEAN began as a strategic alliance toward institutionalization of a "Zone of Peace, Freedom and Neutrality," (ZOPFAN) and by 1987, it progressed into a paradigm of economic regionalization.

Ariff (1994) refers to its "long history", dating back to the 1960s, and notes that ASEAN was preceded by the Association of Southeast Asia (ASA) - Malaysia, the Philippines and Thailand in 1961 - and then in 1963, by MAPHILINDO, consisting of Malaysia, the Philippines and Indonesia, a proposal never acted upon.

The Bangkok Declaration of August 8, 1967 by the designated cabinet members of Indonesia, Malaysia, the Philippines, Singapore and Thailand "*mindful* of the existence of mutual interests and common problems among countries of Southeast Asia" resolved to constitute the Association of Southeast Asian Nations (ASEAN). The lead item on its seven-point objectives was "to accelerate the economic growth, social progress and cultural development in the region through joint endeavors in the spirit of equality and partnership".

On November 27, 1971, came the Kuala Lumpur Declaration by the foreign ministers of Indonesia, Malaysia, the Philippines, Singapore and the special envoy of Thailand, reiterating their joint commitment to the principle of the Bangkok Declaration toward "strengthening the economic and social responsibility of the region". However, the focal point remained the establishment of ZOPFAN.

On February 24, 1976 at Denpasar, Bali, for the first time, the Heads of the five sovereign states - Indonesia, Malaysia, the Philippines, Singapore and Thailand - signed the Declaration of ASEAN Concorde with reaffirmation of their commitment to earlier Declarations of 1967 and 1971. In addition, reference was made to the Charter of the United Nations and the Treaty of Bandung signed in 1955. The signatories to the Concorde made it a point to assure the rest of the world that ASEAN was a regional compact within the framework of the global organization as defined by the United Nations' charter. Indeed, the affirmation of their commitment to regionalism within the framework of globalism was an important step. Reference to the Treaty of Bandung underscored the principle of neutrality for the ASEAN member-states. This Declaration became the main economic blueprint of ASEAN.

At Denpasar, Bali, on February 24, 1976, the Treaty of Amity and Cooperation in Southeast Asia was signed "to promote perpetual peace, *everlasting* amity and cooperation among their peoples which would contribute to their *strength, solidarity and closer relationship*" (italics added). On the same occasion, the contracting parties agreed to establish the ASEAN Secretariat, headed by a Secretary-General, to be appointed by ASEAN foreign ministers.

Brunei Darussalam became a member of ASEAN in 1985, and the heads of the six sovereign nation-states - Brunei Darussalam, Indonesia, Malaysia, the Philippines, Singapore and Thailand - signed the Manila Declaration on December 15, 1987. Encouraged by the achievements of ASEAN since its founding in 1967, the leadership stated in no uncertain terms that they were "convinced that economic development and progress are fundamental to the stability and security of the region". The Manila Declaration went on to emphasize: "member-states shall strengthen *intra-ASEAN economic cooperation* to maximize the realization of the region's potential in trade and development and to increase ASEAN's efficacy in combating protectionism and countering its effects" (italics added). The concept of AFTA was born at the Singapore Summit in January 1992.

As of July 28, 1995, Vietnam has been admitted to ASEAN membership.

TOWARD AN INTRA-ASEAN SUPRANATIONAL ADMINISTRATION

The sovereign participating member-states of ASEAN fully and straightforwardly recognized that a supranational organizational structure was in order, and on February 24, 1976, they resolved to act in this regard. No member-state was concerned about compromising its sovereign authority, nor was there any idle debate. Formal establishment of the intra-ASEAN administrative institution came as a natural corollary.

Indeed, the recent legal verdicts by the highest courts of law in both the United Kingdom and Germany have established that membership of the EU does not compromise the sovereign authority of its member-states. Critiques, however, continue to argue that the debate should be allowed to remain open.

ASEAN has a well-structured, supranational administrative organization (see Table 27.1) and its sovereign member-states accept the duties and responsibilities of its membership as clearly stated by a set of *voluntary* agreements. The supranational institution is known to be expensive and its bureaucracy, of course, has grown as did the agenda of intra-ASEAN cooperation. The ASEAN Secretariat is a very lean organization, especially when compared with that of the EU in Brussels.

Table 27.1 ASEAN organizational structure

Heads of ASEAN member-states

Economic ministers **Foreign ministers** **Other ministers**

ASEAN Standing Committees

Budget Committee

Audit Committee

National Secretariat
- Brunei Darussalam
- Indonesia
- Malaysia
- Philippines
- Singapore
- Thailand

ASEAN Dialogue with
- Australia
- European Union
- New Zealand
- UNDP
- Canada
- Japan
- U.S.
- South Korea
- PRC (China)
- India

ASEAN Committees in
- Bonn
- Brussels
- Canberra
- Geneva
- London
- Ottawa
- Paris
- Tokyo
- Washington, DC
- Wellington

ASEAN Committees on
- Finance and Banking
- Food, Agriculture and Banking
- Industry, Minerals and. Energy
- Trade and Tourism
- Transportation and Communication
- Science and Technology
- Social Development
- Culture/Information
- Drug Matters

ASEAN Secretariat

Source: ASEAN (1990); ASEAN (1995)

The ASEAN Secretariat heads the pyramid with an ASEAN National Secretariat at each member-state - Brunei Darussalam, Indonesia, Malaysia, the Philippines, Singapore and Thailand.

Special missions for "ASEAN Dialogue" with Australia, the EU, New Zealand, the United Nations Development Program (UNDP), Canada, Japan and the U.S. have been established. ASEAN committees have been constituted in various capitals - Bonn, Brussels, Canberra, Geneva, London, Ottawa, Paris, Tokyo, Washington, DC and Wellington. Three new missions for ASEAN Dialogue in South Korea, the People's Republic of China and India have recently been added.

Committees on (i) Finance and Banking, (ii) Food, Agriculture and Banking, (iii) Industry, Minerals and Energy, (iv) Transportation and Communication and (v) Trade and Tourism operate under the ASEAN economic ministers while committees on (i) Science and Technology, (ii) Social Development, (iii) Culture and Information and (iv) Drug Matters operate under an ASEAN Standing Committee, reporting to ASEAN foreign ministers. Over the years the ASEAN committees have appointed a large number of working groups.

ASEAN: A PROFILE OF ECONOMIC DYNAMISM

ASEAN is a market of more than 400 million people. In 1990 the demographic census figures were: Brunei Darussalam - 256,500; Indonesia - 184.28 million; Malaysia - 17.89 million; the Philippines - 62.44 million; Singapore - 2.71 million; and Thailand - 54.68 million (United Nations, 1993, p.107). On July 28, 1995, Vietnam joined ASEAN with its 72 million people. Laos, Cambodia and Mayanmar (populations of 4.20, 8.34 and 41.83 million, respectively, in 1990) are expected to become ASEAN members in the course of time. The probability of the linkage between ASEAN and South Asia continue to be higher, as the push of region-specific geo-economics unfolds.

ASEAN's unique profile of economic dynamism merits attention. For this region from 1960 to 1991, the average growth rate of real GDP at market prices approximating 6 per cent outperformed economies in North America and Europe growing at about 3 per cent, and in Oceana, Africa, and Latin America with growth rates at about 3 to 4 per cent. Select ASEAN members, especially Singapore, compare with Asia's NIEs - South Korea, Taiwan and Hong Kong. Indeed, Singapore's economic status has earned it a place in the group of Asian NIEs.

Brunei Darussalam, a uniquely oil-rich economy with a small population of 256,500 in 1990 in a land area of 5,765 sq. km. became a very special member of ASEAN in 1985. Petroleum and natural gas dominate its economy. Indeed, the mineral fuels have constituted an annual average of 98.3 per cent of its total exports for 1981 to 1988 (Brunei Darussalam Ministry of Finance, 1990, p. 98). The CAB (exports minus imports) has been uniformly positive for 1979 to 1990. For the same period the real GDP (1974 = 100) followed an uneven growth path, albeit within a narrow band of fluctuations. The rate of inflation measured by annual percentage change in the consumer price index (1977 = 100) averaged 3.4 per cent for 1979 to 1990 (ibid., p. 149).

Table 27.2 State of ASEAN economies: GDP and inflation

Panel A: Growth rate of GDP (% per annum)

	Base year	1971-80	1981-90	1991-94
Indonesia	1983	7.7	5.5	6.6
Malaysia	1978	7.8	5.2	8.3
Philippines	1985	6.0	1.0	1.1
Singapore	1985	7.9	6.3	7.4
Thailand	1988	7.9	7.9	7.9

Panel B: Changes in consumer prices (% per annum)

	1971-80	1981-90	1991-94
Indonesia	7.5	8.6	8.3
Malaysia	6.0	3.2	4.2
Philippines	14.8	13.0	11.0
Singapore	7.4	2.3	3.1
Thailand	10.0	4.4	4.3

Source: Asian Development Bank (1994): Panel A, p.231; Panel B, p. 239.

Both by measures of annual GDP growth and the rate of inflation (Table 27.2), the member-economies record exemplary performance, outperforming most others in other regions. Over the 1971 to 1994 time period, in terms of growth rates of real GDP, Indonesia, Malaysia, Singapore and Thailand maintain scores between 6 and 8 per cent. The Philippines, for its unique political reasons, has a poor record in the 1980s; however, in 1994 with a 4 per cent annual growth rate of GDP, it may have turned the corner. Vietnam, the newest member, reports a respectable score (data not reported).

For changes in consumer prices per cent per annum, Singapore excels in its record; Malaysia and Thailand have done as well as South Korea and Taiwan, the newly industrialized economies. For the same period, Indonesia follows closely. The Philippines has yet to stabilize its consumer prices, and the transitional economy of Vietnam appears to have been able to come to grips with its high rate of inflation.

ASEAN member-economies are progressively industrializing (Tables 27.3 and 27.4). Singapore, given its city-state status, began with little agricultural activity and is notable for its dependence on the service sector, which continues to contribute as much as 60 per cent to its GDP. For 1970 to 1993, the economies of Indonesia, Malaysia and Thailand underwent structural changes; traditional agricultural sector's shares to GDP declined to an average of about 15 per cent, while industry-service sectors' shares to GDP, very nearly evenly distributed, rose to some 85 per cent The Philippines is lagging, and it is too soon for Vietnam to report relevant data.

Table 27.3 Manufacturing earnings in selected ASEAN countries

	Average earnings, 1980-91 Average rate of growth (% per annum)	Index 1991 1980 = 100	Output growth 1980-92 Manufacturing	Total
Malaysia	2.4	135	8.0	5.9
Thialand	6.5	173*	10.1	8.2
Philippines	5.8	190	0.7	1.2
Indonesia	4.4	169	14.0	5.5
Korea	7.9	225	11.6	9.5

Source: World Bank (1994). Note * for 1990.

For 1980 to 1992 the rates of growth of manufacturing output in Malaysia, Thailand and Indonesia were 8 per cent, 10.1 per cent and 14 per cent, respectively, and compare favorably with that of South Korea at 11.6 per cent.

Comparison of the total output growth rate in each economy with that of South Korea, for the same period, also presents an interesting profile (Table 27.3). The average annual manufacturing earnings for 1980 to 1991 for these ASEAN economies, however, do not follow the Korean profile. Based on an index 1980 = 100, in 1991, the earnings of manufacturing workers in South Korea have increased phenomenally.

Table 27.4 Sectoral shares of GDP (%)

		Agriculture	Industry	Services	Total
Indonesia	1970	35.0	28.0	37.0	100.0
	1980	24.4	41.3	34.3	100.0
	1993	17.6	42.1	40.3	100.0
Malaysia	1970	na	na	na	na
	1980	22.9	35.8	41.3	100.0
	1993	15.8	44.2	40.0	100.0
Philippines	1970	28.2	33.7	38.1	100.0
	1980	23.5	40.5	36.0	100.0
	1993	22.7	34.4	42.9	100.0
Singapore	1970	2.2	36.4	61.4	100.0
	1980	1.1	38.8	60.0	99.9
	1993	0.2	36.5	63.3	100.0
Thailand	1970	30.2	25.7	44.1	100.0
	1980	20.0	30.1	49.7	100.0
	1993	12.2	40.9	46.9	100.0

Source: Asian Development Bank (1994, p. 236).
Note: na = not available

The pattern of accelerated growth is evident. Singapore began with a lead in 1971 to 1980 and continues to maintain a preeminent position for values of both savings (S) and investment (I) parameters for 1981 to 1994 at 40+ per cent of GDP. For Indonesia, Malaysia and Thailand, performances in the 1970s proved a difficult challenge. However, in the 1980s, the three ASEAN members crossed the 30 per cent mark for the values of the related parameters. Indeed, for 1991 to 1994 the average values of the three economies for both the S/GDP and I/GDP parameters have risen to 35+ per cent and they progressively inch up to be competitive with Singapore. Of course, the Philippines, for its political and related extraeconomic reasons, continue to lag (Table 27.5).

Table 27.5 Savings and investment parameters

Panel A: Gross Domestic Savings (S) as % of GDP

	1971-80	1981-90	1991-94
Indonesia	21.6	31.8	39.9
Malaysia	29.1	33.0	36.1
Philippines	26.5	22.3	15.2
Singapore	30.0	42.6	46.6
Thailand	22.2	27.2	36.5

Panel B: Gross Domestic Investment (I) as a % of GDP

	1971-80	1981-90	1991-94
Indonesia	19.3	30.4	35.1
Malaysia	24.9	30.7	34.7
Philippines	27.8	21.9	23.0
Singapore	41.2	42.2	40.6
Thailand	25.3	30.6	42.4

Source: Asian Development Bank (1994).
Panel A, p. 237. Panel B, p. 238.

If one leaves aside Brunei Darussalam, the Philippines and Vietnam, the three ASEAN members as special cases, the ASEAN-4 - Indonesia, Malaysia, Singapore and Thailand - demonstrate a pattern of convergence in terms of rate of growth of real (GDP), and the savings and investment parameters, the two key behavioral relations (Green, 1994). They also have experienced a course of structural changes of their respective economies. The agriculture-based traditional economies of Indonesia, Malaysia and Thailand have moved to industrialization with necessary support of the service sectors. On the other hand, Singapore, given its initial conditions limiting the role of agriculture, has transformed its economy to a base of strong industry and service sectors, the latter dominating. Singapore shifted from services to industry, and then to services. Indeed, the ASEAN-4 are ready to provide a viable economic base to support and sustain economic regionalization in Southeast Asia.

ASEAN: MONETARY AND FISCAL POLICIES

Each ASEAN member-economy is a sovereign nation-state. They have not been engaged in a debate if they should have an intraregional institutional provision for coordination of *monetary-fiscal* policies. The organizational structure of the overall ASEAN institution provides for regular meetings of the economic ministers and a standing Committee on Finance and Banking working under them. Of course, regular meetings of the heads of central banks of member-countries are held. No intraregional monetary authority has been discussed. We present specific empirical evidence to examine if an ASEAN approach toward an intraregional coordination of monetary-fiscal policies is emerging (Table 27.6).

The monetary policy of each ASEAN member-economy, as measured by changes in money supply per annum, appears to have been firmly targeted to containing inflation so that the growth regime can be sustained. Changes in consumer prices (per cent per annum) for each member-country came to be stabilized approximately at the annual average rate of each for 1981 to 1990 (see Table 27.2, for convenience, partially reproduced at the end of Panel A of Table 27.6).

The figures for the two successive decades, 1971 to 1980 and 1981 to 1990 point to a direction: for Indonesia, 17.5 and 8.6; for Malaysia, 6.0, and 3.2; for the Philippines, 14.8 and 13.0; for Singapore, 7.4 and 2.3; and for Thailand, 10.0 and 4.4. For each country, the annual average rate for the 1980s was lower than the annual average for the 1970s. In the 1990s, each country pursued its monetary policy to maintain inflationary pressure within the bounds attained in the previous decade with varying degrees of fluctuations - albeit

Table 27.6 Monetary-fiscal parameters

Panel A: Money Supply and Changes in Consumer Prices Changes in Money Supply (M2) % per annum - First Row
Changes in Consumer Prices % per annum - Second Row

1988	1989	1990	1991	1992	1993	1994
Indonesia						
23.9	39.8	44.2	17.1	20.2	15.3	16.0
8.0	6.5	7.4	9.2	7.5	9.0	7.5
Malaysia						
7.2	16.1	12.8	14.5	19.1	17.0	18.0
2.6	2.8	2.6	4.4	4.7	3.9	3.9
The Philippines						
23.8	31.6	15.31	5.71	1.01	2.5	16.0
8.7	12.2	14.2	18.7	8.9	7.6	8.9
Singapore						
13.5	22.5	20.0	12.4	8.9	6.1	8.0
1.5	2.4	3.5	3.4	2.3	2.4	4.5
Thailand						
18.2	26.2	26.7	19.8	15.6	16.5	15.5
3.8	5.4	6.0	5.7	4.1	3.1	4.2

Note: For changes in consumer prices (% per annum), 1971-80, 1981-90 and 1991-94, see Table 27.2 Panel B.

Table 27.6 (Continued)

Panel B: Government Expenditure and Budget Government Expenditure (G) as % of GDP - First Row
Overall Budget Surplus/Deficit as % of GDP - Second Row

1988	1989	1990	1991	1992	1993
			Indonesia		
23.2	22.8	25.3	23.0	22.7	20.9
-7.0	-5.6	-5.1	-4.6	-4.2	-3.2
			Malaysia		
27.8	28.0	28.5	28.3	27.4	24.6
-3.6	-3.3	-3.0	-2.0	-0.8	+0.1
			Philippines		
17.1	18.2	20.0	20.1	19.7	19.6
-3.8	-2.1	-3.1	-2.5	-1.2	-1.7
			Singapore		
23.6	22.2	17.8	16.3	18.8	19.2
+6.6	+2.9	+2.9	+5.1	+3.6	+4.0
			Thailand		
14.3	14.2	13.9	14.5	15.8	18.0
+2.3	+3.5	+4.8	+4.3	+2.6	+2.2

Source: Asian Development Bank (1994). Panel A - Money Supply, p. 240; Changes in consumer Prices, p. 239. Panel B - G/GDP, p. 251; and Surplus or Deficit/GDP, p. 253.

within a narrow band in each case - including the Philippines, which has been recovering from its domestic political/extraeconomic shocks.

The fiscal policy as indicated by government expenditure (G) as a percentage of GDP (G/GDP) and overall budget surplus/deficit as a percent of GDP (Panel B of Table 27.6) also indicates a degree of cohesion. For 1988 to 1993 government expenditure as a percentage of GDP (G/GDP) for Indonesia, Malaysia and the Philippines varies between one-fifth to one-fourth, and each has a deficit budget situation. However, the budget deficits in Indonesia and the Philippines are declining, while Malaysia has recorded a marginal surplus in 1993. For the same period, for Singapore and Thailand, the G/GDP ratios are less than one-fifth, and each has uniformly maintained a surplus budget. As to the inflationary impact of the fiscal policy, the evidence supports little pressure.

TRADE/INVESTMENT FLOWS OF ASEAN

Singapore, with a uniform positive balance for the period, stands out as a case by itself. Indonesia, Malaysia, the Philippines and Thailand present a profile of economies struggling to balance their respective balance of payments on current account. The 1988 to 1993 annual averages of negative balances range between -1.22 for Malaysia and -5.77 for Thailand. The relative figure for the Philippines at -2.78 merits attention since its overall economic performance is in no way comparable to that of Thailand (Table 27.7).

Imports of capital goods and exports of newly manufactured products plus traditional merchandise, inclusive of oil, especially for Indonesia, cover the two sides of their balance sheets.

For 1988 to 1993, Singapore presents uniformly each year a negative balance of trade account (merchandise trade only) as against a positive balance of payments on current account; Indonesia reports a positive annual balance of trade account with a negative annual balance of payments on current account; Malaysia has a mixed record - a positive annual balance of trade account with its balance of payments on current account, negative for 1990-92 and positive for the rest of the three years; the Philippines and Thailand record negative annual measures on both accounts. The data as of 1994, however, point to a new direction, Thailand reversing its negative balance.

Direction of exports sheds light on the significance of regionalization (Table 27.8). For Indonesia, Malaysia and Singapore, the shift in direction of export trade to developing Asian economies is to be noted. Excepting the Philippines and Thailand, there is a newly emerging pattern of declining export dependence on Japan and the United States with a concurrent positive shift in

Table 27.7 Balance of payments on current account as percentage of GDP

	1988	1989	1990	1991	1992	1993	Annual Average
Indonesia	-1.7	-1.2	-2.8	-3.5	-2.9	-2.1	-2.37
Malaysia	5.2	0.7	-2.1	-8.9	-2.8	0.6	-1.22
Philippines	-1.0	-3.4	-6.1	-2.3	-1.9	-2.0	-2.78
Singapore	3.6	8.3	5.0	8.2	6.4	2.8	5.72
Thailand	-2.7	-3.5	-8.5	-7.7	-6.0	-6.1	-5.75

Source:Asian Development Bank (1994). Table A-16, p. 246.

Table 27.8 Direction of exports (% share)

	1985	1992	Change
	Indonesia		
DMCs	17.2	24.4	+
Japan	46.2	34.3	-
U.S.	21.7	13.7	-
EU	6.0	12.0	+
ANZ	1.2	2.6	+
ROW	7.6	12.1	+
Total	99.9	99.1	
	Malaysia		
DMCs	38.1	41.1	+
Japan	24.6	13.3	-
U.S.	12.8	18.7	+
EU	13.6	13.7	unchanged
ANZ	1.9	2.2	+
ROW	9.1	11.1	+
Total	100.1	100.1	
	Philippines		
DMCs	19.5	12.9	-
Japan	19.0	20.6	+
U.S.	35.9	41.8	+
EU	13.8	18.2	+
ANZ	2.1	1.2	-
ROW	9.7	5.4	-
Total	100.0	100.1	

Table 27.8 (Continued)

	Singapore		
DMCs	36.7	37.7	+
Japan	9.4	5.7	-
U.S.	21.2	21.2	unchanged
EU	10.1	14.0	+
ANZ	4.5	2.3	-
ROW	18.2	19.1	+
Total	100.1	100.0	
	Thailand		
DMCs	27.1	21.9	-
Japan	13.4	17.5	+
U.S.	19.7	22.5	+
EU	17.8	18.2	+
ANZ	1.9	1.7	-
ROW	20.2	18.1	-
Total	100.1	99.9	

Source: Asian Development Bank (1994). Table A-12, p.242.
Notes: DMCs = Developing member countries of ADB, Hong Kong, South Korea, Taipei (China), People's Republic of China, Mongolia, Cambodia, Indonesia, Laos, Malaysia, Philippines, Thailand, Vietnam, Bangladesh, Bhutan, India, Maldives, Myanmar, Nepal, Pakistan, Sri Lanka, and the Pacific Islands. EU = European Union. ANZ = Australia and New Zealand. ROW = Rest of the world.

Table 27.9 ASEAN trade direction

Panel A: Direction of ASEAN trade flows 1985-90 (%)

	1985	1990	Growth 1985-90
Intra-ASEAN	19.7	17.1	14.8
East Asia	33.8	34.4	17.7
NAFTA	18.7	18.2	16.7
EU	11.5	14.8	23.4
ROW	16.2	15.0	15.5
Total	99.9	99.5	

Panel B: Intra-ASEAN trade profile

	Country share of intra-ASEAN (%)		ASEAN trade/ total trade (%)	
	1985	1990	1985	1990
Brunei	3.0	2.12	2.8	28.4
Indonesia	11.0	8.1	10.2	9.1
Malaysia	25.2	26.4	24.3	24.0
Philippines	4.9	3.5	13.1	8.7
Singapore	45.6	47.1	24.8	22.1
Thailand	10.2	12.8	16.6	12.0

Table 27.9 (Continued)

Panel C: National contribution to total intra-ASEAN exports (%)

	1970-74	1975-79	1980-84	1985-89
Brunei	4.3	2.5	3.3	2.4
Indonesia	16.12	1.7	19.8	12.1
Malaysia	29.82	4.1	23.4	27.6
Philippines	1.2	2.3	2.7	3.0
Singapore	37.6	38.6	43.9	45.2
Thailand	11.0	10.8	6.9	9.7
Total	100.0	100.0	100.0	100.0

Panel D: Intra-ASEAN vis-à-vis ASEAN/world exports

	ASEAN share in total world export	Intra-ASEAN in total ASEAN export
1970-74	2.4	19.1
1975-79	3.2	16.2
1980-84	4.1	21.0
1985-89	3.8	18.3

Source: IMF (1991); Panels A and B adapted from Ariff (1994 pp. 104-5): Panels C and D from Suthiphand (1992).

Table 27.10 DFI ASEAN

Panel A: Total DFI 1986-90 (US$ Million)

	(1)	(2)
Indonesia	15,862.0	20,160.5
Malaysia	10,815.0	5,351.7
Philippines	2,125.0	2,483.5
Thailand	23,467.0	25,174.4
Singapore	4,114.5	

Panel B: Sources of DFI (%): from Japan - 1, U.S. - 2, Singapore - 3, South Korea - 4, Taipei - 5, Hong Kong - 6,

	(1)	(2)	(3)	(4)	(5)	(6)
Indonesia						
1986	39.8	18.6	12.3	1.5	2.2	11.6
1987	36.5	5.0	0.4	1.6	0.5	9.3
1988	5.6	15.2	5.4	4.5	20.6	5.4
1989	16.3	7.4	3.5	9.9	3.3	8.6
1990	13.3	0.3	4.0	6.4	8.5	15.8
Malaysia						
1986	6.9	3.2	10.9	0.3	0.6	3.4
1987	34.7	7.9	12.6	0.2	11.7	4.3
1988	25.1	11.0	8.6	0.9	17.0	6.1
1989	31.1	3.7	10.6	2.2	25.0	4.1
1990	12.0	1.4	2.6	0.7	48.4	3.0

Table 27.10 (Continued)

		(Panel B: continued)				
Philippines						
1986	28.2	28.2	na	0.0	0.4	9.0
1987	17.4	21.6	na	0.6	5.4	16.8
1988	20.3	32.3	na	0.4	23.3	5.7
1989	19.7	16.3	na	2.1	18.5	16.5
1990	37.1	6.0	na	1.7	23.4	5.6
Thailand						
1986	58.2	17.2	6.1	27.3	0.1	7.2
1987	36.6	6.5	4.7	19.0	0.5	11.4
1988	48.7	10.8	8.7	26.9	1.7	13.6
1989	44.1	6.9	7.0	25.2	2.1	10.9
1990	34.6	15.3	13.9	34.7	4.4	7.3

Panel C: ASEAN Cumulative DFI (%) to:
A - Indonesia 1967-87; B - Malaysia 1975-87; C - Philippines 1975-87; D - Singapore (Stock); E - Thailand 1978-87

	(A)	(B)	(C)	(D)	(E)
U.S.	7.3	6.7	38.4	26.8	28.1
Europe	16.3	20.8	18.4	28.4	18.3
Japan	33.2	22.8	14.0	15.3	33.9
NIEs	13.2	11.9	6.3	6.8	8.2
Others	30.0	37.8	22.9	22.7	11.5

Source: Panel A : Column 1 - Tan et al. (1992); adapted from Ariff (1994) p. 105; Column 2 - Chia (1993, p. 80). Panel B: Tan et al. (1992); from Ariff (1994) p. 105. Panel C: Chia (1993) p. 79. NIEs = Hong Kong, South Korea, Taipei.

the direction of the EU. There appears no extreme divergence in the trading patterns of the ASEAN economies, albeit notable differences persist.

An instructive profile of intra-ASEAN trade flows is presented above (Table 27.9). For 1985 to 1990, there is little evidence of significant changes in the relative shares of ASEAN trade to intra-ASEAN region, East Asia, NAFTA, and the rest of the world (ROW) (Panel A). The share of EU, however, rose significantly over the five-year period.

The same phenomenon is to be observed for the shares of an ASEAN member-country in intra-ASEAN trade and in the ratio of a member-country's ASEAN trade as a share of its total trade. Ariff warns that figures presented should be read with due appreciation for the large proportion of "*entrepót* trade" between Malaysia and Singapore, and also for the dominance of oil in the intra-ASEAN trade of Brunei and Indonesia. Suthiphand (personal communication 1995) points to the fact that the recent phenomenon of Thailand-ASEAN trade, consisting mainly of Thailand-Singapore trade, especially for electrical and electronic products, are to be processed for trade with third countries.

The state of relative shares of ASEAN member-economies in intra-ASEAN exports over 1970 to 1989 (Panel C) further points to a corresponding pattern of strength and weakness of each member, with some evidences of negative fluctuations for Thailand in 1980 to 1984 and Indonesia in 1985 to 1989. Both ASEAN's share in total world exports and intra-ASEAN share in total ASEAN exports (Panel D) continue to remain within a limited range of variation for 1970-89. Both in terms of a time-series profile and in terms of an intra-ASEAN cross-section profile, the ASEAN economies appear to be waiting for anticipated changes of substantive high-tech industrialization.

It follows that the ASEAN trade profile is in a process of evolution, and it is too soon to draw any firm conclusion for the emerging intra-ASEAN economic regionalization profile (Ariff, 1994, 1989a and 1989b).

The process of industrialization of ASEAN economies and its consequent deepening are in place, especially in Indonesia, Malaysia and Thailand, and less perceptibly in the Philippines; albeit its manufacturing output/GDP share compares with that of Indonesia. Foreseeably, in the near future, the export-led economic growth regimes of these four ASEAN economies are expected to present a different and more dynamic trade profile. The structure of Singapore's economy is noted for the dominance of its service sector, and Singapore is the one ASEAN member currently engaged in much intraregional investment. Chia (1995, personal communication) and others argue that there are substantial cross investments among ASEAN countries, but statistics are not readily available.

Much of DFI into the ASEAN-4 flows from the United States, Japan, Singapore, South Korea, Taipei and Hong Kong. Two recent studies (Chia, 1993 and Tan et al., 1992) present the estimates for 1986 to 1990 (Table 27.10), total DFI (Panel A) and its major origins (Panel B). The EU has made its competitive share of investment in Southeast Asia (Panel C).

As much as 62 to 88 per cent inflows of foreign investments into ASEAN economies are coming from three competitive sources: the United States, Japan and Western Europe, followed by the NIEs of East Asia. Singapore is an emerging intra-ASEAN investor. Japan has a predominant position in Indonesia, Malaysia and Thailand. The United States is lagging far behind both Japan and Europe in Indonesia and Malaysia, competing with Japan in Thailand, and with Europe in Singapore. Historical ties should explain the dominant position of the U.S. in the Philippines. The pattern is changing fast and in recent years Asian NIEs, especially Taiwan and South Korea, have become leading investors in ASEAN.

Notwithstanding minor discrepancies in the two estimates of total inflows of DFI into ASEAN economies for 1986-90 (Panel A) have been relatively small, especially in the context of economic growth of these economies. The relative figures of foreign investments, direct as well as indirect, in East Asian NIEs - South Korea, Taipei (China) and Hong Kong - given their much smaller population bases, were much larger. If one argues, as we do, that foreign investments provide the platform for export-led growth and also of adaptive innovation paradigm, enabling indigenous economies receiving such inflows of foreign investment to produce goods and services - quality-competitive as well as cost-price competitive - for exports to the world market, the role of ASEAN economies in world trade must await further careful evaluation (Ariff 1989a, 1898b, 1994). It may be too soon to arrive at any definitive conclusion.

GEO-ECONOMICS IN SOUTHEAST ASIA: AFTA

ASEAN, we argue, is a player *par excellence* of geo-economics in Southeast Asia, *a unique presence of economic regionalization.* It has a history of its own. Since 1967 its leaders have enjoyed a high comfort level as they continue to cooperate for a shared intraregional agenda. ASEAN has evolved into a regional economic forum only recently in the 1980s, beginning with the Bali Summit in 1976. In recent years, economic cooperation among its member-states has received priority and intra-ASEAN trade has recorded an upturn.

Adoption of an agenda for an ASEAN free trade area within ten years (originally 15 years), beginning on January 1, 1993, is an important step. Thus, with the new ten-year target date, AFTA will have full intraregional free trade in 2003. A common effective preferential tariff (CEPT) scheme makes the AFTA agenda operational (Lee, 1994; Narongchai and Stifel, 1994).

To this end, a twofold program involving the fast track and the normal track, each track with its two subtracks, has been adopted (Lee, 1994). In the fast track, tariffs at 20 percent is the border line: tariffs on products above the 20 percent limit will be reduced to between 0 and 5 per cent in ten years (January 1, 2003) and those on products below the limit will be so reduced within seven years (January 1, 2000). In the normal track, tariffs above 20 per cent will be reduced again in two stages; first, to 20 per cent in five to eight years by January 1, 2001, and then, further, to between 0 and 5 per cent in the next seven years by January 1, 2008. The CEPT scheme covers all manufactured products inclusive of processed agricultural products, and the list of products published by the ASEAN Secretariat in November 1993 covered about 41,000 tariff lines, approximately 88 per cent of the total tariff lines of ASEAN. It is stated that about 36,000 tariff lines, about 87 per cent of the above list, will have 5 per cent or less tariff in ten years, five years sooner than the 15-year target. Tariff reduction for some 10,000 items came into effect as of January 1, 1994 (see Lee 1994, p. 321).

For ASEAN, the sovereign member-states have much earlier proclaimed that their regional compact is in conformity with global order as embodied in the United Nations Charter. Regionalism of any form must be matched into globalism. For AFTA, with its agenda for intra-ASEAN trade liberalization, three specific issues remain to be addressed.

1. Sovereign member-states of ASEAN are at once members of APEC and also of the WTO. Thus, AFTA must be at once APEC consistent and WTO consistent. The intra-ASEAN free trade area must necessarily be a part of the broader free trade regimes of both APEC and WTO. Hence, the argument is for open regionalism, (Ariff, 1994). The case for fortress ASEAN will fail to maximize economic gains for ASEAN as well as for the rest of the world (Dutta, 1992a, 1992b, 1992c, 1992d, 1994a, 1994b, 1995a, 1995b).
2. AFTA is operational and its effective functioning will have to address the set of problems common to any form of economic regionalization, such as, rules of origin, standardization of tradables and dispute mediation. Given the goodwill and mutual understanding among the participating sovereign member-states, each one of these problems will have a mutually acceptable solution. The EU will be a resource base to look up to, not to replicate what they have done to resolve such issues, but to draw upon necessary learning experience. True, it has been overemphasized that AFTA is not modelled on the EU.

Product standardization is a typical issue. In any international regime - global, regional, subregional - a given product in free trade must be properly standardized. No supranational bureaucratic regimentation can be expected to do the job. It will put a break on the free competitive market, limiting innovation and product differentiation and progressive product-quality enhancement. Indeed, the competitive market forces will work with their full force to do the job as they do in every domestic market. The market will triumphantly force the exit of substandard products. In each national market for necessary consumer concern for health/safety, products are certified/approved for marketing by nationally accepted institutions. Each member-state must accept the product certification by institutions so approved of in each of the other member-states. Thus, the issue is one of standardization of a list of institutions authorized to approve product standards in each member-state, *not one of product standardization by an intraregional authority, so appointed.* Indeed, the EU has adopted this mode of operation. The issue, however, does not appear to have been a point of debate on the AFTA agenda.

Similarly for trade dispute mediation, an intra-ASEAN institution can be helpful. The APEC Bogor Declaration in 1994 proposes a mediation provision while the WTO Charter provides for a more formal international judicial review. The core issue is mutual commitment for member-states, each a sovereign nation-state, to *voluntarily* deny themselves the right to initiate unilateral measures to correct a trade dispute. Even attempts at binational resolution of trade disputes will challenge the foundation of the ASEAN intraregional cooperation. Resolution of all trade disputes should be *multilateralized.*

3. Free trade in final products, and then in services, in an intraregional economic compact must resolve to face the crucial issues of intraregional free flow of factors of production, both human and non-human. Free flow of non-human inputs involving physical capital embodying technology comes with the free flow of investments, especially with free flows of direct investments.

Intraregional free flow of human capital - labor skilled as well as unskilled - faces a host of challenging issues. The EU has adopted its mode of intra-EU free flow of human capital. ASEAN member-states must face the challenge and develop their own mode of intra-ASEAN free flow of labor and human capital. Not to face the issue will be a serious challenge.

AFTA PLUS

The case for an *ASEAN free trade area* must be ready to face two other core issues. Lee (1994, p. 323) very appropriately argues, "what is needed is not *AFTA* per se, *but an AFTA-plus*" (italics ours).

First, will a free trade area of sovereign nation-states be operationally successful if each member-nation continues to uncompromisingly exercise its sovereign authority to frame its economic policies? It has been argued that a supranational common economic policy regime alone can provide long-term support to a free trade regime. The sovereign member-states must be able to formulate a common intraregional economic policy in the context of a shared macroeconomic framework with well-specified monetary and fiscal policy guidelines. If each ASEAN member-state is too anxious to exercise its unlimited sovereign authority to formulate its own individual economic policies, then the foundation of an intraregional economic regime will collapse.

Second, ASEAN membership to non-member sovereign nation-states in Southeast Asia must remain open. Belonging of an economy to the specific geographic region is a necessary condition. Of course, there will be a set of well-defined terms for membership and a member-state belonging to a region, able and willing to satisfy those conditions, should be welcome to join ASEAN. The principle of *inclusion, not exclusion*, should be the governing principle. Vietnam's becoming a member of ASEAN, as of July 28, 1995, will remain a benchmark in this regard. Next, Laos, Cambodia and Mayanmar are expected to be candidates for ASEAN membership. It is expected that there will be occasions to revisit the question for other non-member regional economies in the near future.

Naturally, it is instructive to refer to the EU and its positive experiments with respect to both the above issues. ASEAN will, of course, draw upon its own history and find its own answers to both the issues. Narongchai and Stifel (1994, p. 337) argue that "unless visionary action is taken in ASEAN", the intra-ASEAN free trade regime will be unable to fulfill its promises. An economic system, as is ASEAN, is dynamic, not static. The law of economic dynamics merits a robust response to Lee's call for an agenda for "AFTA plus". Any speculation as to what it will be is unwarranted.

28 Australia and New Zealand Closer Economic Relations (ANZ-CER)

Australia and New Zealand (ANZ) are both members of APEC. Indeed, Australia joined Japan in the leadership role in economic regionalization in the Asia-Pacific as early as the 1960s. Long before APEC was officially instituted in 1989, the first non-official Asia-Pacific economic grouping - the Organization for Pacific Trade and Development (OPTAD) became an entity in the 1970s with Japan, Australia, New Zealand, Canada and the United States. Eventually, the five-member OPTAD broadened its membership to countries in East and Southeast Asia, and then in 1991 to Hong Kong, China and Taiwan - and the non-official forum, Pacific Economic Cooperation Conference (PECC) came into being.

We have argued that much of this Asia-Pacific happening was due to the push factor, originating in the fast-evolving economic regionalization in Western Europe. The movement was reinforced by the pull factors from the high rate of economic growth of NIEs in East Asia and in Southeast Asia.

In this general context, the economic grouping of Australia and New Zealand in the South Pacific presents yet another facet of region-specific common economic regime. Both Australia and New Zealand are resource-rich, high-income economies with small population bases. Thus, the economic structures of Australia and New Zealand "with a specialization in primary commodities" differ very much from those of most East and Southeast Asian economies.

It is interesting to compare the population and land area figures of Australia, New Zealand and Japan. In 1990, Australia had a population base of 17.09 million in its vast land area of 7,687,000 sq. km. The corresponding figures for New Zealand in 1990 are 3.39 million people and 269,000 sq km. In 1990, for Japan, the population base was 123.54 million with a land area of 372,000 sq km. In 1990, China's 1.15 billion people lived in a land area larger only by some 2,000 sq. km. of that of Australia, while India's 846.19 million people made their homes in less than one half of Australia's land area (3,288,000 sq. km.) (United Nations, 1990, 1991, 1994).

In the South Pacific, Australia and New Zealand constitute a region-specific, intra-APEC economic union.

MACROECONOMIC INDICATORS

Historically, the economies of both Australia and New Zealand have developed as models of free-enterprise market economy, open to the rest of the world.

Macroeconomic performances of the two economies point to their relative compatibility (see Figure 28.1).

Figure 28.1 Annual growth in GDP, 1983-84 to 1993-94

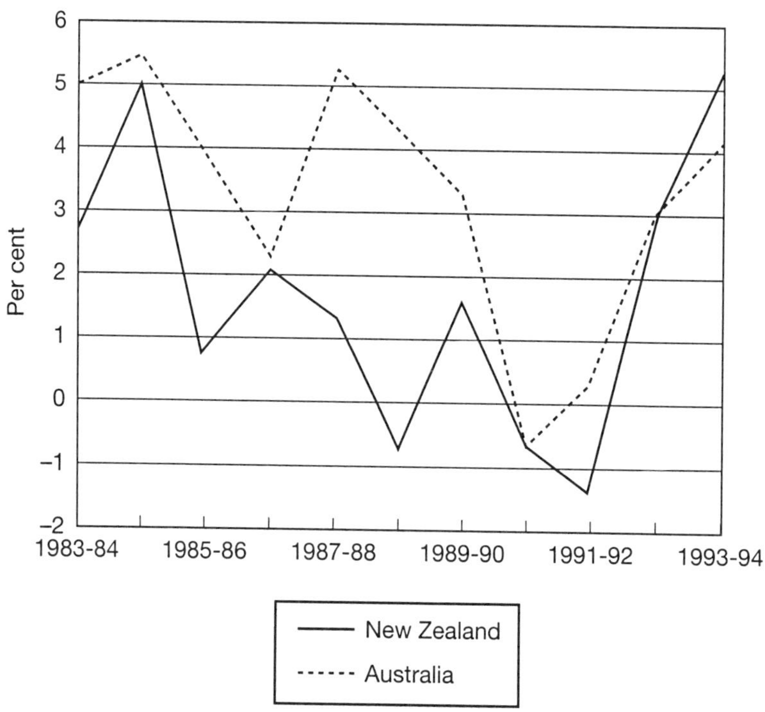

Sources: Australian Bureau of Statistics (1995), Statistics New Zealand (1995). Adapted from Bureau of Industry Economics, 1995, p. 55.

Annual average rate of real GDP growth for Australia at about 3 per cent for the 1986 to 1991 six-year period corresponds more to the rates of growth of major industrialized economies. Of course, it is much behind Japan, a fellow APEC member, and not to be compared with those of the NIEs in East Asia, also members of APEC. For the same time period, with an annual average rate of GDP growth at about 1.5 per cent, New Zealand presents a much lower

Table 28.1 Australia and New Zealand (1986-1991)

	1986	1987	1988	1989	1990	1991
Australia						
Real GDP growth	2.4	4.3	3.5	4.5	3.6	-1.1
Saving/GDP	21.4	23.4	25.0	26.1	23.5	..
Investment/GDP	24.0	23.7	24.8	28.7	23.0	..
CAB/GDP	-5.4	-4.0	-4.1	-6.2	-5.0	
Budgetary balance/GDP	2.3	-1.2	0.5	..	..	..
Money supply growth	11.4	20.3	29.6	7.5	7.9	..
Changes in CPI	9.0	8.3	7.6	7.1	7.4	5.3
New Zealand						
Real GDP growth	3.5	0.5	-1.3	1.3	1.0	0.5
Saving/GD	24.5	22.2	21.5	22.4	..	..
Investment/GDP	24.2	22.2	20.0	23.8	..	..
CAB/GDP	-6.1	-4.5	-1.1	-2.9	..	..
Budgetary balance/GDP	-3.7	1.1	2.1	..	..	..
Money supply growth	13.7	42.8	..			
Changes in CPI	13.2	15.7	6.4	5.7	6.1	..

Source: United Nations (1991, p. 32).
Notes: CAB = current account balance, export minus import, and CPI = consumer price index. Money supply is measured by M1.

profile. Both Australia and New Zealand came out of the recessionary downturns in the early 1990s and sustained recovery at moderate rates of real GDP growth for 1992-1993-1994. GDP growth rates moved up to 5 per cent in New Zealand, and 4 per cent in Australia, in 1993 to 1994 FY.

A comparison of economic performances of Australia and New Zealand, as measured by the selected macroeconomic indicators (Table 28.1), makes it evident that these two member-economies of APEC have a structural compatibility. Given the historical relationships between the two economies in the South Pacific, the level of mutual interdependence between Australia and New Zealand merits attention. Both economies present a comparable profile of savings/GDP and investment/GDP ratios, with no evidence of significant gaps for the five-year period, 1986 to 1990. Australia's average annual

Table 28.2 Australia-New Zealand trade: imports (per cent of total imports)

	Australia's from New Zealand	New Zealand's from Australia
1965	1.51	18.36
1970	2.35	19.38
1975	2.62	19.05
1980	3.41	18.48
1981	3.27	18.81
1982	3.03	19.02
1983	3.54	19.29
1984	3.75	20.38
1985	4.08	17.25
1986	3.86	16.33
1987	4.13	20.28
1988	4.41	21.60
1989	4.09	20.96
1990	4.40	20.19
1991	4.59	22.02
1992	4.63	21.19
1993	4.93	21.68

Source: Lloyd (1994, p. 343).

savings/GDP and investment/GDP ratios are at 24 and 25 per cent, respectively. For New Zealand for the four-year period, 1986 to 1989, the annual averages of both savings/GDP and investment/GDP ratios are at about 23 per cent. Money supply in both the economies follow an erratic path and the pressure of inflation as indicated by changes in CPI is evident in both cases. A negative CAB/GDP ratio is recorded for both for the time period. Government budget balancing appears to remain an artful performance.

A time profile of trade relationships may be noted from their respective shares of imports from each other (Table 28.2). Since the ANZ-CER Agreement in 1983, trade between the two countries has increased. The mutual shares are relatively stable for 1980 to 1993; the annual average of Australia's imports from New Zealand as a percentage of its total imports centers at about 4 percent, while for New Zealand, the corresponding average is about 18 per cent.

ANZ-CER

By the signing of the Agreement for Closer Economic Relations (CER) by the two countries, effective from January 1, 1983, the Australia-New Zealand common economic region or ANZ economic union may have been formally instituted. It replaces the New Zealand-Australia Free Trade Agreement of 1966, which created "a free trade area", albeit quite limited in its scope.

Article 1 of the 1983 CER Agreement calls for (i) strengthening "the broader relationship" between Australia and New Zealand, and (ii) developing "closer economic relations" between the two countries "through a mutually beneficial expansion of free trade", eliminating all "barriers" to trade "under an agreed timetable and with a minimum of disruption", of course, "under conditions of *fair competition*" (Lloyd, 1994).

The Agreement provided for bilateral free trade involving removal of all tariffs in five years by 1988, export incentives in four years by 1987, and of all quantitative restrictions and quotas in 12 years by 1995. The Agreement provided for periodic ministerial reviews. The ministerial review of the CER Agreement in June 1988 approved of "a comprehensive package of arrangements" toward implementing "the *full* free trade area and open a new chapter in the closer economic relations between the two countries".

The Ministerial Review of 1992 records CER as "a resounding success". Lloyd (1994, pp. 342-3) argues that "The CER Agreement was a major accomplishment, given the long history of failed attempts at freeing trade between the two countries". By July 1, 1990, five years ahead of the target date, "all tariffs, import licensing, and quantitative restrictions, and export incentives restricting trade between the two countries were removed", writes Lloyd.

Free trade in commodities was followed by an agreement in 1989 for free trade in services with *specific stipulations*. Following ministerial reviews in 1988 and 1992, agreement has been reached on "national subsidies, government purchases and antidumping provisions". For Australia, the average effective rate of assistance for all manufactures in 1982 to 1983 was 23 per cent and this rate fell to only 12 per cent in 1992 to 1993. For New Zealand, the more limited measures which are available show that the average effective rate of assistance for the manufacturing sector fell from 39 per cent in 1981 to 1982 to 26 per cent in 1987 to 1988, and it has fallen sharply since then (Lloyd, 1995). Export subsidies for trade between the two countries have ended. In addition, they have agreed to discontinue "production bounties or like measures" for exports to third countries.

Progress has also been reported for harmonization of business laws, customs policies and procedures, and quantitative administrative and technical barriers to trade. As of 1990, Australia and New Zealand have amended their respective legal systems to ensure "fair competition". The Joint Understanding on Harmonization of Customs Policies and Procedures require both countries to adopt "common approaches wherever appropriate".

Standardization of traded products, we argue, must satisfy consumers' revealed preferences for product differentiations. For Australia and New Zealand, the stated goal is neither "uniformity" nor "replication". In 1991, the institution of the Joint Accreditation System of Australia and New Zealand (JAS-ANZ) was examined. Following further review, the EU arrangement in this regard has been preferred, and an agreement for mutual recognition of each other's standards and also of labor qualifications has been ready in 1995. The ANZ-CER Agreement on "rules of origin" has been uniquely simple. However, dissent and dispute on its interpretation and enforcment have been reported.

The ANZ-CER is "a successful and far reaching trade liberalization agreement", ahead of the Canada-United States Free Trade Agreement of 1989, which has been limited by so many exclusions and exceptions, and "second only to the EU in terms of range of measures which relate to, or bear upon trade" between Australia and New Zealand (Lloyd, 1991, 1994, 1995). CER is unique in having achieved "free trade in goods and in labor but not in capital", adds Lloyd.

AUSTRALIA-NEW ZEALAND: SINGLE MARKET/ ECONOMIC UNION: ANZ-CER/WTO/APEC

The ANZ-CER approximates the Western European economic regionalization model, but certainly lags behind the EU, after the Maastricht Treaty of 1992. ANZ-CER does not provide for a common external tariff and freedom of movement of capital. The Agreement makes no specific provision for free labor movement, albeit free movement of citizens and residents are guaranteed by modified versions of the arrangements prevalent under the British colonial era. Under the Trans-Tasman Travel Arrangements, formally adopted in the 1920s, free movement of citizens and residents provides for intraregional labor mobility, and hence optimization of allocation of a resource - labor - which has been relatively scarce in the two countries.

The CER Agreement does not stipulate common excise and value-added taxes. In addition, the ANZ-CER arrangement for free trade for services *continues to be conditioned by specific stipulations*. Unlike the Single European Act of 1985 in the EU, the ANZ-CER has not adopted the One Nation Statement, although the two countries have elected to examine the issue in the context of travel and aviation. The EU certainly outperforms on each count and presents a unique model of economic regionalization. Lloyd (1994, p. 359) argues that "there is a strong case Australia and New Zealand should proceed to form a single market" across the Tasman. Australia and New Zealand should in general "*unashamedly* emulate" the paradigm of economic union or single market the EU presents, he adds.

The core question for the South Pacific region-specific ANZ-CER Agreement to answer will involve defining its relations with the global trade institution and also with economic regionalization in the Asia-Pacific. Both Australia and New Zealand are members of APEC and also of the WTO and, as such, they must accept the rules of the respective trade regimes. Can the performance of ANZ-CER, a specific regional group of two sovereign nation-state-based economies, be APEC consistent as well as WTO consistent? Of course, as per Article XXIV of GATT, the EU is WTO consistent, and ANZ-CER, if it models itself as an economic union, will be eligible for the same standing. As members of APEC, they will have an opportunity to debate the issue with the 18 other fellow members.

There is absolutely no case for a fortress - an ANZ single market or economic union. Indeed, the case for open regionalism has been forcefully argued (Ariff, 1994; Arndt, 1993; Elek, 1992; Garnaut, 1994; Garnaut and Drysdale, 1994; Kim, 1992). Economic regionalization of any form must belong to the global order. Heinz Arndt (see Part II) argues that an ANZ-CER FTA with its intraregional free trade arrangements has little negative impact on its trade with third countries. A closer examination of the shares of ANZ trade - intraregional and interegional - merits further attention.

ANZ AND INTERREGIONAL LINKAGES

Will the ANZ-CER Agreement exclude any other sovereign economies in the specific region? In this specific South Pacific region, Australia and New Zealand are the only two major sovereign nation-state-based economies. Absence of any other major country may preempt the issue of acceptance of new membership into the group. Thus, for ANZ, as a single market or as an economic union, the issue may be moot.

On the other hand, these two resource-rich economies with some 20 plus million people are expected to optimize deepening of their respective economies by a much broader and progressive regional widening. One possibility is to consider an extension of the ANZ-CER Free Trade Agreement to interlink it with AFTA in a joint regional market. Earlier in 1983, the subject was raised at a meeting in Thailand. Australia's proximity and economic ties with Indonesia have also been extensively studied.

For Australia and New Zealand, an effort to institute an APEC-consistent regional market with Chile and Mexico may be yet another option toward widening the intraregional economic relationships. The four are APEC members, and with the United States and Canada, they may present a special reverse-L shape APEC profile, not inclusive of APEC members on the eastern shore of the Pacific.

The possibility of ANZ-CER and ASEAN institutional linkage, following earlier discussions in Thailand in 1983, continues to merit attention. The two free trade regimes - one of South Pacific and another of Southeast Asia - do meet the logic of geo-economics; the two sets of free-enterprise sovereign market economies jointly share a specific region on the map of the world, and internalization of their interregional economic cooperation and the related externalities are expected to optimize economic gains for all households and businesses in the member-economies of all countries.

Only recently, concerned scholars of Australia, India and South Africa have proposed yet another option for trans-oceanic economic regionalization, the Indian Ocean Area Regional Grouping. In June 1995, at Perth, Australia, the International Forum of the Indian Ocean Region resolved to establish the Indian Ocean Research Network (IORN). In December 1995, the IORN convened a meeting in New Delhi, India to further examine the feasibility of constituting a regional economic group consisting of 47 littoral economies on the Indian Ocean rim. Participants at the New Delhi conference came from Australia, Bangladesh, India, Iran, Malaysia, Maldives, Mauritius, New Zealand, Pakistan, Singapore, South Africa and Sri Lanka, and were joined by representatives of ESCAP, a United Nations body. These non-official efforts would expectedly complement the formal intergovernmental Indian Ocean Rim Initiative initiated earlier in Mauritius (Personal Communication, K.P. Kalirajan, Australian National University, Canberra, August 19, 1996; see also, Kalirajan and Shand, 1996). The role of geo-economics will certainly continue to manifest its expression in many and varied ways.

As members of APEC, ANZ common market or economic union will be linked with its other neighbors - the Pacific Island and member economies of ASEAN. ANZ- CER is an important step toward the region-specific economic integration under the trans-Pacific "big tent" of APEC.

ANZ-CER BEYOND AN FTA

Can there be optimization of microeconomic welfare, that is, satisfaction for the households and profit for the business firms in each member-economy in the ANZ-CER economic compact without a shared macroeconomic agenda (Dutta, 1992a, 1992b, 1992c, 1992d, 1994a, 1994b, 1995a, 1995b; Lorenz, 1992; Lloyd, 1995)? We have argued that there is a strong case for an effective coordination of monetary-fiscal policies by the sovereign member-countries of an intraregional economic grouping in any form.

The EU has offered a unique paradigm of its own answering the issues. The EU is more than a free trade agreement and it is WTO consistent. In addition to intraregional free flows of trade and investment, it has made provisions for free intraregional movement of labor and human capital. It has accepted the principle of "mutual recognition" of each others' standards. Its membership is open to sovereign nation-state-based economies belonging to the region, willing and able to accept the Union's membership.

The ANZ-CER, as noted earlier, has no agenda for an order of integration at the EU level. If the goal is limited to a free trade agreement, one can argue that ANZ-CER has accomplished it. On the other hand, others argue that the ANZ-CER free trade agreement is essentially incomplete as it remains limited to trade in goods and movement of labor with no provision for free flow of capital and free trade in services. Lloyd (1995) writes that both Australia and New Zealand have "unilaterally" engaged in substantial liberalization of foreign investment. Can the ANZ-CER limit its economic integration to a free trade agreement in its limited framework?

The issue is at the core of any form of economic regionalization. I have argued that a supranational macroeconomic core with specific guidelines toward coordination of intraregional monetary-fiscal policies is a necessary framework. The process of trade liberalization in a free trade agenda necessarily addresses to varied microeconomic issues. A necessary and sufficient condition will have been established if both macro- and micro-economic issues were allowed to be coordinated.

New Zealand and Australia seem to have different views, the former being more proactive. We conclude that the process of higher-order intraregional integration in South Pacific will evolve over time, as it did in Western Europe.

One notes that there is an absence of a supranational institution for ANZ-CER. The EU has its Commission in Brussels. APEC has its Secretariat in Singapore. ASEAN, with its Secretariat in Singapore, has its supranational institutional arrangement (as described earlier). ANZ-CER works without any such arrangement. Common membership of the British imperial family provided a historical togetherness for Australia and New Zealand. The shared background facilitated ANZ-CER communications and there has been much direct negotiations between the two governments. It may be too soon to conclude that there will be no need for an intraregional institutional arrangement.

The common economic region of Australia and New Zealand following their Agreement for Closer Economic Relations is in the historic process of evolution and its progress appears to be irreversible. The ANZ economic union in the South Pacific provides a unique meeting point for the 18 sovereign APEC member-economies on the two shores of Lake Pacific. Indeed, the role of geo-economics will continue to seek its expression in many and varied ways.

29 The North American Free Trade Area (NAFTA)

Following fast track action by the President and Congress of the United States and parallel actions by Canada and Mexico, the North American Free Trade Area of the three sovereign economies became operational on January 1, 1994. Indeed, it broadened the Free Trade Area Agreement of Canada and the United States, signed in 1988, effective from January 1, 1989. The only other Free Trade Area Agreement the United States had signed was with Israel in 1985. The U.S.-Isreal Agreement is beyond the framework of region-specific economic regionalization.

Our review points out that AFTA has reported significant progress in intra-ASEAN trade liberalization by 1994, and is forging ahead with a well-specified agenda for progressive trade liberalization five years sooner than the 15-year target; and that ANZ-CER has very much accomplished its goal of Australia-New Zealand trade liberalization by July 1, 1990, five years ahead of the target date. The EU, of course, is indeed a program beyond the typical FTA and has accomplished liberalization of trade in final products - goods as well as services - and also in an intraregional free flow of factors of production - capital and labor.

NAFTA is at its initial stage, and it begins with a much lower threshold of intra-NAFTA trade barriers. However, NAFTA will have to accomplish a great deal more before intra-North American trade liberalization achieves a comparable performance.

With a population base of 360 million, commanding a GDP total of $6+ trillion in 1990 (the United States $5.4 trillion, Canada $600 billion and Mexico $300 billion), NAFTA creates a regional economic regime of immense magnitude. In population, NAFTA compares with EU and ASEAN. Its economic potential in terms of intraregional free trade remains to materialize.

ECONOMICS OF NAFTA DEBATE

Debate over NAFTA in the United States covered economic as well as extraeconomic issues (Brown et al., 1992a, 1992b; Hufbauer and Schott, 1992, 1993; Krugman, 1993; Orme Jr., 1993). It is to be noted that the Canada-U.S. FTA in 1988 was agreed upon with little public debate and such was the case with the Israel-U.S. FTA in 1985. Thus, it has been suggested that much of the debate in 1993 over NAFTA was for its Mexican content.

The cost for containment of communism in Cuba *vis-à-vis* the cost for construction of the "Great American Wall" to prevent illegal immigration of poor neighbors from Mexico must remain beyond the scope of this study. Students of economics have been taught about the irrelevance of the "beggar-thy-neighbor" policy.

The "big sucking sound from the south" became an empty threat and added little of substance to rational economic discourse. In a free-enterprise capitalist market economy, international flows of capital to command competitive shares of the world market for long-term profit maximization, given specific cost-benefit analyses, have been a familiar phenomenon. Analyses of firm-level, private sector international investment behavior will show that the larger shares of available funds flow into the high-productivity, high-wage economies of Japan, North America and Western Europe. The rest finds its way into investment in high-growth economies with records for high rates of savings and investments relative to their respective GDP. Absence of threats of inflation within a macroeconomic framework of stability, as may be indicated by monetary-fiscal policies of a given economic regime, must at once be issues for rational decision making.

The balances of Mexico-U.S. cross-border trade, plus or minus, will always be real and will have to be explained by a duly specified multivariate behavioral function. The fact remains that Mexico and the United States share borders. The same is true for Canada and the United States. The three sovereign economies belonging to a shared geographic region will have to be able to forge their economic activities together.

Paul Krugman (1993, p. 14) summarized the "truth" about NAFTA in five simple propositions:

(i) NAFTA will have no effect on the number of jobs in the United States:
(ii) NAFTA will not hurt and *may* help the environment;
(iii) NAFTA will, however, produce *only* a small gain in overall U.S. real income;
(iv) NAFTA will also *probably* lead to a slight fall in the real wages of unskilled U.S. workers; and
(v) for the U.S., NAFTA is *essentially* a foreign-policy rather than an economic issue. (italics added)

THE PUSH FACTOR OF GEO-ECONOMICS IN NAFTA

During the post-World War II Cold War years, geo-politics became the catch word. In the post-Cold War regime, *geo-economics* has become the point of focus, of course, with its emphasis on rational economic decision making in the context of a supranational arrangement, not on an act of political balance of a superpower hegemony. To quote Scalapino, "to an unprecedented extent, economics has taken command of international relations" (Scalapino, 1991/92, p. 20).

Indeed, one can argue that geo-economics with its agenda for the optimization of economic gains for all intraregional sovereign member-states is the core point for the North American Economic Union, beginning with the institution of NAFTA. Indeed, eventual progression of NAFTA by way of broadening its membership to include all the sovereign national economies of the American hemisphere into an American economic union or a Free Trade Area of the Americas (FTAA) cannot be ruled out (Dobson 1990; Dutta 1992a, 1992b, 1992c, 1992d).

The conference of all sovereign nations in the North and South Americas, excepting Cuba, hosted by the United States, December 1994 in Miami was an important step. The Miami Initiative certainly points to the potential of the FTAA, and then the American Hemispheric Union.

The root of geo-economics can be traced to the economics of *location theory*. In the post-World War II period, geo-economics first found its robust expression in economic regionalization in Western Europe following the Treaty of Rome signed in 1957, effective January 1, 1958, and in 1995, the EU with its membership of 15 sovereign nation-state-based economies in Western Europe is a reality. The OECD with its headquarters in Europe, however, continues to function as a forum for two dozen-plus rich, high-income, industrialized economies. The OECD is a club of rich nations and its membership may be extended to nations as they become appropriately rich.

The EU limited its membership to the regional map of Europe and thus did not invite Japan, Australia, New Zealand, Canada and the United States to become members. It zealously maintained its Europeanness, allowing its membership to expand only within the specific region of Europe. Soon after this European phenomenon of geo-economics became a fact in the 1960s, Japan and Australia took the initiative to sponsor a parallel forum in the Asia-Pacific, eventually institutionalizing APEC in 1989. To begin with, the United States joined Japan and Australia seemingly with less enthusiasm. However, the U.S. is now a leader of APEC. Geo-economics has become a dominant facet of international economic relations in the Asia-Pacific.

Was APEC a response to the EU? Did Europeanization of Europe, *à la EU's* Single European Act of 1985, prompt the multi-continental innovative economic regionalization in the Asia-Pacific, now encompassing membership of 18 sovereign economies in the Americas, Asia and the Oceana? No definitive answer to the question is on record. That geo-economics has emerged as a dominant phenomenon is beyond dispute.

One must hasten to add that the EU is a much more integrated common economic market while APEC is a much simpler forum for economic cooperation and trade liberalization. However, the essence of geo-economics is singularly manifest. The cyberspace-based information super-highway has reduced the vast water mass of the Pacific Ocean into the Lake Pacific, and expansive trans-Pacific economic regionalization of APEC can easily accommodate such region-specific economic integration of many and varied forms. NAFTA is indeed a region-specific manifestation of geo-economics. ASEAN and ANZ-CER are the two important geo-economic groups of sovereign members in specific regions, within the APEC umbrella arrangement. In 1988, the United States signed its Free Trade Area Agreement with Canada, its northern neighbor. Across the Atlantic geo-economics found expanded connotation, as membership of the EU, limited to the richer economies of Western Europe, progressively extended to its poorer neighbors including Greece, Portugal, Spain and Ireland. The EU made specific provisions to help expedite economic restructuring of the poorer members of the Union. The expansion of the U.S.-Canada Free Trade Area Agreement to include Mexico, its poorer southern neighbor, as a member of NAFTA, became a necessary geo-economic engagement.

NAFTA will not establish a common trade wall against other non-member economies and will function as another *open* subregion, fully APEC consistent and WTO consistent. On a timetable agreed upon, it will eliminate all intraregional trade barriers and barriers for financial flows.

THE PULL FACTOR IN NORTH AMERICA

The pull factors of North American geo-economics, anchored to its multi-trillion dollar market, are very real. Given its population size and its resource endowment, Mexico is potentially a large market, and its economic development will substantially add to the volume of intra-NAFTA trade. Opportunities for DFI, real *not* speculative, must be noted.

Economic lessons of the recent Mexican debacle are twofold: first, financial flows of foreign speculative funds into Mexico's newly industrializing economy proved very much destabilizing; second, absence of a stable macroeconomic framework in Mexico contributed to much instability. Time will tell if remedial measures will help sustain stable economic growth.

The fact is that Mexico has never defaulted on interest payment for the $12+ billion financial accommodation, which was offered by the United States. In addition, a repayment of $700 million on capital account as early as fall 1995 certainly adds to the credit standing of Mexico, and, of course, to the basic soundness of intra-NAFTA economic integration.

NAFTA's pull factors go beyond Mexico. The geo-economics in North America may be viewed in the larger context of the American hemisphere. The Miami Initiative of December 1994 may have been the first crucial step for the hemispheric FTAA. It is an open invitation for an American agenda for intra-hemispheric economic cooperation and free trade, never to be confused with the fortress Americas.

The Miami Initiative, successful as it was, became at once a question and an answer. It is a robust positive answer to the call for geo-economics in the American hemisphere . At the same time, it does raise the question whether an FTA of the Americas, once institutionalized, will truly be compatible with APEC. One view is that the Americas' hemispheric free trade area, as it becomes a reality, not unlike NAFTA, AFTA and ANZ-CER, will be APEC consistent as well as WTO consistent. A robust interpretation of Article XXIV of GATT may be the answer.

The concern in Western Europe is whether the United States will be able to provide concurrent leadership for both the hemispheric FTA (FTAA) and the trans-Pacific economic cooperation (APEC). Quoting an unnamed prominent German, R.W. Apple Jr. writes:

> We are starting to feel isolated. It used to be Europe and America, the Atlantic nations, taking on all comers, especially the Communist bloc. Now we are afraid it's you and the Asian, the Pacific nations, who are setting the pace, with us off by ourselves (*The New York Times*, January 9, 1994).

Lorenz (1989, 1991, 1993) questions whether the United States will opt for leading economic regionalization longitudinally in the American hemisphere or latitudinally across the Pacific.

Bergsten (see Part II) forcefully argues that neither Europe nor Asia should have any valid reason to question the U.S. commitment to a global free trade regime.

SOME REMARKS

The final output of the emerging new paradigm of geo-economics in North America, and in the American hemisphere, to be specified by a simultaneous system of relationships relative to both push and pull factors, remains to be estimated. Preliminary remarks are, however, in order.

After reviewing several economic studies (Adams et al., 1992; Bachrach and Mizrahi 1992; Brown et al., 1992a and 1992b; Hinojosa-Ojeda and Robinson 1991; McCleery 1992; Robinson et al. 1992; Sobarzo 1992; Young and Romero 1992), Congressional Budget Office (1993) quotes Barry Bosworth in summing up that no definitive results are yet to be reported.

> Since Mexico's economy is about one-twenty-fifth the size of the U.S. economy, NAFTA could not possibly have much effect on the U.S. economy for a long time, and it would be likely to have substantial effect rather quickly on the Mexican economy (p. 56).

In general, the significance level of reported statistical findings of most models, as reviewed above, are unsatisfactory. Or, economic interpretations of the reported findings relate to a much too distant future, or to a magnitude of change which at best is of second order (p. 57). Cox and Harris (1992) reported their findings from the Canadian perspective. Prestowitz and Cohen (1991) reported results of a study on NAFTA, based on modified extrapolation of current trends.

One must add that over time, NAFTA will foreseeably impact upon intra-NAFTA productivity growth rates, investment flows, wages and employment and balance of trade. Needless to add that specific industries, hitherto sheltered by protectionist policies in any NAFTA country, will be more directly impacted. The goal, of course. is optimization of gains for consumers and maximization of profits for businesses in all three NAFTA member-economies.

30 The South Asian Association for Regional Cooperation (SAARC)

We take a map-of-the-world view of Asia and examine the South Asian region-specific institutionalized cooperation of India and six other sovereign nation-state-based economies. Belonging to the map of the region is the core argument for geo-economics. The sovereign economies of Laos, Cambodia and Mayanmar wait to become members of one or another regional association.

The South Asian Association for Regional Cooperation (SAARC) is another institutionalized expression of a specific regional grouping of seven sovereign member-economies - Bangladesh, Bhutan, India, Maldives, Nepal, Pakistan and Sri Lanka - with a population base of 1.12 billion in 1990. (Bangladesh - 113.68 million; Bhutan - 1.54 million; India - 846.19 million; Maldives - 213, 000; Nepal - 19.57 million; Pakistan - 118.12 million, and Sri Lanka - 17.23 million) (United Nations, 1994, p. 108).

The push factor of geo-economics has been evident. In 1985, the Western European economic community adopted the Single European Act. It was evident that the economic regionalization movement in Western Europe would continue to gather momentum and the rest of the world was anticipating what then came as the Maastricht Treaty in 1992, followed by the institution of the EU. The ANZ-CER agreement was signed in January 1983. In neighboring Southeast Asia, ASEAN - Indonesia, Malaysia, the Philippines, Singapore and Thailand - encouraged by their achievements of intraregional cooperation since 1967, signed the Bali Declaration in 1976 with a more pronounced intraregional economic agenda. In 1985, Brunei Darussalam became a member of ASEAN. Vietnam, as of July 1995, is a member of ASEAN. The trans-Pacific economic regionalization steadily progressed through the 1970s and 1980s, and the formal institutionalization of APEC in 1989 was very much anticipated.

EVOLUTION OF SAARC

For South Asia, the virtue of geo-economic cooperation became a pressing lesson. The first step was the meeting of the foreign secretaries of seven South Asian nations in Colombo in 1981, followed by a series of working meetings of the foreign secretaries in Kathmandu, Islamabad and Dhaka in 1981, 1982 and 1983, respectively. The summit meetings of SAARC member-countries' leaders have been an instructive feature (SAARC Summit, 1990, 1996).

To begin with, nine specific areas of intraregional cooperation were identified: (i) agriculture, (ii) rural development, (iii) telecommunications, (iv) meteorology, (v) health and population, (vi) postal services, (vii) science and technology, (viii) sports, arts and culture, and (ix) transport. Over time the list was expanded to add on other areas of cooperation, such as drug abuse and drug trafficking, and the role of women in economic development.

The initiative that originally came from Bangladesh in 1980 failed to receive enthusiastic support from either India or Pakistan, the two larger economies in South Asia. The foreign ministers again met in New Delhi and Male in August 1983 and July 1984, respectively. Finally, in 1985, at the summit in Dhaka, capital of Bangladesh, the SAARC Agreement was signed by the heads of the seven sovereign member-states; since then the summit meetings have become a fairly regular feature. A SAARC Secretariat in Kathmandu has been established with the support of technical committees and standing committees (SAARC Documents, 1991, 1993, 1995).

From its founding, SAARC proclaimed its commitment to what is referred to as open regionalism, as it would not be "a substitute for bilateral and multilateral cooperation". SAARC activities will be WTO consistent. SAARC member-countries are not APEC members.

SAARC performance has received mixed reviews. A catalogue of events for its performance since 1985 has been compiled. One hastens to emphasize that the mutual comfort level among the leaders which made ASEAN in neighboring Southeast Asia a lively and successful geo-economic compact was singularly absent among the heads of the seven South Asian nations. We identify *two* specific factors that may have been responsible for its limited impact globally.

First, the political relationships among the member-countries continue to overwhelm any and all discussions of substantive intraregional economic cooperation. Intra-SAARC political disputes are allowed to dominate its effective functioning and the member-countries finally seem to have elected to remain *poor together*, rejecting the option of becoming *rich together*.

Second, there is an absence of economic pull factors in South Asia. For India, which covers 73.36 per cent of the region's estimated total land area of 4,482,000 sq. km. with a population share of 76.80 percent (total estimated population at 1.12 billion in 1990) and GDP share of 78.85 per cent (total estimated regional GDP at U.S.$322.83 billion in 1990) (World Bank, 1992), the initiative to reverse its economic policy of import substitution, in effect since 1950s, to one of export-led growth paradigm came haltingly through the 1980s and failed to become adopted until 1990s.

In addition, India's policy of neutrality as leader of the "non-aligned" nations during the post-World War II Cold War regime made its access to the Western industrialized markets somewhat fractured. Led by the United States, which contributed to the spectacular success of the export-led growth regimes, the strategic friendly alliance of nations in East and Southeast Asia has been known to be responsible for its open economic relations with the nations in the Western alliance, and in the Asian miracle. Even after the collapse of the Cold War regime, India moved at a slow pace.

Immediately after the normalization of political relationships with the United States in 1978, the PRC promptly adopted its open economic policy aggressively pursuing the export-led growth regime as was tried with much success in its neighboring economies in East and Southeast Asia. China's *socialist market* economy successfully courted foreign investments with provisions for 100 per cent foreign ownership for specific DFIs to accelerate its economic growth. India's new economic policy as adopted in 1993 will foreseeably move the pace for India as well as for South Asia.

THE STRUCTURE OF SOUTH ASIAN ECONOMIES

India's predominant economic position in South Asia is indeed a crucial point for consideration. For extraeconomic reasons, the natural intra-SAARC geo-economic linkages remained fractured. Politics apart, the fact of economic predominance by virtue of the size of its economy, 78.85 per cent of the South Asian region's total GDP, added to much resentment for India's neighbors in South Asia. In terms of shares of regional GDP Pakistan and Bangladesh, with their respective shares of 11 and 6.9 per cent of GDP in 1990, are the two next major economies. Their shares of land area in the region are 17.76 and 3.21 per cent, respectively. The four other members of the South Asian region - Bhutan, Maldives, Nepal and Sri Lanka - shared a meager 4.25 per cent of regional GDP in 1990. In 1990, Pakistan's shares of population and GDP were 10.16 per cent and 11 per cent, respectively. For Bangladesh, its shares in the same year were 9.65 per cent of the population and 6.90 per cent of GDP. In 1990, the shares of GDP of Sri Lanka, Nepal, Bhutan and Maldives were 2.25, 0.90, 0.09, 0.02 per cent, respectively (World Bank, 1992).

Failure to accelerate economic growth on India's part certainly contributed to the immobilization of the South Asian regional economy. Could the relatively smaller size economies of its six neighbors independently or jointly make a difference? We shall not speculate on an answer to the above question.

Soon after 1947, when India became an independent sovereign nation-state-based economy, India instituted a series of Five Year Economic Plans. Its main thrust was self-sustained economic growth for its millions within the framework of a "mixed" market economy. A sector of the economy consisting of "key" industries - much of the financial sector, transportation and heavy industries - was designated the exclusive field of government ownership and management, while the private sector corporations were given 100 per cent ownership and management rights for the market sector of its vast economy.

India's "mixed" economic strategy and its emphasis on import substitution must have been responsible for a limited inflow of DFI to India. Indeed, a further specific disincentive to inflows of DFI came from *limitations of ownership to 49 per cent or less for a given foreign joint venture.* Limited supply of indigenous savings naturally resulted in limited investments. Insulation of India's nationalized industries from open market competition eventually made them inefficient and their products failed to be competitive in terms of consumer satisfaction in the home market. India's private sector, much sheltered from foreign competition, also failed to be quality and cost competitive in the world market.

The average annual growth rate of India's GDP remained as low as it was. The total product was relatively low, and its exportables were increasingly unable to compete internationally. An exposition of the state of the economy of the economies of South Asia (Table 30.1) points to the fact that there has been a notable absence of the pull factors, as would successfully invite the rest of the world to engage in robust economic relations with economies in South Asia.

Macroeconomic performances of the economies of South Asia have been relatively poor. Independent of an analysis of the possible contributing factors, their rates of growth of real GDP (Panel A) for the time period, averaging some 5 per cent have remained below that of their ASEAN neighbors, whose average annual rate of growth for the same time period was about 7 per cent and who in their turn lagged one notch behind that of Asia's NIEs - South Korea, Hong Kong and Taipei - reporting an annual average rate of growth of 8+ per cent. The PRC closely approximates the rate of growth of the NIEs, albeit with periodic jolts of inflation.

As for the rate of inflation, measured by annual percentage change of CPI (Panel B) for 1971-93, the South Asian average at 8-9 per cent per annum follows a parallel profile. The ASEAN average at 7-8 per cent per annum is better, albeit marginally. The Asian NIEs did still better. South Korea began with a high annual average of 16.5 per cent in the 1970s, and progressed successfully to stabilize its price level for 1981-93 at an annual average of 6.5

Table 30.1 South Asian economies

Panel A. Growth rate of GDP, % per annum

	1971-80	1981-90	1992-93	1994-95
Bangladesh (base 1985)	5.8	4.1	4.3	4.3
Bhutan (base 1980)	na	7.5	4.7	6.9
India (base 1980)	3.7	5.6	3.0	7.1
Maldives (base 1985)	na	12.1	6.7	6.7
Nepal (base 1975)	3.2	4.7	3.2	4.5
Pakistan (base 1981)	5.2	6.2	5.4	5.3
Sri Lanka (base 1982)	4.3	3.8	5.0	4.7

Panel B. Changes in consumer prices, % per annum

	1971-80	1981-90	1992-93	1994-95
Bangladesh	20.6	10.7	4.5	2.5
Bhutan	na	9.2	11.9	na
India	8.2	9.0	11.4	8.3
Maldives	na	na	17.2	na
Nepal	7.8	10.2	13.6	7.1
Pakistan	12.4	7.0	10.2	8.4
Sri Lanka	8.9	12.4	11.9	10.5

Table 30.1 (Continued)

Panel C. Gross domestic savings % of GDP, S/GDP

	1971-80	1981-90	1992-93	1994-95
Bangladesh	2.4	2.1	5.7	7.9
Bhutan	na	12.6	13.7	na
India	20.1	21.4	23.6	24.6
Maldives	na	na	na	na
Nepal	11.8	10.4	8.9	10.0
Pakistan	9.1	7.5	14.5	15.6
Sri Lanka	13.2	14.2	15.3	17.5

Panel D. Gross domestic investment % of GDP, I/GDP

	1971-80	1981-90	1992-93	1994-95
Bangladesh	9.1	13.1	12.1	14.0
Bhutan	na	37.6	36.4	na
India	20.5	22.8	24.7	25.7
Maldives	na	na	na	na
Nepal	16.3	20.1	20.2	22.7
Pakistan	16.4	18.7	19.8	20.8
Sri Lanka	19.0	24.7	24.2	24.4

Source: Asian Development Bank (1994). Panel A p. 231; Panel B p. 239; Panel C p. 237; Panel D p. 238.

Table 30.2 Structural shift in SAARC economies

	1970	1980	1993
Bangladesh			
- Agriculture	na	49.4	36.0
- Industry	na	14.8	18.1
- Service	na	35.8	45.9
Bhutan			
- Agriculture	na	56.7	43.0
- Industry	na	12.2	23.7
- Service	na	31.1	33.3
India			
- Agriculture	44.5	38.1	30.5
- Industry	23.9	25.9	28.1
- Service	31.6	36.0	41.4
Maldives			
- Agriculture	na	na	20.6
- Industry	na	na	17.1
- Service	na	na	62.3
Nepal			
- Agriculture	na	61.8	49.3
- Industry	na	11.9	18.4
- Service	na	26.3	32.3
Pakistan			
- Agriculture	40.1	30.6	24.4
- Industry	19.6	25.6	26.7
- Service	40.3	43.8	48.9
Sri Lanka			
- Agriculture	30.7	26.6	21.2
- Industry	27.1	27.2	29.3
- Service	42.2	46.2	49.5

Source: Asian Development Bank (1994, p. 236).

Table 30.3 Money supply, fiscal balance and current account balance

	1988	1989	1990	1991	1992	1993	Average
Panel A. Changes in money supply (M2) - % per annum							
Bangladesh	9.1	16.3	16.9	12.1	14.1	10.6	13.2
Bhutan	31.0	34.9	10.5	29.6	13.5	16.2	22.6
India	17.6	19.6	15.1	19.4	14.2	14.1	16.7
Maldives	14.3	19.7	18.7	24.9	12.9	36.4	21.2
Nepal	22.4	24.2	18.6	19.5	21.1	30.2	22.7
Pakistan	12.2	4.6	12.6	19.4	24.6	18.7	15.4
Sri Lanka	16.5	12.5	19.1	23.2	16.6	20.0	18.0
Panel B: Balance of payments on current account, % of GDP							
Bangladesh	-1.5	-5.4	-1.9	0.3	0.8	0.9	
Bhutan	-27.7	-18.0	-6.8	-4.5	-6.8	-20.8	
India	-2.6	-2.5	-2.4	-2.0	-2.4	-1.0	
Maldives	8.3	9.2	7.0	-6.1	-18.7	-24.7	
Nepal	-9.2	-8.5	-9.3	-10.9	-6.1	-7.1	
Pakistan	-3.8	-3.6	-4.2	-3.3	-4.2	-4.7	
Sri Lanka	na	na	na	na	na	na	
Panel C: Overall budget surplus/deficit, % of GDP							
Bangladesh	-7.1	-7.3	-7.7	-6.8	-5.0	-5.3	
Bhutan	0.8	-10.7	-7.9	-0.8	-4.1	4.6	
India	-8.0	-7.9	-8.5	-6.1	-5.5	-7.3	
Maldives	3.5	-3.6	-13.5	-14.9	-20.4	-17.2	
Nepal	-9.8	-13.2	-11.4	-12.3	-10.2	-11.1	
Pakistan	-8.5	-7.4	-6.5	-8.7	-7.4	-7.9	
Sri Lanka	-15.3	-11.0	-10.0	-11.7	-7.5	-7.8	

Source: Asian Development Bank (1994). Panel A, p. 240; Panel B, p. 246; Panel C, p. 253.

per cent. Hong Kong has uniformly maintained an annual average rate of about 8 per cent matched, of course, by a high growth rate. Taipei's performance with an annual rate of inflation less than 4 per cent for 1981 to 1993 with a sustained high rate of growth of GDP must be a learning experience. The PRC performance for 1981 to 93 at an annual inflation rate of some 10 per cent with bursts of double-digit inflations in 1988, 1989 and again in 1993, of course, poses a serious question mark.

For the S/GDP and I/GDP ratios (Panels C and D), South Asia again is far outperformed by its ASEAN neighbors - especially Singapore, Indonesia, Malaysia and Thailand. Asian NIEs - Hong Kong, South Korea and Taipei are, of course, established leaders, the PRC approaching the NIEs. The PRC's high growth rate of GDP, even when punctuated by periodic inflationary inflections, can be explained by its high-saving and high-investment economic strategy. India with its annual averages of both S/GDP and I/GDP ratios for 1971-93 at 20+ percentage points rate is an exception at the low end. The fact that the two ratios in general match for the time period should point to an absence of any notable gap.

The intersectoral contributions to GDP have been a familiar pedagogic way of studying structural shifts in given economies (Table 30.2). Over 1970-93, in all seven South Asian economies, the shift follows the pattern of industrialization - the agricultural sector's contribution to GDP declining, while contributions of the two other sectors (industry and service) recording corresponding increases. It remains to be noted that in South Asia the shift is more in favor of the service sector, and less pronounced in the industry sector. Still to be examined is how much increases in service sectors' contributions relate to what may be called "soft jobs" or jobs in service enterprises, known for their suboptimal capitalization. Thus, the process of structural shifts in South Asian economies may not be comparable with that in the NIEs in East and Southeast Asia.

In 1993, for Indonesia, Malaysia, Thailand, South Korea and Taipei contributions of their respective industry sectors to their respective GDPs were above 40 per cent with matching increases in their service sectors' contributions to GDP. For the PRC, in 1993, the contributions of agriculture, industry and service sectors to its GDP were 22.6, 52.0 and 25.4 per cent, respectively. The decline in the agricultural sector's contributions from 42.2 per cent in 1970 to 22.6 per cent in 1993 is notable. However, the contributions of its service sector to GDP at 22.6 and 25.4 per cent, respectively in 1970 and 1993, have been rather static, causing intersectoral imbalance, and thus hurting its stable growth.

The profile of annual percentage changes in the money supply (M2) of South Asian economies (Table 30.3), especially SAARC-4 (Bangladesh, India, Pakistan and Sri Lanka) for 1988-93 (Panel A) compare with that of ASEAN-4 (Indonesia, Malaysia, the Philippines and Thailand). The PRC's profile for 1988-93 with an annual average M2 at 25.3 per cent has been quite different.

For 1988-93, overall performances, based on balance of payments on current accounts as a percentage of GDP place SAARC-4, ASEAN-4 and PRC in the same scale (Panel B). Again for the same time period, with the notable exception of Thailand, all SAARC and ASEAN economies as well as the PRC report negative balances of their respective national governments. Malaysia did inch out to a positive balance in 1993. It must be added that the negative budget balances in South Asian economies have been a few percentage points higher (Panel C).

The presentation above of a general outlook of monetary and fiscal policy and current account balance of South Asian economies must be read in the context of general economic growth and the rate of inflation. Performances of the SAARC economies, especially SAARC-4, compared to that of economies in East and Southeast Asia, point to a state of low growth, low saving and low investment.

The low level of economic activity of SAARC economies has been responsible for their insignificant role in the world trade, with a dismal record of their respective shares of world exports. For 1988 to 1990 the annual average share of world exports for India, the predominant economy of South Asia, has been as low as 0.75 per cent while that of Pakistan was only 0.25 per cent. Bangladesh and Sri Lanka scored less than one-tenth of 1 per cent each. The flow of SAARC intraregional trade has continued to be low (IMF, 1991).

The generally low level of economic activity and GDP became responsible for the bleak situation in the South Asian economies.

EMERGING NEW REGIME IN SOUTH ASIA

Two recent events merit attention. First, the post-World War II Cold War regime is behind us. Consequently, India's policy of non-alignment will have been reevaluated by India's policy makers. Second, as late as 1993, India has adopted a new economic policy, dismantling its regime of mixed economic planning, and reversing its earlier policy of import substitution. An open economic policy with a competitive access for inflows of foreign investment will help accelerate India's economic growth.

The lessons from the neighboring economies in NIEs, ASEAN and China are on record. India's new economic policy must have received much impetus from the experiences of its Asian neighbors. The PRC recently elected to join its neighbors in East and Southeast Asia in this regard.

Inflows of DFI have been known to be a platform for accelerated growth in Asian economies. Should this inflow of investments result in adaptive innovation producing cost-and quality-effective exportables - goods and services - for the world market with its competitive price tags - then the regime of export-led growth should follow. The economic changes in India covering 79 per cent of the region's GDP and 77 per cent of the region's population will instantaneously relate to the rest of South Asia.

True, the change of economic policy has come late in India. India and China are the two largest economies in the world. Their potential market size commands the profit-earning motivation of investors from the rest of the world. In addition, the resource endowment and availability of human capital - inclusive of skilled and unskilled labor plus one of the world's largest pools of scientists and engineers - are points of attraction for sufficient and sustained inflows of DFI.

Both China and India are late entrants into their respective new economic regimes and they will competitively invite foreign investments. The limitation of availability of investment funds globally is only real. The debate over the limitations of export-led growth remains open. Counterbalancing factors must not be ignored. In the 1960s, sources of funds for DFI and markets for export from NIEs were all too limited. The world situation in the 1990s has changed for the better. The Asian NIEs, as their respective domestic economies progressively *deepen*, are aggressively seeking to *widen* their economic engagements in the neighboring Asian economies. In addition, these economies have become markets for sustaining the export-led growth model for others who have come late to join the process.

In 1994, India was already receiving an inflow of DFI as its new economic policy expanded the scope of foreign ownership, no longer constrained by the statutory limit of 49 per cent or less. As in China, there are now specified provisions for 100 per cent foreign ownership. The Indian rupee has been made convertible (only on current account, not on capital account).

SAARC: INTRAREGIONAL ECONOMIC COOPERATION AND INTERREGIONAL LINKAGES

It is no longer an idle speculation to suggest that the intraregional feuds among SAARC member-countries may change as economic dynamics begin to play its role. As India with its predominant position in the regional economy will have been viewed as able to deliver its share of economic opportunities, a new and proactive order of intraregional economic cooperation will be in order.

India's open economic policy will be reinforced by competitive opening up of other SAARC member-economies. Pakistan, Bangladesh, Sri Lanka and Nepal have already elected to adopt their respective forms of open economic policy, very much welcoming the export-led growth models of economic development.

The dialogue for a SAARC free trade agreement (SAFTA) is on the agenda. The SAARC Secretariat at Kathmandu, Nepal has been actively engaged in pursuing an intraregional economic agenda.

Broader economic regionalization is on the map. The ASEAN-SAARC economic dialogue has recently gained momentum and the ASEAN Dialogue Mission in New Delhi, India is a specific step. With a "big tent" view of the map of Asia, the 18-member APEC may consider inviting India and other South Asian nations to join its regional compact.

An innovative economic regionalization framework of the Indian Ocean Trading Area under the joint initiative of Australia, India and South Africa is being actively explored. Indeed, exploratory conferences of the Indian Ocean countries have been convened.

In all cases, the point for consideration will belong to the paradigm of open regionalism. As members of the WTO, India and other SAARC member-countries will accept economic regionalization which will be WTO consistent.

31 The Golden Triangle of China: Mainland, Taipei, Hong Kong

ASEAN, ANZ-CER and NAFTA are formal institutionalized expressions of specific geo-economic regionalization within APEC. So is SAARC, but it does not belong to APEC. The Golden Triangle of Mainland China, Taipei and Hong Kong (the three independent members of APEC) and also of the Pacific Economic Cooperation Conference (PECC) - is a very special outcome of geo-economics, with no formal agreement.

With no special institutional arrangement, the Golden Triangle has, however, become a viable subregional economic grouping. Economic relationships among the three neighboring economic entities of Hong Kong, China and Taipei, a market of a billion-plus people, have worked successfully, independent of any and all political debates. The World Bank, following its special estimates of own-price-adjusted GDP, ranked China as the third largest economy, next only to the United States and Japan.

Hong Kong's political tie with China under the Treaty Agreement with the British Crown has been historically defined. Sovereignty of Hong Kong reverted to China in 1997. The present discussion will focus on economic relationships between Taipei and China.

Extraeconomic factors - common language, religion, culture, culinary art and lifestyle - do play a role for a unifying influence in the Golden Triangle. They help cut down the cost of trade and investment. Mutual appreciation of economic practice is a plus, eliminating the cost of learning a foreign language or an alien accounting/bookkeeping system. The legal system, albeit different can be more easily comprehended. Thus, per unit of trade/investment, the cost of legal and accounting fees will be much less. Common religious/cultural values also help to cut down the cost of market creation per unit of economic activity. In addition, geographical contiguity makes the cost of transportation minimal (Dutta, 1995a, p. 184). However, these factors alone cannot contribute to the push of geo-economics. Some 300+ million people in the 15-nation EU speak different languages and enjoy different lifestyles and culinary arts. They go to many different churches and temples and say their prayers in many different ways. A shared economic agenda for the optimization of individual economic gains for households and business firms in each sovereign member-economy within a stable macroeconomic framework brought them together in the Union. "The impact of extra-economic factors on Taipei and Mainland China's economic relations may have been a contributing factor, only marginally. The potential for profit China's market offers is the key inducement for foreign investors, inclusive of those from Taiwan" (ibid., p. 190).

The three economic entities belonging to a common geographic region share real economies of the locational advantages and have accepted the push factors of geo-economics, combined with the pull factors of mutual economic gains.

MACROECONOMIC PERFORMANCES OF THE THREE ECONOMIC UNITS

The comparative macroeconomic performances of the three economies merit attention (Table 31.1). For all three, annual average rates of growth of real GDP for 1970-90 at high single digits point to their compatibility. In the 1990s, the growth rates of GDP for Hong Kong and Taipei at 4 to 7 per cent point to a stability and demonstrate the state of economic maturity. For the PRC, the growth path has been unstable. With major downturns in 1989 and 1990, the PRC experienced a recovery in the 1990s, which soon proved to be unsustainable. The PRC's economic reform - marketization and open economic policy - began in 1978 and it is struggling to design a stable growth path. The course of events was not unexpected.

With high annual S/GDP and I/GDP ratios at 30+ percentage points, all three economies are on a course of accelerated industrialization. Hong Kong and Taipei, ahead in their respective scores of industrialization, record S/GDP greater than I/GDP ratios and they are ready to make DFIs. For China, the ratios on an average have remained comparatively high and are in balance. In addition, it is important to note that the economic structure of Hong Kong is dominated by its service sector, as much as four-fifths of its GDP originating in the service sector alone. Hong Kong's historic relationship with Mainland China, especially in relation to the PRC's foreign trade, merits much closer attention in this regard.

For the rate of inflation as measured by changes in consumer prices, per cent per annum, the records are far different. Performances for 1970-93 point to the fact that Taipei has been able to contain it successfully, and that Hong Kong has stabilized the rate of inflation at about 8 per cent a year, paralleling its rate of growth of GDP.

For the PRC, the rate of inflation has been the challenge. In the 1970s, its inflation rate at an annual average of 1.1 per cent was, of course, the result of official price control. As the experiment in its *socialist market* progressed and China engaged in its economic planning for an accelerated growth, inflation

Table 31.1 Comparative macroeconomic performances

Panel A: Growth rate of gross domestic product (GDP)			
	Hong Kong	Taipei	China
Base year	1980	1986	1978
1971-80 (annual average)	9.3	9.3	7.9
1981-90 (annual average)	7.2	8.5	10.4
1991	4.1	7.2	8.0
1992	5.3	6.6	13.2
1993	5.5	6.2	13.4
Panel B: Gross domestic saving (S) as % of GDP			
1971-1980 (annual average)	28.4	32.1	35.8
1981-1990 (annual average)	31.0	32.9	34.4
1991	31.2	27.8	38.3
1992	31.0	26.7	35.9
1993	30.2	27.0	35.5
Panel C:Gross domestic investment (I) as % of GDP			
1971-1980 (annual average)	27.8	30.5	33.9
1981-1990 (annual average)	28.2	22.6	32.1
1991	28.2	22.8	35.4
1992	29.1	24.2	34.1
1993	29.7	25.1	36.7

Table 31.1 (Continued)

Panel D: Changes in consumer prices (CPI) - % per annum			
1971-1980 (annual average)	8.71	1.1	1.1
1981-1990 (annual average)	8.3	3.1	7.5
1991	12.0	3.6	5.1
1992	9.4	4.5	8.6
1993	8.5	2.8	14.5
Panel E: Changes in money supply (M2) - % per annum			
1988	21.8	17.9	21.0
1989	19.9	9.8	18.3
1990	22.4	9.8	28.0
1991	13.3	19.3	26.4
1992	10.8	19.3	31.3
1993	7.9	14.8	28.0
Panel F: Balance of payments on current account - % GDP			
1988	na	8.3	-1.6
1989	na	7.8	-1.9
1990	na	6.9	2.2
1991	na	6.8	3.5
1992	na	3.8	1.5
1993	na	3.0	-1.9
Panel G: Overall budget surplus/deficit of gov as % GDP			
1988	3.0	1.1	-2.4
1989	2.2	1.4	-2.4
1990	0.7	1.9	-2.1
1991	3.5	-2.3	-2.4
1992	2.9	-5.6	-1.0
1993	-0.4	-5.8	-1.0

Source: Asian Development Bank (1994, pp. 231-53).

Table 31.2 Taipei-Mainland trade interdependence

Year	TE/TTE (%)	TM/TTM (%)	TM/MTE (%)	TE/MTM (%)
1979	0.13	0.37	0.13	0.40
1980	1.22	0.40	1.24	0.43
1981	1.72	0.36	1.80	0.35
1982	0.94	0.47	1.10	0.41
1983	0.67	0.47	0.79	0.43
1984	1.40	0.58	1.64	0.51
1985	3.21	0.58	2.32	0.42
1986	2.03	0.60	1.88	0.46
1987	2.28	0.83	2.84	0.73
1988	3.70	0.96	4.05	1.00
1989	4.37	1.14	4.90	1.13
1990	4.88	1.40	6.36	1.21
1991	6.13	1.79	7.32	1.77

Source: Transfer Trade Statistics Department, Hong Kong Government, Monthly Statistics of Exports and Imports, Taiwan, and Director of Trade Statistics, International Monetary Fund. Adapted from Yu (1992).

Notes: TE Taipei's commodity exports to Mainland China.
TTE Taipei's total commodity exports.
TM Taipei's commodity imports from Mainland China.
TTM Taipei's total commodity imports.
MTM Total commodity imports of Mainland China.
MTE Total commodity exports of Mainland China.

surged to 20.7 and 16.3 per cent in 1988 and 1989, respectively. Again in 1993, the rate crossed the double digit mark at 14.5 per cent. For money supply growth, a parallel pattern is evident. For 1988-93, average annual rates of money supply growth are 16, 15.2 and 25.5 per cent for Hong Kong, Taipei, and the PRC, respectively, pointing to the basic structural differences of the three economic units. For the PRC to sustain its accelerated economic growth, with high savings and high investment, its ability to manage money supply and the rate of inflation has been a challenge. For Taipei and Hong Kong at their respective levels of industrialization and maturity, management of monetary policy has been a relative success story. For fiscal policy, as indicated by overall budget surplus/deficit, and also for its balance of payments on current account as a per centage of GDP, the PRC continues to lag behind the two neighboring economies.

ECONOMIC CALCULUS: TAIPEI / MAINLAND CHINA

In what follows, the focus of discussion will center on Taipei and China in the overall context of geo-economics. It is argued here that economic calculus defines the paradigm.

The PRC's economic reform since 1978 has produced spectacular results (Dutta and Zhang 1991; Dutta and Merva, 1990; Zhang et al., 1991; Chow, 1985, 1994; Garnaut and Ma, 1993). For 1979-90, average annual growth rates of China's net national product, and of the five sectors of its economy, agriculture, industry, architecture, transportation and commerce at 8.4, 5.6, 10.1, 9.6 and 7.2 per cent, respectively, support the above statement (Dutta and Shi, 1992).

For 1980-86, China's average annual growth rates of GDP and its constituent sectors - agriculture, industry and service, at 9.37 (6.71), 6.11 (2.34), 11.85 (7.73) and 8.83 (6.73) per cent, respectively, score a competitive ranking with the corresponding rates of (in parentheses) Asia's NIEs (Hong Kong, Taipei, South Korea and Singapore).

For 1979 to 1988, China's economy has experienced a structural shift in favor of economic development. Its share of agriculture in GDP has declined from a high of 70.14 per cent in 1979 to a low of 26.08 per cent in 1988. Contributions of the industry sector rose from 41.62 per cent of GDP in 1979 to 48.06 per cent in 1988; and that of the service sector from minus 11.76 per cent in 1979 to 25.86 per cent in 1988 (Garnaut and Ma, 1993). One notes that the increases in the contributions of industry and service sectors in recent years have not been in balance.

It has been noted above that the PRC's management of its monetary-fiscal policies has remained suboptimal and the situation calls for urgent attention to defining its macroeconomic parameters. In addition, an evaluation of its intersectoral growth in terms of each sector's contribution to GDP point to the fact that contributions of the service sector to its GDP fail to match that of its industry sector, resulting in an imbalance. The rapid industrial development needs to be supported by a matching growth in its service sector.

Notwithstanding all its limitations, the PRC has emerged as a high-growth economy. China's domestic market of a billion-plus people is yet another point of attraction for economies which are relatively savings surplus, willing and able to capture its competitive share of the world market. Taipei fits the bill and the Taipei mainland trade and investment must be examined in this context. The economic calculus of maximization of mutual gains very much govern the revealed behavioral relationships.

TAIPEI AND MAINLAND CHINA TRADE FLOWS

Taipei's exports to Mainland China as a percentage of its total exports (TE/TTE) have increased from 0.13 in 1979 to 6.13 in 1991, with a sharp upturn in 1985, and the increase has been steady except in 1982 and 1983 (Table 31.2). Its share of imports from Mainland China as a percentage of its total commodity imports (TM/TTM) rose from 0.37 to 1.79 for the same period, again a steady growth pattern. Taipei's commodity imports from Mainland China as a percentage of China's total commodity exports (TM/MTE) have increased from 0.13 in 1979 to 7.32 in 1991, a fairly steady growth except in 1983. Finally, Taipei's commodity exports as a percentage of total commodity imports of Mainland China (TE/MTM) rose from 0.40 in 1979 to 1.77 in 1991, recording a fairly steady progress. The trade picture can be fully appreciated if and only if the trade flow between the two economies via Hong Kong is accounted for (Kao and Yen, 1992).

INVESTMENT FLOWS: TAIPEI TO MAINLAND CHINA

A preliminary analysis of investment flows from Taipei to Mainland China points to a parallel pattern of economic engagement between the two economies across the Taiwan Straits (Chiu, 1992; Chiu and Ching Chung, 1992).

It is instructive to note that for the period 1975 to 1985, as high as 81.3 per cent of inflow of DFI into Mainland China came from Hong Kong and Macao.

Taiwan's contribution to this total, if any, however, remains undocumented. The remaining 18.7 per cent came from Japan (5.1), the United States (3.4), Singapore (1.5), the Philippines (0.5), Germany (0.5), the United Kingdom (0.5), Australia (0.5), Thailand (0.4), France (0.4), Italy (0.3), Canada (0.2) and others (5.4) (Dutta and Merva 1990, p. 179).

The amount of foreign capital utilized, in the form of foreign loans or foreign investments, increased steadily from 1979 to 1986, totaling U.S. $29.93 billion during these eight years, with $20.92 billion being loans and $8.31 billion being foreign investment. In the year 1986, foreign loans utilized amounted to $5.01 billion and foreign investments $2.24 billion. Of the $2.24 billion of foreign investment utilized in 1986, however, $1.33 billion came from Hong Kong (Chow 1994, p. 142). In 1986 a little more than 50 per cent of foreign investments in Mainland China came from Hong Kong.

Several studies in foreign investments in Mainland China from Taipei have recently been reported. Taipei's share of new ownership industry in Mainland China is about one-third nationally, and in the top five provinces of Guangdong, Fuijang, Hainan, Shanghai and Hebei, ranked in order of output share in 1990, is 62.1, 58.4, 79.0, 5.1, 9.8 per cent, respectively (Table 31.3). The percentage computations are, however, subject to error "due to the usage of mix of different statistical definitions" (Chiu, 1992). However, the figures do reflect the fact that the majority of investors, especially in DFI in specific regions, are from Taipei.

Table 31.3 National total and top five provinces with fastest growth of new ownership industry in China

(ranked in order of output share, 1990)	Total number of firms Taipei	Number of Taipei DFI firms	Share of new type (%)
National total	7,403	2,503	33.8
Provinces			
- Guangdong	1,946	1,208	62.1
- Fuijang	1,024	598	58.4
- Hainan	62	49	79.0
- Shanghai	1,529	78	5.1
- Hebei	112	11	9.8

Source: Chiu, (1992).

Table 31.4 Top overseas investors

Panel A: 1979-92		
Countries/ regions	Number of actual projects invested	Percentage share in total (in US$ billion)
Hong Kong	61,07820,842	60.8
Japan	3,6943,879	11.3
U. S.	5,2693,174	9.3
Taipei	10,0341,917	5.6
Germany	2490,471	1.4
France	2420,461	1.3
Singapore	1,3710,441	1.3
Macao	2,2010,400	1.2
U. K.	2680,357	1.0
Australia	5410,228	0.7

Panel B: 1992		
Countries/ regions	Number of projects contractual	Investment (in US $ billion)
Hong Kong	30,781	40,044
Taipei	6,430	5,543
U.S.	3,265	3,121
Japan	1,805	2,173
Macao	1,111	1,487
Singapore	742	0,997
Thailand	407	0,723
South Korea	650	0,417
Canada	394	0,316
France	140	0,289

Source: Huang (1995 p. 224).

Table 31.5 Approved Taipei investment: ASEAN-4 and Mainland China (U.S.$ million)

	Annual Value	Units	Average
ASEAN-4			
1986	92.42	44	2.10
1987	404.04	185	2.21
1988	2,177.87	522	4.17
1989	1,992.69	645	3.09
1990	3,902.66	666	5.86
1991	2,949.89	417	7.07
total	11,523.56	2,479	4.65
Mainland China			
1986	--	--	--
1987*	100	80	1.25
1988	520	435	1.20
1989	437	552	0.79
1990	892	1,103	0.81
1991(estimate)**	1,200	830	1.45
total	3,241	3,000	1.08

Source: Chiu (1992), based on figures reported by DFI-receiving economies

Notes: * Accumulated investment up to 1987.
**According to the estimate of the PRC the accumulated investment by the end of 1991 was ASEAN-4 US$2.1 billion = Thailand, Malaysia, the Philippines and Indonesia.

One observes that both trade and investment flows between Mainland China and Taipei have increased in recent years. We have argued that the economic factor is the key. For both Mainland China and Taipei, their respective shares of trade with the rest of the world have also increased for the same time period. Both have emerged as significant trading partners in the Asia-Pacific region. In recent years, Taipei has emerged as a leading source of DFI and its share of DFI in China has been noted. China's billion-plus people market size, resource endowment, and labor force of some 500 million with a good mix of skilled and unskilled human capital certainly attracts foreign investors. Notwithstanding its many problems, foreign investors inclusive of Taipei must compete for a fair share of China's market and its potential profitability.

Huang (1995, p. 224) presents instructive data on the top ten overseas investors in the PRC for 1979-92 with an annual breakdown for 1992 (Table 31.4, Panels A and B). Over the period from 1979 to 1992 Taipei accounts for 5.6 per cent of total foreign investment, ranking fourth next to Hong Kong, Japan and the United States. Hong Kong tops the list and Macao with its eighth place, outranks the United Kingdom and Australia. In 1992, Taipei ranks second only to Hong Kong, while Macao moves up to fifth place. It is also noted that at the beginning of the 1990s, direct investment from Taipei to Mainland China increased rapidly. Huang adds that, after Hong Kong and Macao, Taipei, "a member of China's big family", has become "the second largest source of overseas direct investment".

There is more to the "big family" argument. A rational appraisal of the emerging pattern of "the Golden Triangle" must take into consideration the economic norm of profit maximization within the paradigm of market economics. Marketization and internationalization of China's economy is the key to the success.

The immediate point for us to consider is that Taipei has elected to make rational economic decisions for its share of investments in mainland China Extraeconomic factors - language, religion and culture - have not been the end point in its decision. A comparative evaluation of Taipei's foreign investment in the Mainland China and Southeast Asia may help bring this argument more into focus. For 1986 to 1991, the accumulated total of Taipei's approved investment in the four Southeast Asian economies - Thailand, Malaysia, Philippines and Indonesia - is estimated at U.S.$ 11.52 billion, while the total for Mainland China is U.S.$ 3.24 billion. (Table 31.5). The average size of investment in ASEAN-4 at U.S.$ 4.65 is much larger than that in Mainland China at U.S.$ 1.08. ASEAN-4, given its comparatively superior performances by relevant macroeconomic indicators, such as rate of GDP growth, S/GDP and I/GDP ratios, inflation rate and monetary-fiscal policy management, has been more competitive in terms of receiving foreign investments.

In the context of Asia-Pacific economic regionalization, a subregional Golden Triangle of Taipei, Mainland China and Hong Kong is an option, as is ASEAN, ANZ-CER and NAFTA. The sanction for a subregional or a regional economic group can be traced to the concept of geo-economics. The optimum size of a region or a subregion cannot be defined *a priori*.

Two core conditions to be noted are: first, economic factors must play a competitive role so that total economic gains of all intraregional member-economies will have been maximized, with no non-member economy becoming poorer; second, a subregional or a regional economic market must be open, not a fortress group.

The Golden Triangle should meet the conditions to become an idealized geo-economic entity. Our findings point to the fact that the three constituent economies are engaged in a competitive market relationship, and the norm of profit maximization, not togetherness of extraeconomic ties of belonging to "a family", define their respective behavioral relations. Of course, a well-defined formal structure is yet to come.

As independent members of APEC, the three economic entities are committed to the APEC-consistent free trade regime. The APEC Bogor agenda for liberalization of trade by 2010/2020 was accepted by all three members in 1994. Sooner or later, hopefully sooner, the issue of China's membership of the WTO will have been settled.

Bibliography

Adams, F. Gerard, Mario Alanis and Abel Beltran del Rio (1992), "The Mexico-United States free trade and investment area proposal: a macroeconometric evaluation of impacts on Mexico", *Journal of Policy Modeling* 14 (1), February, 99–119.

Allen, Polly Reynolds (1990), "The ECU and the transition to European monetary system", Paper presented at the University of Pennsylvania-Rutgers University Colloquium on the European regional economic integration of 1992, November 15–16.

APEC (1991), *Declaration of APEC Ministers*, Seoul, Korea.

APEC (1993), *A Vision for APEC: Towards an Asia-Pacific Economic Community*, Report of the Eminent Persons' Group (EPG), APEC Secretariat, Singapore, October.

APEC (1994), *Achieving the APEC Vision: Free and Open Trade in the Asia-Pacific Region*, Second EPG Report, APEC Secretariat, Singapore, August.

APEC (1995a), *Implementing the APEC Vision*, Third EPG Report, APEC Secretariat, Singapore, August.

APEC (1995b), *Selected APEC Documents*, APEC Secretariat, Singapore.

APEC (1995c), *Asia-Pacific Economic Cooperation*, Annual Report of the APEC Secretariat, APEC Secretariat, Singapore.

APEC (1996), *Asia-Pacific Economic Cooperation*, Annual Report of the APEC Secretariat, APEC Secretariat, Singapore.

Apple, R.W. Jr. (1994), *New York Times*, January 9.

Ariff, Mohamed (1989a), "The US-ASEAN free trade option: scope and implications", in Schott (ed.), *Free Trade Areas and U.S. Trade Policy*, 201–16.

Ariff, Mohamed (1989b), "The changing role of ASEAN in the coming decades", in M. Sinohara and F.C. Lo (eds), *Global Adjustment and the Future of Asian-Pacific Economy*, Tokyo, Institute of Developing Economies.

Ariff, Mohamed (1994), "Open regionalism *a la* ASEAN", *Journal of Asian Economics*, 5 (1), 99–117.

Arndt, H.W. (1993), "Anatomy of regionalism", *Journal of Asian Economics*, 4 (2), 271–82.

ASEAN (1990), *ASEAN Economic Cooperation: A Handbook*, ASEAN Secretariat, Singapore.

ASEAN (1995), *ASEAN UPDATE*, ASEAN Secretariat, Singapore.

Asian Development Bank (1994), *Asian Development Bank Outlook*, (1994) Hong Kong: Oxford University Press, 231-53.

Brunei Darassalam Ministry of Finance, Statistics Division (1990), *Brunei Darussalam Statistical Yearbook*, Brunei Darussalam: Government Printing Department.

Bachrach, Carlos and Loris Mizrahi (1992), "The economic impact of a free trade agreement between the United States and Mexico: a CGE analysis", in U.S. International Trade Commission, *Economy-wide Modeling of the Economic Implications of a FTA with Mexico and a NAFTA with Canada and Mexico*, USITC pub. No. 2508.

Balassa, Bela (1987), "Japanese trade policies toward developing countries", in *Asia-Pacific Economies: Promises and Challenges*, M. Dutta (ed.), Greenwich, CT:, Jai Press, Part A, 49-68.

Bergsten, C. Fred (1994), A recorded conversation on Asia-Pacific Economic Cooperation, this volume, pp. 112-23.

Bergsten, C. Fred (1995), APEC: *The Bogor Declaration and the Path Ahead*, Washington DC: Institute for International Economics.

Bergsten, C. Fred (1996), *APEC After Osaka: Toward Free Trade by 2010/2020*, Washington, DC: Institute for International Economics.

Bradford, Colin I., Jr. and William H. Branson (eds) (1987), *Trade and Structural Change in Pacific Asia*, National Bureau of Economic Research: University of Chicago Press.

Bradsher, Keith (1992), "As global talks stall, regional trade pacts multiply", *New York Times*, August 23.

Brown, Drusilla, K., Alan V. Deardorff and Robert M. Stern (1992a), "North American free trade agreement: analytical issues and a computational assessment", *World Economy*, January, 15-29.

Brown, Drusilla, K., Alan V. Deardorff and Robert M. Stern (1992b), "A U.S.-Mexico-Canada free trade agreement: sectoral employment effects and regional/occupational employment re-alignments in the United States", in National Commissions for Employment Policy, *The Employment Effects of the North American Free Trade Agreement: Recommendations and Background Studies*, Special Report No. 33.

Bureau of Industry Economics, Government of Australia (1995), *Impact of the CER Trade Agreement - Lessons for Regional Economic Cooperation*, Government of Australia, Canberra, 55.

Chia Siow Yue (1993), "Foreign direct investment in ASEAN economies", *Asian Development Review*, 11 (1), Asian Development Bank, Manila, Philippines.

Chiu, Lee-in Chen (1992), "The economic reunion of Taiwan and the

Mainland China – the impact on industrial development", Discussion paper No. 9203 (mimeo), Chung-Hua Institution for Economic Research, Taipei.

Chiu, Lee-in Chen and Chin Chung (1992), "An assessment of Taiwan's indirect investment toward Mainland China", Discussion paper No. 9201 (mimeo), Chung-Hua Institution for Economic Research, Taipei, January.

Chow, Gregory C. (1985), *The Chinese Economy*, New York: Harper & Row Second Edition, World Scientific, 1988.

Chow, Gregory C. (1994), *Understanding China's Economy*, Singapore: World Scientific Publishing Co.

Congressional Budget Office (1993), *Estimating the Effects of NAFTA: An Assessment of Economic Models and Other Empirical Studies*, Washington, DC: CBO.

Cooper, Richard (1974), "Worldwide Versus Regional Integration: Is There an Optimal Size of the Integrated Area?" Yale Economic Growth Center Discussion Paper, No. 220, November.

Cox, David and Richard G. Harris (1991), "North American free trade and its implications for Canada: results from a CGE model of North American trade", paper presented at conference, Washington, DC, June 27-28; also in U.S. International Trade Commission, *Economy-wide Modeling of the Economic Implications of a FTA with Mexico and a NAFTA with Canada and Mexico*, USITC publication No. 2508, May 1992.

Dertous, Lester, Solow, et al. (1989), *Made in America*, Cambridge, MA, MIT Press.

Dobson, Wendy (1990), *Economic Policy Coordination: Requiem or Prologue*, Washington, DC: Institute for International Economics.

Dornbusch, Rudiger (1980), *Open Economy Macroeconomics*, New York: Basic Books.

Dornsbusch, Rudiger (1987), "Exchange rates and prices", *American Economic Review*, 77 (1), March 9, 3–106.

Dornbusch, Rudiger (1990), "The dollar in the 1990s: competitiveness and the challenges of new economic blocs", in *Monetary Policy Issues in the 1990s*, Kansas City: Federal Reserve Bank of Kansas City.

Drysdale, Peter (1968), "Pacific economic integration: an Australian view", in Kojima (ed.), *Pacific Trade and Development*, Tokyo, Japan; Economic Research Center.

Drysdale, Peter (1988), *International Economic Pluralism: Economic Policy in East Asia and the Pacific*, New York, Columbia University Press.

Drysdale, Peter and Ross Garnaut (1989), "A Pacific free trade area", in Schott (ed.), *Free Trade Areas and U.S. Trade Policy*, 217–54.

Drysdale, Peter and Hugh T. Patrick (1979), *An Asian-Pacific Regional Economic Organization: An Exploratory Concept Paper*, Washington, DC: U.S. Congressional Research Service, U.S. Governmental Printing Office, July.

Dutta, M. (ed.) (1985), *Studies in United States-Asia Economic Relations*, Durham, NC: The Acorn Press, 578.

Dutta, M. (ed.) (1987a), *Asia-Pacific Economies: Promises and Challenges*, Greenwich, CT: JAI Press, Part A, 308, Part B, 308.

Dutta, M. (1987b), "The Asia-Pacific Economic Community: some comments", in M. Dutta (ed.), *Asia-Pacific Economies: Promises and Challenges*, Greenwich, CT, JAI Press, 93–100.

Dutta, M. (ed.) (1988), *Asian Industrialization: Changing Economic Structures*, Greenwich, CT: JAI Press, Part A, 359, Part B, 377.

Dutta, M. (1990), "The United States an Asian economy: new dimensions in U.S.-Asia economic relations", an invited lecture at the 14th International Symposium of Hosei University at Tama Campus, Tokyo, September 26–28.

Dutta, M. (1992a), "Economic regionalization in Western Europe: Asia-Pacific economies (macroeconomic core: microeconomic optimization)", *American Economic Review, Papers and Proceedings*, 82 (2), 67–73.

Dutta, M. (1992b), "Economic regionalization: macroeconomic core and microeconomic optimization" (mimeo), Paper presented at the first conference on APEC: ASEAN/SAARC, sponsored by ACAES jointly with Chulalongkorn University, Thailand, 1992. Revised and published in *Journal of Asian Economics*, 5 (1), 1994.

Dutta, M. (1992c), "Asia-Pacific Economic Cooperation: Structure of a Common Economic Region", *Journal of Asian Economics*, 3 (1), Spring, 1–28.

Dutta, M. (1992d), "The United States: an Asian economy: new dimensions in U.S.-Asia economic relations" (in Japanese). A revised and abridged version of invited lecture at the 14th International Symposium of Hosei University at Tama Campus, Tokyo, Japan, September 26–28, 1990, in Yoshihiko Hirata (ed.), Sekai-Keizai no Seicho Senta-Azia Taiheiyou Chiiki (*Asia-Pacific Region as a Center for Growth in the World Economy*), Tokyo, Japan: Taga Publishing Company, 13–31.

Dutta, M. (1994a), "Economic regionalism in the Asia-Pacific: macroeconomic core and microeconomic optimization", *Journal of Asian Economics*, 5 (1), 15–42.

Dutta, M. (1994b), "Toward a supra-national macroeconomic core", *Journal of Asian Economics*, 5 (4), 443–58.

Dutta, M. (1995a), "Economic relationships between Taiwan and China", in C.F. Lee (ed.), *Advances in Pacific Basin Business, Economics and Finance*, Greenwich, CT: JAI Press Inc., 183–95.

Dutta, M. (1995b), "Macroeconomics and supra-national macroeconomic core", in M. Dutta et al. (eds), *Economics, Econometrics and the LINK, Essays in Honor of Lawrence R. Klein*, Amsterdam: North-Holland/Elsevier, 59–73.

Dutta, M. and Mary Merva (1990), "U.S.-China joint ventures", in M. Dutta, Pei-kang Chang and Shao-kung Lin (eds), *China's Modernization and Open Economic Policy*, Greenwich, CT: JAI Press Inc., 171–96; 466.

Dutta, M. and L. Shi (1992), "China's economic development with stability and efficiency" (mimeo), paper presented at the Fourth International Conference on "China's economic development", sponsored by American Committee on Asian Economic Studies (ACAES), Chinese Academy of Social Sciences (CASS) and Shanghai Academy of Social Sciences (SASS), Beijing, China, November 10–12.

Dutta, M. and Daniel Tantum (1988), "Industrialization of Japan and selected East Asian countries: The structural divergence hypothesis", in M. Dutta (ed.), *Asian Industrialization: Changing Economic Structures*, JAI Press, Part A, 17–46.

Dutta, M. and Zhongli Zhang (eds) (1991), *China's Economic Reform 1978-1988*. Greenwich, CT: JAI Press Inc., 300.

Elek, Andrew (1992), "Trade policy options for the Asia-Pacific Region in the 1990s: the potential for open regionalism", *American Economic Review, Papers and Proceedings*, 82 (2), 74–8.

Emmerij, Louis (ed.) (1989a), *One World or Several*? Paris: OECD, Development Center, 301.

Emmerij, Louis (1989b), "One World or Several? An Introductory Statement", in Emmerij (ed.), *One World or Several*?, 25–30.

European Commission (1989a), *Committee for the Study of Economic and Monetary Union in the European Community*, Brussels: EC.

European Commission (1989b), *Report on Economic and Monetary Union in the European Community* (Delors Commission Report), by the Committee for the Study of Economic and Monetary Union, Luxembourg: EC.

European Commission (1990), *Report on Economic and Monetary Union in the European Community* (Delors Commission Report), Luxembourg: EC.

Fieleke, Norman S. (1992), "One trading world, or many: the issue of regional trading blocs", *New England Economic Review*, May/June, 3–20.

Forrestal, Robert P. (1993), "The role of central banks in a global marketplace: exchange rates and policy coordination", *Journal of Asian Economics*, 4 (1), Spring, 131–7. (A revised version of the author's presentation at the 5th special financial conference, on "Managed exchange rate regime – yen, dollar and ecu", sponsored by American Committee on Asian Economic Studies in cooperation with Federal Reserve Bank of Atlanta, Atlanta, GA, October 29–30, 1992.)

Frankel, Jeffrey A. and Miles Kahler (eds) (1993), *Regionalism and Rivalry: Japan and the United States in Pacific Area*, Chicago: University of Chicago Press for National Bureau of Economic Research.

Freeman, G.P. and J. Mo (1996), "Japan and the Asian NICs as new countries of destination", in Lloyd and Williams (eds), *International Trade and Migration in the Asia-Pacific*, Melbourne: Oxford University Press.

Garnaut, Ross (1994), "Open regionalism: its analytic basis and relevance to the international system", *Journal of Asian Economics*, 5 (2), 273–90.

Garnaut, Ross and Peter Drysdale (1994), "Asia-Pacific regionalism: the issues", in Ross Garnaut and Peter Drysdale (eds), *Asia-Pacific Regionalism*, Harper-Education, a division of Harper Collins in association with the Australia-Japan Research Center and the Australian National University, Australia, 1–7.

Garnaut, Ross and Guonan Ma (1993), "Economic growth and stability in China", *Journal of Asian Economics*, 4 (1), Spring, 5–24.

Gray, H. Peter (1989), "The mechanics of international economic location", in Khosrow Fatemi (ed.), *International Trade: Existing Problems and Prospective Solutions*, New York: Taylor & Francis, 24–34.

Green, David Jay (1994), "Convergence and cohesion within the ASEAN-4", *Journal of Asian Economics*, 5 (1), 119–44.

Hesse, Helmut (1993), "ECU – now and later: some considerations after Maastricht", *Journal of Asian Economics*, 4 (1), Spring, 139–52. (A revised version of the author's presentation at the 5th Special Financial Conference, on "Managed exchange rate regime – yen, dollar and ecu", sponsored by ACAES in cooperation with Federal Reserve Bank of Atlanta, Atlanta, GA, October 29–30, 1992.)

Hinojosa-Ojeda, Raul and Sherman Robinson (1991), "Alternative scenarios of U.S.-Mexico integration: a computable general equilibrium approach", Working Paper No. 609, Department of Agricultural and Resource Economics, University of California at Berkeley.

Huang, Fanzhang (1995), "China's utilization of foreign capital and the related policies", *Journal of Asian Economics*, 6 (2), Spring, 224. (A revised version of a paper presented at the conference on "Which way APEC?" Indonesia, August 29–September 1, 1994.)

Hufbauer, Gary C. (ed.) (1990), *Europe 1992: An American Perspective*, Washington, DC: Brookings Institution.

Hufbauer, Gary Clyde (1995), "Whither APEC?", *Journal of Asian Economics*, 6 (1), 89–94.

Hufbauer, Gary and Jeffrey Schott (1992), *North American Free Trade: Issues and Recommendations*, Washington, DC: Institute for International Economics, 51–7.

Hufbauer, Gary and Jeffrey Schott (1993), *NAFTA: An Assessment*, Washington, DC: Institute for International Economics.

International Monetary Fund (IMF) (1991), *Direction of Trade Statistics*, Washington, DC: IMF.

Ito, Takatoshi and Anne O. Krueger (eds) (1997), *Regionalism versus Multilateral Trade Arrangements*, Chicago, University of Chicago Press.

Kalirajan, K.P. and Ric T. Shand (1996), "Towards an Indian Ocean grouping: prospects for economic cooperation", *Journal of Asian Economics*, 6 (3), fall.

Kao, C. and T. Yen (1992), "The current condition and development trend of economic exchange across the Taiwan straits" (mid-term report: mimeo), January, Chung-Hua Institution for Economic Research, Taipei.

Kim, Duk-Choong (1992), "Open regionalism in the Pacific: a world of trading blocs?", *American Economic Review, Papers and Proceedings*, 82 (2), 79–83.

Kindleberger, Charles F. (1986), "International public goods without international government", *American Economic Review*, March, 1–13.

Klein, Lawrence R. (1990), "Can export-led growth continue indefinitely? An Asia-Pacific perspective", *Journal of Asian Economics*, 1 (1), 1–12.

Kojima, Kiyoshi (ed.) (1968), *Pacific Trade and Development*, Tokyo; Japan Economic Research Center.

Kojima, Kiyoshi (1971), *Japan and a Pacific Free Trade Area*, London, Macmillan.

Kojima, Kiyoshi (1978), *Direct Foreign Investment: A Japanese Model of Multinational Business Operations*, London: Croom Helm.

Kojima, Kiyoshi (1990a), *Japanese Direct Investment Abroad* (monograph), Tokyo: International Christian University.

Kojima, Kiyoshi (1990b), "Proposal for a multiple key currency gold-exchange standard", *Journal of Asian Economics*, 1 (1), 19–33.

Krause, Lawrence B. (1987), "A second-best strategy for Pacific dynamism", in Dutta (ed.), *Asia-Pacific Economies: Promises and Challenges*, 11–22.

Krugman, Paul (1993), "The uncomfortable truth about NAFTA", *Foreign Affairs*, November/December, 13–19.

Kuroda, Makota (1989), "Strengthening Japan-U.S. Cooperation and the Concept of Japan-U.S. Free-Trade Arrangements", in Schott (ed.), *Free Trade Areas and U.S. Trade Policy*, 121–30.

Lamfalussy, A. (1989), "The ecu banking market", in European Commission (1989), *Report on Economic and Monetary Union in the European Community*, 201–7.

Lee, Tsao Yuan (1994), "The ASEAN free-trade area: the search for a common prosperity", in Ross Garnaut and Peter Drysdale (eds), *Asia-Pacific Regionalism*, 319–26.

Linder, Staffan Burenstam (1986), *The Pacific Century: Economic and Political Consequences of Asian-Pacific Dynamism*, Stanford, CA: Stanford University Press.

Linder, Staffan Burenstam (1987), "Economic and political consequences of Asia-Pacific dynamism", in Dutta (ed.), *Asia-Pacific Economies: Promises and Challenges*, Part A, 69–81.

Linnemann, Hans (1966), *An Econometric Study of International Trade Flows*, Amsterdam: North-Holland.

Lipsey, Richard G. (1992), "Growth, erosion, and restructuring of the multilateral trading system", *Journal of Asian Economics*, 3 (1), 121–39.

Lipsey, Richard G. and Murray G. Smith (1989), "The Canada-US free trade area: special case or wave of the future", in Schott (ed.), *Free Trade Areas and U.S. Trade Policy*, 317–36.

Lloyd, Peter J. (1991), *The Future of CER: A Single Market for Australia and New Zealand*, Committee for Economic Development in Australia and the Institute of Policy Studies, Victoria University of Wellington, Wellington, New Zealand.

Lloyd, Peter J. (1994), "The future of the CER Agreement: a single market for Australia and New Zealand", in Ross Garnaut and Peter Drysdale (eds), *Asia-Pacific Regionalism*, Harper-Education, a division of Harper Collins in association with the Australia-Japan Research Center and the Australian National University, Australia.

Lloyd, Peter J. (1995), "CER free trade only or economic integration" (mimeo), *Agenda* (forthcoming).

Lorenz, Detlef (1989), "Trends towards regionalism in the world economy – a contribution to a new economic order?", *Intereconomics*, March/April, 64–70.

Lorenz, Detlef (1991), "Regionalization versus regionalism – problems of change in the world economy", *Intereconomics*, January/February, 3-9.

Lorenz, Detlef (1992), "Economic geography and the political economy of regionalization: the example of Western Europe", *American Economic Review, Papers and Proceedings*, 82 (2), 84-7.

Lorenz, Detlef (1993), "Europe and East Asia in the context of regionalization: theory and economic policy", *Journal of Asian Economics*, 4 (2), Fall, 255-70.

McCleery, Robert K. (1992), "An intertemporal, linked, macroeconomic CGE model of the United States and Mexico focusing on demographic change and factor flows", in U.S. International Trade Commission, *Economy-wide Modeling of the Economic Implications of a FTA with Mexico and a NAFTA with Canada and Mexico*, USITC publication No. 2508.

MIT Commission (1989), Made in America, MIT Press, MA, USA.

Monnet, Jean (1978), *Memoirs*, Garden City, NY: Doubleday.

Narongchai Akrasanee and David Stifel (1994), "The political economy of the ASEAN free trade area", in Ross Garnaut and Peter Drysdale (eds), *Asia-Pacific Regionalism*, Harper-Education, a division of Harper Collins in association with The Australia-Japan Research Center and The Australian National University, Australia, 327-36.

Okita, Saburo (1989), "Policy approaches to the problem", in Emmerij (ed.), *One World or Several?*, 41-50.

Orme, Jr. William A. (1993), "Myths versus facts. The whole truth about the half-truths", *Foreign Affairs*, November/December, 2-12.

Park, Yung Chul and Jang H. Yoo (1989), "More free trade areas: a Korean perspective", in Jeffrey J. Schott (ed.) *Free Trade Areas and U.S. Trade Policy*, 141-58.

PECC (1992), Proceedings of the 9th Council Meeting, Pacific Economic Cooperation Council (PECC), Singapore. (The 5th Ministerial Meeting of Asia-Pacific Economic Cooperation (APEC) voted to accept the PECC recommendations.)

Prestowitz, Jr. Clyde V. and Robert B. Cohen (with Peter Morici and Alan Tonelson) (1991), *The New North American Order*, Washington DC); Economic Strategy Inst., 45-52.

Robinson, Sherman, Mary E. Burfisher, Raul Hinojosa-Ojeda and Karen Theirfelder (1992), "Agricultural policies and migration in a U.S.-Mexico free trade area: a computable general equilibrium analysis", in U.S. International Trade Commission, *Economy-wide Modeling of the Economic Implications of a FTA with Mexico and a NAFTA with Canada and Mexico*, USITC publication No. 2508.

Rosen, Howard (1989), "The US-Israel free trade agreement: how well is it working and what have we learned?", in Schott (ed.), *Free Trade Areas and U.S. Trade Policy*, Washington, DC: Institute for International Economics, 97-190.

Rostow, Walt W. (1985), "Is there need for economic leadership? Japanese or U.S.?", *American Economic Review* (Proceedings Volume), 75 (2), 285-91.

Scalapino, Robert A. (1991/92), "The United States and Asia: future prospects", *Foreign Affairs*, winter.

Schott, Jeffrey J. (ed.) (1989a), *Free Trade Areas and U.S. Trade Policy*, Washington, DC: Institute for International Economics.

Schott, Jeffrey J. (ed.) (1989b), "Free trade areas and U.S. trade policy", in Schott (ed.), *Free Trade Areas and U.S. Trade Policy*, 141-58.

Shinohara, Miyohei (1987), "Patterns and backgrounds of dynamics in the Asia-Pacific economies", in Dutta (ed.), *Asia-Pacific Economies: Promises and Challenges*, Part A, 23-48.

Snape, Richard H. (1989), "A free trade agreement with Australia", in Schott (ed.), *Free Trade Areas and U.S. Trade Policy*, 167-96.

Sobarzo, Horacio (1992), "A general equilibrium analysis of gains from trade of the Mexican economy of a North American free trade agreement" in U.S. International Trade Commission, *Economy-wide Modeling of the Economic Implications of a FTA with Mexico and a NAFTA with Canada and Mexico*, USITC publication No. 2508.

South Asian Association for Regional Cooperation (1990), *SAARC Summits: 1985-1988*, Kathmandu, Nepal. SAARC Secretariat.

South Asian Association for Regional Cooperation (1991), *SAARC Documents*, Kathmandu, Nepal. SAARC Secretariat.

South Asian Association for Regional Cooperation (1993), *SAARC Documents*, Kathmandu, Nepal. SAARC Secretariat.

South Asian Association for Regional Cooperation (1995), *SAARC Documents*, Kathmandu, Nepal. SAARC Secretariat.

South Asian Association for Regional Cooperation (1996), *SAARC Summits: 1990-1995*, Kathmandu, Nepal. SAARC Secretariat.

Stek, Pieter (1992), "Impact of European integration on financial markets", *Journal of Asian Economics*, 2 (2), 325-36.

Suthiphand, Chirathivat (1992), "ASEAN: prospects for growth, requirements of structural adjustment, directions for policy", Bangkok: Chulalongkorn University; Taiwan: Chung-Hua Institute for Research, Mimeo.

Tan, K.Y., M.H. Toh and Linda Low (1992), ASEAN and Pacific economic cooperation, *ASEAN Economic Bulletin*, 8 (3).

Trigueros, Ignacio (1989), "A free trade agreement between Mexico and the United States", in Schott (ed.), *Free Trade Areas and U.S. Trade Policy*, 255–67.

Tsiang, S.C. (1989), "Feasibility and desirability of a US-Taiwan free trade agreement", in Schott (ed.), *Free Trade Areas and U.S. Trade Policy*, 159–66.

Ungerer, H., O. Evans, T. Mayer and P. Young (1986), *"The European Monetary System: Recent Development"*, Occasional Paper No. 48, Washington, DC, International Monetary Fund, December.

United Nations (1990), *Economic and Social Survey of Asia and the Pacific*, New York: United Nations.

United Nations (1991), *Economic and Social Survey of Asia and the Pacific*, New York: United Nations.

United Nations (1993), *Economic and Social Survey of Asia and the Pacific 1993*, New York: United Nations.

United Nations (1994), *Economic and Social Survey of Asia and the Pacific*, New York: United Nations.

Viner, Jacob (1950), *The Customs Union Issue*, New York: Carnegie Endowment for International Peace.

Wade, Robert (1990), *Governing the Market: Economic Theory and the Role of Government in East Asian Industrialization*, Princeton: Princeton University Press.

World Bank (1992), *The World Development Report:* Washington, DC.

World Bank (1994), *The World Development Report:* Washington, DC.

World Bank (1996), *The World Development Report:* Washington, DC.

Wonnacott, Paul and Mark Lutz (1989), "Is there a case for free trade areas?", in Schott (ed.), *Free Trade Areas and U.S. Trade Policy*, 59–84.

Yamazawa, Ippei (1994), "Asia-Pacific Economic Community: new paradigm and challenges", *Journal of Asian Economics*, 5 (3), 301–12.

Yoo, Jang-Hee and Chang-Jae Lee (eds) (1994), *Northeast Asian Economic Cooperation, Progress in Conceptualization and in Practice*, Seoul, South Korea: Korea Institute for International Economic Policy, 298.

Yoo, Jang-Hee and Keuk-Je Sung (1994), "APEC: U.S.-Asia cooperation", *Journal of Asian Economics*, 5 (4), 471–84.

Young, Leslie and Jose Romero (1992), "Steady growth and transition in a dynamic dual model of the North American free trade agreement", in *U.S. International Trade Commission, Economy-wide Modeling of the Economic Implications of a FTA with Mexico and a NAFTA with Canada and Mexico*, USITC publication No. 2508.

Yu, Tzong-shian (1992), "The two sides of the Taiwan Straits: economic interdependence and cooperation", Discussion paper No. 9203 (mimeo), *Chung-Hua Institution for Economic Research*, 1 March, Taipei.

Zhang, Zhongli, M. Dutta, Gary Jefferson and Tingang Yao (eds) (1991), *Retrospect and prospect (views on China's economic reform: Chinese and American economists)*, Shanghai, China: Shanghai Academy Press, (in Chinese).

Index